Language and National Ident
in Greece 1766–1976

'There can be little doubt that this work is a major contribution to the cultural history of Greece. Peter Mackridge has written a book that is authoritative, hugely informative, an inexhaustible source of useful detail and sound judgement, that makes complete and fair use of all available literature on an important and controversial subject. For all this we should be grateful.'
Paschalis M. Kitromilides, Professor of Political Science, University of Athens, and Director of the Institute for Neohellenic Research, National Research Foundation

'This book provides the first authoritative, nuanced, and analytical account of the notorious language question in modern Greece. Drawing copiously on original sources that have often been overlooked, even by specialists, Mackridge coherently and convincingly explains why the "correct" form of their national language mattered so much to Greek-speakers for more than two centuries. In doing so he also argues powerfully for the role of language to be better studied as part of the global phenomenon of nation-formation.'
Roderick Beaton, Koraes Professor of Modern Greek and Byzantine History, Language, and Literature, King's College London

'Modern Greek, a more extraordinary language even than English, reaches back to Homer, Sophocles, Plato, and Sappho. For Greeks, the demotic language of today is part of a three-thousand-year continuum that buoys their sense of pride and identity. "What a joy it is to fashion our language!" says Kazantzakis. Peter Mackridge's incisive examination shows why.'
Peter Bien, Professor Emeritus of English and Comparative Literature, Dartmouth College

'Despite its methodological foundation in linguistics and social sciences, the study has a great scholarly accomplishment that is basically historical ... Peter Mackridge's book should be read by all students in all the social sciences.' **Anna Frangoudaki**, *The Athens Review of Books*

'For centuries the Greek language has been the focus of struggles and conflicts, few truly about the language itself and most essentially cultural, social and political. Peter Mackridge is the world's leading authority on the topic. In this masterly, comprehensive, and timely work, he untangles the tortuous path these struggles have taken over the past two and a half centuries and reveals the profound intertwining of the history of Greek with the national identity of Greece.' **Peter Trudgill**, Professor Emeritus of English Linguistics at the University of Fribourg; Honorary Professor at the University of East Anglia

Language and National Identity in Greece 1766–1976

PETER MACKRIDGE

OXFORD
UNIVERSITY PRESS

OXFORD
UNIVERSITY PRESS

Great Clarendon Street, Oxford ox2 6DP

Oxford University Press is a department of the University of Oxford.
It furthers the University's objective of excellence in research, scholarship,
and education by publishing worldwide in

Oxford New York

Auckland Cape Town Dar es Salaam Hong Kong Karachi
Kuala Lumpur Madrid Melbourne Mexico City Nairobi
New Delhi Shanghai Taipei Toronto

With offices in

Argentina Austria Brazil Chile Czech Republic France Greece
Guatemala Hungary Italy Japan Poland Portugal Singapore
South Korea Switzerland Thailand Turkey Ukraine Vietnam

Oxford is a registered trade mark of Oxford University Press
in the UK and in certain other countries

Published in the United States
by Oxford University Press Inc., New York

© Peter Mackridge 2009

British Library Cataloguing in Publication Data

Data available

Library of Congress Cataloging-in-Publication Data
Mackridge, Peter.
Language and national identity in Greece, 1766–1976 / Peter Mackridge.
   p. cm.
Includes bibliographical references.
ISBN 978–0–19–921442–6
1. Greek language, Modern–Political aspects–History.
2. Nationalism–Greece–History. 3. Language policy–Greece. I. Title.
PA1050.M33 2009
306.44'909509–dc22   2008041406

Typeset by SPI Publisher Services, Pondicherry, India
Printed in Great Britain
on acid-free paper by
MPG Books Group, Bodmin and King's Lynn

ISBN 978–0–19–921442–6(hbk.)
     978–0–19–959905–9(pbk.)

1 3 5 7 9 10 8 6 4 2

The debate...concerning the genuineness of our National Dialect and the examination of its natural form and character is no longer simply a literary or grammatical debate, but a national debate, a public problem, and a postulate that is constitutive of the most sacred rights of the Nation.

(Kodrikas 1818)[1]

Just as each individual has a different facial character from everyone else, so naturally he must have a different character of language. But this character cannot manifest itself as it truly is except when a person writes in his natural language—that is, in the language which he suckled with his mother's milk and which he speaks every day, or at least more regularly than other, acquired languages....Just as it is true concerning each individual person that 'a man's character is known by his language', so the character of an entire nation is known by its language.

(Korais 1804)[2]

Was the language question merely literary? On the contrary, it was also, and chiefly, political..., containing...the solution...to the Greek destiny, that is to say the final and absolute solution to the Eastern Question.

(S. Zambelios 1852)[3]

The son of a great poet used to say that the profitless burden that he was condemned by irrevocable ill fortune to bear on his shoulders throughout his life was his father's name. The great and useless load which we Greeks are condemned by irrevocable ill fortune to bear on our puny shoulders is the great and glorious, but heavy and burdensome name of our great forefathers, with all the obligations that it entails.

(Vernardakis 1884)[4]

Language and homeland are one and the same. To fight for one's homeland or one's national language is one and the same struggle.

(Psycharis 1888)[5]

La battaglia per la lingua è prima di tutto battaglia di idee.

(Rotolo 1965)[6]

---

[1] Kodrikas 1988: p. iii, used as epigraph in Sathas 1870.
[2] Korais 1984b: 43–4, 52, quoting Menander.   [3] Zampelios 1852: 368.
[4] Vernardakis 1884: 441.   [5] Psycharis 1971: 37 [=Psycharis 1888: p. i].
[6] Rotolo 1965: 55.

[I]dentity crisis is the central problem of modern Greek society, the constituent feature of contemporary Hellenism and the axis around which our modern history revolves.

(Tsaousis 1983)[7]

[T]he conflict between demoticism and purism/archaism can be viewed as a conflict for the appropriation of the authority to form the national identity.

(Tziovas 1986)[8]

[7] Tsaousis 1983: 17.   [8] Tziovas 1986: 5.

Contents

Preface

In the film *My Big Fat Greek Wedding* (2002) the heroine's Greek-American family have modelled the façade of their house on the Parthenon, and her father claims that the Japanese word *kimono* is derived from the Greek word *cheimonas* [winter] on the grounds that a kimono keeps the wearer warm in winter.

Comically exaggerated as they are, these two instances of architectural and verbal language, as cultural features that distinguish Greeks from other nations and enable them to be proud of their own culture, illustrate the importance of language and other aspects of culture to a nation's sense of identity.

Greek national identity has been chiefly defined by two criteria that have been held to distinguish Greeks from non-Greeks. The first is membership of the Orthodox Church. The second is the possession of the Greek language. While there are other peoples in the world who are predominantly Orthodox Christian, the Greek language is clearly distinguished from all other languages in the world by its alphabet, its vocabulary, and its grammar. The Modern Greek language has constantly been associated in the minds of educated Greeks with the Ancient Greek language, together with the unique civilization (including the great achievements in literature and philosophy) that was expressed through it. In the minds of almost all Greeks, their language has also been connected, in an unbroken continuity upheld by the traditions of the Orthodox Church and by the chanting of texts in the liturgy, with the New Testament and other early ecclesiastical texts.

This has given educated Greeks a sense that their nation possesses a unique cultural heritage. Their language both distinguishes them from all other modern nations and connects them with the civilization of ancient Hellas, early Christianity, and Byzantium. It is largely this complex connection between contemporary and older culture that has given rise to the development of the Greek national identity in modern times. In no other area has this connection been so problematic as in language. It is the question of the Greek language that is the subject of this book.

Roderick Beaton has written that the story of the Greek language question 'tends to be told piecemeal and there is no single, authoritative history of the debate from the late eighteenth century to the late twentieth'.[1] I cannot claim that my book is that single, authoritative history, but Beaton's statement has been both a challenge and an incentive to me.

[1] Beaton 1999: 296.

Transliteration from Greek and pronunciation of Greek words

In most cases I have transliterated Greek words into the Roman alphabet. There is no single internationally recognized system for transliterating Modern Greek. I have adopted a procedure that normally reproduces the Greek letters rather than the pronunciation. This allows the reader to gain an approximate visual image of the word and is also useful when looking up a Greek writer's name in a library catalogue.

I have normally transliterated:

αυ as av or af according to the pronunciation in each particular case
γγ as ng
γι as gi, not y
γκ as nk
ευ as ev or ef according to the pronunciation in each particular case
η as i, not e
υ (without preceding α or ε) as y, not i
φ as f, not ph
χ as ch, not h

As far as pronunciation is concerned:

ai is pronounced *e*
ch is pronounced like Scots or German, not English
g is pronounced [ɣ] before *a*, *o*, or *u* (no equivalent in English), but *y* before *e* or *i*; however, after *n* it is pronounced *g*
gi is usually pronounced *y* before a vowel
d is pronounced like *th* in English *there*
ei, *oi*, and *y* are all pronounced *i* as in English *thin*
mp is pronounced *mb* or *b*
nk is pronounced *ng* or *g*
nt is pronounced *nd* or *d*
th is pronounced like *th* in English *thin*
x is pronounced like English *x*

I have made some exceptions in personal names, especially those of certain authors whose work has been published extensively under a different form of their name in languages other than Greek, e.g. G. N. Hatzidakis, C. P. Cavafy rather than G. N. Chatzidakis, K. P. Kavafis. In transliterated Greek words (but not names or titles) I have usually used an acute accent to mark the stressed vowel unless the stress falls on the penultimate syllable. I have placed broad phonological transcriptions of Greek between slashes / /, while I have placed English glosses of foreign words or phrases between square brackets [ ]. In most cases I have used English translations of the titles of Greek publications in the main text of the book. The reader will find the Greek titles (transliterated into Roman) in the Bibliography.

Maps and illustrations

Acknowledgements

Some of the research for this book was carried out while I held a visiting fellowship at the Program in Hellenic Studies at Princeton University in 2005 and a visiting fellowship in Athens funded by the Onassis Foundation in the same year. I would also like to express my gratitude to the staff at the Firestone Library at Princeton, the Gennadeios Library in Athens, and the Slavonic and Greek Section of the Taylor Institution Library in Oxford for their unfailing assistance.

Individuals who have helped me directly with the research and writing of this book, by supplying me with their own published and unpublished work, or by directing me to read certain works or to investigate various avenues, or by discussing the whole or part of my project include Anna Anastasiadi-Symeonidi, Stephen Batalden, Josep Maria Bernal, Peter Bien, Philip Carabott, Richard Crampton, Rea Delveroudi, Olga Demetriou, Damla Demirözü, Alex Drace-Francis, Georges Drettas, Anna Frangoudaki, Stathis Gauntlett, Alexandra Georgakopoulou, Vasilis Gounaris, Constanze Güthenke, I. K. Hassiotis, Martin Hintenberger, Renée Hirschon, David Holton, Marjolijne Jansen, Maro Kakridi-Ferrari, Nikolaos Kalospyros, Alexander Kazamias, Maxim Kisilier, Paschalis Kitromilides, John Koliopoulos, Paraskevas Konortas, Angeliki Konstantakopoulou, Asterios Koukoudis, Ioannis Kourboulis, Elena Koutrianou, Emmanouil Kriaras, Marc Lauxtermann, Mary MacRobert, Io Manolessou, Elli Droulia Mitrakou, Spiros Moschonas, John Nandriş, Vasilis Nitsiakos, Yannis Papadakis, Katerina Papatheu, Socrates Petmezas, Kostas Petropoulos, N. K. Petropoulos, Ioanna Petropoulou, Alexis Politis, Walter Puchner, Effi Rentzou, Julian Roberts, Michael Silk, Sir Michael Llewellyn Smith, Dimitris Stamatopoulos, Nicolae Şerban Tanaşoca, Mihai Ţipău, Arturo Tosi, Peter Trudgill, Karen Van Dyck, Gonda Van Steen, Nasos Vayenas, Peter Vejleskov, Pantelis Voutouris, Katerina Zacharia, and Anna Zimbone. In addition, I am immensely grateful to Roderick Beaton for reading a complete draft of this book and making a large number of suggestions for improvement. I am also grateful to Dimitris Gounelas, Dimitris Livanios, and Elina Tsalicoglou for reading and commenting on a number of draft chapters.

While supervising Dimitra Karoulla-Vrikki's 2005 thesis, I learned a great deal from her about the relationship between language and national identity. With specific reference to Cyprus, she provided me with important insights into the conflicting pulls of ethnic and state identity among the Greek-Cypriot community since 1960. It was working with her that made me realize that I wanted to write this book. I very much regret having been unable, for reasons of space, to give the sociolinguistic situation in Cyprus the attention it deserves in my book.

The image on page 248 was kindly supplied by the Library of the Hellenic Parliament.

Lastly, I would like to acknowledge my gratitude to the late Geoffrey Lewis for his enthusiasm, encouragement, and advice, and to Jackie for her support and tolerance.

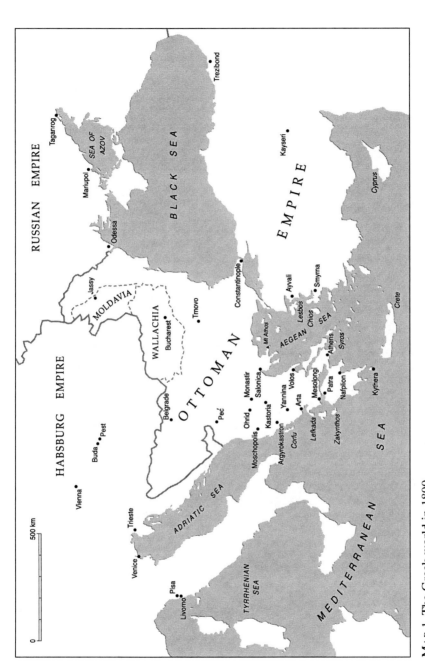

MAP 1 The Greek world in 1800

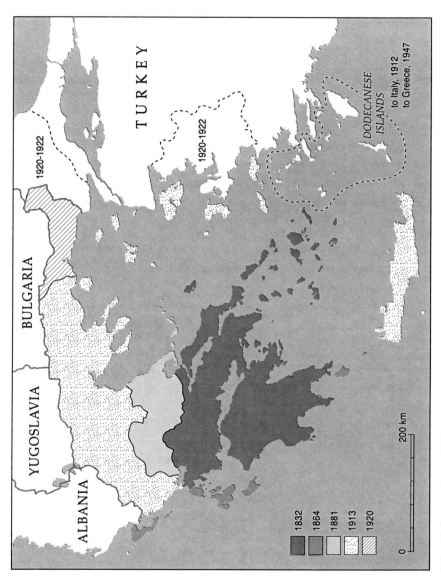

MAP 2 Greece since 1832

1

Theoretical background

Aims and approach

Over the last two centuries or so, Greek identity has usually been defined in terms of language and religion, with territory and landscape as additional factors. My aim in this book is to analyse the Greek language question within the context of nation-building and identity formation. Drawing on a variety of sources (literary, historical, and combative), I am presenting a historical study of the Greek language question with the help of the disciplines of linguistics, literary studies, and anthropology. In addition, I aim to identify the historical, political, social, and linguistic causes and ramifications of the controversy. It is no coincidence that the beginnings of the Greek language question lie in the late eighteenth century, at the point when a number of Greek intellectuals, under the influence of the European Enlightenment, were beginning to develop a new, specifically national, identity for themselves and their compatriots as Hellenes – a national identity that came to co-exist in a dialectical relationship with their traditional religious identity as Orthodox Christians.

The most intense phases of the Greek language debate have taken place during periods of crucial social transition. The first of these was the period from the 1760s to 1821, when – though many of the participants in the debate were unaware of it – the economic, intellectual, and political ground was being prepared for the Greek national revolution against the Ottomans. The second, a century later (1880s–1920s), coincided with the consolidation of the Greek bourgeoisie, the beginnings of industrialization, and the growth of the national expansionist movement, all of which demanded a more efficient education system. Perhaps the third was the period from 1974 to the early 1990s, with the return to democracy after a particularly inane dictatorship, and the entry of Greece into the European Economic Community (since renamed European Union) in 1981. This book focuses particularly on the first and second of these periods. I deal with the third period very briefly in the Epilogue.

My investigation takes account of both the language-planning policies of the Greek state (status planning) and the standardization efforts of cultural elites (corpus planning), in the context of the competing varieties of Greek and of the other languages (Turkish, Italian, Albanian, Aromanian, Slavonic, and others) that were spoken in areas in which Greek culture was dominant. Of these, Turkish (in the Ottoman empire) and Italian (in the Ionian Islands) were languages of political authority, and the other languages named above were for the most part confined to the status of local spoken vernaculars, while the status of Greek was somewhere between the two.

At the heart of the Greek language question was the desire to develop a written language that would reflect an ideal national image that would in turn embody and express the relationship of the modern Greeks to the ancients. The problem was that different members of the Greek elite entertained different versions of this national image. Archaists and purists claimed that the best way to demonstrate the modern Greeks' connection with the ancients was to imitate Ancient Greek linguistic models (chiefly in vocabulary and morphology), while vernacularists (later known as demoticists) argued that they could best demonstrate their direct cultural descent from the ancients by writing in a variety of Greek that was as close as possible to the spoken tongue, since, they asserted, the spoken language was the outcome of the natural and continuous development of the Greek language from ancient to modern times. I am using the term 'vernacular' (in Greek, *dimodis*) in preference to 'demotic' when talking about the spoken language before the demoticist movement in the late nineteenth century.[1]

This book is about how Greek cultural leaders have contributed to the formation of national identity by means of language, and how the language itself, in its turn, has been influenced by competing concepts of Greek national identity. It examines the ways in which language contributed to the building of the Greek nation out of the heterogeneous membership of the *Millet-i Rum* (the Orthodox Christian community of the Ottoman empire). I am focusing particularly on those Orthodox Christians who either spoke Greek or lived in the region that was to become what is now the Greek state.[2]

---

[1] Suleiman (2003: 10) uses the term 'colloquialists' as the equivalent of my 'vernacularists'. However, the term 'vernacular' has the advantage of meaning 'native language' as a whole, while 'colloquial' is restricted to informal spoken styles.

[2] For more on Greek nation-building see the essays collected in Beaton and Ricks (ed.) 2009.

In the title of this book, 'Greece' refers to the Greek *Kulturraum* or *Sprachraum*, which became exceptionally extensive from the 1760s onwards, as I shall explain in Chapter 2, where the geographical space that I am referring to will be more clearly defined. While I refer to Greeks scattered across Europe in the eighteenth and nineteenth centuries, there is no space in this book to deal with the twentieth-century Greek diaspora.[3]

As the title of the book makes clear, I am focusing on the particular relationship between language and national identity in Greece. Ideally, there should be a companion volume on religion and national identity, treating religion as a social phenomenon, particularly in terms of an attachment to rituals and a sense of group belonging rather than in terms of beliefs and dogmas. On this aspect, confining myself to publications in English, I can refer the reader to Clogg 1976a, Just 1988, Hirschon 1989, Stewart 2001, Molokotos-Liederman 2003, Kitromilides 2007, and various contributions to Beaton and Ricks (ed.) 2009. My references to religion will be largely confined to the attitude of the Orthodox Church hierarchy towards the Greek language question and to the multiplicity of languages spoken by its Balkan and Anatolian Orthodox flock. I cannot deal in this book with the strictly political aspects of church history, such as the relationship between the Ecumenical Patriarchate, the Sublime Porte, and the Greek state (together with its autocephalous Church).

In addition, my book should be read in conjunction with studies on literature and national identity (see Lambropoulos 1988 and Güthenke 2008), geography and national identity (see Peckham 2001), historiography and national identity (see K. Th. Dimaras 1986, Kitromilides 1998, Huxley 1998, and Koubourlis 2009 on Paparrigopoulos, Koubourlis 2005 on Spyridon Zampelios, and Liakos 2008), archaeology and national identity (see Hamilakis 2007), and folklore and national identity (see Herzfeld 1982).

Language is, among other things, the means by which its speakers make sense of their culture and express their feelings of belonging to a community. For this reason the study of a culture – whether by way of historical, anthropological, literary, or other approaches – needs to begin from the study of language, in terms of its vocabulary and grammar, of the ways in which it is used in social interaction, and of the ways in which

---

[3] For the more recent Greek diaspora see the contributions in Clogg (ed.) 1999a, especially Hirschon 1999 on identity and the Greek state.

it is viewed by its speakers. My book is chiefly about the third of these aspects.

I am not an anthropologist (though my thinking is influenced by a certain amount of anthropological writing), and I do not infer the attitudes of contemporary people by observing their behaviour. Rather, I base myself on the writings of individuals in the past who were by definition relatively privileged, in that they had access to print, albeit in some cases well after their death. By and large, they were members of cultural elites who could be described as opinion formers. It is not within my competence to investigate how these elite messages were received by the broad masses of the people. Suffice it to say that much of the nationalist discourse about language came to be incorporated into school teaching and therefore exerted a profound influence on the way large numbers of people in Greece came to think and talk about their language.

One of the many other things I am not qualified to do is to investigate the social forces at work in the language controversy: the role of various social and political interest groups in the controversy and the correlation between a person's class allegiance and political ideology and which language variety they supported. This has been ably carried out by Rena Stavridi-Patrikiou (1976, 1999) and Anna Frangoudaki (1977a, 1977b, 1987, 1992, 2001, 2002).

For my purposes, the term 'language question' covers the social and political aspects of the language situation in general and the debate about it, while 'language controversy' refers to explicit disagreements about the Greek written language. The *glossikó zítima* [Greek language question] has generally been seen in terms of the controversy about the different varieties of the Greek language. This has often obscured the broader question of languages in the plural, by which I mean the social relationship between Greek and other languages spoken in the same area. As far as this book is concerned, the Greek language question includes not only the controversy within the Greek language but also comparative attitudes to Greek and other languages.

According to Pierre Bourdieu, linguistics 'treats language as an object of contemplation rather than as an instrument of action and power'. In reality, he argues, linguistic exchanges are 'relations of symbolic power in which the power relations between speakers or their respective groups are actualized'.[4] In the two grammars of Modern Greek which

---

[4] Bourdieu 1991: 37.

I co-authored, I studied language more as an 'object of contemplation',[5] whereas in this book I am studying the ways in which language has been viewed and the ways in which it has been used to construct and disseminate national identities and to exert cultural authority and even political power.

One of the most recent scholars to discuss the Greek language question at length in English, Roderick Beaton, divides his treatment into three sections: 'The "Language Question" in theory', in which he sets out the main lines of the debate; 'The "Language Question" in practice', in terms of its influence on the language of modern Greek literature; and 'Beyond the "Language Question": words and things'.[6] In this book I aim to cover the first two aspects, though more the first than the second. Beaton writes that 'the "Language Question" can be seen as just one part of a continuing and complex dialogue between words and things, in which literature, naturally, has an important part to play'.[7] Whereas Beaton's book, like those of Bien (1972) and Tziovas (1986) before it, is centrally about literature, mine is not.

Nor am I attempting to make generalizations (as Beaton trenchantly does) about attitudes to the relationship between 'words and things' in Greece and about Greek perceptions of language from a philosophical or an anthropological point of view. It is telling that, whereas Beaton explicitly connects the phrase 'words and things' with Michel Foucault's book of the same name, I discuss it particularly in connection with an article by the late nineteenth-century poet and fiction writer Georgios Vizyinos (see Chapter 7). Be that as it may, as Beaton points out, in Greece, perhaps more than in other countries, words are, in an important sense, considered to be things.

Like other authors who have studied the Greek language question, Beaton displays a keen awareness of widespread Greek attitudes towards their language. As he puts it,

[l]anguage, in the dominant terms of the linguistic debate in Greece, is . . . a thing rather than a process, and moreover a thing with talismanic properties. Possession of it is a prerequisite for the survival and prosperity of the nation . . . ; conversely, as a thing, it is subject to the risks of damage and loss.[8]

---

[5] Holton, Mackridge, and Philippaki-Warburton 1997, 2004.

[6] Beaton 1999: 296–365. There is also a succinct survey of the language question in Horrocks 1997: 344–62.

[7] Beaton 1999: 365.   [8] Ibid., 350.

According to Beaton, the Greek language debate is 'a symptom of . . . a "reification" or "objectivization" of language, developed to an unusually high degree'.[9] A result of this is that 'attention is diverted from the meanings of words to their substance'; another is that '[b]oth sides in the debate invested language-as-thing with extraordinary power: the power to create or destroy the foundations of the state'.[10]

These are the aspects of the Greek language question that particularly interest me, namely language ideologies and their practical consequences. As Kathryn A. Woolard has written, language ideologies arise when speakers 'see language as a collection of words, commodified objects to be brought out and displayed'.[11] Language ideologies are the offspring of the union between speakers' linguistic awareness and the non-referential functions of language.[12] According to Jan Blommaert, they are '[t]he socioculturally motivated ideas, perceptions and expectations of a language'.[13] He and the other contributors to his edited volume wanted 'to add to the history of language and languages a dimension of human agency, political intervention, power and authority, and so make that history more *political*'.[14] It is noteworthy that Greece and Greek do not figure in the index of that volume; yet, in the case of Greek, one does not have to tell oneself and others to make the history of the language political. In Greece it is all too obvious that language ideologies, like identities, are the result of interaction, including the contestation of other ideologies or identities.

As John Joseph writes, 'it makes little sense to imagine one English language evolving over many centuries, rather than different English languages existing at different stages'.[15] One of the most pervasive language ideologies in Greece is the belief that Greek is a single language from antiquity to the present. This belief has greatly influenced its actual development and current use, since those who subscribe to this ideology have felt free to insert features from earlier stages of the language into their own discourse.

'A language is not a thing,' writes Joseph, 'but a practice always characterised by diversity, into which attempts at imposing unity are introduced'.[16] Thus synchronic linguistic unity is as much a matter of ideology as is diachronic unity. In the nineteenth and early twentieth centuries, Greek vernacularists asserted that there was a common spoken language, while their purist opponents argued that the spoken language

---

[9] Ibid., 351.   [10] Ibid., 352.   [11] Woolard 1998: 14.   [12] Kroskrity 2000: 5.
[13] Blommaert 1999: 1.   [14] Ibid., 5.   [15] J. Joseph 2006: 7.   [16] Ibid., 9.

was split into regional dialects. The likelihood is that it was neither the case that there was a common spoken language nor that there was not, but that the situation was somewhere in between. That is, despite the differences between regional dialects, Greek speakers were able to make themselves understood orally by Greek speakers from other regions.

In approaching the Greek language question I aspire to be both a 'critical analyst' and a 'sympathetic observer',[17] as Herbert C. Kelman described the great sociolinguist Joshua Fishman. Nevertheless, I need to make clear what direction I have come to the Greek language question from.

I studied Medieval and Modern Greek, at undergraduate and graduate level, at the University of Oxford. During the course of my studies, however, in the period 1966–73, I spent a total of four years in Athens. Most of this time coincided with the Colonels' dictatorship (1967–74). It was a period during which the eyes of the world were turned on Greece in a way that they never have been since, and living there at that time was an intense experience. One of the most obvious manifestations of the Colonels' ideology was their insistence that *katharévousa* (at that time the official language variety; the term literally means the language that 'tends towards purity') was the only variety of Greek worthy of being called the 'national language', whereas demotic was no more than a debased, corrupt, and barbaric idiom (the word *idíoma* is often used in Greek to denote a language variety that is claimed to be something less than a proper language). Meanwhile, almost all of the Greek literary texts I was studying for my Oxford degree courses were in demotic. They included the novels of Nikos Kazantzakis, which were being avidly read all over the world, and the poetry of Giorgos Seferis (who had recently been awarded the Nobel Prize in 1963) and Odysseas Elytis (who was to receive the same prize in 1979). My teachers at Oxford, Robin Fletcher and Constantine Trypanis, left their students in no doubt that, in their view, demotic was the proper language of the modern Greeks – proper in the double sense that it was their genuine and authentic language, and that the adoption of demotic for all communicative purposes was the only sensible solution to the language question. Fletcher had written a book on Kostis Palamas and lectured on the Greek poet's contribution to the language controversy.[18] Ever since my student days I have shared my teachers' attitudes on this subject.

---

[17] Kelman 1975: p. ix.
[18] The book was eventually published, after a long delay, as Fletcher 1984.

National identity and language

> The only way for us to become great and possibly even inimitable is for us to imitate the Ancients.
>
> (Winckelmann 1755)

> [T]he [ancient] Greeks never wholly were 'one people', but were ever in the process of becoming.
>
> (J. L. Myres)[19]

The terms 'national identity' and 'national consciousness' are often used interchangeably, or at least without an explicit distinction being made between them. However, Margaret Majumdar has recently made a useful distinction:

the notion of national identity remains predominantly a static one, in which the nation is presumed to be what it is. In its turn, this usually, but not inevitably, implies a degree of uniformity, in which national identity is taken to be the same for all citizens of the nation. National identity is thus often invoked with a conservative purpose in view: to maintain, to restore, the traditional elements that constitute this 'identity'. As such, it should be distinguished from the more dynamic, mobilising concept of 'national consciousness', which defines the coming together of the people as a collective subject with the common goal of a future project.[20]

While the raising of Greek national consciousness could indeed be a liberating force during the period before the War of Independence, it was the more conservative features of Greek national identity that soon predominated. However, as we have seen, there were at least two competing versions of the Greek national identity – represented by at least two different versions of the written language – that viewed the relationship between the modern Greeks and their ancient ancestors in strikingly different ways.

For the purposes of this book I define national consciousness as the belief or awareness that one belongs to a particular nation. By contrast, national identity consists of beliefs about what defines one's nation. National identity, then, refers to the content of a particular nationality. In my book I deal with the role of language in the development of national identity – what it means to be Greek, as preached by cultural and political elites – rather than in the development of national consciousness,

---

[19] Myres 1930: 538.   [20] Majumdar 2007: 127.

although both of these concepts constantly interact. I take consciousness to be more subjective, more related to feeling. It is often said to be 'awoken' or 'raised', but it is not necessarily articulated. By contrast, identity is a more intellectual concept, which is often expressed, analysed, and debated, chiefly by members of cultural and political elites.

National identity consists of a set of specific components that supposedly identify a particular nationality and distinguish it from others. These components can be inferred by outside observers, and they can be taught by educators. For most Greeks today, being Greek is chiefly defined by speaking the Greek language, being a member of the Orthodox Church, and living in lands that were inhabited by Greek ancestors. Beyond this, Greeks feel that their Church membership connects them particularly to the Byzantine empire, while their language connects them to Classical Hellas as well as Byzantium.

My outlook is existentialist rather than post-structuralist. I believe, like Jean-Paul Sartre, that 'existence precedes essence'.[21] I am convinced, in other words, that national identity is not a primordial and essential characteristic of individuals or groups, but is created and developed by a mixture of certain adventitious factors (living in a particular area, speaking a particular language, practising a certain religion) and influenced by certain goal-orientated activities, which are manifested especially in the education system and in the speeches and writings of political and cultural elites. Identity is not who or what people are in essence but who or what they think they are, who or what they say they are, and who or what they aspire to be.

Equally, identities are subject to manipulation. One is not born with a Greek (or any other) identity; one becomes a Greek through a complex process of acculturation, which normally includes one's own desire to espouse the dominant national identity. In some cases, however, to parody Shakespeare's Malvolio, 'some have Greekness thrust upon them': this applies particularly to non-Greek-speaking communities who found themselves, willy-nilly, living on Greek national territory as a result of the revolution of 1821 or later territorial wars. Gender identity, national identity, religious identity, social identity, regional identity – all these are acquired and developed through upbringing. Identities can change, and one can feel oneself to be situated in between the normally recognized categories. In each person who 'possesses' the same cluster of identities as other individuals, these identities may not exist in the same way.

---

[21] Sartre 1946: 17.

Each identity, though called by the same name, may be experienced in different ways – there is a wide variation in how strongly a person feels (s)he possesses a certain identity – and the relationship among the identities in the cluster may also differ from individual to individual.

As Joseph writes, it is now commonplace to assert that all group identities are 'claims made through performance. An identity exists by virtue of the assertions of the people who make it'. Yet, as he says, 'essentialism versus constructionism is not as mutually exclusive a distinction as it is normally taken to be'.[22] Language may not be a primordial constituent of nationality, but it is the chief medium through which speakers are acculturated into nationhood and one of the chief means by which they articulate their sense of it.

Yasir Suleiman rightly argues that 'national identity is a construct, in both the intellectual and the historical senses. It is fashioned out of history, or, more correctly, interpretations of history. The involvement of the elite in fashioning it is absolutely fundamental to formulating its intellectual foundations and, also, to popularizing it as the basis of mass political action.' Yet '[i]magination, invention and mythologizing work only to the extent that they can successfully exploit authentic and highly significant aspects of the culture of those for whom a particular national identity is being constructed'. For Suleiman's 'popularizing' I would prefer to say disseminating and propagandizing, while for his 'highly significant' I would prefer 'revered and cherished'. Suleiman notes the importance of aspects of nationalist discourse that are characterized by 'authenticity, rootedness, continuity, dignity and destiny'.[23]

Benedict Anderson, Eric Hobsbawm, and John Breuilly stress that national and ethnic identities – and national languages too – are largely a political creation.[24] The Greek case leads me to challenge this: the linguistic and educational crusade carried out by Adamantios Korais before 1821, for instance, was not primarily political; it was largely cultural. Before the revolution, Korais seems to have had remarkably little contact with the political and military figures who were to carry it out. Anderson argues that nationalism was made possible by directing appeals towards increasingly literate masses via print media written in the popular language.[25] This was not the case in Greece, where the popular language was largely marginalized until very late in the nation-building

[22] J. Joseph 2004: 20, 90.   [23] Suleiman 2003: 7.
[24] Anderson 1991; Hobsbawm 1992; Breuilly 1993.
[25] Anderson 1991: 80–2; also Hobsbawm 1992: 104.

process. Anderson and Hobsbawm portray language and nationalism in instrumental terms. Anthony D. Smith attacks this 'instrumentalist' view of culture as well as the 'primordialist' view, arguing that one needs to 'reconstitute the notion of collective cultural identity in historical, subjective and symbolic terms'.[26] This is what I am trying to do.

In this book I am dealing with nationalism in the sense of nation-building, that is, the effort to instil, in a certain community of people, a sense of nationhood (a term which I take to include both national consciousness and national identity, as I have defined them above), both before and after the creation of the nation-state. According to the anthropologist Anastasia Karakasidou, nation-building is 'a process of cultural revolution' through which 'education, religion, and institutions and symbols of state control shape the creation of a national identity, a new conceptual or intellectual framework for interpreting historical experience'.[27]

National identity is a complex matter, typically based on a sense of sharing the same language, religion, geography, history, descent (genealogy), nationality/citizenship, and culture/customs (or at least some of these features) with the other members of the same nation. I am not convinced, however, by other shared phenomena that scholars often include together with these components, such as 'common myths and historical memories',[28] since all national myths, as well as national memories that go back more than two or three generations, can be invented, manipulated, and disseminated. However, nationalists often claim that national identity involves a common cultural heritage, a common 'past' ('history'), and even a common 'future' ('destiny'), which emerges as a 'necessary' extension of the (constructed) shared past.

Pre-nationalist identities were normally defined by one's religion and one's social status within the local community. In post-medieval Europe, language became the chief defining factor of collective identity in the West, while religion remained the defining factor in Eastern Christendom.[29] The language controversy began when Greeks started to enter the West (and consequently to experience modernity) in significant numbers during the Enlightenment period, which was, for the Balkans, the equivalent of the European Renaissance. It was then that many Greek

---

[26] Smith 1991: 25.   [27] Karakasidou 1997: 18.

[28] See Smith 1991: 14. Renan (1882) too talks of 'la possession en commun d'un riche legs de souvenirs' as one of the two essential components of a nation (the other being a common desire to live together), but he fails to discuss how far back in time these memories might feasibly go.

[29] Koliopoulos 2003: 32.

intellectuals began to see language rather than religion as the primordial defining characteristic of the nation. Yet this defining characteristic had itself to be defined. As Paschalis Kitromilides writes, 'the language question formed the essence of the debate on cultural change in the Neo-Hellenic Enlightenment'.[30]

Fishman has stressed the importance of people's perception of the authenticity of their language. Authenticity implies the need to find 'roots', which imply both origins in past history and a physical and metaphorical groundedness in a certain place.[31] Korais probably felt that the written language variety he developed in the early nineteenth century was the 'true expressive vehicle of perfected nature'.[32] Language reformers such as Korais thought it necessary to fashion an 'apparently unified, authenticated and modern-problem-oriented nationality' and an 'apparently unified, authenticated and modern-problem-oriented language' out of manifest diversity.[33] According to Fishman, nationalism struggles to achieve a compromise between traditionalism (authenticity) and innovation (modernization) in language. This is what Korais thought he was doing in devising and disseminating his preferred variety of the Greek language. He was in favour of the importation of western European concepts, but not of the use of foreign words; he wished Greeks to see the modern world, but to see it though Greek eyes.[34]

In the West, Fishman writes, 'language (specifically, a society's perceived "own" language) has been elevated to the stature of a prime consideration in the life of most human collectivities. In other words, we have made language into something more important than might otherwise have been the case.'[35] The Greek language has been invested by its speakers with even more significance than most other European languages; a widespread Greek belief that they are privileged to possess their native tongue underlies not only the creation and use of *katharévousa* but also the widespread doom and gloom among Greeks today about the present state and future fate of their language.

André Mirambel concisely summed up the psychological factors underlying modern Greek purism as 'le prestige de l'antique' and 'la primauté de l'écrit', adding that the two factors cannot be separated, since Ancient Greek is known only through the written word. He goes

---

[30] Kitromilides 1983: 57.   [31] Kelman 1975: ix.

[32] Louis Ambroise de Bonald's description of French in the seventeenth century (1796), quoted in Ludassy 2004: 28.

[33] Fishman 1975: 62.   [34] Some of these thoughts are inspired by Fishman 1975: 73.

[35] Fishman 2001b: 2–3.

on to compare Greek purism with religious dogma: the 'sacred texts' of Hellenism were those of antiquity, while the modern vernacular was considered to be a 'profane' language.[36] Greek purism, like purism in other nations, was motivated, to a significant extent, by 'shame, insecurity and a collective inferiority complex about the blemishes and inadequacies of the national language'.[37] Moreover, Greek purism saw all deviations from Ancient Greek in the modern language as being the result of foreign influences. This goes together with the nationalist view of Greek history as the constant struggle of the Greek nation to defend its existence and its character against foreign occupiers.

Evangelos Petrounias has succinctly laid out three reasons for the creation of *katharévousa*: a national sense of cultural inferiority vis-à-vis both the ancient Greeks and modern western Europeans; the existence of an indigenous ruling group that felt alien to the majority of the population; and false linguistic premises.[38] With reference to the last of these factors, it was not sufficiently understood by Greek intellectuals in 1800 (and well afterwards) that it was possible to elaborate any spoken language in order to render it suitable for all purposes. In other words, they did not realize that all languages are 'poor' (particularly in terms of abstract vocabulary and of logical connectives such as 'therefore', 'however', and 'nevertheless') before they have been 'enriched'. In particular, they did not realize that it was unnecessary to use the morphological system of Ancient Greek in order to enrich the modern language.

R. B. Le Page and Andrée Tabouret-Keller entitled one of their books *Acts of Identity*.[39] In these terms, speaking and writing Greek has long been an act of national identity. In the nineteenth century, *katharévousa* and demotic were used in order to proclaim and enact competing versions of national identity. In the twentieth century, as we shall see from Chapter 8 onwards, each of these varieties was often used for the performance of a specifically *political* identity, that is, either 'conservative' or 'progressive'. As Rena Stavridi-Patrikiou has pointed out, the demoticist movement was constantly accused of 'anti-religiousness, anti-nationalism and immorality'. The threat posed to the political and cultural *status quo*, she concludes, 'did not concern a language variety but a view of life, which had to be protected by all means: ideological, political, legislative and constitutional'.[40]

[36] Mirambel 1964: 408, 434–5.
[37] Thomas 1991: 45, with reference to linguistic purism in general.
[38] Petrounias 1978: 198.   [39] Le Page and Tabouret-Keller 1985.
[40] Stavridi-Patrikiou 1999: 175.

Language and nationalism

A nation is an imagined community whose members believe that they are linked by a shared culture.[41] Nationalism is both an ideology and a political movement,[42] ideology being defined by the anthropologist Lloyd A. Fallers as 'that part of culture which is actively concerned with the establishment and defense of patterns of belief and value'.[43] Smith defines nationalism as 'an ideological movement aiming to attain or maintain autonomy, unity and identity for a social group which is deemed to constitute a nation'.[44]

Greek nationalism has been particularly intense because of the real or perceived rival claims of the Greeks' neighbours. From the outset, however, it did not stress the importance of common ancestry: you could become a Hellene even if you were an Aromanian or an Arvanite, provided you were a Christian and espoused the Hellenic cause.[45] Nor would it be accurate to claim that the modern Greek nation 'formed in the first place around a dominant *ethnie*, which annexed or attracted other *ethnies* or ethnic fragments into the state to which it gave a name and cultural character'.[46] In fact, ethnicity was hardly an issue in early Greek nationalism, which is why I avoid using the term in this book. This is because the Hellenic nation developed out of a religious community, the Orthodox Christian *millet* of the Ottoman empire, which gradually metamorphosed from a pan-Orthodox Balkan and Anatolian community into a number of distinct national communities: Greeks, Bulgarians, Romanians, and Albanians. It was precisely because it was originally a multi-ethnic movement that grew out of the Greek Enlightenment, which was itself a pan-Balkan enterprise, that early Greek nationalism did not stress vernacular language and culture; vernacular lexicographers and ethnographers came at a later stage. Later, state institutions, particularly education, spread the national idea further and deeper, both within the confines of the state and beyond its boundaries, until finally, as a result of the victorious Balkan wars of 1912–13 and the disastrous Asia

[41] Although I am borrowing the term 'imagined community' from Anderson, I am providing a looser definition of 'nation' than he does (Anderson 1991: 6).

[42] Jaffrelot 2005: 34.   [43] Fallers, quoted in Jaffrelot 2005: 36.   [44] Smith 1991: 51.

[45] Despite this, as Hirschon 1999: 161 notes, among Greeks today 'the belief in a shared and common blood is a key notion, one which is based on folk notions of biology'. This belief seems to have grown up independently of the discourse enunciated by political and cultural elites.

[46] The quotation is from Smith 1991: 39, though he is talking generally, rather than specifically about Greece.

Minor campaign of 1919–22, it confined itself to the borders of the now much enlarged state, which meant incorporating a large number of Slav, Albanian, and Aromanian speakers.

Nevertheless, for most of its history as an independent state, Greek national identity was based on language and religion rather than on shared institutions. Like Germany, Greece was a case of 'cultural nationalism' in the terminology of Hans Kohn (1946), as opposed to – or rather in tandem with – political nationalism: the beginnings of a cultural nationalist movement – as in the case of the two rival projects of Korais and Doukas in Greece (see Chapters 4 and 5) – preceded the founding of the state. In situations where a nation is based on language and religion, nationalists tend to think of other people, outside the boundaries of the nation-state, who either speak the same language or practise the same religion as those within it, as belonging equally to the same nation; this is the origin of Greek irredentism.

Studies of colonialism and nationalism rarely deal with nations emerging from the Ottoman empire. None of the contributors to Dieckhoff and Jaffrelot (2005) mentions Greek nationalism, for instance. Unlike the leaders of nations emerging from European imperial rule (including Greek Cypriots in the twentieth century), Greek cultural leaders in the eighteenth and nineteenth centuries were able to deploy European criteria in order to assert that their people were superior to their non-European masters. Indeed, it could be asserted that the reason why Greek intellectuals were able to shun their own vernacular was that they did not feel the need to rescue it from the domination of a colonialist language that was deemed to be superior.

In Greece, as elsewhere, nationalism began by being liberal (aiming at the liberation of peoples) but went on to become oppressive and divisive. Greek nationalism went through two overlapping stages: liberation nationalism began before the founding of the nation-state, while state nationalism began after the formation of the state. The first stage continued, in the form of irredentism, after the beginning of the second, often with little or no input from state institutions, as in the case of efforts to 'liberate' Macedonia and Crete in the mid-nineteenth century. Liberation nationalism is by definition dynamic, and in Greece it went together with enthusiasm for a new version of the language, whether that be the revival of Ancient Greek, which would symbolize the rebirth of the Hellenes, or the compromise variety elaborated by Korais, which attempted to bring Greek discourse closer to those of western European nations and which was the variety adopted for most written purposes.[47] State nationalism within Greece was static for most of the nineteenth century, generally occupied in consolidating the country's nationhood and citizenship through education and land reform, and it is not surprising that the language variety bequeathed to the nation by Korais was gradually rendered more antique as the decades passed.

Is national identity possible without nationalism? Ernest Gellner argues that nationalism creates nations, and not vice versa.[48] Is national identity possible without a state? A nation only begins to come into being when people begin to be conscious of it and feel loyalty and allegiance towards it as an 'imagined community'. Romantic nationalists claim that their national movement is the awakening of their nation to self-consciousness. Suleiman asserts that '[t]he existence of the state is necessary for the creation of a national identity in the political sense'[49] There is clearly a distinction to be made between Greek national identity before and after the creation of the Greek state, and thereafter between national identity in the Greek state ('free Greece') and in what was often called *ypódoulos ellinismós* [enslaved Hellenism] which meant, essentially, the unredeemed Greeks.

According to Michael Hechter, nationalist activities 'aim to make the boundaries of the nation – a culturally distinctive collectivity aspiring to self-governance – coterminous with those of the state'.[50] This is helpful, except that the concept of 'nation' is too reified here, too homogenized, and endowed with feelings and desires: it is precisely nationalist rhetoric that attributes feelings and desires to nations and peoples. Nationalist activities also aim to bring about national integration (what was commonly called in Greek *apokatástasis* [restoration, reinstatement, rehabilitation] and *oloklírosis* [completion, integration]). National integration has an external (physical) and an internal (psychological) dimension. In physical terms it entails the liberation of the national homeland and (in cases where only a portion of the national homeland has been liberated) the integration into the already liberated area of any other areas of the national homeland that still remain outside its borders. In psychological terms, national integration entails the cultural nationalization and homogenization of the populations that are considered to constitute the particular nation, including the nationalization and homogenization of the national language (i.e. efforts aimed both at standardizing the language itself and at getting everyone to be able to speak and read it),

---

[47] *Pace* Anderson 1991: 72, Korais was not young in 1803; he was 55 years old.
[48] Gellner 1983: 55–6.   [49] Suleiman 2003: 7.   [50] Quoted in Jaffrelot 2005: 12.

the nationalization and homogenization of national history, and in some cases the nationalization and homogenization of the national religion. One of the most important ways in which nationalists carry out the process of cultural homogenization is by creating a national consciousness and a national identity, which they disseminate among the people who are supposed to form part of that nation.

As far as language is concerned, it is significant that the French revolution saw linguistic diversity as a characteristic of the *ancien régime* that had to be eradicated.[51] In Greece too, the Greek language (albeit usually in its more archaic forms) was seen as a force of progress, while other languages were sometimes viewed as signs of backwardness. Modern spoken Greek was also considered by many Greek intellectuals to be a shameful reminder of the 'Ottoman yoke', but even they considered it to be superior to the other languages spoken in the region. Just as the French revolutionaries realized they had to 'franciser les français',[52] Greek intellectuals believed the Greeks, as well as other Orthodox Christians, had to be Hellenized. This meant not only getting all Greek citizens to speak Greek but also marginalizing the Greek spoken language, which was perceived by many Greek intellectuals to be split into diverse dialects, a phenomenon that threatened national unity.

Greek nationalism aimed at maximal national homogeneity. Jan Blommaert and Jef Verschuren talk of

the dogma of *homogeneism*: a view of society in which differences are seen as dangerous and centrifugal and in which the 'best' society is suggested to be one without intergroup differences. In other words, the ideal model of society is monolingual, monoethnic, monoreligious, monoideological. Nationalism, interpreted as the struggle to keep groups as 'pure' and homogeneous as possible, is considered to be a positive attitude within the dogma of homogeneism. Pluriethnic or plurilingual societies are seen as problem-prone, because they require forms of state organization that run counter to the 'natural' characteristics of groupings of people.[53]

Nationalism is tremendously assisted by the existence of a single language through which cultural homogeneity and the mobilization of the masses can be achieved. This single national language is useful both as a symbol of belonging to a single nation and as a practical channel for the dissemination of the nationalist ideology. The national language should be such that all members of the nation, whatever their origin or

---

[51] Thiesse 2005: 128.   [52] See Marcellesi 1981: 7.
[53] Blommaert and Verschuren 1998: 195.

social class, should be able to understand and use it;[54] yet this was not the case with *katharévousa*, which was used *de facto* as Greece's official language from 1830 to 1911 and *de jure* from 1911 to 1976.

In many countries, nationalists extolled and elaborated a single national language, 'liberated' their people and their homeland, set up a state, and continued a process of cultural homogenization. Why did this not happen in Greece? Why was the national language such a contentious issue, both before the first phase of liberation (i.e. before 1821), during the irredentist period (1844–1922), and for another half-century after that? Since Greek is an *Abstand* language (i.e. it differs radically from all the languages spoken around it),[55] there should, linguistically speaking, have been no difficulty in elaborating a written language on the basis of spoken varieties. The answer to this question, as I have already suggested, is that the disagreements about which variety of Greek was and should be the national language were due to disagreements over the definition of Greek national identity.

John Plamenatz talks of the 'rejection of ancestral ways which are seen as obstacles to progress yet also cherished marks of identity'.[56] In Greece there was a disjunction between these two outlooks. The purists tended to reject most aspects of recent traditional Greek culture – which they saw as 'obstacles to progress' – for the sake of the culture of ancient Greece (to which Byzantium was added later). It was the vernacularists who saw aspects of traditional modern Greek culture as 'cherished marks of identity'.

According to Gerhard Masur, 'nationalist movements have been invariably populist in outlook and sought to induct lower classes into political life'.[57] Yet in Greece, despite a law providing for compulsory primary education as early as 1834, purist nationalism failed to attempt this. It was in the nature of Greek linguistic purism to be elitist. A 'normal' cultural nationalism, influenced by Herder, did not become fully fledged in Greece until the second half of the nineteenth century. It was then that Greek cultural nationalists – language builders, ethnologists, folklorists, historians, and literary writers – set out to collect and protect the cultural heritage of the Greek folk before it was swamped by modernity. They investigated the history of the Greek language and recorded its dialects (focusing especially on those features that appeared to demonstrate that the dialects were more archaic than the language spoken by the urban

---

[54] Thiesse 2005: 128.   [55] For *Abstand* languages and *Ausbau* languages see Kloss 1967.
[56] Quoted in Jaffrelot 2005: 30–1.   [57] Quoted in Anderson 1991: 48.

middle class), studied the ethnological past of the populations that made up the nation, discovered the 'national epic', and gathered folk songs, folk tales, proverbs, and traditions, while the literary writers among them sought to embody much of this material in poems and works of fiction. The result was that the Greek people were now given 'a systematised culture which testified to its "primordial unity"'. Cultural entrepreneurs everywhere try to distinguish their people from all others in order to 'give legitimacy to their inclination for independence'[58] – and in Greece's case for their inclination towards irredentism. All this was typical of nationalist movements in many countries; what came extraordinarily late in Greece was the standardization of the national language.

The mutual influence of language and national identity

John Joseph points out that Benedict Anderson 'gives all his attention to how languages shape national identities, but none to how national identities shape languages, which they do profoundly'.[59] This is clearly apparent in the Greek case. For many Greeks, Saussure's distinction between the synchronic and diachronic dimensions of language (and particularly his privileging of the synchronic over the diachronic) has not applied and does not apply to their language.[60] Ever since late antiquity, the synchronic use of the Greek language has constantly been influenced by writers' recourse to material belonging – from a strictly, and therefore ideally, synchronic viewpoint – to earlier forms of the language. The use of lexical and grammatical features from older stages of the language in preference to their more recent equivalents is a function of Greek language ideologies.

Michael Silverstein has argued that a grasp of language ideology is essential to understanding the evolution of linguistic structures.[61] Again, this is clearly valid for the Greek language. An account of the specific influence of language ideologies on the vocabulary and grammar of Modern Greek – apart from the section entitled 'The linguistic consequences of the learned/popular distinction' in the Epilogue – is beyond the scope

---

[58] Much of this paragraph so far was inspired by Dieckhoff (2005: 71–2), from which the quoted passages are taken.

[59] J. Joseph 2004: 13, with reference to Anderson 1991.

[60] For treatments of these issues across the diachronic perspective see Georgakopoulou and Silk (ed.) 2009.

[61] Mentioned by Woolard 1998: 11.

of this book.[62] Instead, I will now look briefly at some of the ways in which language and national identity have interacted in Greece.

It is not necessary to subscribe to the Sapir–Whorf hypothesis – that different languages view the world in subtly different ways – in order to realize that different languages have slightly, but sometimes significantly, different ways (in both the semantics of their vocabulary and the structures of the grammar) of representing the world, and that these influence the ways in which a speaker or writer thinks. The differences between *katharévousa* and demotic were not as great as those that tend to subsist between two related but separate languages, but they were sufficient to influence the thought patterns of their users. Some Greek intellectuals have talked about a '*katharévousa* mentality' – a tendency towards clichés, empty rhetoric, and the pretentious display of lexical and grammatical virtuosity – which both influenced and was influenced by the nature of *katharévousa* itself. We also have the testimonies of a number of literary writers who, at some point in their careers, shifted from writing in *katharévousa* to writing in demotic. Subsequently, these writers tended to present their feelings at the moment of language shift in terms of a sense of liberation, a sense that at last they could express themselves freely, without the restrictions of a lexical and grammatical rigidity imposed from outside. Literature then went on to become demotic's Trojan horse that eventually enabled demotic to take over the citadels of power in Greece in 1976.

In a sense, the language shift brought about a change of identity among the Greeks from being constantly anxious to obey explicitly stated linguistic rules to feeling free to follow rules that they had internalized during their earliest childhood. When the reign of *katharévousa* came to an end in 1976, many Greeks felt, in their everyday lives, a kind of linguistic liberation and a greater sense of personal and national self-respect at the realization that the language they had imbibed with their mothers' milk was not only something to be cherished but something to be proud of – a sense of liberation and pride that was, rather paradoxically, not unlike the feelings that Ottoman Orthodox Christians before and during the Greek revolution must have experienced when they 'discovered' that they were not Greeks or Romans but 'Hellenes'.[63]

National identity can be instilled through what the social psychologist Michael Billig has famously called 'banal nationalism', the everyday

---

[62] For more details see Horrocks 1997: 362–5 and Mackridge forthcoming.
[63] See section 'Romans, Greeks, or Hellenes?' in Chapter 2.

performance of nationalism that comes to be perceived as a natural part of life. As Billig writes, 'an identity is to be found in the embodied habits of social life. Such habits include those of thinking and using language.'[64] In Greece banal nationalism includes the naming of infants, the replacement of place-names of non-Greek origin with Greek names (mostly ancient), and the naming of streets almost exclusively after persons or places from the past history and geography of Greece.

Whereas almost all Greeks were traditionally baptized with the names of saints recognized by the Orthodox Church, since the years immediately preceding the revolution it has been fashionable to name infants after Greek figures (whether deities or mortals) dating from the pre-Christian Greek past. There are even a couple of oft-quoted stories of Greek pupils in the 1810s being encouraged to replace their Christian names with the names of illustrious ancient Greek figures – at least within the confines of the school.[65] Today a significant proportion of Greeks bear given names associated with pagan antiquity. Such names are a constant reminder of, and a source of pride in, one's belonging to a three-thousand-year-old Greek nation. This is an instance in which the development of a Greek national identity has had a profound impact on the language.

The renaming of places is a striking component of the process whereby Greek cultural and political leaders have attempted to reflect and impose an already formulated national identity through changes in the language that would in turn help to fashion the national identity of their compatriots. Immediately after the Greek state was founded, a long-drawn-out process began whereby many place-names of non-Greek origin were replaced by ancient or pseudo-ancient names that were supposed (sometimes erroneously) to have some connection with the area – a trend that has continued until the present day. The renaming was carried out by both central and local government. To take two striking examples from the Athens area, the port known as Drakos to the Greeks, Porto Leone to the Venetians, and Aslan Limanı to the Turks – all after the large ancient marble lion that had stood on the harbour's edge until it was removed to Venice by Francesco Morosini in 1687 – reverted to its ancient name

---

[64] Billig 1995: 8–9.

[65] These are mentioned by K. Th. Dimaras 1985: 59–60, one involving the teacher Dionysios Pyrros in Athens in 1813, another the pupils of the school at Kydonies (Ayvali) in 1817. Clogg (1985: 17) points out that in the latter case the pupils' decision to change their names seems to have been due to the encouragement of the French printer and Philhellene Ambroise Firmin Didot, who reported the incident.

of Piraeus, while the island of Koulouri became Salamis again. As the authorities were well aware, changing names is not only an explicitly ideological act, it also changes the nature of the named item.

The renaming of places was carried out on an *ad hoc* and sometimes arbitrary basis until measures were taken to place the process on a systematic footing. In 1909 a committee was established by Royal Decree, chaired by the folklorist Nikolaos Politis, 'to study the toponyms of Greece and ascertain their historical rationale'. The text accompanying the decree, probably drafted by Politis himself, set out the justifications for this enterprise. The changes of place-names since ancient times often reflected 'national calamities and humiliations', and for this reason 'offended the patriotic sentiments of the educated'. By contrast, 'the obliteration of every trace of earlier national discomforts' from the topography of Greece had complemented the process of liberation. The government's effort to replace the old names had been an attempt 'at the resurrection of the old names of Greece'. Barbarian names, as well as ugly-sounding Greek ones, not only 'distress the linguistic sense' but 'have a harmful cultural effect on the inhabitants, somewhat reducing and humbling their *frónima* [national pride]'. Furthermore, foreign names erroneously suggested that the inhabitants were of the same 'national composition' as the names themselves. The only foreign names that should be preserved were those that had been 'sanctified by heroic actions' in the War of Independence. Tellingly, not only 'barbarous' names, but also 'insignificant' ones had been or were to be replaced, 'insignificant' meaning 'without national historical significance'. 'The historical knowledge that is enclosed in place-names is important and valuable, since it sheds light... on dark periods of our national history; indeed, one of our geographers [Antonios Miliarakis] has compared them with inscriptions carved into the very *édafos* [territory, ground, soil].'[66] After the Balkan wars (1912–13) there was a further spate of renaming in Greece's newly-acquired territories in Macedonia and Thrace, where a significant proportion of the place-names were Slavic or Turkish.

In this way the topography and cartography of Greece have become one vast lesson in Greek national history, which is physically inscribed

---

[66] The quotations and paraphrases in this paragraph relate to the text of the 1909 decree and its accompanying explanatory text, reproduced in Chouliarakis 1973: 207–10. This text was also included in the final report of the committee, published by the Ministry of the Interior as N. G. Politis 1920: 3–6. The definition of 'insignificant' is given ibid., 9. For the renaming of places see also Triantafyllidis 1938: 570–9.

in the landscape. The new names are an attempt to purify the landscape,[67] reconstructing Hellas (or in some cases a Hellenized Byzantium) on the landscape and on the map and effacing more recent or more heterogeneous aspects of Greek history and culture, including Slav settlements and Ottoman domination.

Language planning and power

The emergence of new nations and new states normally involves a certain amount of language planning. Robert Cooper has attacked Einar Haugen's view that language planning occurs 'wherever there are language problems', arguing instead that 'language planning is typically motivated by efforts to secure or maintain interests, material or nonmaterial or both'.[68] This has clearly been the case in Greece.

However, Greece is unusual in that it has been through two distinct, but chronologically overlapping, stages of language planning. The first (which could be called the *katharévousa* project) was pioneered by Korais in the early years of the nineteenth century and continued for about a century. The second (the demotic project) was carried out in two different versions, the first by Psycharis from 1888 onwards and the second by Manolis Triantafyllidis and other indigenous Greek intellectuals since the first half of the twentieth century.

Haugen divided language planning into status planning and corpus planning.[69] Status planning refers to the choice as to which language, and which variety of this language, to use as the standard. Corpus planning refers to the interventions aimed at rendering the chosen variety adequate to the functions it is called upon to perform. The aim of corpus planning has been expressed as 'minimising variation in form and maximising variation of function'.[70] Cooper added a third dimension, namely acquisition planning, which refers to the efforts to disseminate the chosen variety, chiefly through education.[71]

Charles Ferguson listed the following processes that constitute what he called 'language development', that is, corpus planning: graphization; standardization, i.e. the development and codification of a single norm

---

[67] Hamilakis 2007: 85–6. Hamilakis also talks about the 'retrieval' of the ancient names of towns (ibid., 82), which suggests that they are perceived as having been won back from the grasp of foreign occupiers.

[68] Cooper 1989: 34–5, 183.

[69] According to Wright (2004: 42), these terms were apparently invented by Haugen 1968. Cooper 1989: 31 attributes them to Kloss in 1969.

[70] Wright 2004: 48, paraphrasing Haugen 1966.   [71] Cooper 1989: 33–4.

(unification across registers and across dialects); and modernization (a process known to other scholars as elaboration[72]), namely the expansion of the vocabulary and the development of new styles and forms of discourse. Graphization hardly applies to the Greek case, since numerous varieties of Greek had been written for well over two millennia.

Standardization could not really be carried out on *katharévousa* because it was dependent – even parasitic – upon both Ancient Greek and the spoken language rather than being a distinct variety with its own system and its own rules. Since *katharévousa* was both distant from common usage and not standardized, it was to be expected that there would be a reaction that would lead to a written language closer to common usage being put in its place. The development of *katharévousa* took place empirically and unsystematically at the hands of non-linguists, while the planning of demotic was carried out in a systematic manner by linguists as well as by literary writers.

Modernization entails 'the development of intertranslatability with other languages in a range of topics and forms of discourse characteristic of industrialized, secularized, structurally differentiated modern societies'.[73] In Greece modernization was carried out first in *katharévousa*, then in demotic. In the *katharévousa* project, semantic modernization or renovation went hand in hand with formal archaization, as new concepts imported from the West were clothed in ancient or apparently ancient words and morphological forms.

Elaboration is carried out with the aim of counteracting the perceived inadequacy of a variety. Joseph distinguishes between 'remedial' and 'cosmetic' elaboration, examples of the latter being the baroque over-elaboration of spelling in seventeenth-century France and England. Remedial elaborations fill an apparent (or real) gap in languages' use, whereas cosmetic elaborations, while unnecessary for purely communicative purposes, 'may give the elite avant-garde in particular a sense of the "worthiness" of the language'.[74] This is exactly the situation with Greek linguistic purists: by equating 'correction' with 'embellishment', they conflated the remedial with the cosmetic. The continuing process of embellishment, which the purists inherited from the written tradition of Greek, led to a baroque tendency in the writing of *katharévousa* (and preserved to a lesser degree in demotic), which is manifested in the supposedly etymological system of orthography and in the use of a

---

[72] Ibid., 150.   [73] Ferguson 1968: 28.
[74] Millar 2005: 68, referring to J. Joseph 1987: 104–6.

more complex system of diacritics than is functionally significant. The combination of these two factors led to a situation in which there were 24 ways of writing the sound [a] and at least 55 ways of writing the sound [i] in lower-case – only one of which was considered to be correct in the context of a particular word.[75] Most – though by no means all – of the purists insisted on preserving all of these complexities, while there has been a tendency for demoticists to call for gradual orthographic simplification.

There is no space in this book to deal in detail with orthography. It is, however, an important aspect of the Greek language question, since most educated Greeks over the centuries have believed that the visual appearance of Modern Greek should be as similar to Ancient Greek as is practicable. Implementing radical changes in the traditional orthographic system of Greek, which had remained the same (apart from the diacritics) since the fifth century BC,[76] has been seen by many Greeks as making the modern language independent from Ancient Greek. Some saw this a positive step, but most did not.

The written language variety elaborated by Korais, and which developed into what became known later as *katharévousa*, was the outcome of his lexical expansion of Modern Greek combined with what he called 'correction', that is, a process of morphological archaization in keeping with an arbitrary selection of the rules governing the phonology and morphology of the ancient language. Psycharis' version of written demotic was the outcome of his own quite different process of lexical expansion of Modern Greek, coupled with his own 'correction' in keeping with the rules governing the phonology and morphology of the modern spoken language. While Greek as a whole can be considered to be an *Abstand* language, Psycharis' demotic was like an *Ausbau* language in the sense that he systematically set about making it as different as possible from *katharévousa*, which was the Other that helped his demotic to define itself.

Of the two rival language-planning projects in Greece, the demotic project has received a huge amount of scholarly attention. This is partly because the planning of demotic in the first half of the twentieth century

[75] In the case of [a], this figure is due to the possibility of writing alpha alone or with one or more of the following diacritics: one of three accents, one of two breathings, and the iota subscript. In the case of [i], the possibilities are increased because this sound can be represented by several different individual letters and combinations of letters.

[76] The system of diacritics remained virtually the same from the ninth century AD, when minuscule (lower-case) letters were introduced, up to the twentieth century, the only innovation being the iota subscript, which was introduced in the thirteenth century.

was carried out by specific individuals, often in collaboration with the state. What has been little studied is the *katharévousa* project. Aside from Korais, little is known about the agents who planned *katharévousa* in theory and by what processes it was developed in practice. There is an urgent need for further research in this area, but it lies beyond the scope of this book.

Sue Wright has written that '[c]odification and standardisation are... usually state initiatives, undertaken by prestigious language academies at the behest of the government or sovereign'.[77] This has not been the case in Greece, where language planning was usually a matter of *laissez-faire* and private enterprise. As far as *katharévousa* is concerned, the process that took place was not so much language planning as such (which conjures up images of state committees whose proposals are immediately and permanently put into practice) as language-building (on the analogy of nation-building) – an ongoing process to which a large number of individuals and institutions have made their contributions. Kathryn A. Woolard has written that 'new emphasis on the ideological dimension of language practices has given rise to analyses of language standardization as a discursive project, treating "standard" more as ideological process than as empirical linguistic fact'.[78] In this sense the term *katharévousa* (literally meaning 'language in the process of becoming pure') was honest and transparent, since it denoted not so much a standardized form of a language as a gradual process of linguistic purification.

As John Joseph has pointed out, the question as to who has authority over a language is a political issue.[79] Many of the insights into the relations between language and power expressed by Bourdieu are already familiar to those working on modern Greece. This is due to the fact that Greeks have explicitly discussed the social aspects of language (e.g. the correlation between language and power) that in other countries (such as Britain) have been ignored or suppressed. *Katharévousa* was a *performative* language *par excellence*: its users were 'legitimized', by virtue of their language, to make authoritative statements that brought into existence what they asserted.[80]

In view of this, it is a curious fact that, until recently, the concept of language planning has been very little known about and acknowledged in Greece. Those who have written about Greek language planners have tended to deny that they have exerted any practical influence on the

---

[77] Wright 2004: 53.   [78] Woolard 1998: 21.   [79] J. Joseph 2006: 9.
[80] See Bourdieu 1991: 70, 222.

language. The literary and cultural historian Alkis Angelou, for instance, writes: 'Language...is not susceptible...of either regulation or correction during the course of its development'.[81] On the contrary, the Greek case demonstrates quite clearly – more clearly perhaps than most – that language planning can be highly effective.

Diglossia

In 1885 the novelist and essayist Emmanouil Roïdis coined the term *diglossía* to denote the use, by the same speakers in different circumstances, of two lexically and grammatically distinct varieties of Greek. He asserted that it was not simply a distinction between written and spoken discourse, or between the language of the educated elite and the language of the populace. He illustrated his argument by pointing out that members of parliament used one variety of the language when delivering their prepared speeches and another during the cut-and-thrust of debate.[82] Two years before the publication of his demoticist manifesto *My Journey*, Psycharis used the term *diglossía* in a paper written in Greek in 1886, where he defined it (though not explicitly in terms of the coexistence of demotic and *katharévousa*) and claimed that it appeared to be an Oriental phenomenon, since it was found in Arabic, Chinese, and Sanskrit as well as Greek.[83]

As defined by Ferguson (1959), diglossia denotes the complementary use, by the same speech community, of two forms of the same language, each of which has a restricted range of registers (different varieties used in different social situations). Ferguson contrasted diglossia with bilingualism (the use of two different languages by the same speech community), although later scholars have tended to subsume 'societal bilingualism' (as opposed to the existence of bilingual individuals) under diglossia. He also contrasted diglossia with the existence of different dialects, i.e. different varieties of a single language used in different geographical regions. The ideal diglossic situation would be one in which there were two linguistic varieties (which Ferguson labelled 'low' and 'high' respectively) that were perceived to be distinct, and in which, say, one of the two linguistic varieties were reserved for informal speech, and the other for formal speeches and for the law, the administration, education, and literature.

---

[81] Angelou 1998: 79*.   [82] Roïdis 1885: 116–17.
[83] Psichari 1888 [= Psycharis 1902: 129, 155]. Psichari 1885: 211, n. 1, using *diglossie* for the first time in French, acknowledges Roïdis 1885: p. xvii as the inventor of the term.

Ferguson's dualistic pattern has been criticized for being too schematic and for not taking sufficient account of the differences between cultures; indeed, some years ago, Georges Drettas called – rightly but, as it turns out, unsuccessfully – for the concept to be abandoned on the grounds that it is inadequate for the description of Greek, which was the focus of one of Ferguson's principal case studies.[84] The concept of diglossia tends to reify two distinct varieties, which are supposed to be formally contrasted and socially complementary. Ferguson does not allow for hybrid varieties, such as are to be found in societies that he described as diglossic.[85]

Furthermore, linguists and speakers may have different perceptions and different criteria for distinguishing between the two 'varieties'. In Greece, for instance, linguists distinguished between *katharévousa* and demotic chiefly on the level of morphology, secondarily on the level of phonology, and thirdly on the level of vocabulary, whereas ordinary speakers tended to distinguish them more by 'feel', paying attention not only to vocabulary but also to discursive phenomena such as style, complexity or simplicity of sentence structure, and impersonal or personal expression, which are distinctions that fall outside the criteria used by traditional linguistics. In this book I am using narrowly linguistic criteria (lexis and grammar) for making the distinction between the two varieties.

All languages have different registers for different purposes; the difference between Greek and, say, English is that, whereas in English it is mostly a matter of details (e.g. 'do not' vs. 'don't', 'enter' vs. 'go in'), the two recognized varieties of Greek were systematically distinguished in phonology and morphology, somewhat less systematically in vocabulary and syntax, and in some cases in semantics. For example (A = Ancient Greek, K = *katharévousa*, D = demotic):

- phonology: AK ανοικτός /aniktós/ vs. D ανοιχτός /anixtós/ [open];
- morphology: AK κυβερνήσεως /kiverníseos/ vs. D κυβέρνησης /kivérnisis/ [government (gen. sg.)];
- vocabulary: AK οίκος /íkos/ or οικία /ikía/ vs. D σπίτι /spíti/ [house, home];

---

[84] Drettas 1981: 66. Among the many more recent critiques of Ferguson's concept see Daltas 1994 and the contributions to Fishman (ed.) 2002. For diglossia in Greece see, among others, Petrounias 1978, Alexiou 1982, Browning 1982, Frangoudaki 1992, Kazazis 1993, and Holton 2002.

[85] For instance, Martinet 1982: 11, 16 warned against any 'opposition binaire simpliste' and against 'les simplifications abusives, les réductions formalisantes'.

- syntax: από /apo/ [from] with the genitive case in AK, but with the accusative in D; K ο προαναφερθείς υπουργός /o proanaferθís ipurγós/ [the aforementioned minister], using the aorist passive participle that in spoken Greek is hardly used outside fixed expressions, vs. D ο υπουργός που μόλις αναφέραμε /o ipurγós pu mólis anaférame/ [the minister we have just mentioned];
- semantics: AK πόλις /pólis/ [city], D Πόλη /póli/ [Constantinople]; πολιτεία /politía/ ΛK [state, polity], D [town]; άρματα /ármata/ A [chariots], K [tanks], D [weapons] (cf. AK όπλα /ópla/ [weapons]); καταλάβω /katalávo/ (perfective form) AK [capture], D [understand]; απομάθω /apomáθo/ (perfective form) AK [unlearn] (cf. D ξεμάθω /ksemáθo/ (perfective form) [unlearn]), D [learn completely].

However, the Greek situation was never as simple as Ferguson's binary opposition – or the above examples – would suggest. In the early stages of the period covered in this book, it is more helpful to talk about polyglossia than diglossia, while today Greeks live in a situation not of diglossia but of monoglossia. Yet the fact that Beaton can describe this monoglossia as polyphony[86] shows how much variety and freedom of choice there is to be found in contemporary Greek – a healthy and normal situation that contrasts with the earlier pathological situation in which the Greek language found itself.

Although the words *katharévousa* and *dimotikí* [demotic] were first used as feminine adjectives qualifying *glossa* or *diálektos* [language] by Nikiforos Theotokis (1796) and Panagiotis Kodrikas (1818) respectively,[87] they did not become key terms as nouns until the crucial period of the language controversy that began with the publication of Psycharis' book *My Journey* in 1888; only then did it become usual for Greeks to take opposing sides and view the language question in terms of two more or less well-defined alternatives. Diglossia is as much a matter of speakers' perceptions (including the labels used) as of the actual sociolinguistic situation, which is always more messy; actual language used in Greece covered a continuum of linguistic registers ranging from 'pure' demotic to 'extreme' *katharévousa*, with hybrid varieties in between.

---

[86] Beaton 1999: 346.
[87] Papazoglou 1991 plausibly claims that Kodrikas based this term on the distinction made by Herodotus – and by French Egyptologists of Kodrikas' time – between 'hieroglyphic' and 'demotic' Egyptian.

From about 1880 to 1976 many Greek literary authors were diglossic in their writing; for instance, in his capacity as general secretary of Athens University, the demoticist poet Kostis Palamas drew up official documents in impeccable *katharévousa*; similarly Giorgos Seferis wrote in *katharévousa* as a diplomat and civil servant, whereas all of his literary writings are in demotic. Until 1976, all educated Greeks had been taught Ancient Greek at school, and even today Greek churchgoers are used to listening to archaic Greek being chanted and recited. It is inevitable that these experiences would influence actual language use. Hybrid varieties could be interpreted by observers as the result of interference from one variety in the use of the other, but the speakers or writers themselves may not have seen it that way. As Margaret Alexiou puts it, 'the two forms [*katharévousa* and demotic] interpenetrate continuously, yet exclude each other consciously'.[88]

Another complicating factor is that, as Anna Frangoudaki points out, 'demotic' properly denotes not the actual spoken language but a 'codified and normalized form of the "natural" language'.[89] From this point of view, which I share, contrary to the perceptions of many observers, demotic is primarily a written language. In fact, demotic was supposed by its supporters to be a standardized written version of a common spoken language (often known as 'Panhellenic *koine*'), as opposed to dialects and other regional varieties.

According to Ferguson, the 'high' variety is typically more standardized than the 'low' one.[90] As we have seen, however, *katharévousa* could never be as standardized as written demotic. This is because *katharévousa* is a hybrid consisting of lexical and grammatical features belonging to different historical stages of spoken Greek from Classical times to the present day, and writers of *katharévousa* differed from each other (and were often inconsistent with themselves) in the proportions and the categories of the archaic features that they used.

Once demotic had been planned as a written language from the late nineteenth century onwards, it ceased *de facto* to be 'low', and its supporters challenged the *de jure* monopolistic privilege of *katharévousa* to be thought of as 'high'. From the late nineteenth century until 1976, when demotic and *katharévousa* co-existed as written varieties usable, actually or potentially, for all written purposes, two rival standard varieties of the language competed for the same social functions. In this respect the

[88] Alexiou 1982: 178.   [89] Frangoudaki 1992: 360.
[90] This is repeated by Millar 2005: 4.

situation in Greece was somewhat similar to that in Norway, where there are also two standard written varieties that compete to 'represent the nation'.[91] Nevertheless, neither of the two written varieties of Norwegian is as artificial as *katharévousa*, since each of them is based, to a greater or lesser extent, on a spoken variety. Moreover, since 1885 both varieties have received legal recognition as being of equal value, whereas in Greece *katharévousa* alone was the official language of the state from 1911 to 1976, and demotic alone from then on.

In Cyprus, by contrast, since independence in 1960, the Greek Cypriots have fitted the Fergusonian model of diglossic community more closely than the Greeks of Greece. Whereas the official language of the Republic of Cyprus, alongside Turkish, has been the same as in Greece itself (*katharévousa* until 1976, demotic since then) and most writing and official oral communication is carried out in standard Greek, Greek Cypriots speak amongst themselves informally in Cypriot Greek, which is markedly different from the standard written variety and is not normally used even in literature, except when recording or imitating folk poetry or for comic purposes.[92]

---

[91] Haugen 1966: 305.

[92] Karoulla-Vrikki 2005: 13–14. For the relationship between the Greek dialect of Cyprus and Greek-Cypriot identity see Karoulla-Vrikki 2004, 2005, and 2008/9.

2

The preconditions for the Greek
language controversy

In order to understand how and why the Greek language controversy
materialized in the late eighteenth century one needs to investigate the
geographical spread of the Greek language, the places where the Greeks
lived, and who was considered to be Greek. In this chapter I aim to
sketch out the historical, geographical, social, cultural, and ideological
background to the emergence of the controversy.

Greek political and cultural geographies, real and imagined

During the period between 1760 and Greek independence around 1830,
Greeks found themselves caught up in power struggles and realignments
among no fewer than six empires: the Ottoman, Venetian, Russian,
Holy Roman (in practice, the Habsburg monarchy), French, and British.
The Ottoman empire was home to the vast majority of the Orthodox
Christians who lived outside the Russian empire. The Venetian empire
controlled the Ionian Islands until it was destroyed by France in 1797.
The Russian empire, the only Orthodox Christian state in the world, was
constantly fighting wars with the Ottomans and in 1770 encouraged a
revolt in Greece with the aim of detaching the country from the Ottoman
empire and eventually capturing the Ottoman capital, Constantinople. The
Habsburg empire controlled lands to the north and west of Greece. France
occupied the Ionian Islands for varying periods between 1797 and 1814
and Egypt from 1798 to 1801, and seemed set to try to liberate Greece
from the Ottomans before its forces were defeated by the British.[1] The
British empire took all of the Ionian Islands under its 'protection' from

---

[1] Solomos (1961: 135), in a note to his unfinished poem on the death of Lord Byron, written in
or soon after 1824, quotes Napoleon as having exclaimed: 'La Grèce attend un libérateur!...Je
n'en ai peut-être pas été loin'. As his source Solomos cites Emmanuel Las Cases, *Mémorial de
Sainte-Hélène*, vol. 2, p. 366. This work was first published in 1823.

1815 to 1864 and later went on to rule Cyprus from 1878 to 1960. When Greece eventually became an independent state in 1830, it did so under the official protection of Britain, France, and Russia. It was within this geographical and political environment that the Greeks had to develop both the cultural identity and the geographical extent of their nation.

For pious Orthodox Christians in the Ottoman empire in the eighteenth century the only alternative to tolerating their subjection to the Ottoman regime was to hope and pray for 'salvation' by Russia, which would have meant being subsumed into an Orthodox Christian empire instead of a Muslim one. Greeks largely abandoned what Kitromilides calls the 'Russian expectation' in 1792 after their hopes had been disappointed by the peace concluded between Russia and Turkey in the face of the French revolution.[2] This eventually led to a sense that the Greeks would have to liberate themselves on their own initiative.

In the late eighteenth and early nineteenth centuries, Orthodox Christians with religious allegiance to the patriarchate of Constantinople lived in the domains of all of the empires that have been mentioned above. The Ottoman empire included what is now Greece, Albania, Serbia, the Former Yugoslav Republic of Macedonia, Bulgaria and parts of Romania as well as present-day Turkey, and large numbers of Orthodox Christians lived in all of these regions; indeed, they formed an overall majority of the population in all of these areas except Asia Minor. An indication of the geographical extent of those who spoke and read Greek in the late Ottoman period is the fact that, of those individuals whose names appear on the lists of subscribers to the publication of books in Greek between 1749 and 1821, only 7 per cent lived in areas that were to form part of the new Greek state whose borders were determined in 1832. The largest number of subscribers lived in Constantinople, Vienna, and Bucharest, followed by Jassy, Smyrna, and Mount Athos.[3]

Since the patriarch of Constantinople was the spiritual leader of all of the Orthodox Christians in the Ottoman domains, the patriarchate was like an empire within an empire, dominating not only the religious life of the Orthodox Christians but their educational and cultural life as well. The Ottoman empire also included the three other eastern patriarchates, those of Antioch, Jerusalem, and Alexandria, but, among the four patriarchs, the patriarch of Constantinople was considered to be *primus inter pares*. While the patriarch of Antioch resided in Damascus, the patriarchs of Jerusalem and Alexandria resided in Constantinople, which

---

[2] See, for example, Kitromilides 1996: 169, 190, 288.   [3] Iliou 2005: 118.

meant that the religious authorities of the vast majority of the Christians of the empire were concentrated in the Ottoman capital. According to Douglas Dakin, by the end of the eighteenth century the patriarch of Constantinople was the spiritual – and some extent temporal – ruler of some thirteen million Christians, representing about one quarter of the empire's inhabitants.[4] The official language of all four of the eastern patriarchates – the language in which they conducted their business as well as the language of the liturgy in the majority of churches – was Greek, and in practice almost all of the incumbents of the four patriarchates during this period, together with the majority of the bishops, were native speakers of Greek.

It is often claimed that the Orthodox Church preserved a sense of Greek national consciousness under Ottoman rule. In reality, the Church was concerned to preserve the Orthodox tradition, with its accompanying dogma, ritual, and institutions, and to perpetuate and, if possible increase, its own authority vis-à-vis both the Ottoman Porte and its own flock. Inasmuch as Greeks identified themselves as belonging to the Orthodox Church rather than to any national group, the Church did indeed preserve a sense of Greek communal identity. However, this does not mean that the Church preserved a sense of Greek nationhood in the modern sense of the word.

The fact that Muslims in the Ottoman empire were liable to be summoned for military service at any time favoured the Greeks, Jews, and Armenians in the sense that they were able to engage in trade as merchants and artisans unimpeded by military call-ups. In the seventeenth and eighteenth centuries a number of members of the subject peoples in the Ottoman empire involved themselves in the European maritime trade and in the overland caravan trade with Central Europe. Businessmen from these peoples established themselves in cities on the Mediterranean, in Central Europe and (a little later) in Russia, chiefly in order to bring goods into and out of the Ottoman empire, and Greeks became the necessary middlemen in the commerce of all the European states with the empire. Many Greeks, especially in Constantinople and some of the islands, also became shipowners and sea captains, whose merchant vessels plied the Mediterranean and, from the 1770s onwards, the Black Sea. Greek merchants rapidly displaced the French in the Levantine trade and came to control three quarters of this French commerce. Greeks gradually gained almost total control over the import and export trade of the Balkan

---

[4] Dakin 1972: 11–12.

peninsula, and they succeeded in establishing almost complete maritime and commercial supremacy in Constantinople.[5] The Greek diaspora, that is, the Greeks who lived outside the Ottoman lands and the Ionian Islands, consisted to a large extent of merchants and their families.

Venice had controlled large areas of the Greek-speaking world since the Fourth Crusade of 1204. These included Crete from 1210/11 and Cyprus from 1489 until these islands were captured by the Ottomans in 1669 and 1571 respectively. Venice also controlled the Ionian Islands for most of the period until 1797, as well as other areas of the Greek world at various times. For this reason, the city of Venice attracted a large number of Greek immigrants over the centuries, many of whom engaged in mercantile activities both within Venetian lands and between the Venetian and other empires. The Greek presence in Venice was so large and long-lasting that the seat of the Orthodox bishopric of Philadelphia was transferred there from Asia Minor in 1571, and two years later the great Orthodox church of San Giorgio dei Greci was completed; this was the only see of the Greek Orthodox Church to be situated outside Ottoman lands and the Ionian Islands.[6] Greeks settled in other Italian cities too, particularly Livorno, but it was in Venice that they were granted the greatest freedom to practise their religion. In particular, the University of Padua, which was situated in Venetian lands, was the only Italian university where Greeks were allowed to study without (at least nominally) becoming Catholics. The result of this was that thousands of Greeks studied at Padua over the centuries.

Venice was thus an important economic, spiritual, educational, and cultural centre for the Greeks, and this was both reflected in and bolstered by the fact that it was also the most important centre for the printing, publishing, and dissemination of religious and secular books in Greek. Several Greek publishers had long been established in Venice, as well as Italian publishers who published significant numbers of Greek books. During the period 1801–20, well after the primacy of Venice as the centre of Greek book production had begun to be seriously challenged by Vienna and after the capture of the *Serenissima* and its territorial possessions by the French in 1797, more than half of all Greek books

---

[5] Todorov 1983: 193, 198, 58. For more on Balkan Orthodox merchants during the Ottoman era see Stoianovich 1960.

[6] Another, later, exception was the metropolitanate of Karlovci [Carlowitz], which from 1713 onwards had jurisdiction over Orthodox Serbs, Greeks, Romanians, and Aromanians in Habsburg lands.

were still being published there.[7] By contrast, very few Greek books were published within the Ottoman domains.

The vast Russian empire was another magnet for the Greek diaspora. From the sixteenth century onwards, Greek merchants and others established themselves in modern Ukraine (especially Nezhin [Nizhyn]), where they were granted special privileges such as reduced tariffs. During the Russo-Turkish War of 1770, Count Orlov, commander of the Russian naval forces of the enlightened despot Catherine II, fomented an unsuccessful rebellion in parts of Greece (particularly the Peloponnese) against Ottoman rule. The treaty of Küçük Kaynarca (1774), which ended this war, brought southern Ukraine and the Crimea into the Russian empire, thus ending Ottoman control over the north coast of the Black Sea. Under the treaty, after three hundred years during which the Black Sea was effectively an Ottoman lake,

> the Ottomans at last agreed to allow Russian merchant vessels to sail the [Black] sea unimpeded, a concession that would be extended over the next several decades to include other foreign merchantmen as well. . . . Russian merchant ships were given the right to sail 'free and unmolested' all the way across the sea and through the Straits into the Mediterranean.[8]

From then on, Greek ships were permitted to sail the Black Sea under the Russian flag. Greek merchants and captains took advantage of the shortage of cereals in Europe in the wake of the French revolution and the Napoleonic wars, exporting grain especially from southern Russia.

In 1775 Catherine placed a Greek, Evgenios Voulgaris (1716–1806), on the throne of the newly created archbishopric of Kherson and Slavyansk, with its seat at Poltava, under the jurisdiction of the patriarchate of Moscow. The diocese covered the whole of 'New Russia' from the river Bug to the river Don and beyond; most of this region is now in Ukraine.[9] After the treaty of Jassy (1792), which marked the end of the next Russo-Turkish War, Russia permanently occupied the coastal regions of the Black Sea from the mouth of the Danube to Taganrog on the Sea of Azov. From 1774 onwards, Greeks were encouraged to settle in these new regions, especially in the port of Odessa, which was founded in 1794. In the places where they settled, Greeks encountered little commercial competition. As Russia's only southern port, Odessa afforded access to the rest of the Black Sea and to the Mediterranean and very quickly developed into an important mercantile centre, soon becoming Russia's

---

[7] Iliou 1997: p. xxxvii.   [8] King 2004: 140–1, 147.
[9] Batalden 1982: 34; for a map of the diocese see ibid., fig. 3 (unnumbered page).

third city after Moscow and St Petersburg and attracting a significant number of Greeks, some of whom became fabulously rich within a very short time. The secret society that prepared the Greek revolution of 1821, the *Filikí Etaireía*, was founded by three Greek merchants in Odessa in 1814. Odessa also became a centre of Greek cultural production, hosting performances of patriotic plays in Greek, also beginning in 1814 and including the first performance by Greeks of Classical Greek drama in Greek since ancient times.[10]

In the east, places such as Taganrog provided Greek merchants with large fortunes from the wheat and caviar trade. Greek education and culture gained such prestige and predominance in Taganrog that the seven-year-old Anton Chekhov and his two bothers were sent to a Greek school by their father, a shopkeeper, who, according to Rosamund Bartlett, 'hoped that fluency in the language would be his sons' passport to wealth and prosperity, or at the very least a job as a clerk'. Anton only tolerated it for a year, after which he persuaded his father to place him elsewhere;[11] one can imagine how the future playwright and short-story writer must have chafed under the triple burden of having to learn Ancient Greek and 'corrected' written Modern Greek as well as the colloquial language.

But the Greek diaspora did not consist only of leading mercantile, spiritual, and cultural figures. One exception was the Orthodox Christians of the Crimea, who were divided into Tatar speakers, most of whom lived in towns, and the speakers of a Greek dialect presenting a mixture of features from Pontus (the southern coast of the Black Sea) and northern Greece, who were mostly peasants. After the Russians took over the Crimean Khanate, these Orthodox Christians were removed in 1779 to the north coast of the Sea of Azov, where they established the city of Mariupol and a number of outlying villages. This was part of Catherine's project of peopling the newly conquered steppe with Orthodox Christians. The town of Mariupol was largely settled by Tatar speakers, while the villages were established by Greek speakers. Another exception, at the geographically opposite extreme, was the Greek speakers of southern Italy (Calabria and Terra d'Otranto). However, since they had gradually espoused Catholicism since the medieval period, they were hardly considered (or considered themselves) to be members of the Greek nation.

Since the early seventeenth century Orthodox Christians from the southern Balkans, many of them of Aromanian origin, settled in the

---

[10] This was a prose adaptation in Modern Greek of Sophocles' *Philoctetes* by Nikolaos Pikkolos, first performed at Odessa in February 1818.

[11] Bartlett 2004: 2–3; see also 39.

Habsburg domains, especially in Vienna and in Trieste (the only sea port in the Habsburg empire), but also in a number of towns in present-day Hungary and Romania (Transylvania), where they were, however, living in a predominantly German-speaking environment. Many of them conducted trade between Habsburg and Ottoman lands. As in other regions where Greek merchants operated, a typical business was run by a number of brothers, some of them remaining in Ottoman territories and others settling in Habsburg lands, who traded goods back and forth by land or sea. Another enlightened despot, the emperor Joseph II, issued a series of Patents of Toleration, beginning in 1781, which granted freedom of worship to communities of Greek Orthodox and removed the restrictions on their buying property, joining guilds, and attending universities in Habsburg lands. Vienna became home to the largest Greek community in the diaspora. Greeks were able to build two churches in Vienna (St George for Ottoman subjects and Holy Trinity for Austrian subjects)[12] and set up printing presses and a school there.[13] During the period 1801–20, almost a quarter of all Greek books were published in Vienna;[14] a significant proportion of these books were of a secular educational content, in contrast to Venice's bias towards religious works. Greek books were also printed in Trieste from 1787 onwards. Some of the Greek merchants in Habsburg lands made immense fortunes and went on to become significant benefactors, founding schools, hospitals, and other institutions both in the diaspora and in their own places of origin within the Ottoman empire, and in the Greek state after 1821.

There was an important Greek trading community in Marseille, which became especially rich during the 1790s as merchants took advantage of the food crisis in France. Ships from the Greek islands, in particular Hydra, Spetses, and Psara, brought grain to Marseille from the Black Sea. Paris became important for Greek culture in the twenty years leading up to the Greek War of Independence largely because of the presence of Adamantios Korais, who lived there from 1788 until his death in 1833

[12] The Orthodox church of St George was transferred from Serbian to Greek jurisdiction in 1776 (Charilaou 2002: 36). Neofytos Doukas, Anthimos Gazis, and Theoklitos Farmakidis all served as parish priests there. The present church of St George was built in 1804. Holy Trinity church was built in 1787, but in 1836 it was replaced by a magnificent new church built by the Danish architect Theophil Hansen in neo-Byzantine style at the expense of the banker Simon Sinas.

[13] Georgios Vendotis founded a press in Vienna in 1788, and the brothers Markides Pouliou in 1792. There was also an increasing number of non-Greek printers of Greek books in Vienna, especially Baumeister from 1775 onwards. The first Greek school there, financed and overseen by the Greek community of the Holy Trinity, was founded in 1804.

[14] Iliou 1997: p. xxxvii.

and who became a pole of attraction for other Greek intellectuals before 1821.

The Ionian Islands were an important Greek cultural centre orientated towards western Europe; indeed, they could be called Greece's window on the West. They were part of the Venetian empire until 1797, when they were briefly taken over by France. During the Venetian period, Italian alone was used for official purposes in those islands. From 1800 to 1807 there was a Septinsular Republic, under Ottoman suzerainty and Russian protection, whose first constitution, approved in 1800, was printed in Greek by the patriarchal press in Constantinople, using many loanwords from Italian for technical terms.[15] However, the new constitution approved in 1803 was drafted in Italian, though a Greek translation by Dimitrios Venieris was also published, in a more archaized language. The text of the constitution is prefaced by the report of the committee that drafted it, which states that:

the noble, rich and harmonious Greek dialect, having been exiled by the long dominion of the Venetians, should be recalled to the State and become the language of government and the interpreter of the active citizens.[16]

In fact, Greek became, with Italian, the joint official language of the Septinsular Republic.

The United States of the Ionian Islands, under British protection, was the first nominally independent Greek state. The 1817 constitution stipulated that Greek should be the sole official language, but that, since Italian had been used for all official purposes for so long, its use was allowed to be continued temporarily. In practice, the British often communicated with the local populations in Italian, a language known and prized only by a small elite, and the official government gazette was written entirely in Italian until the end of 1830, after which it was written in Greek and Italian.[17] By contrast, the English language had little impact on the population, including even the elites. It was in Corfu in 1824 that Lord Guilford established the Ionian Academy, an institution of higher education with Greek as its chief language of instruction and administration, and he ran it till his death in 1827. The Heptanese, as the Ionian Islands are collectively known, was the home of Dionysios Solomos (1798–1857), who became the author of Greece's national anthem and the country's national poet, and of a number of other intellectual leaders

---

[15] *Geniki* 1801.

[16] *Costituzione* (1803). The translator of the Greek version calls the republic's citizens 'Hellenes' (*Katastasis* 1804: 17).

[17] Konomos 1964: 90–2

who shared his Italian education, his romantic outlook, and his passionate attachment to the spoken Greek language.

Before 1821 the chief places where Greeks could wield political power were Constantinople and the Danubian principalities. Most of the leading figures involved here came from the small group of families known as the Fanariots, who lived in the Fanar quarter of Constantinople, where the patriarchate is situated, and who exercised considerable power not only within the patriarchate and the Orthodox Christian community as a whole but also within the Ottoman administration. Most of the Fanariots were of Greek origin, though some originated from Albanian, Romanian, or Slav families, but in every case Greek was their language of culture.[18] In the Ottoman administration they held posts such as Grand Dragoman (chief interpreter to the Sultan) and Dragoman of the Fleet (which virtually entailed being governor of the Aegean Islands). The vitally important duties of the Grand Dragoman included negotiating and drawing up treaties with Christian states. The first Christian Grand Dragoman, from 1669 onwards, was Panagiotis Nikousios.[19]

The chief areas where the Fanariots wielded power were the principalities of Wallachia (with its capital at Bucharest) and Moldavia (with its capital at Jassy [Iaşi]), which covered parts of present-day Romania and Moldova. Until the early eighteenth century these predominantly Romanian-speaking principalities were governed by princes (known as hospodars or voivodes), who were vassals of the Sublime Porte but were elected by the local landowning nobles (boyars). From the 1710s until the outbreak of the Greek revolution in 1821, however, the Danubian principalities, as they are known, were governed by Christian princes appointed directly by the Sublime Porte. Most of these princes were Fanariots.

According to Kitromilides, Nikousios' successor Alexandros Mavrokordatos (1641–1709), who studied philosophy and medicine at Padua, appears to have had no national identity, while Alexandros' son and successor Nikolaos (c. 1670–1730), who went on to become the first Fanariot hospodar of Moldavia and Wallachia, possessed a 'fully developed Ottoman consciousness': in his writings he defends Ottoman society against the misunderstandings of European observers, and he identifies himself with the Ottoman political environment. However, this did not prevent both Alexandros and Nikolaos from having a

---

[18] For the origins of some of the Fanariot families see Zallony 1824: 239–40.
[19] Zallony 1824: 16; Kitromilides 1996: 30.

'cosmopolitan European consciousness'.[20] Dimitris Livanios describes them as 'essentially, although not exclusively, Christian Ottomans'.[21] For all that, Bucharest and Jassy soon became important centres of Greek culture, education, and learning. The Fanariot administration in Wallachia and Moldavia was a kind of privatization of Ottoman rule in the region; the princes acted as the Sultan's agents with a concession to rule, which they bought at a high price, recouping their expenses through taxation. In these wealthy communities, free from direct Ottoman control, Greek culture was able to flourish. The official court languages in Bucharest and Jassy were Greek and Romanian, Greek being predominant in education too. Wallachia and Moldavia held a particular attraction for people of Aromanian background, since they were easily able to learn to communicate in Romanian, which is closely related to their own language.

As early as the sixteenth century, well before the beginning of Fanariot rule, the princes and many of the boyars spoke and read Greek. The presence of Greek merchants in Romanian lands provided an economic incentive for the use of the Greek language.[22] For almost two centuries (seventeenth to nineteenth) Greek held supremacy as the language of culture in Wallachia and Moldavia,[23] where it superseded Slavonic as the language of the Church and of secular high culture. The princely academy at Bucharest was founded around 1689, with Greek as the language of instruction, though Slavonic and Romanian were taught there too.[24] This and the other higher schools in the Danubian principalities provided a secular education, based on the teaching of Ancient Greek and later also of modern scientific subjects, to both Romanians and Greeks as well as other Orthodox Christians of the Ottoman empire.[25] Many Romanian intellectuals gained access to Enlightenment ideas and writings through their studies in Greek, and they proceeded to transfer both ancient Greek and modern European thought into their own language.[26] At the same time, as Ariana Camariano-Cioran puts it, Romanians created a Romanian literature in Greek just as previously they had created a Romanian literature in Slavonic.[27] Until the 1810s, Greek education in Romania was pan-Balkan rather than nationalistic,[28] and Greek continued to enjoy high prestige in Romanian lands until the mid-nineteenth century.

---

[20] Kitromilides 1996: 35–40.   [21] Livanios 2000: 18, 6.
[22] Camariano-Cioran 1974: 10–19.   [23] Ibid., 10.   [24] Ibid., 23–36.
[25] By contrast, those Orthodox Christians from the Ionian Islands who went abroad for their education tended to go to Italy.
[26] Camariano-Cioran 1974: 288.   [27] Ibid., 341.   [28] Ibid., 349.

The princes and the higher clergy in the Danubian principalities favoured Greek partly because they saw themselves as defenders of Orthodoxy against the Latin of the Catholics, against Protestantism, and against Slavism; it was for this reason that they founded academies and set up presses. As Nicolae Iorga put it, Greek was 'un instrument du progrès intellectuel, c'était la grande langue de culture de l'Orient'. Eventually, merchants in Romanian provincial towns asked for Greek schools to be set up, because Greek was the medium of business transactions.[29] Nevertheless, Camariano-Cioran claims that Greek education in Romania was encouraged more by the feudal boyars than by the princes, since the boyars wanted to retain their superiority over the Romanian masses, to whom Greek culture was inaccessible.[30]

The Danubian principalities were the first places since the fall of Byzantium where Greek was used as an official language of state. Various legal codes were drawn up in Greek in the principalities during the eighteenth and early nineteenth centuries. Michail Foteinopoulos' *Nomikón prócheiron* was drawn up 'in simple Hellenic dialect' (i.e. in Modern Greek) at the behest of prince Ştefan Racoviţă of Wallachia in 1765.[31] The *Syntagmation nomikón* of Wallachia drafted under Alexandros Ypsilantis and printed in 1780 was originally written in vernacular Greek and was subsequently translated into Romanian by Ienăchiţă Văcărescu.[32] The Moldavian *Civil Code* of prince Skarlatos Kallimachis (1816) was in a rather more conservative Greek and included a glossary in which archaic Greek terms and neologisms were rendered into Modern Greek, Latin, Turkish, Romanian, or French.[33] The short-lived *Nomothesía* (Civil Code) of 'Hungro-Wallachia' (i.e. Wallachia), written by Athanasios Christopoulos in vernacular Greek and approved by prince Ioannis Karatzas, was published in both Greek and Romanian in 1817 and 1818.[34] This was written in a slightly archaized version of the vernacular, which was not averse to using words of non-Greek origin.[35]

The Fanariots gained a bad reputation, not only among Romanians but among Greeks too, for collaborating with the Ottoman government.

---

[29] Ibid., 256; Karathanassis 2004: 253–6, including the quotation from Iorga.

[30] Camariano-Cioran 1974: 664–5.

[31] Foteinopulos' code was not printed at the time; it was published in Zepos 1959.

[32] Zepos 1936: 33–4.   [33] *Kodix* 1816–17.

[34] Ţipău 2004: 167 ff.; Iliou 1997: 557.

[35] Christopoulos' legislation would have been rendered obsolete by the so-called Règlement Organique (Organic Statute) that became the basic law of Wallachia in July 1831 and of Moldavia in January 1832; both of the principalities were under Russian occupation (protectorate) 1829–56.

Although an intense desire for personal gain was undoubtedly among the motivations of the Fanariot princes, they were also inspired by modern western ideas of enlightened despotism, and some of them were keen to introduce enlightened legislation and to encourage high culture and education in their domains. They patronized schools and monasteries and funded the publication of books. During this period the Danubian princely courts provided numerous positions for talented Orthodox Christians from throughout the Ottoman empire, among whom were important and influential writers in both literary and other intellectual spheres. Nevertheless, the princes generally ruled for only a couple of years at a time, a practice that has been attributed to the fact that the Sublime Porte received payment every time a hospodar was enthroned.[36] Combined with the fact that Wallachia and Moldavia were on the front line between Turkey, Russia, and Austria, and were subject to several periods of Russian and Austrian occupation between 1769 and 1812, this inevitably resulted in discontinuities in policy-making and funding within the principalities.

Unlike most of the nations that gained independence in the nineteenth and twentieth centuries, the Greeks, Serbs, Bulgarians, Albanians, and others emerged into nationhood from the Ottoman empire rather than from European colonial rule. This makes the development of these nations strikingly different from the usual transition from a colonial to a post-colonial situation. Through their experience of living abroad, members of the Greek diaspora were able to compare the way they lived and worked in western or central Europe or in Russia with conditions of life in the Ottoman empire. In Russian and Habsburg lands, Greek communities typically enjoyed special protection and financial incentives from the authorities, including a degree of internal self-administration and exemptions from certain taxes and from military service. Nikolai Todorov has drawn attention to the growing gap, during the late eighteenth and the early nineteenth centuries, between the economic role of the non-Muslim Ottoman bourgeoisie and its lack of political rights, between its own cultural level and the ignorance of the Ottoman rulers. It was an awareness of this gap that gradually led to the conviction that Ottoman domination was no longer tolerable.[37] One of the motives of the movement for Greek independence was economic. Merchants, in particular, came to value the rule of law, the respect for life and property, the freedom to practise their profession, and the explicitly codified tariffs that

[36] Zallony 1824: 21–2.   [37] Todorov 1983: 195.

they encountered in other countries, which compared favourably with the arbitrary justice and capricious taxation that they had experienced in their homeland. Cultural nationalists too resented living as second-class subjects in the Ottoman empire and the limited access to power that this entailed. These considerations led many Greeks to wish to throw off Ottoman rule at home and establish their own national state, which would by definition be well governed and prosperous. Among Greek intellectual leaders, the culture of the imperial rulers was generally thought to be vastly inferior to their own, and (unlike the situation in former European colonies) nobody wished to continue using the old imperial language for official purposes after independence. Since the time of the first Greek revolutionary proclamations of 1821, the sole official language of the Greek state has been Greek.[38]

The diaspora Greeks living in Italy (especially Venice), the Romanian lands, the Habsburg territories (especially Vienna and Trieste), the Russian empire (Black Sea) and elsewhere broadened their experience and their imaginative and intellectual horizons, exploring a wider world, learning the ways of foreign peoples (and thereby learning about themselves as a people) and extending the social, economic, political and intellectual possibilities available to them. The origins of modernization, liberal and revolutionary ideas, and nationalism – a greater self-consciousness, gained through being abroad, of belonging to a wider nation, and an ancient and glorious one at that – are to be found in these experiences. Success in commerce, in particular, must have led many Greeks to abandon the traditional fatalistic outlook (summed up in the belief that God had sent the Turks to punish the Greeks for their sins and to protect their religion from the Catholics) and to acquire a sense that everything was possible – including the liberation of oneself and one's people, the liberation of one's place of origin and of the whole of the national territory – provided one had the courage to take the initiative. This material and intellectual success was a remarkable achievement for a people who were, for the most part, living as second-class subjects of a Muslim-dominated empire.

Finally, Cyprus has occupied a special position within the Greek-speaking world since its church became autocephalous as early as the year 431. From 1191 it was ruled by western European Catholics (until 1489 by the French Lusignan dynasty, then by Venice), until it was captured by

---

[38] The earliest constitutions of the Greek state (1844 and 1864) contain no clause specifying an official language; this was not introduced until 1911.

the Ottomans in 1571. From 1878 onwards it was governed by Britain, initially on a leasehold basis from the Ottoman empire, then (after the defeat of Turkey in the First World War) as an integral part of the British empire. While the Greek state won its independence in a period shortly after the American and French revolutions, Cyprus became independent in 1960, during the same period as the Asian and African colonies of European empires.[39] Cyprus faced the problem of the widespread use of English, which was and is instrumentally valuable yet, to many Greek Cypriots, ideologically unacceptable, because it was the language of the island's occupiers.

During the period of the Greek Enlightenment, Kitromilides traces a transition from a 'geography of faith' (descriptions of the Holy Land, the monasteries of Mount Athos and Mount Sinai) to a secular view of space, a 'geography of culture'.[40] Greek geographers who wrote before 1821 disagreed as to whether 'Hellas' covered only Classical Greece or the whole of European Turkey.[41] Those who included the latter in the terms 'Hellas' and *Graikía* did not, however, imply territorial claims on the part of Greeks against other peoples of the Balkans.[42] It is not my purpose to cover this vast subject here; I shall confine myself to a few instances of writers whose work is relevant to language and national identity.

In the first (and only) volume of their book *Modern Geography* (1791) Daniil Filippidis and Grigorios Konstantas give a precise delimitation of 'European Hellas' in their day as being between 36.5 and 43 degrees north, an area that would include not only present-day Greece but Albania, the former Yugoslav Republic of Macedonia, and the southern half of Bulgaria as well; this corresponds to the area ruled by the Macedonian kings rather than to the extent of Classical Hellas.[43] Since their volume only covers Europe, it contains no definition of what the authors call 'Asiatic Hellas'.[44] In his *Map of Hellas* (1797), Rigas Velestinlis includes not only what is Greece today, but also parts

[39] For an overview of British rule in Cyprus see Holland and Markides 2006: 162–88 and 213–40.

[40] Kitromilides 1996: 126, 164.   [41] Gounaris 2007: 48–51.

[42] Hatzopoulos 1999: 366–8. For the Greek geographical imagination see Peckham 2001, Koliopoulos 2003, and Gounaris 2007: 47–63.

[43] Cf. Sigalas 2001: 12–14.

[44] Filippidis and Konstantas 1988: 109. Filippidis devoted much of his life to a study of geography, and it is perhaps not surprising that the word and concept *Roumounia* [Romania] should have been first used in a modern sense in his work, which was written in Greek (Ţipău 2007).

of Romania, Bulgaria, Serbia, and Montenegro as well as the western portion of Asia Minor.[45]

The writer of the period who laid the maximum claim to the geographical extent of the Hellenes was the cleric, teacher, and grammarian Neofytos Doukas (*c.* 1760–1845), born in Ano Soudena (now Ano Pedina) in the Zagori region of Epirus. Kitromilides has described Doukas as 'one of the earliest exponents of romantic nationalism in southeastern Europe'.[46] In a pamphlet published in 1811 he wrote:

> When I utter the sweet thing and name 'Hellenes' I mean not only those few inhabitants of ancient Greece, but the whole region in which is spoken the modern dialect of the Hellenes, through which each person is cultivated and reaches his own perfection. Such people are almost all those who inhabit the area between the river Prut and the Nile.[47]

The absurdly large extent of the region that Doukas claimed to be inhabited by 'Hellenes' – which covers present-day Romania, Bulgaria, and parts of former Yugoslavia and Albania as well as part of Egypt – is based on the presence there of people who speak Modern Greek. For him, allegiance to the Greek language and the culture associated with it, rather than speaking it as mother tongue, is the criterion for being a Hellene. His conception of the geographical extent of the Hellenes, as expressed in this passage, coincides with the extent of the Balkan Orthodox Christians. Although Doukas does not mention Asia Minor here, he includes the western part of it within his conception of the Hellenic world in other writings.[48]

After the establishment of the Greek state around 1830, with Athens as its capital from 1834 onwards, its intellectual and political leaders set up institutions for the production of a new national culture, including the Church of Greece (established in 1833), the University of Athens (founded in 1837), and a network of schools. For some time Athens could be seen as one of the three capitals of the Greek nation, often attempting to outdo its rivals, namely Constantinople, seat of the patriarch, and Corfu, capital of the British-protected United States of the Ionian Islands. Each of these capitals also continued to produce Greek culture, sometimes in collaboration with Athens and sometimes in parallel with it (or even in

---

[45] Kitromilides 1996: 308, 326–7. For Rigas' map see Tolias 1998.

[46] Kitromilides 1989: 157.

[47] Doukas n.d. [1811]: 17, reprinted in K. Th. Dimaras 1953: 259.

[48] For instance, he calls for Greek to be spread wherever 'the dogma of the Orthodox is preached', from Moldavia to Caesarea [Kayseri] and the river Halys [Kızılırmak] in Asia Minor (Doukas 1812a: 43).

opposition to it). It is no coincidence, for instance, that most of those who supported the written use of the spoken language after 1821 were from the Ionian Islands, and that Psycharis, leader of the demoticist movement from 1888 onwards, grew up partly in Constantinople and never lived in Greece.

Who were the Greeks?

Romans, Greeks, or Hellenes?[49]

Because Greek was the predominant language of the Orthodox Church in the Ottoman empire, the term 'Greeks' was often applied by foreigners to the Orthodox Christians of the Ottoman empire in general, in contrast to 'Latins' (i.e. Catholics). I am doing the same in parts of the present chapter. The fact that Europeans used the same term to denote both the ancient and the modern Greeks helped the Greeks themselves to make the connection between the ancient and modern inhabitants of Greece.

According to Kitromilides, the old chronographic tradition of the Orthodox East held that the Christian peoples had a common Biblical descent: it traced the destinies of the Christian flock from the Creation, through Jewish history to the Christian Roman empire and the empire of the Ottoman Sultans. By contrast, the Enlightenment pointed to a separate national history for each Balkan people.[50] This revolutionary conception broke with the Christian cultural tradition. The new secular approach to history that emerged among Greek intellectuals cultivated a developing sense that the modern Greeks had a special origin – a consciousness of their cultural descent from Classical Hellas. Greeks began to see the restitution of a real relationship with their ancestors as an essential precondition for national revival.[51]

Greek geography and history books of the period tend to compare the systems of government of ancient Hellas with modern Europe and with Ottoman-occupied modern Greece.[52] In 1796 the doctor and poet Georgios Sakellarios laments the passing of the ancient Greek city-states and the tyranny of the Macedonian kings, which was followed by the 'Roman yoke'.[53] The author of an anonymous history book of 1814 shows a sense of the continuity of Greek culture from ancient Greece

---

[49] There is a considerable literature on the historical use of these three ethnonyms, e.g. Dimaras 1985: 82–6; Beaton 2007; see also the critical bibliography on the topic in Mantouvalou 1983.

[50] Kitromilides 1996: 224.   [51] Ibid., 83–7, 104, 114.   [52] Ibid., 126, 164.

[53] Sakellarios 1796, quoted in Kitromilides 1996: 100–1.

through Byzantium to the Ottoman period.[54] As Kitromilides writes, 'The patriotic enthusiasm that took hold of the Greek world on the eve of the national revolution seems to have been inspired by the study of ancient history' and by a consciousness of the freedom enjoyed by the ancient Greeks. 'The discovery of the ancient descent of the Greeks and the awareness of their special national past constituted the decisive component in the formation of their sense of their historical identity'. Greeks conceived a desire to regain not only their ancestral glory but also their ancestral wisdom and virtue.[55]

The development of Greek identity since the eighteenth century has been complicated by the fact that Greeks used three different names for themselves. Since Constantinople was founded as the 'New Rome', that is, the eastern capital of the Roman empire, and because, after the collapse of the western empire, it became the sole capital, its emperors and their subjects normally called themselves *Romaioi* [Romans].[56] Eventually the Greek spoken language came to be called *romaíika* [Romaic].[57] Nevertheless, during the Ottoman period, the term *Romaios* (together with its colloquial form *Romiós* and its Turkish equivalent *Rum*) often denoted an Orthodox Christian subject of the Ottoman empire, irrespective of language and region.

Orthodox Christians defined themselves by their differences from the members of the other chief religious communities that made up the population of the Ottoman empire, namely Muslims, Jews, and Armenians. For most Ottoman Orthodox Christians of that time, the world was chiefly divided, at a popular level, into *Romioí* (Orthodox Christians, among whom Greek speakers might or might not be distinguished from Vlachs, Albanians, and Bulgarians), *Tourkoi* (which referred to all Muslims in general), *Ovrioi* (Jews), and *Arménides* (Armenians). To the west of the empire lived the *Frangoi* (Catholics and – since the Reformation – Protestants).[58] These distinctions were based on

---

[54] *Apologia* 1814, quoted in Kitromilides 1996: 108–9.   [55] Ibid., 109–11, 113–14.

[56] The use of the adjective 'Byzantine' to refer to the eastern Roman empire did not become current in European languages until the first half of the nineteenth century. In Greek, the adjective may have been first used by Korais in 1805 (Korais 1805a: 33).

[57] *Romaíika* is used as an adverb to mean 'in Greek' in the fourteenth-century *Chronicle of the Morea*, line 4130. According to De Boel (2003: 178), the use of this word as a noun denoting vernacular Greek dates from the Ottoman period.

[58] In this scheme of things there was a double division, between Christians and non-Christians within the Ottoman empire, and between Ottomans and non-Ottomans. It was not only Christians who applied the term 'Turk' to Muslims in general; Balkan Muslims identified themselves as Turks too.

religious rather than ethnic criteria, specifically the way in which one worshipped.[59]

Many Greeks living outside Greece used the word *Graikós*. This term, of ancient Greek origin, passed into Latin as *Graecus* and from there gave rise to the equivalents in all modern European languages, including those of the Greeks' Christian neighbours in the Balkans: Aromanians (known by Greeks and others as Vlachs), Romanians, Albanians, and Slavs.

For eastern Christians since the time of the Gospels, the word *Ellin* [Hellene] had meant a non-Christian, that is, a pagan.[60] Nevertheless, some writers during the late Byzantine period and afterwards used the term 'Hellenes' to refer to Orthodox Christians. Some of these were even senior churchmen, but they were using the term in an antiquarian way, in texts written in Ancient Greek, as the counterpart of 'Latins' (Roman Catholics).[61] Such uses were a rhetorical conceit confined to a small intellectual elite, and they were hardly ever intended to imply that the authors felt that they and their compatriots were to be identified with the ancient Hellenes.[62] Nevertheless, from the seventeenth century onwards there was an increasingly expressed assumption that the modern speakers of the Greek language were the descendants of the ancient Hellenes.[63] This assumption or assertion was not originally based on any elaborated theory of racial descent but simply on the fact that they inhabited the same region (called Hellas) and spoke a version of the same language.

Writing in Bucharest in the 1780s, Dimitrios Katartzis insists that the correct phrase to describe his own identity is *Romiós Christianós*

[59] It is significant that in his *New Political Administration* (1797), Rigas Velestinlis lists *tourkismós* (literally 'Turkism') as a religion, along with *christianismós* and *ioudaïsmós* [Judaism] (Velestinlis 2000: 37). In English too, 'Turcism' was used to denote Islam; the *Oxford English Dictionary* gives this meaning for the word, as used from 1566 onwards, often in conjunction with the word 'Judaism'. In French, Littré's *Dictionnaire de la langue française* cites a passage from Bossuet (1627–1704) that includes the term *turcisme* with the same meaning. For an English translation of extracts from the *New Political Administration* see Clogg 1976b: 149–62.

[60] In e.g. Mark 7.26 it is used to mean 'gentile', i.e. non-Jew.

[61] See e.g. Antonios Eparchos in a letter to the Catholic bishop of Mylopotamos in Crete, Dionysios II, about 1547, and a letter from Dionysios to the Hellenist Ermodoros Listarchos; see Ziogas 1974: 68–74. Dimaras (1985: 83) suggests that Byzantine historians called the modern Greeks 'Hellenes' in the same way that they called the Turks 'Persians'.

[62] Mango 1965: 33.

[63] See, for instance, the dedication in Kontaris 1675, a book covering the history of Athens from its mythical founder, Cecrops, to St Dionysios the Areopagite (supposedly baptized by St Paul in Athens and martyred in AD 96). The author views Christian history as the culmination of ancient Greek history rather than as the continuation of Jewish history. He refers to the Greeks of his time as 'neoi Ellines' [new Hellenes] (Apostolopoulos 2005).

(adding the Turkish equivalent, *Urum Hristiyan*). He criticizes those who have such an inclination towards Hellenic culture and language that they think it an honour to call themselves Hellenes; this, he writes, is unworthy of a *Romiós* Christian, for whom the Hellenes are pagans. We were originally called *Graikoí*, he continues, and then we took the name Hellenes; later, when Constantine the Great moved the capital to Constantinople, we called ourselves Romans and called the pagans 'Hellenes'. Only when we have enriched and cultivated our Romaic (Modern Greek) language will it not be shameful for us to say we have the Hellenes as our ancestors: '[T]hat we had the Hellenes as our ancestors is a very great honour, without claiming their name'.[64] As K. Th. Dimaras points out, Katartzis distinguishes identity from descent.[65]

Konstantinos Koumas claimed that the Fanariots insisted on calling themselves *Romaioi* rather than *Graikoí* or *Ellines*.[66] If this is true, then Katartzis was no doubt influenced by this usage. However, the Fanariot Iakovos Rizos Neroulos begins a mock-heroic poem with the following invocation to the Muses: 'Now begin in the living language of the *Graikoí*'. In the same poem he refers to himself and his hero as *Graikoí*, and even to the country they inhabit as *Graikía*.[67]

By contrast, in their *Modern Geography*, Katartzis' pupils Filippidis and Konstantas refer to their contemporary compatriots as 'the modern Hellenes' or simply as 'Hellenes'. They write that 'The Hellenes of today are improperly called [or 'call themselves'] *Romaioi*' and go on to state that in Byzantine times 'all the ... Hellenes began to call themselves *Romaioi* and to appropriate the name of their tyrants, especially since they thought, out of ignorance, that "Hellenes" was a name that belonged to the idolaters'.[68] Their retrospective naming of the Byzantines as 'Hellenes', unusual at the time, became *de rigueur* in Greek historiography from the mid-nineteenth century onwards.

Adamantios Korais normally preferred to use *Graikós*. One of the reasons why he favoured *Graikós* is that it seems to have meant specifically a Greek speaker. He avoided *Romaios*, explicitly because it was a shameful reminder of the subjugation of the Greeks to the Romans, and implicitly because it was connected with Byzantium and Orthodox

---

[64] Katartzis 1970: 43–4, 50, 105.   [65] K. Th. Dimaras 1985: 219.

[66] Koumas 1832: 535, quoted in Mantouvalou 1983: 35. However, Koumas, being a faithful disciple of Korais, was not an impartial witness.

[67] Neroulos 1816. Theodoros Negris too, in his prologue to Neroulos 1813, addresses readers as *Graikoí*, while Neroulos in the same text describes the characters in his play as coming 'from various regions of *Graikía*'.

[68] Filippidis and Konstantas 1988: 114–15, 120.

Christianity rather than with a Greek identity that looked back directly to Classical antiquity. Nevertheless, he did sometimes use *Ellines*, notably in the prologues to the volumes of his *Hellenic Library*, each of which is addressed 'To the Hellenes'.

The predominant language that was spoken in what is now Greece, and was known colloquially as Romaic, was clearly distinct from any other modern language. At the same time, it was obvious that Romaic was closely related to the ancient language of Greece, which was known in Greek as *elliniká* [Hellenic] and was still employed by some learned writers, as Latin was in the West. The term *Romaios/Romiós* was used to denote both people who spoke Romaic and Ottoman Orthodox Christians in general. Language was used as a marker of identity more by certain elites than by the broad masses of the people (and, it should be added, by the patriarchate of Constantinople). Thus the distinction between the two meanings of *Romioí* – 'the Greeks' (or at least Greek speakers) and the Ottoman Orthodox Christians as a whole – may coincide with the distinction between the different conceptions held by popular and elite groups. Apart from this semantic ambiguity, the problem with the term *Romaios* was that, in Ancient Greek, it referred to a different people, namely the ancient Romans, who were referred to in Romaic as *Romanoi*; this was the reason that Evgenios Voulgaris gave in 1768 for using *Graikós* rather than *Romaios* in a translation of Voltaire, justifying it in addition by the fact that this name existed before the word 'Hellene', which, besides, was associated in people's minds with idolatry.[69] Yet some intellectuals felt *Graikós* to be a name imposed on the Greeks by foreigners. A further complicating factor was that the Latin speakers of the Balkans called themselves *Rumâni/Români* [Romans or Romanians] and *Armâni* [Aromanians]. The only possible way out of this impasse was for the modern Greeks to call themselves Hellenes and their modern language Hellenic. Thus this change of appellation was not carried out solely for the purpose of raising the prestige of the modern Greeks in the eyes of western Europe; it clarified a semantic confusion. At the same time, the change of name provided the modern Greeks with a new history and new models for behaviour (the great intellectual, military, and political figures of Classical Greece) – in short, a new identity of which they could feel proud and of which they could aspire to be worthy.

---

[69] Voulgaris in Voltaire 1768, quoted in K. Th. Dimaras 1985: 84. Voulgaris is referring to the story told by, among others, Apollodorus (*Library and Epitome*, 1.99), that Hellen, son of Deucalion, named the *Graikoí* after himself.

The period between the late eighteenth century and the early nineteenth is marked by the transition from the '*genos* of the *Romaioi*' to the Hellenic *ethnos*. Although the two nouns *genos* and *ethnos* were often used interchangeably to mean either a religious community (*millet* in the Ottoman sense) or a political community (nation in the modern European sense), there are a few instances where they are clearly distinguished. It is significant that one of those who distinguished them was Evgenios Voulgaris: in his Greek translation of a text by Catherine II, published in 1771, he writes about the Greek and other *ethni* that make up the Orthodox *genos*.[70]

By the 1810s the words 'Hellene' and 'Hellenic' were being increasingly used to denote the modern Greeks and their language. As we have seen, the writer who claimed the greatest extent for the geographical area inhabited by Hellenes was Neofytos Doukas. Not surprisingly, he was also one of those who did most to promote the Hellenic ideal. In 1812 he addressed an open letter, in the form of a preface to his edition of Demosthenes, 'To the most holy and venerable Hierarchs of the Orthodox Hellenes everywhere'.[71] Here and in other prefaces to pre-Christian texts, Doukas announces an evangelical mission to extend the use of the Greek language among the Orthodox Christians of the Balkans and Asia Minor.[72] The purpose of Doukas' mission was to transform all the Orthodox Christians into Hellenes. Doukas likens himself to St Paul sending his epistle to the Christians in Rome; yet his message is radically different:

Two things most demand your philanthropy and diligence today, . . . the increase of our *genos* [nation], and application in philosophy, that is, the extension of our language throughout the domain of the Ecumenical throne [i.e. the patriarchate of Constantinople], and the establishment of schools in all the towns and large villages, so that in so far as the language, as the closest and particular characteristic of the *genos*, is extended, so the *genos* too must in fact increase throughout all the provinces in which it was spoken in the beginnings of Christianity.

By 'our *genos*' Doukas means a nation consisting of all those who can speak Greek, whether as their mother tongue or as a second language.

'The Church has guarded our ancestral language from above until today', Doukas continues. Yet circumstances have confined our language to 'the circle of ancient Hellas', by which he means Classical Greece

---

[70] Quoted in Batalden 1982: 18–19.
[71] The open letter is published in Doukas 1812b: pp. v–xxviii.
[72] Kitromilides (1994: 156–7) talks of Doukas' 'cultural crusade' and 'cultural evangelism'.

as opposed to the far larger area in which Greek was spoken and written after the conquests of Alexander the Great and at the peak of the Byzantine empire. Outside this circle, he writes, the Greek language has been swamped by Slavonic, Vlach, and Albanian. Previous ages, he proclaims, were 'dead times,...But now that the fullness of time has come,[73] a shining day has dawned, and the voice of the fatherland is crying and seeking its own members for itself'. Doukas quotes St Paul: '[F]or now is the day of our salvation;...let us therefore cast off the works of darkness and let us put on the armour of light'.[74]

In 1824, during the revolution, Doukas sees the imminent achievement of national liberation in terms of the triumph of Christianity and in words that once again echo St Paul:

[O]nce the *Graikoí* have become fused with the Hellenes in the same melting-pot of language..., once we, the present-day metics [resident aliens] of ancient Hellas, become worthy of taking possession of our citizenship,...there will no longer be *Graikós* and Hellene, slave and free, but one and the same in the strength of the word, all Hellenes, the same Attic, the same Athenians.[75]

It is clear that Doukas was a religious nationalist who saw the advent of the Hellenic state as a messianic event in which divine providence would bring about the rebirth of the Hellenic nation, thus vouchsafing its members earthly bliss.

Elsewhere Doukas complains that many *Graikoí* (by which, in the context, he means native Greek speakers in contrast to Greeks of Aromanian origin)[76] boast that they should enjoy the rights due to people of Hellenic descent even though they are not adorned with Hellenic culture and virtue. To be a Hellene, in Doukas' view, it was not enough to speak Greek, or to be racially descended from Hellenes, or to claim that one is a Hellene; one must demonstrate that one is a Hellene through one's actions, that is, through the espousal of Hellenic *paideia* [culture] and

---

[73] Galatians 4.4.

[74] Romans 13.11. The quoted passages are in Doukas 1812b: pp. vii–x. Kitromilides dates the beginning of Doukas' 'cultural crusade' as 1815, but it is clear that it had begun shortly before this.

[75] Doukas 1834: p. vii; cf. Colossians 3.9–11: '[Y]e have put off the old man with his deeds; And have put on the new man, which is renewed in knowledge...; Where there is neither Greek nor Jew,...Barbarian, Scythian, bond nor free: but Christ is all, in all'. According to Paul's schema, the 'Hellenes' are equivalent to the unconverted Jews, whereas, according to Doukas', the fulfilment of the process of Christianization will result in the Greeks becoming Hellenes.

[76] The term *Grecu* is still used in Aromanian to refer to someone of Greek (as opposed to *Armânu* [Aromanian]) origin: see Koukoudis 2003: 27. Koukoudis reports an Aromanian telling him that the Hellenes consist of Greeks and Aromanians: ibid., 33.

Hellenic virtue.[77] However, the fact that Doukas' brand of Romantic nationalism was based primarily on language is shown by his attitude to the Greek language as being 'the most divine mother of all languages and for this reason acknowledged by all to be the language of the gods'.[78] Here we witness the extraordinary phenomenon of an Orthodox Christian priest promoting a Greek nationalism that proudly connects Greek culture with the pagan pre-Christian past.

From the revolutionary constitutions of the 1820s onwards, the term 'Hellenes' is the only one to be used to denote citizens of the emerging state. As Dimitris Livanios writes:

During the period of the Greek revolution the meaning of the term ['Hellenes'] was unclear, as both language and religion were employed as criteria for denoting the 'Greek'. According to the first Greek revolutionary constitution voted in 1822, all Christians shared this appellation, for it was stipulated that 'Greeks' [Έλληνες] are those 'who believe in Christ', and were born within the insurgents' domains. The second national assembly [held at Astros in April 1823], in addition to religion, inserted also the criterion of language, stating that Greeks are also those 'who have the Greek language as their native tongue and believe in Christ'. It is indicative of the relative strength of religion over language, however, that the third and last Greek national assembly, convened at Troezen in 1827, deleted the reference to the Greek language, and argued that Greeks are simply those born in the country who 'believe in Christ', as well as those who came to Greece from Ottoman-occupied lands and 'believe in Christ' and wish either to fight with the insurgents or live in Greece.[79]

In fact, the 1823 citizenship law was the only one that specified the speaking of Greek as a precondition for becoming a citizen of Hellas.[80]

Once the revolution broke out, the use of the terms 'Hellene' and 'Hellenic', hitherto confined to the discourse of an intellectual elite, suddenly became so widespread as to be almost universal.[81] With reference

---

[77] Although he does not mention it specifically, Doukas may have had in mind the passage in Isocrates (*Panegyrikos*, 50), which is much quoted in an adapted form in modern Greece: 'In thought and speech our city [i.e. Athens] has left other people so far behind that its pupils have become teachers of others, with the result that the name Hellenes is thought of no longer as that of a nation but as that of a way of thinking, and that those who are called Hellenes are those who participate in our culture rather than in our common nature [i.e. descent].'

[78] Doukas 1810: pp. xxxiii–xxxviii.

[79] Livanios 2006: 55. The quoted passage has a reference to *Ta ellinika* 1998: 108, 122, 136, and Koliopoulos 2003: 65. For more details on language, religion, descent, and place of birth as criteria for Greek citizenship during the revolution and in the early years of the Greek state see Vogli 2007.

[80] Vogli 2007: 141–7.

[81] However, as late as 1842, Evangelinos Sophocles – albeit writing in America – claimed that the mass of the people call themselves *Romaioi* and that the term Hellenes 'is used chiefly

to General Makriyannis, one of the heroes of the War of Independence, Ioannis Kakridis pointed out that in the early part of his memoirs, relating to the pre-revolutionary period, he uses only the term *Romaioi*, whereas once the war begins he uses only 'Hellenes'. Kakridis also points out that, in the charter of the *Filikí Etaireía*, the Greeks who have taken up arms against the Turks are referred to as 'Hellenes', while those who live at a distance call themselves *Graikoí*. Again, in a request written from Odessa to the Russian tsar for assistance in the revolution, Konstantinos Oikonomos calls the warriors 'Hellenes', while those who signed his document call themselves *Graikoí*.[82] This suggests that the word 'Hellenes' had both a geographical and a chronological dimension: the Hellenes were particularly those who found themselves on Hellenic territory during and after the outbreak of the revolution.

Thus the *Romioí* or *Graikoí* appear to have been born again in 1821 as Hellenes, having realized, as it seemed to them, who they truly were. Many Greeks today do not realize that, in the second verse of their National Anthem (whose words were written by Dionysios Solomos during the War of Independence, in 1823), the word 'Hellenes' refers to the ancient Greeks:

> Emerging from the sacred
> bones of the Hellenes,
> valiant as of old,
> hail, o hail, Liberty![83]

They tend to assume that the word refers to the modern Greeks. This is also why it is difficult to write about the language question around 1800, because the key terms and their meanings have changed in the intervening two centuries. In this book I tend to use the terms *Romaios/Romiós*, *Graikós* and 'Hellas'/'Hellene'/'Hellenic' as I find them in Greek texts written before 1821, whereas I use 'Greek' with reference to the same period in contexts where a distinction between the different terms would have no relevance. For the period from 1821 onwards I normally use 'Greece'/'Greek' where *Ellás* [Hellas]/*Ellin* [Hellene] is used in the Greek texts, though I occasionally use 'Hellas'/'Hellene'/'Hellenic' in cases where the relevant author is stressing the unity of the ancient and

by the inhabitants of Bavarian Greece, who perhaps do not constitute more than one fourth of the Greek nation' (Sophocles 1842: iv). Sophocles' use of the term 'Bavarian Greece' to refer to the Greek state is highly derogatory.

[82] I. Th. Kakridis 1963: 252–3 [1956]. For a more nuanced account of Makriyannis' use of the terms *Romaioi* and *Ellines* see Holton 1984/5: 142–9.

[83] Solomos 1961: 71.

modern Greeks. By contrast, Greek historians since the mid-nineteenth century have used the term 'Hellenes' with reference to all periods of Greek history, thus abolishing the distinctions between the multiplicity of terms (and the concomitant attitudes) that were available for use before the revolution.

Greeks and others

Apart from the question of the national name there was also the question as to which communities could be identified as Greek and which could not. In this respect, religion was used as a more powerful criterion than language. Despite the existence of a Catholic minority on some of the Cycladic islands, all Greeks were generally assumed to be Orthodox Christians; but were all Ottoman Orthodox Christians assumed to be Greeks?[84] Ottoman Orthodox Christians spoke many different languages: Greek, Latin languages (Aromanian and Romanian), Slav languages (Serbian and Bulgarian), Albanian and Turkish. There were also Greek-speaking Muslims, who were not normally thought of as being Greek, nor did they consider themselves to be.

The situation is further complicated by the fact that what we might nowadays think of as ethnic labels often corresponded to the division of labour. Vasilis Gounaris argues that 'the cultural division of labour' was the most basic factor of other-identification in the Balkans after religion: 'In broad terms, every transhumant shepherd was thought to be a "Vlach", just as merchants were invariably called, or perceived as, "Greeks", and peasants were "Bulgarians" '.[85] The Habsburg authorities in Transylvania called members of the Orthodox merchant companies 'Greeks', while in Macedonia the term 'Bulgarian' tended to be used to denote a poor Slav peasant.[86] In the Danubian provinces, Greeks, Bulgarians, and Serbs who were professional soldiers were known as *Arvanitai* or *Arnaoútides*, i.e. Albanians.[87] Greek-speaking was associated with commerce and vice versa. In Macedonia, as late as the early twentieth century, both 'Greek' and 'Bulgarian' denoted professions, the latter often being applied to 'poor, Slavic-speaking, Orthodox Christian peasants, shepherds, or laborers of lower social status to whom were ascribed a "peasant" culture.

---

[84] It is significant that the Greek-speaking Catholics of the Cycladic islands, like the Greek-speaking Muslims, did not take part in the Greek revolution against the Ottomans. Nevertheless, according to Vogli 2007: 191, it was never subsequently alleged that they were not Greek.

[85] Livanios 2008: 248–9.   [86] Livanios 2006: 46–7.   [87] Koliopoulos 2003: 145.

The *bakal* (Turkish: "grocer"), on the other hand, was generally known as a Greek, regardless of the language he spoke'.[88]

As we have already seen, before 1821 the terms *Romaios/Romiós* and *Rum* seem to have been used in two different ways, though the two meanings were hardly ever explicitly distinguished by writers at the time. In their wider sense they referred to every Orthodox Christian under the jurisdiction of the patriarchate of Constantinople, that is, every member of the Ottoman *Millet-i Rum* ['nation' of the Orthodox Christians], which was sometimes known in Greek as *to genos ton Romaion*.[89] Also included among the *Romaioi* were the Orthodox Christians of the Ionian Islands and those who lived outside the Ottoman domains. In the narrower sense of the word, however, these terms often denoted a Greek-speaking Orthodox Christian.

In his famous poem entitled 'Thourios' [War song] (1797), in which he calls upon the subject peoples of the Ottoman empire to join forces to overthrow the Ottoman regime, Rigas Velestinlis addresses

> Bulgarians and Albanians, Armenians and *Romioí*,
> blacks and whites, with a common impulse.[90]

Rigas came from an area of Thessaly inhabited by mixed Greek- and Aromanian-speaking populations, where there was widespread bilingualism. It therefore seems strange that he does not specifically refer to Aromanians (Vlachs) at all in this couplet.[91] Here the term *Romiós* appears to exclude those who do not have Greek as their mother tongue – unless Rigas included the Aromanians among the *Romioí*. In the constitution that he proposed for the 'Hellenic Republic' that he envisaged in his book *New Political Administration* (1797), Rigas specifies Vlachs along with 'Hellenes', Bulgarians, Albanians, Armenians, and Turks (i.e. Muslims).[92]

---

[88] Karakasidou 1997: 72, referring to Vermeulen 1984: 232, 234.

[89] For more in English on the *Millet-i Rum* see Clogg 1982; for its organization and functions see Augustinos 1992: 33–8.

[90] Velestinlis 2000: 75.

[91] While it has been claimed by some Romanian nationalist historians that Rigas was of Aromanian origin (e.g. Arginteanu 1904: 245–7), there is no sure evidence to support this, and many Romanian scholars today reject it: see the English version of Lambru 2001: n. 49. Nevertheless, Clogg 1992b: 29 calls Rigas 'a Hellenised Vlach'.

[92] While Rigas stated that 'the simple language of the Hellenes' (i.e. Modern Greek) should be the sole official language of the future state, he did not propose that the other languages be abolished (Konstantakopoulou 1988: 35; Gounaris 2007: 44). On Rigas' solution to the ethnic problem see Kitromilides 1996: 328–32.

The priest Daniil of Moschopolis uses the term *Romaios* in a similar way in his *Introductory Teaching*, which was published in 1802 at the expense of the Metropolitan of Pelagonia (based in Monastir [now Bitola] in what later became Yugoslav Macedonia). Moschopolis was a prosperous Aromanian-speaking town in Albania which was destroyed by Ali Pasha in 1788. Daniil's book was intended to persuade the Aromanian-, Bulgarian-, and Albanian-speaking populations of the southern Balkans to abandon their mother tongues in favour of Greek (Romaic).[93] In a spirit of what Kitromilides calls his 'cultural evangelism',[94] Daniil's book promotes the learning of Greek ('the Mother of wisdom') as a passport to material, spiritual, and intellectual betterment; it begins with the following appeal:

> Albanians, Vlachs, Bulgarians, speakers of other languages, rejoice,
> and prepare to become *Romaioi*.

It is clear that Daniil, like Rigas, intends the term *Romaioi* to mean exclusively Greek-speaking Christians, i.e. those whose mother tongue is Romaic.

In the cases of Rigas and Daniil we see educated Orthodox Christians appearing to distinguish Greek speakers from the rest of their co-religionists according to linguistic criteria. Yet the aim of Daniil's Greek-teaching book was precisely to encourage and enable non-Greek speakers to become Greeks (*Romaioi*). He was a representative of those educated Aromanian speakers (probably the majority) who felt an allegiance to Greek language and culture. We can associate his intention with the work of the priest Kosmas the Aetolian (1714–79) some years earlier. In 1759 Kosmas left his monastery and, with the blessing of several successive patriarchs,[95] set out on tours of western and northern Greece and Albania, encouraging the Orthodox Christians to found schools. During these tours he also encouraged Albanian- and Aromanian-speaking Christians to abandon their mother tongue and to become Greek speakers, 'because our church is in Hellenic'.[96] By this he meant that the liturgy is in Ancient

[93] Daniil 1802: 8 of unnumbered prelims.
[94] Kitromilides 1989: 153. As we have seen, he uses the same phrase about Doukas.
[95] Kitromilides 1996: 177.
[96] Ever since Michalopoulos 1940: 47, this phrase, when quoted, has often been followed by an additional phrase: 'and our nation is Hellenic'. Several scholars have followed Michalopoulos in this, including K. Th. Dimaras 1985: 83. It is likely that this additional phrase is a nationalist fabrication by Michalopoulos. Michalopoulos claims he is quoting from a manuscript in his possession, but this manuscript is not extant today (Menounos n.d.: 46–7). In his edition of Kosmas' teachings, which were recorded in writing only by members of his congregations, Menounos (ibid., 209–10) wisely but tacitly omits it. Elsewhere, according to Menounos,

Greek and that, in order to be able to understand it, one has to know some sort of Greek. Nevertheless, it is unlikely that Kosmas' exhortations were inspired by Greek nationalism. Rather, he was painfully aware that large numbers of the Orthodox flock were unable to understand the scriptures and the liturgy because they did not know Greek of any kind; he saw Greek as the language of Orthodox Christianity, not the language of the Greek nation. If he was inspired by some kind of political motive, it was to try to ensure that the Orthodox populations remained faithful to the patriarchate of Constantinople rather then converting to Islam, as many Christians in the region had done. Like Daniil, Kosmas was trying, with the blessing of the local Orthodox establishment, to persuade the speakers of Aromanian, Albanian, and Slavonic to learn Greek and become fully-fledged *Romaioi* capable of understanding the liturgy (in the case of Kosmas) and becoming merchants (in the case of Daniil).

When it came to converting the Orthodox Christians into Hellenes, Greek nationalists were keen to include speakers of other languages within the Hellenic nation, arguing that they were related to the Greeks either by descent or by way of their shared religion, customs, and manners. One of these was Neofytos Doukas, whose evangelical mission, as we have seen, was far more radical than that of Kosmas and Daniil. In 1810 Doukas published an appeal to the Vlachs of Metsovo in which he urged them to use only Greek and to abandon what he called their 'filthy and squalid' language – 'if it is permitted for the name language to be given to this totally lame thing, which is probably not the offspring of any other language and which gives off a disgusting and malodorous stench'. Doukas points out that Vlachs have been among the foremost proponents of Greek culture, having set up the only Greek printing press in the Ottoman empire, at Moschopolis, in the early eighteenth century. Doukas claimed that the Vlachs should not be proud of their Roman descent, since they know nothing of the Romans. Instead, Doukas continues, Fate has brought them to live in Hellas, whose milk they have suckled, whose fruits they have eaten and whose language, customs and manners they have embraced. In a word, irrespective of their racial descent, the Vlachs have become acculturated in the ways of the Hellenic nation. The Vlachs, who are united with the Hellenes by religion, should also unite with them through language rather than try to set up a separate nation (*genos*).[97]

Kosmas tells his congregation: 'You are not Hellenes, you are not impious, heretics, atheists; you are pious Orthodox Christians' (ibid., 115–16).

[97] Doukas 1810: p. xxxvii.

Doukas, who may himself have come from an Aromanian background though he never mentioned it, was writing in response to the first stirrings of Aromanian nationalism that were taking place among a number of Aromanian expatriates in the Habsburg empire such as Georg Constantin Rosa (Rozha), who urged his compatriots to distance themselves from Greek language and culture and to develop an Aromanian consciousness.[98] The danger of Aromanians asserting their cultural independence from the Greeks was a real one before and after 1821, since many of them were living in Transylvania, where they came into contact with Protestant and Catholic propagandizers who had published the Bible in Romanian. In this way, Aromanians became accustomed not only to seeing a language similar to theirs printed in books but also to thinking of themselves as belonging to the same nation as the Romanian-speaking populations of Wallachia and Moldavia.

Another of these was Michail Boyadji (Boiatzis), who was born in Pest into a family of Aromanian-speaking refugees from Moschopolis and became a teacher of Greek at the Orthodox community school in Vienna. The Orthodox community in Pest was riven by rivalry between supporters of the Greek *status quo* and those who wanted to have Aromanian used in church, a rivalry that eventually led the community to split in two in 1809.[99] In Vienna in 1813 Boyadji published the first ever grammar of the Aromanian language, entitled *Grammar of Romanian or Macedono-Vlach*, written in Greek and German. In the introduction to his book, in which he explicitly counters Doukas' ideas, Boyadji writes that '[o]ur Vlach language is spoken by four million souls' and ends by claiming that, 'even if the Vlachs were Hottentots, they would still have the right and the duty to perfect themselves by means of their own language, as being the most suitable means towards this end; but the figure of four million is not to be despised, especially by a Greek (*Graikós*), the number of whose co-linguals does not exceed it by very much'.[100] Boyadji explains Doukas' Greek chauvinism by claiming that Doukas does not know any language but Greek and for this reason wants to

---

[98] In his impressive *Investigations Concerning the Romans or so-called Vlachs who Reside Beyond the Danube* (1808), written in German and Greek, Rosa, who was born in Bitola in what later became the Yugoslav republic of Macedonia, calls the Aromanians *Romaioi* (thus appropriating this name from the Greeks) and asserts that they are descended from the '*palaioí Romanoi* [old Romans]'; see Iliou 1997: 242–3.

[99] Konstantakopoulou 1988: 39–40.

[100] Boiatzis 1813: pp. x–xiv. Note the early use of the concept of ethnic rights here. It is significant that Boyadji differentiates the 'Macedono-Vlach' language from 'the north Danube idiom', as he calls the Romanian language.

destroy all other languages in the world. Nevertheless, the progress of Aromanian cultural nationalism was greatly impeded by the fact that most of the influential people of Aromanian origin became integrated into Greek culture and presented themselves as Greeks.

Doukas' nationalist impulse was also rejected in an anonymous pamphlet published in 1815 by Ignatios, former Metropolitan of Wallachia, who must have been perturbed by the fact that Doukas was an ordained priest and was therefore perceived as being a representative of the Church. The author expresses regret that Vlach was being used in the liturgy among Epirot Vlachs in Pest, but he opposes Doukas' proposal to send monks to teach Greek to those Orthodox Christians who do not speak the language. He dismisses Doukas' proposals as impracticable, arguing that language is a crucial differentiating characteristic of peoples:

[T]he Hellenes, the Bulgarians, the Vlachs, the Serbs and the Albanians today form Nations, each of which has its language. All of these peoples, however, and all those others who inhabit the East, united by faith and the Church, form one body and nation under the name Greeks or Romans.[101]

Here the author distinguishes between linguistic and religious identity; he acknowledges that Vlachs, Serbs, Albanians and 'Hellenes' (by which he must mean Greek speakers, as Rigas did in his *New Political Administration*) constitute separate peoples or cultural nations on the basis of their distinct languages, yet at the same time he claims, as the Orthodox establishment had always done, that all of these peoples make up a single religious nation, by which he means what the Ottomans called the *Millet-i Rum*. Under the term 'Vlachs' the author seems to subsume both Aromanians (the Romance speakers living south of the Danube) and Wallachians (the Romance speakers living north of the Danube who are today called Romanians); this is another indication of his concern to define each people by its language.[102]

One of the reasons why many Aromanian- and Albanian-speaking Orthodox Christians espoused the Hellenic national project was that their languages were almost entirely unwritten and had not produced a body of literature. These languages were therefore held – even by their own speakers – to be inferior to Greek, which was not only the language

---

[101] K. 1815: 108–9. The name 'Kyrillos K.' may have been intended to give the impression that the text was written by 'Kyrillos [Patriarch] of Constantinople', whereas the author was probably Kyrillos Liverios (see Iliou 1997: 413). For an account of Ignatios' life and work see Kyriakis 2007.

[102] For discussions of the Doukas–Ignatios exchange see Kitromilides 1989: 156–9 and Gounaris 2007: 42–3.

of a venerated pre-Christian literature and of the New Testament and the liturgy but also that of education and commerce in their own time. As for the Albanians, their language was hardly written, and they did not develop a sense of national identity until the late nineteenth century, by which time a large number of Albanian-speaking communities had been integrated into Greek culture. It seems to have been a widely held belief in the late eighteenth and early nineteenth centuries (and in the Balkan region much later too, especially among Greek nationalists) that an independent nation could not exist in modern times unless it had already existed in the past: western European intellectuals often made a distinction between 'historic nations' and 'nations without history'.[103] The phenomenon of Greeks harking back to ancient Greece for national legitimacy is only one instance of a widespread activity that responded to the West's expectations that any modern people that aspired to be recognized as a nation should have a historical past. It was held that nationhood and national identity were not invented but rediscovered and revived, and that 'nations without history' would benefit from being absorbed into 'historic nations'.[104] Thus, given that they could not base a claim to nationhood on the historical past, many Aromanian- and Albanian-speaking Orthodox Christians were content to embrace the Hellenic national cause.

To be a Hellene was felt by some to be such a special privilege (or at least to entail such social prestige and economic success as well as national pride) that they either actively suppressed or passively neglected (first in front of others and later even among themselves) their own non-Greek origin; in this way they gained greater self-respect through identification with the larger Hellenic cultural community at the expense of their solidarity with their smaller linguistic community. The new orientation towards Classical Greece, diligently and successfully promoted by Korais, had the effect of encouraging modern Greeks to become acquainted with and to espouse modern readings of Classical humanist ideals such as liberty, democracy, the rule of law, and civic duty. These noble ideals were something for them to aspire to – to make themselves into modern Hellenes. These ideals were not available in such a direct manner to peoples who did not call themselves Hellenes, who did not speak and write a language descended from Ancient Greek, and who did not inhabit the same geographical area as the ancient Greeks.

[103] These terms seem to have been first used by Friedrich Engels; cf. Fishman 1975: 26.
[104] Cf. Sigalas 2001: 19.

The Greeks were fortunate that assiduous research into the ancient Greek past was already being carried out by non-Greeks, and they were not left to do the job all by themselves. As Marc Lauxtermann has written,

While the other European nations largely had to create their own national symbols, stories and monuments (which Hobsbawm has aptly called 'invention of tradition'), the Greeks on the contrary received their national identity from Western Europe as a ready-to-use package.[105]

The ancient component of their 'national history' was already written, and they could take it over ready-made. In addition, the cultural prestige of Greek language and culture in the modern Balkans (what is sometimes called, after Dimitri Obolensky, the Orthodox Commonwealth) was also ready-made, although this prestige was not necessarily attached to the modern spoken varieties of the Greek language.

According to Vincenzo Rotolo, it was precisely their 'extravagant national pride', linked with their worship of ancient Greece, that enabled Greeks to prepare the revolution after many centuries of servitude. The greatest source of inspiration for the revolutionary movement was antiquity, with its illustrious heroes, its literature and its language.[106] Thus the Greeks' worship of antiquity and their claim to be descendants of the ancient Greeks were far from being solely for foreign consumption.

Greek nationalists were usually content to let the Serbs develop their own national identity. As for the Bulgarians, although they could lay claim to a historically-based nationhood, they did not do so until the middle of the nineteenth century. In his *Slavyano-Bulgarian History*, written in 1762, Paisii Khilendarski had already rehabilitated the glorious Bulgarian medieval imperial past and complained that in his day the patriarchate of Constantinople imposed central ecclesiastical and educational control on the Bulgarians, including Greek priests and Greek teachers, yet the earliest studies on his book date from 1871, and it was not published till 1914.[107]

In the second half of the eighteenth century and the first half of the nineteenth, education in Bulgaria was almost entirely in Greek.[108] For this reason, several intellectuals of Bulgarian background espoused the Greek national cause. One of these was the doctor and Classical scholar Nikolaos Pikkolos (1792–1865), born to Bulgarian parents in Trnovo

---

[105] Lauxtermann 2007: 127.   [106] Rotolo 1965: 56.

[107] Ivanov 1914. The dates are significant: 1871 was the year after the Bulgarian Exarchate was established, while 1914 fell between the second Balkan war and the First World War, in each of which Greece and Bulgaria were on opposing sides.

[108] Camariano-Cioran 1974: 357.

in Bulgaria, who became an associate of Korais in Paris, where he taught Modern Greek to Claude Fauriel and became one of his leading assistants in his publication of Greek folk songs. He donated much of his wealth to the Greek revolution and taught in Chios and Corfu. He spent the last twenty-five years of his life in Paris, where he lobbied for Bulgarian autonomy at the Congress of Paris in 1856, yet he was still writing letters in Greek to his nephew Petar Protich, inspector of hospitals in Bucharest, as late as 1861.[109] Such cases show how much choice was available to talented Christians in the Balkans during the late Ottoman period – choice of identities, choice of careers – and also that competence in the Greek language was a key to this kind of social mobility.

The final group of non-Greek-speaking Orthodox Christians of the Ottoman empire that should be mentioned are the Turkish-speaking Christians of central and southern Asia Minor, popularly known as *Karamanlides*, a term that properly refers to the inhabitants of Karaman province in south central Turkey.[110] These communities were geographically far removed from communities of Greek-speaking Christians. There were Turkish-speaking Orthodox Christians in other parts of Anatolia too, particularly in western Pontus in north-east Turkey. It is not clear whether these people were descended from Greek-speaking Christians who changed their language, or from Turkish speakers who changed their religion, or originate from a mixture of the two. Those of them who wrote in their own language normally used the Greek script. There is a significant body of printed texts in what is called *karamanlídika*, i.e. Turkish language written in the Greek alphabet. The first book printed in *karamanlídika* dates from 1718, while the last was printed in Salonica in 1929.[111] The publication of books in *karamanlídika* was promoted by the patriarchate not only to discourage Turkish-speaking Christians from converting to Islam but also to counteract Catholic propaganda in the areas where they lived.[112] One of the first novels to be published in the Turkish language was written in *karamanlídika* by the teacher and journalist Evangelinos Misailidis and published in Constantinople in 1871–72.[113] The most highly educated *Karamanlides*

---

[109] For Pikkolos' life and work see Beshevliev et al. (ed.) 1968; A. Politis 1984. Todorov (1964: 80) has no hesitation in asserting that Pikkolos was 'de nationalité bulgare'.

[110] For more on the *Karamanlides* in English see Clogg 1999b.

[111] Salaville and Dalleggio 1958: 3–4; Balta 1987a: 150.   [112] Sigalas 2004: 129.

[113] Misailidis 1871–72. Misailidis' novel is an adaptation of one of the earliest modern Greek novels, *O polypathis* (Athens 1839), by the Constantinopolitan Grigorios Palaiologos; see Kechagioglou 1995–96.

became bilingual in Turkish and Greek and literate in Greek; some wrote in both languages, and a few of them were even able to write Turkish in Arabic script.[114]

By and large, with some notable exceptions, the *Karamanlides* did not espouse the Greek national cause. According to Evangelia Balta, the authors of prologues to books in *karamanlídika* call their readers 'Christians' (i.e. not Muslims), 'Orthodox Christians' (i.e. not Catholics or Protestants), or 'Christians of Anatolia' (i.e. not inhabitants of Greece), but never 'Hellenes'. The prefatory verses to one book, published in 1896, state that

though we are *Rum* we don't know our language, but speak Turkish. Yet we don't read and write Turkish [i.e. Arabic script], just as we don't speak Greek. So we are a mixture. Our alphabet is Greek but we express ourselves in Turkish.[115]

Greek-speaking Muslims have not usually been considered as belonging to the Greek nation. Some communities of Greek-speaking Muslims lived in Macedonia. Muslims, most of them native speakers of Greek, formed a slight majority of the population of Crete in the early nineteenth century. The vast majority of these were descended from Christians who had voluntarily converted to Islam in the period following the Ottoman conquest of the island in 1669.[116]

In this book, for reasons of space, I am largely confining myself to the national identity of Orthodox Christians. For religious minorities in Greece I refer the reader to the volume edited by Clogg (2002), especially the chapters by Charles Frazee on Catholics, John O. Iatrides on Evangelicals, Steven Bowman on Jews, and Ronald Meinardus on Muslims. For the co-existence of Christians, Muslims, and Jews in Salonica see Mazower 2004. Among the contributions on Orthodox

---

[114] For the prolific local historian, geographer, and archaeologist Anastasios M. Levidis (formerly Kazantzoglou, 1834–1918), the historian Pavlos Karolidis (1849–1930, formerly Karloglou, born at Enderelik [Androniki] near Kayseri, professor of history at the University of Athens, translator into Ottoman Turkish of Kritovoulos' history of Mehmet II (1912) and member of the Ottoman Parliament), and other bilingual *Karamanli* authors see Petropoulou 1988–89 and Strauss 1995. For the bilingual sociologist and economist Dimosthenis Daniilidis (1889–1972) see Kriaras 2004: 218–31.

[115] Balta 1987b: 232, quoting from *Kaisareia* 1896.

[116] All Greek-speaking Muslims living in Greece were removed to Turkey together with the rest of the Muslims under the Lausanne exchange agreement in 1923–24, the largest number coming from Crete. Exceptions to the compulsory exchange were the Muslims of Eastern Thrace and the Albanian-speaking Chams of Epirus. For the fate of the Chams see Margaritis 2005: 133–215.

Christian minorities in the same volume are those by T. J. Winnifrith on the Vlachs and Anastasia Karakasidou on the 'Slavo-Macedonians'.[117]

The prehistory of the Greek language question

According to Rotolo, the Greek language controversy in the late eighteenth century did not continue earlier disputes about the Greek language.[118] For this reason it is not necessary to deal at length with earlier periods. Suffice it to say that, ever since the artificial revival of Classical Attic Greek in the movement known as the 'Second Sophistic' (during the Roman period, from late first century AD onwards), which in turn influenced the language of Christian texts from the late second century onwards, most Greek writing had been carried out in a variety of language significantly removed, in vocabulary and grammar, from everyday speech.[119] A contempt for the spoken language and a desire to emulate the language of the ancient authors remained prevalent well into the twentieth century, being manifested in an effort either to write in Ancient Greek or to archaize the modern language when writing it.

Between Hellenistic and modern times, spoken Greek has changed remarkably little. The pronunciation went through a series of radical changes from the end of the Classical period in the fourth century BC until about the ninth century AD, but it has remained stable ever since. There has been a certain amount of morphological simplification, but not nearly so much as occurred between Latin and the modern romance languages. Unlike Italian, for instance, Modern Greek has retained all of the three ancient genders and a highly inflected nominal system, with up to four morphologically distinct cases, having lost only the dative. The morphology of Modern Greek, coupled with the traditional orthography, makes the language look very close to Ancient Greek when it is written. Greeks seeing a sentence in Ancient Greek can immediately recognize which words are nouns and which are verbs (and in most cases which is the subject and which the direct object), even if they do not know what the words mean. For this reason the gap between the ancient and the modern languages has appeared to many to be bridgeable. In these

---

[117] Some members of this group like to be called 'Macedonians' rather than 'Slavo-Macedonians', hence my use of quotation marks. Karakasidou avoids using the term 'Slavo-Macedonians' on the additional grounds that it was coined by the Greek Communist Party (Karakasidou 1997: 22).

[118] Rotolo 1965: 53–4.

[119] For a brief survey of Atticism and the Second Sophistic see Horrocks 1997: 79–83.

circumstances, given the enormous prestige enjoyed by ancient Greek language and culture, the temptation to 'correct' the modern written language by making it look even closer to Ancient Greek is understandable. Most Greeks failed to take account of the pronunciation changes from Ancient Greek to Modern Greek: they assumed that the ancients pronounced Greek as they themselves did, and some of them tried to refute the claim of western Classical scholars since Erasmus that the Classical Greeks pronounced their language differently. It is not coincidental that some of the exceptions to this rule were proponents of the written use of the spoken language.

There was no language controversy in Byzantium, where various levels of written Greek co-existed harmoniously.[120] In the twelfth century, efforts were made in Constantinople to begin writing in vernacular Greek, and these efforts spread elsewhere in the empire and beyond its borders in the fourteenth and fifteenth centuries. Yet even most of this vernacular literature was 'macaronic', that is, it consisted of a preponderance of colloquial features with a haphazard admixture of archaic or learned features. Moreover, it was confined to fifteen-syllable verse. It is nevertheless highly significant for the study of the development of the Greek language. By contrast, in lands ruled by Catholics of western European origin, such as Cyprus and Crete, education in Ancient Greek was not widely available, while vernacular models for writing were accessible to those Greeks who were educated in the language of the occupiers. Cretan dramatic and narrative poetry produced under Venetian rule in the sixteenth and seventeenth centuries was written in a literary version of the spoken dialect under the influence of Italian literary movements during the Renaissance and after. The authors of these works developed an eloquent literary vernacular closely based on the lexis and morphology of spoken Cretan dialect and deliberately avoiding archaic words and forms. This language variety was confined to verse literature, albeit of a highly sophisticated kind, whose production was cut short by the gradual Ottoman conquest of Crete, which was completed in 1669. As in the Byzantine period, the vernacular literary language in Venetian-dominated Crete had no impact on education, which was either in ecclesiastical Greek or Latin for would-be clerics, or in Latin and Italian for laypeople. In addition, even though Cretan texts in printed form were widely read in various parts of the Greek-speaking world, the fact that their language was based on a local dialect made it unsuitable for adoption outside Crete.

---

[120] Beck 1978: 147; Toufexis 2008.

In prose, the Cretan contemporaries of these authors wrote either in
Ancient Greek or in a slightly archaized version of the modern language.
Only Cypriots, under Lusignan and Venetian rule during the fourteenth
to sixteenth centuries, wrote both verse and prose in a non-archaized
vernacular, with abundant dialect features.

In the 1540s Nikolaos Sofianos (*c*.1500–*c*.1550), a Corfiote settled in
Italy, devised a Greek educational programme based on the vernacular language, including vernacular translations of ancient Greek texts.
However, his project was discontinued, perhaps because of its association
with Catholicism. As part of his project, Sofianos wrote the first grammar
of modern spoken Greek, but failed to publish it.[121] His *Grammatical
Introduction* is prefaced by a dedication in Latin to Cardinal Giovanni
Lotharingio, in which he says that the writing of his grammar was
influenced by similar efforts devoted to national languages in Europe.[122]
If not actually a Catholic himself, Sofianos was very close to the Catholic
hierarchy.[123] At all events, the connection between his linguistic ideas
and the Catholic Church were bound to alienate many Greeks both in his
time and later. Sofianos' life and work coincided chronologically with
the early stages of printing in vernacular Greek, starting with the Cretan
poem *Apokopos* (first published in Venice in 1509), which provided cheap
and plentiful copies of widely read secular books and began to lend a
certain prestige to the spoken language by accustoming Greek readers to
seeing it written down.

From the late sixteenth century onwards, collections of sermons and
other books intended for a popular audience, mostly the work of clerics
from Crete and Ionian Islands, were written and published in a slightly

---

[121] Sofianos' grammar was written forty years before the first published English grammar
(1586); see Crystal 2006: 56. It remained unpublished until 1870. I am grateful to David Holton
for pointing out to me that Sofianos uses the same title as the famous grammar of Ancient Greek
by Theodore of Gaza (d. 1478). Some later scholars have referred to Sofianos' grammar by
the misleading title that its editor gave it in 1870: 'Grammar of the Common Language of the
Hellenes'; Sofianos does not use the term 'Hellenes' to refer to the modern Greeks. The first
published grammar of contemporary Greek by a Greek was Venieris 1799 (Manolessou 2008:
73, n. 40). The author was later the translator of the constitution of the Septinsular Republic. Io
Manolessou (personal communication) informs me that Venieris' grammar is a version of the
famous grammar of Ancient Greek by Konstantinos Laskaris (1476), but with examples taken
from Modern Greek. Venieris' grammar is in Greek ('in dialetto greco volgare') and Italian. In
his preface (reproduced in Ladas and Hatzidimou 1973: 217–20), the author states that his aim
is to bring 'our language' closer to 'ancient Hellenic'.

[122] For the place of Sofianos' grammar within his overall educational project see Ziogas
1974: 270–4.

[123] For instance, he chose as his cultural model the Catholic bishop Dionysios II of Mylopotamos in Crete, who was well known for subjecting the Eastern Church to the Western; see Ziogas
1974: 300–3.

archaized version of the vernacular. Such publications were exceptions to the rule that works produced by the Greek intellectual leadership were in archaic Greek.[124] The clerics who wrote books in the vernacular were attempting to counter Jesuit propaganda publications, which were being produced in vernacular Greek within the context of the Counter-Reformation in order to undermine Protestant efforts to propagandize in the vernacular. In such a complex situation it was difficult to avoid controversy. The first complete translation of the New Testament into Modern Greek (in a very slightly archaized vernacular) was undertaken by Archimandrite Maximos Kallioupolitis at the suggestion of the Ambassador of the Netherlands to Constantinople and published in Geneva in 1638 in a luxury edition at the expense of the States General of the United Provinces of the Netherlands (i.e. the Dutch government) with a preface by the patriarch of Constantinople, Kyrillos I (the Cretan Kyrillos Loukaris). But, even before the translation was published, Kyrillos was executed by the Ottomans following allegations from French Jesuits that his contacts with Protestant countries were undermining the security of the Ottoman state, and very few copies of the translation were distributed. The fact that vernacular Greek was used by both Protestant and Catholic propagandists continued to be an obstacle to its acceptance in Orthodox circles.

As in China, so in the Ottoman empire, low literacy abetted the tendency towards the preciosity and antiquarianism of inbred scholarship.[125] The Fanariot Alexandros Mavrokordatos wrote in Ancient Greek; indeed, he specifically instructed his sons to avoid 'the coarse and vulgar dialect',[126] although in the event his son Nikolaos wrote some of his work in Ancient Greek and some in the modern language.[127]

During the Greek Enlightenment in the late eighteenth century the Greek language became a focus of attention for the Orthodox populations of the Balkans. Greek was the language of the New Testament, the Orthodox liturgy and the patriarchate of Constantinople, as well as that of the pre-Christian ancient Greeks. By that time it had also become the language of commerce, education, and the new learning. It did not take long for people to be troubled by the fact that 'Greek' did not take a single form but that there were almost as many varieties of Greek as there were writers and communities of speakers. Which kind of Greek should

---

[124] Kitromilides 1996: 61–2.   [125] For China see De Francis 1950: 8.

[126] Kitromilides 1996: 61; Angelou 1998: 84*.

[127] See e.g. his *Nouthesiai* [*Admonitions*], addressed to his son Konstantinos, which remained unpublished till modern times.

be used for written expression, especially when it came to transfusing the new secular learning from the West through original works and through translations and adaptations of foreign works? Was it more appropriate to use Ancient Greek or the vernacular? And if the vernacular, then which variety of the vernacular?

As Alkis Angelou has written, 'Perhaps in no other European country was the Enlightenment such a complex matter as in Greece'. In contrast to western Europe, as Kitromilides has observed, 'In modern Greek culture the Enlightenment provoked rather than resolved the quarrel of the ancients and moderns'.[128] The Enlightenment in Greece and the Balkans was to some extent the equivalent of the Renaissance in western Europe, including the struggle for dominance between the ancient and the modern languages. For this reason it was inevitable that the Greek language controversy – initially in the form of the dilemma between Ancient and Modern Greek rather than between rival versions of the modern language – should have begun during the period of the Greek Enlightenment and should have been a crucial component of it.

Nasia Yakovaki sees the influence of print culture in this movement, as had been the case previously in the West, where printing led to the final victory of the vernaculars over Latin as written languages. In the eighteenth century we observe the emergence of a new readership, besides the *lógioi*, the teachers and the higher clergy, and the audience for the traditional popular printed books. This new readership included especially merchants, and it went together with the subscription method of financing the publication of Greek books, which began in the mid-eighteenth century as a result of initiatives coming from printers acting as entrepreneurs.[129] As Todorov points out, the importance of the subscription method was that it obviated the need for capital subsidies, whether from the Church or from elsewhere, to pay for the publication of books.[130] K. Th. Dimaras has shown that, as the eighteenth century proceeded, the number of Greek printed books increased, while a larger proportion of those published were of a secular nature, especially books of grammar. Thus, for instance, while in 1701–25 one hundred and seven Greek books were published, 75 per cent of which were religious, in 1776–1800 seven hundred and forty-nine books were published, of which 53 per cent were religious.[131] By contrast, in 1800–21 over 1300 Greek

---

[128] Angelou 1998: 116*; Kitromilides 1996: 223.

[129] Yakovaki 2005: 199. For details of the subscription method for financing the publication of Greek books during the period 1749–1832 see Iliou 2005: 111–317.

[130] Todorov 1985: 66.   [131] K. Th. Dimaras 1985: 30, 122.

books were published, while only 34 per cent of the books produced during the five-year period 1816–21 were religious.[132] The first successful periodical publication in Greek, the twice-weekly newspaper *Efimerís*, was published in Vienna 'in the simple Romaic language' from 1790 to 1797 by the brothers Markides Pouliou, who came from an Aromanian background in Siatista in Macedonia.[133] In sum, Modern Greek came to be used in writing and in print for a wide variety of different purposes.

Finally, there was the problem of converting Greek from the common language of Balkan clerics, intellectuals, and merchants into the language of the Greek nation. This is where the need for standardization was felt: but should the direction of standardization be upward (whether based on out-and-out archaism or purist 'correction') or downward (based on the common features of the spoken dialects)? Present-day written Greek is the result of a long, tortuous, and arduous process of compromise between these two directions.

Attitudes to language

Attitudes towards the Greek language in the late eighteenth century can be summed up as a combination of the tremendous prestige of the Greek language in general and a general contempt for its everyday spoken varieties. The reverence for Ancient and Biblical Greek in the Orthodox world was similar to the reverence for Latin in the West, but with one crucial difference. The fact that Greek never split into separate languages means that Greek speakers have always been tempted to view the whole of Greek as a single language, from antiquity to the present.

Contemptuous attitudes towards the spoken language are not confined to Greece. In eighteenth-century England Samuel Johnson and others were determined to differentiate their own 'refined' diction from that of the 'vulgar' mob. They argued that writing and polite conversation should employ a more 'durable' language than the 'fugitive cant' of 'the laborious and mercantile part of the people', which differed from place to place and from time to time.[134] 'Durability' implied both standardization and conservatism, both of which in turn, in their view, necessitated prescriptive rules that would bring English closer to Latin and Greek

[132] Clogg 1979: 74, referring to Iliou 1973: 38–9.

[133] For the background and the content of the *Efimerís* see Sofou 2007. The *Efimeris* was preceded by an unsuccessful attempt to publish a Greek newspaper in Vienna in 1784.

[134] Johnson 1755, in Johnson 2000: esp. 323. The phrase 'grocers' language' used by Kodrikas against the variety of Greek used and proposed by Korais and others is reminiscent of this phrase of Johnson's.

and thus give it a separate grammar from that of colloquial speech. Just as Johnson argued that one needed to know Latin so as to 'grammaticalize' one's English,[135] many Greeks have believed their language would become more grammatical if they were taught Ancient Greek. Men like Johnson also claimed that the way a person used language reflected their intelligence and their moral character: one could not be moral, civilized, rational, and capable of abstract thought if one used a 'base' (i.e. vernacular) language. It is indicative that opposition to these views from vernacularists in Britain and elsewhere (e.g. poets such as Wordsworth) arose around the turn of the nineteenth century, with the rise of romanticism, which claimed that 'natural' and 'artless' language was morally superior because it was 'genuine' and 'truthful'.

Apart from the adulation of Classical and early Christian culture, a factor that led to the prejudice against spoken Greek was the fact that it had not been properly studied and analysed, and the systematic nature of its grammar had not been understood. Before the time of the Swiss linguist Ferdinand de Saussure (1857–1913), language was normally studied primarily in its written form; for one thing, before sound recording, it was difficult to study spoken language precisely. Spoken language was generally thought of as inherently inferior. Connected with this is the fact that, before Saussure, language tended to be studied primarily in its historical (diachronic) development rather than in its present (synchronic) form: it was not sufficiently understood that every natural language at any one time presents a systematic structure.

When Adamantios Korais came to study vernacular Greek around 1800, his research was almost totally confined to vocabulary, which is the least systematic of the various linguistic categories, since it is open to loans from other languages as long as these are made to conform to the phonological and morphological rules of the borrowing language – which was the case in spoken Modern Greek. Ancient Greek was known solely through a prestigious body of written texts and was codified in numerous school grammars, while Modern Greek was spoken by all, yet little written and even less studied. Thus, despite the fact that it was split into dialects, Ancient Greek was perceived as a system, while spoken Modern Greek was perceived to be bewilderingly unsystematic.

The presence of many words of non-Greek origin in spoken Greek gave the impression that the whole language had been 'barbarized'; to the non-linguist, individual words tend to be more noticeable than grammatical

---

[135] Boswell 1791 in Boswell 1980: 1078.

structures, which are what constitutes the essence of a language. The loanwords from Turkish were thought to be too shameful a reminder of Turkish domination to be allowed to remain in the written language. As Michael Herzfeld has written, it seemed that under Ottoman rule 'the Greeks... had acquired a shamefully Turkish patina which now had to be scraped away'.[136] Examples of Turkish words in common use in the early nineteenth century that have since been replaced by Greek equivalents are as follows (with Turkish etymons in italics and native Greek equivalents in brackets):

αλισβερίσι < *alışveriş* [(business) dealings] (συναλλαγές)
γιολτζής < *yolcu* [traveller, wayfarer] (οδοιπόρος, ταξιδιώτης)
μουστερής < *müşteri* [customer] (πελάτης)
μπερεκέτι < *bereket* [abundance] (αφθονία)
οντάς < *oda* [room] (δωμάτιο)
σερμαγιά < *sermaye* [(financial) capital] (κεφάλαιο)
τζελάτης < *cellât* [executioner] (δήμιος)[137]

But it was not only loanwords from Turkish that were 'purged' from written Greek by purists; many pan-European words that had entered Greek from Italian, in particular, were also replaced by new or revived Hellenic terms:

πόστα < *posta* [postal service; post office] (ταχυδρομείον: neologism)
βίζιτα < *visita* [visit] (επίσκεψις)
φαμελιά < *famiglia* [family] (οικογένεια)
μινίστρος < *ministro* [(government) minister] (υπουργός)

Ironically, the purging of loanwords from Italian made Modern Greek less like other European languages in terms of its vocabulary, while at the same time its semantics and syntax were being brought closer to these languages.

Both the history of the Greek language question and the history of the Greek language itself since the late eighteenth century are about the way the Greeks have moulded their language to make it reflect their image of their own identity, and especially their relationship with the Greek past. The purging of a large number of loanwords from the language has diminished the obvious traces of foreign influences on Greek culture, while the insistence on historical orthography and the 'correction' of many phonological and morphological features according to Ancient Greek

---

[136] Herzfeld 1982: 17.
[137] These examples are taken from the list drawn up by S. Vyzantios 1835 of words to be expunged from the language.

rules reflects Greeks' idea of their close connection with ancient Greece and with the learned linguistic and literary tradition of Byzantium. This is why the language question has been so crucial in the history of Greek culture, and why its study is essential for an understanding of that culture. Moreover, the modern language controversy is in a sense a replay of the controversy during the Second Sophistic, and is therefore in itself a manifestation of a Greek sense of cultural continuity.

The Greek language controversy, both before and after the revolution, has been a competition for cultural dominance and the control of knowledge. All sides in the controversy, whether they supported the continued use of Ancient Greek or whether they argued for the use of a 'natural' or a 'corrected' version of the vernacular, felt that they were seeking what was genuine and authentic. The members of the conservative elite tried to hold on to their cultural privileges, helped by the Orthodox Church.[138] By contrast, the vernacularists aimed at the democratization of knowledge by attempting to open up high culture to larger numbers of people; in this respect they resembled Protestants, who promote universal literacy in order to enable universal access to the text of the Scriptures.

Rotolo sums up the opposing linguistic arguments of the archaists and the vernacularists as follows. On the one side, '[t]o preserve the use of the ancient language seemed to many to be the best way of demonstrating, both to themselves and to foreigners, that the modern Greeks are the legitimate sons of the ancients'; on the other side, 'the argument that seemed more incontrovertible was that the language of the Greeks had for over twenty-five centuries continued to be the same, save for a few insignificant phonetic and lexical changes'.[139]

The immediate historical and intellectual background to the beginning of the language controversy

In the late eighteenth century, no one envisaged a Greek nation-state in the modern (romantic) sense, made up of a single people speaking a single language. Even the most revolutionary, Rigas Velestinlis, envisaged a broad republic replacing the Ottoman empire, which would embrace citizens of all religions and all mother tongues but whose official language would be Greek.

The year 1766 saw the publication of Voulgaris' *Logic*, in which the author attacked those who wrote about philosophical subjects in the

---

[138] Rotolo 1965: 55.   [139] Ibid., 56–7.

'vulgar language'. This attack marks the beginning of the language controversy, which was to last almost exactly two hundred years. The beginning of the language controversy took place during a period of rapid change in the political and cultural history of the Orthodox Christians of the Balkans and Anatolia. The same year marked the beginning of a new era in Greek and Balkan history. The patriarchate of Constantinople abolished the autocephaly of the Serbian patriarchate of Peć (now in north-west Kosovo; Pejë in Albanian) and the Bulgarian archbishopric of Ohrid (now in FYROM) in 1766–67. Thus the patriarchate of Constantinople came to exert direct control over all of the Orthodox Christian communities in the Balkan domains of the Ottoman empire, and mostly Greek bishops were installed in the sees of these regions.[140] As Victor Roudometof writes, 'The abolition of the two autocephalous seats further expanded patriarchal authority over the Balkan peninsula and enhanced the prestige and power of the Grecophone elites controlling the patriarchate.'[141] It was also about this time that the Ottoman *millet* arrangement was systematized, with the patriarch of Constantinople explicitly recognized by the Ottoman state as the leader of a unitary community consisting of all the Orthodox Christians of the empire.[142] According to Dennis P. Hupchick, Greek cultural hegemony within the Orthodox *millet* went unchallenged until the middle of the nineteenth century.[143] These developments led to the even greater prestige of the Greek language in Ottoman lands.

A huge number of clergymen needed to be trained to occupy senior and junior positions throughout the Orthodox Christian world under the jurisdiction of the patriarchate of Constantinople. Whether they were to become clergymen or not, all Orthodox Christians in the Balkans who aspired to education needed to learn Greek, but some educated people were beginning to turn away from the traditional learning, dominated by the Church, to modern philosophical ideas and approaches emanating from the West. It is no coincidence that the language controversy began in the realm of philosophy, since the term 'philosophy' came to be applied by Greeks to secular Enlightenment ideas in general, often with particular reference to the natural sciences as opposed to the study of grammar.

---

[140] The motive for the abolition of autocephaly seems not to have been political but to have been due to the inability of these archbishoprics to support themselves financially; see Konortas 1998: 217–27.

[141] Roudometof 1998: 20.

[142] Konortas 1998: 299–300. According to Ursinus 1993: 62, the term *Millet-i Rum* [Nation of the Orthodox Christians] first appears in an Ottoman document of 1757.

[143] Hupchick 2001: 206.

By the 1780s, Dimitrios Katartzis was elaborating the connection between Enlightenment, language, and nationality.[144] However, the French revolution – and especially the execution of Louis XVI in 1792 – proved to be a setback for the Greek Enlightenment, as the Church and the Fanariots distanced themselves from it. The French revolution, followed by Napoleon's campaigns in the Mediterranean, polarized Greek intellectual leaders, encouraging some of them to call for revolution and liberation, while the Church hierarchy, justifiably fearing that its authority and even its very existence were in jeopardy, issued condemnations of the new philosophically and politically revolutionary ideas. The patriarchate of Constantinople issued a series of encyclicals condemning the dissemination of modern western ideas. In 1793 it condemned 'Voltaires' as 'instruments of impiety and atheism'.[145] In 1798 patriarch Grigorios V urged that all copies of Rigas' revolutionary pamphlet, the *New Political Administration*, be withdrawn from circulation.[146]

The chief attack on the importation of modern Western secular ideas into the Christian East, entitled *Paternal Teaching* (1798), was written in a mildly archaized version of the vernacular and published in Constantinople in response to the French landings in Corfu and Alexandria. It condemned the French revolution and ideas of social equality and progress as being inspired by the devil, and it exhorted Christians to be obedient to their monarch and to avoid being tempted by foreign teaching, arguing that the Ottoman empire had been created by God to protect the Orthodox from the Latin heresy.[147] Korais' riposte to it, *Fraternal Teaching* (also published in 1798) attempted to demonstrate that true Christianity is compatible with the new philosophical ideas, arguing that liberty is a God-given right.[148] As Kitromilides puts it, the Orthodox hierarchy made a common front with the Sublime Porte against the West, at a time when the hope – shared by Rigas as well as Korais – for French intervention in the affairs of Greece had superseded the 'Russian expectation'.[149]

---

[144] Kitromilides 1989: 153.   [145] K. Th. Dimaras 1985: 156.

[146] For an extract of Grigorios' letter to the metropolitan of Smyrna on this subject see Ladas and Hatzidimou 1973: 72–3. Stavridi-Patrikiou 1999: 10 points out that Grigorios condemned Rigas' pamphlet not only because of its revolutionary content but because it was written in 'simple Romaic phrase'.

[147] Anthimos 1798. The *Paternal Teaching* was written by (or at least published under the name of) Anthimos, Patriarch of Jerusalem. For an English translation of the text and an account of its background see Clogg 1969. In their *Rudder of the Figurative Ship*, a compendium of Orthodox canon law, the monks Agapios and Nikodimos of the Holy Mountain make the same assertion about the Ottoman empire: Agapios and Nikodimos 1800; see Clogg 1979: 73.

[148] Korais 1798; Rotolo 1965: 26; Kitromilides 1996: 276–9.

Despite the best efforts of the Church hierarchy, the commercial bourgeoise gradually took over the role of the Orthodox Church as leader, inspirer, and organizer of educational and cultural activity.[150] Nevertheless, during this period, the Church continued its own educational and spiritual mission. At the same time that western secular ideas were being disseminated in books, printing was exploited by Orthodox churchmen in order to propagate specifically Orthodox Christian ideas. An upsurge in Orthodox spirituality was expressed and encouraged at this time by the ambitious project of the monk Nikodimos of the Holy Mountain, who was born in 1748 (the same year as Korais) and died in 1809. Among the fifteen or so books by Nikodimos that were published in his lifetime, his chief work was his first, entitled *Philokalia*, an anthology of ascetic and mystical texts dating from the fourth to the fifteenth centuries, which he compiled in collaboration with Makarios, Metropolitan of Corinth, and published in Venice in 1782. According to Kitromilides, '[t]he *Philokalia* could be considered, without risk of serious exaggeration, as the most important achievement in the spiritual tradition of the Orthodox world in the eighteenth century'. In reaction to the secularization preached by the Greek Enlightenment, Kitromilides continues, the compilers 'pointed to an alternative form of "enlightenment", illumination by the inner light of God, that became visible to the faithful by means of purification of the soul through prayer and meditation on the mystical wisdom of the fathers'.[151]

The language question and society

Regarding the social allegiances of the chief participants in the language controversy before 1821 – contrary to the received wisdom, which seems to have originated from the Marxist Gianis Kordatos (1927) – there is no simple correlation between conservatism or radicalism in social attitudes and their apparent counterparts in linguistic matters. The patriarchate itself and the majority of the clergy were, linguistically speaking, more conservative than reactionary; they were simply reluctant to change the linguistic *status quo*, which meant continuing to write in a fairly macaronic language.

Linguistic conservatives tended to be supporters of the ecclesiastical and Fanariot establishment, who feared the challenge to their cultural

---

[149] Kitromilides 1996: 27, 280, 312.   [150] Todorov 1985: 65–6.
[151] Kitromilides 2000: 341–2.

hegemony. Yet by no means all the members of the Fanariot circle were archaists or even linguistic conservatives. Indeed, some of the courtiers and officials attached to the Fanariot princes of Wallachia and Moldavia, who were in turn close to the patriarch and even to the Sultan, were in the forefront of the vernacularist movement. The political ideal of the vernacularists Katartzis and Christopoulos was enlightened despotism, according to which not only the Danubian princes but perhaps even the Sultan too would benefit both themselves and their subjects through a kind of top-down enlightenment. As Alexis Politis points out, the later vernacularists Vilaras and Psalidas too were adherents of enlightened despotism – in this case the despotism of Ali Pasha of Yannina, whose enlightenment was more a matter of hope than reality. Indeed, none of the enthusiastic vernacularists joined the secret revolutionary society, the *Filikí Etaireia*.[152]

The fact that the leading archaists were both clerics and schoolteachers, who feared that their educational authority was being undermined by radical linguistic proposals, did not prevent them from being progressive in their social outlook. The archaist Neofytos Doukas, who became a member of the *Etaireia*, passionately believed in justice, freedom, and equality, and he saw linguistic archaism as a liberating and enabling force. In 1812 he published an open letter to the princes of Wallachia, calling upon them to release the Gypsies from serfdom and invoking 'the rights of man'. Far from being an elitist, he expressed his desire for the whole of the nation to be enlightened, or at least the inhabitants of the towns. After he was attacked and severely beaten in a Bucharest street one morning in 1817, he attributed this attempt against his life to the fact that 'it is not in the interests of the Fanariots that the Dacians [= Romanians] be educated'. Doukas made a decisive contribution to the creation of a Romanian elite, which in turn played a leading role in the cultural leadership of the Romanians after 1821.[153]

The role of clerics in the debate is perhaps not surprising: the most educated Greeks tended to become deacons, since it was the most convenient way of gaining an education; we can compare the enlightened French *abbés* of the eighteenth century, as well as Oxford and Cambridge dons, who at that time were obliged to be in holy orders. Thus the archaists Voulgaris and Doukas, the purist Theotokis, the self-styled modernist Moisiodax, and the vernacularists Konstantas and Filippidis were all clerics; Voulgaris and Theotokis even became bishops. All these clerics

---

[152] See A. Politis 2007.   [153] Charilaou 2004.

were also teachers, while among the teachers who were not clergymen were Lampros Fotiadis in Bucharest and Psalidas in Yannina.

Another typical profession practised (or at least studied) by the participants in the language debate was medicine, which was the only real profession in the Ottoman empire: among the so-called *iatrofilósofoi* (the local equivalent of the English 'natural philosophers') were the arch-vernacularist Vilaras, personal physician to Muhtar Pasha, son of Ali Pasha of Yannina, and the anti-clerical republican and linguistic compromiser Korais (though he had previously been a merchant and subsequently became a full-time literary and philological scholar and publicist). Korais claimed that he had decided to study medicine because it was only to doctors that the Turkish nation was 'obliged to feign a certain mildness'.[154] It is not surprising that two of the leading vernacularists, Vilaras and Solomos, were poets.

In terms of geographical origin, almost all the participants in the language controversy before 1821 came from and/or were active in northern areas of the Greco-Turkish world (Constantinople, Romania, Bulgaria, Macedonia, Epirus, and Thessaly). Most of those who have been named above were or had been active in Bucharest, which, as we have seen, was one of the chief centres of Greek culture and a magnet for Greeks, Romanians, Bulgarians, Serbs, and Albanians who wished to acquire a Greek education.[155] Those, such as Psalidas and Vilaras, who lived in predominantly Greek-speaking areas were sufficiently close to everyday linguistic reality to support the use of the spoken language in writing, leaving those who were far away to support the various utopian proposals: Korais and Kodrikas settled in Paris, while Doukas spent decades of his career in Bucharest and Vienna.

[154] Quoted from Korais' autobiography in Korais 1984b: p. xxi.
[155] Charilaou 2004: 179.

3

The early stages of the controversy, 1766–1804

Language use in the late eighteenth century

In the late eighteenth century, Greek speakers spoke one or other of the modern Greek dialects, and/or probably some local *koine*. These dialects were not widely divergent and were mutually comprehensible, with the exception of some peripheral dialects such as those of central and north-eastern Asia Minor (Cappadocian and Pontic) and to a lesser extent Cyprus. All of the Modern Greek dialects (except Tsakonian, spoken in the south-east Peloponnese) derive from the Hellenistic *koine*, the language in which the New Testament was written.

Since Byzantine times, Greek education had been more or less confined to the study of Ancient Greek grammar and ecclesiastical texts; the typical course began with the Psalter, then went on to the *Octoechos* (a book containing the Resurrectional material for Sunday services), the *Horologion* (Book of Hours, providing the fixed portions of the Daily Cycle of service), and other liturgical texts. The 'common schools', also known as schools 'of sacred letters', as well as the monastic schools, all of which provided this teaching, were primarily aimed at educating priests, cantors and monks, and the initiatives for founding and running these schools came from local priests and monasteries.[1] It is not surprising that, after all their exposure to Ancient Greek at school and in church, many authors went on to use a number of archaic features in their written language.

There was no Greek language controversy until after the middle of the eighteenth century: everyone simply wrote as they thought fit. Writers were faced with a choice, which can be roughly summed up in terms of three options: a few (the archaists) attempted to write in Ancient Greek, an even smaller number (whom I call vernacularists) wrote in

---

[1] Patrinelis 2005: 323–4.

colloquial spoken Greek, while most (the compromisers) attempted to use a 'purified' or 'elevated' version of spoken Greek by replacing certain features of the spoken language with ancient (or at least older) equivalents. Each of these different language varieties was often known as an *yfos*, a term that nowadays means 'style' but was used at that time to denote a variety that was distinguished from other varieties not only by such factors as the choice of vocabulary and the structure of the sentences but by a different set of grammatical rules.[2]

By the second half of the eighteenth century, then, most books being published in Greek employed a mildly archaized version of the spoken language. Increasingly, the purchaser or reader of a Greek book would be informed on its title page that it was written in 'simple language' or 'common style', or some such phrase; in the absence of any sense of the historical development of the language, the word 'modern' was hardly used at the time to describe contemporary Greek.[3] 'Simple language' or 'common style' (or, as its detractors called it, 'vulgar style') was based on vernacular Modern Greek, but with Ancient Greek final -*n*, the ancient prepositions *eis* 'to, at, in' (instead of spoken *s[e]*) and *diá* 'for' (instead of *gia*), and various other phonological and morphological archaisms. Writers of the 'common style' differed among themselves in details of orthography, phonology, morphology, and syntax. For instance, differences can be found in the use of the accusative or genitive case (as in the spoken language) as against the dative case (as in Ancient Greek) for the indirect object pronoun, in the use or avoidance of the ancient 'strong aorist' (e.g. the ancient and modern forms of the simple past tense of the verb 'say', respectively *eipon* and *eipa*), in the use of various other prepositions and conjunctions, and in vocabulary (for instance, in their tolerance of words of foreign origin, or in their substitution of an Ancient Greek word even where a word of native origin was used in speech).

As this sketchy outline suggests, the 'common style' consisted of a mixture of living and obsolete elements and consequently involved a wide variation in the actual language used: the proportions of modern and older features in the mixture varied according to the writers' level

[2] It is telling that when Kodrikas (1817, in Dimaras 1953: 284) translates Buffon's famous saying, 'Le style c'est l'homme même', he renders *style* not by *yfos* but as 'trópos tis ekfráseos', literally 'mode of expression'. Nevertheless, Voulgaris, in the passage quoted on p. 86, uses the same word to denote style.

[3] With few exceptions (again including Voulgaris), the distinction between 'Ancient' and 'Modern' Greek started to be made explicitly (albeit not systematically) by Doukas and Korais in the 1820s.

of education and the ideological and social purpose of their writing, including their intended readership. Nevertheless, as Ariana Camariano-Cioran has pointed out, a number of writers in the pre-1821 period succeeded, in their translations and paraphrases of scientific works, in devising Modern Greek terminology in various areas of study, including physics, philosophy, law, and astronomy.[4]

Traditional orthography, even among the vernacularists, attempted to make morphemes that were not Ancient Greek look as much like Ancient Greek as possible, or at least to display what was thought to be their etymology: thus ἡ κόραις [the girls] (the feminine plural article being spelled like the feminine singular and the noun being spelled like the ancient dative plural; cf. modern spelling οι κόρες), 'ς ταῖς κόραις [to the girls] (the apostrophe in 'ς indicated that the preposition was derived from ancient εἰς; modern στις κόρες), ὁποῦ [which, who] (a mixture of the relative adverb ὅπου [where] and the interrogative adverb ποῦ [where?]; modern που), 'γλίγωρα [quickly] (by false etymology from the non-existent phrase *ἐκ λίγη ὥρα, literally 'from a little time'; modern γρήγορα). Orthography did not necessarily represent pronunciation: writers who spelled ἀνοικτός rather than ἀνοιχτός [open] might well have pronounced it /anixtós/ rather than /aniktós/, yet they wished to preserve the ancient appearance of the word.

The predominant use of the vernacular was slow to undermine the prestige and use of Ancient Greek in philosophical and scientific discourse. Apart from sheer inertia, the reasons why this situation was preserved included psychological, social, and cultural factors. Educated Greeks admired ancient Greek culture; they were aware of the gap between the excellence of 'free' ancient Greece and modern Greek squalor in 'enslavement' to the Turks; and they were conscious that such adulation was fashionable among western Europeans. Such writers felt that ancient Greek culture was their heritage, and they believed that only the ancient form of their language was sufficient for the expression of philosophical ideas. For many other writers, though, this admiration for antiquity was orientated not so much towards Classical Greece as towards the New Testament, the writings of the Fathers of the Church, the liturgy, and other ecclesiastical texts. In each case, however, the language of the ancient texts was considered to be canonical and worthy of imitation or emulation, in a similar way to the language of the Koran for Arabic-speaking Muslims. In addition, learned writers wished to differentiate

---

[4] Camariano-Cioran 1974: 442.

themselves from the vulgar, unlettered rabble, to display class solidarity, and to impress by their erudition.

It was the influence of the Enlightenment – the challenge presented by the 'moderns' to the authority of the 'ancients' – that led certain Greek authors to challenge the continuing use of Ancient Greek for scholarly writings. This in turn led to the three general tendencies in written language (archaism, compromise, and vernacularism) being seen not simply as a matter of choice but in terms of rivalry and conflict. We shall now examine the three chief theoretical and practical tendencies of the language question in this period, as represented by a number of influential figures who wrote on philosophical and other scholarly subjects.

Archaism: Evgenios Voulgaris

The illustrious Corfiot cleric and teacher Evgenios Voulgaris wrote in markedly different language varieties according to his subject matter and intended audience. These included varieties of Ancient Greek, varieties of Modern Greek involving differing degrees of archaization, and a colloquial variety. This shows that before 1800 there was a situation of Greek polyglossia accompanied by a sense that different varieties of language were appropriate to different subjects. What initiated the language controversy was disagreement about the most appropriate variety for use in a particular discourse, namely philosophy.

The beginning of the modern Greek language controversy can be precisely dated to 1766, when Voulgaris, in the preface to his *Logic*, argued that in order to study philosophy it was necessary to know Ancient Greek, adding that 'the worthless little books that profess to philosophize in vulgar language should be hissed off the stage'.[5] By 'vulgar language' he meant any variety of Modern Greek as opposed to the ancient language. Although he did not name them, the targets he had in mind probably included both his teacher Vikentios Damodos

---

[5] Voulgaris 1766: 49. Even though Voulgaris' preface is quoted by Sathas 1870: 146–7, Megas seems to have been the first to identify Voulgaris as 'the instigator of the language controversy' (A. E. Megas 1927: 5). Korais implied that Voulgaris' *Logic* and Theotokis' *Elements of Physics*, both published in 1766, signalled the beginning of the regeneration of Greek culture (Coray 1803: 12–13). The argument proposed by Psimmenos (1995) that the intention behind Voulgaris' famous words was not strictly linguistic is irrelevant for our purposes, particularly since Moisiodax took them as being a criticism of the language of his own books.

(1700–52) from Cephalonia[6] and, more pointedly, his own pupil Iosipos Moisiodax (*c*.1725–*c*.1800), about whom I shall have more to say below. Voulgaris did not seem to be aware of the incongruity of a situation in which he used Ancient Greek even when expressing his approval of innovative modern European philosophers who challenged the authority of the ancients.

Kitromilides describes Voulgaris as the 'patriarch of the Greek Enlightenment' and the first recognized leader of the Enlightenment in south-east Europe. In fact, his views were reactionary compared with some of his Greek predecessors in philosophical writings, such as Damodos, and his use of Ancient Greek gives his Enlightenment an aristocratic character.[7] Throughout his career, Voulgaris struggled unsuccessfully to strike a balance between Enlightenment ideas and Orthodox dogma.

Voulgaris studied at Padua and went on to teach for twenty years in Yannina, Kozani, the Athonite Academy and Constantinople. He taught John Locke's *Essay Concerning Human Understanding* (originally published in English in 1690) at school in Yannina in 1742, probably in his own abridgement, which was written in archaic Greek.[8] He was the first to produce Greek translations of works by Voltaire, whom he met in Leipzig and whom he praised in his *Logic* but whom he later denounced for his impiety.[9] He translated and published two of Voltaire's works: the philosophical tale 'Memnon, ou la sagesse humaine'[10] and the pro-Russian *Essai historique et critique sur les dissensions des églises de Pologne* against the persecutions suffered by the Orthodox and Protestant populations at the hands of the Catholic Church in Poland.

After spending seven years in Leipzig and Halle, Voulgaris settled in Russia. He hoped that Russia would liberate the Balkans and Anatolia from the Ottomans, thus uniting all Orthodox Christians in a single

---

[6] Damodos taught philosophical texts in the vernacular at the school in Cephalonia that he founded in 1721 (Kitromilides 1996: 50–1). His book *Concise Logic* (1759), published after his death, contains a prologue in which the author states that he wrote his book in the common language 'for the common benefit', arguing that knowledge of the sciences does not depend on a particular language (Bompou-Stamati 1982: 350).

[7] Kitromilides 1996: 195, 54, 62–3.   [8] Angelou 1954.

[9] K. Th. Dimaras 1985: 150, 155.

[10] Voltaire's tale was first published in French in 1749; Voulgaris' Greek paraphrase appeared in 1766. He included it in his edition of the comic poem *Vosporomachia* [Battle of the Bosporus], written in Greek by Caspar Ludwig Momarz, interpreter at the Habsburg embassy in Constantinople. For a new edition of Voulgaris' paraphrase of 'Memnon', with an introduction, see Tomadakis 1989; for further details of Voulgaris' text and its publication see Henrich 2007.

Russo-Greek empire.[11] Voulgaris also translated Virgil's *Georgics* and *Aeneid* (published by the Russian Academy of Sciences in St Petersburg in 1786 and 1791–92 respectively) into Homeric language and Ancient Greek hexameters; one wonders what the intended readership of these demanding achievements might have been, and indeed how many people read the translations from end to end. He was carried away by the anti-revolutionary fervour that dominated the Russian court after 1789. In the last years of his long life he published the handbooks he had been using as a teacher in the 1740s and 1750s: by then, as Kitromilides puts it, he had outlived his own influences.[12] In some respects, Voulgaris marks the end of an era rather than the beginning of a new one.

Voulgaris introduced himself to the Russian empress in 1771 by referring to himself as 'Slaviano-Bulgarian by origin, Greek by birth, Russian by inclination'.[13] It is clear that his aim was to ingratiate himself with the empress by asserting that he too, like the majority of her subjects, was of Slav origin; it is not certain how seriously he took this himself, but his surname does imply Bulgarian origin. Be that as it may, in his published writings Voulgaris showed little or no interest in languages spoken in the Greek region other than Greek itself.

The linguistic arguments put forward by Voulgaris and others in favour of the use of Ancient Greek can be summarized in the following extended syllogism: Ancient Greek has been thoroughly elaborated for the purpose of philosophical discourse; all educated Greeks can read Ancient Greek, since Greek education is based on the teaching of the ancient language; only educated people can understand philosophy and science; therefore works of philosophy and science should be written in Ancient Greek – or at least in a variety of language approximating to it.

Even though Voulgaris' *Logic* is written in Ancient Greek, some of his other writings are in a 'purified' version of the vernacular. An open letter addressed to the patriarch of Constantinople that he published in 1752 is written in 'simple' language, that is, a moderately archaized version

[11] His vision of the establishment of a Greek principality, now that the Ottoman empire was beginning to collapse, is expressed in his *Thoughts on the Present Critical Times of the Empire of the Ottomans* (first published *c.* 1771–72): see Kitromilides 1996: 183–4, 553. The legends mentioned by Angelou (1963: 99) concerning Voulgaris' clandestine nationalist activity while he was teaching at Yannina and on Mount Athos are implausible.

[12] Kitromilides 1996: 187.

[13] Quoted from an unpublished manuscript by Batalden (1982: 22), who points out the irony that Catherine was not Russian but German by birth. I am grateful to Elka Bakalova for informing me that 'Slaviano-Bulgarian' refers to the Slav Bulgarians as distinct from the Turkic proto-Bulgars.

of the vernacular.[14] He uses an only slightly more archaized version of Modern Greek in his translation of the *Essai historique*. His paraphrase of 'Memnon', published in the same year as the *Logic*, is, exceptionally, in colloquial language with a dialectal tinge, which includes a number of loanwords from Italian and Turkish. Voulgaris probably considered that these liberties were licensed by the moderately frivolous nature of the content (indeed it is more frivolous than Voltaire's original) and by the popular fifteen-syllable metre, which Voulgaris chose to use even though the original was in prose.

Especially interesting is a passage from a book published in 1770, in which Voulgaris promotes a variety of language that foreshadows the linguistic theory and practice of Korais. This is the introduction to his translation of the *Nakaz* [*Decree*] issued in Russian by Catherine II in 1767;[15] Voulgaris' translation is written in a slightly archaized version of the vernacular:

One may reasonably add here the weakness and imperfection of our common Dialect. The language which we, the Hellenes of today, speak, if it happens to be that of the streets such as the vulgar people have in use, is insufferable and monstrous for those who know the old Hellenic. On the one hand, it is impossible to listen to it, because of the admixture of foreign and barbaric words, and on the other, it is incapable of representing a relevant meaning, because of the lack of necessary words and phrases. In order to cure somewhat that roughness and unevenness, and this weakness and indigence, one must often resort to the more ancient language, from which the newer has deviated and become corrupted; so that a middle language will be created, less barbarizing and solecistic, yet more effective and fulfilling the need; a language that is more Hellenic as regards its words [vocabulary], and approaching the peculiarity of European languages in its syntax and style. Such a Dialect is used for the most part by our educated men, and this is what I have preferred to use for the present.[16]

Voulgaris' opposition to philosophizing in the vulgar language did not apply to a work on a non-philosophical subject.

What is particularly interesting about this passage is that Voulgaris makes it obvious that he encountered two difficulties in using Modern Greek: first, that the language was insufficiently expressive for abstract discourse and, second, that he found it ugly. Yet he does not seem to have realized that these two factors – the expressive weakness of the

---

[14] Quoted in Sathas 1870: 139–40.

[15] The *Nakaz* (*Eisigisis* in Greek) was addressed by Catherine II to the representatives who were charged with drawing up a new legal code for the Russian empire.

[16] Voulgaris 1770, quoted by Angelou 1994: 30*–31*.

language and its negative aesthetic aspect – are unrelated. At all events, here Voulgaris provides a definition of what came, almost a century later, to be called *katharévousa*; the major element missing from his definition is *katharévousa*'s use of most of the features of Ancient Greek morphology. The conflation of the expressive with the aesthetic aspect came to be a crucial and recurrent feature of the arguments deployed against the written use of the vernacular over the next two hundred years. It is noteworthy that both Voulgaris and Korais, coming at the Modern Greek language from rather different directions – Voulgaris from the Church as well as the Classics, and Korais from the Classics alone – arrived at the same conclusion about how a 'middle language' should be developed for written use. Nevertheless, thirty years after the publication of his *Logic*, Voulgaris continued to defend its archaic language against attacks from Iosipos Moisiodax and Athanasios Psalidas by arguing that serious philosophical discourse cannot be adapted to the common idiom of the everyday language.[17]

Compromise: Moisiodax and others

According to Kitromilides, Voulgaris' aristocratic version of the Enlightenment was challenged by those who argued for the creation of a Modern Greek written language that could make the new learning accessible to more people.[18] The first to pose the language question explicitly – and the man who elicited the first salvo in the language controversy from Voulgaris – was the cleric and teacher Iosipos Moisiodax, whose archaic surname denotes 'a Dacian from Moesia', in other words an Aromanian from Bulgaria; he was born at Cernavodă on the south bank of the Danube, now in Romania. Moisiodax studied at the Athonite Academy under Voulgaris and spent some time in Venice and Padua before becoming headmaster of the Princely Academy at Jassy, after which he divided most of his time between Jassy and Bucharest. Despite this, as Nikos Sigalas points out, Moisiodax never once refers to the language spoken in his native village or in the Romanian cities where he lived and taught.[19]

In his preface to his translation (1761) of Lodovico Antonio Muratori's book *La filosofia morale esposta e proposta ai giovani* (1735), Moisiodax defended his own use of the 'common style'. By doing so, according to

---

[17] Voulgaris 1797; see Kitromilides 1996: 195–6, 555.   [18] Kitromilides 1983: 59.
[19] Sigalas 2004: 120.

Anastasios Megas, Moisiodax became 'the first advocate of the Modern Greek language'.[20] Indeed, Nasia Yakovaki claims that the 1761 preface by Moisiodax is 'the oldest publicly communicated defence of the spoken Greek language', in which the author sees the cultivation of Modern Greek as the cure for *amátheia* [ignorance].[21] Yet the language Moisiodax uses is a highly archaized version of Modern Greek. It seems that for him, as it was later for Korais, the 'correction' of the modern language was a *sine qua non* for its defence and its cultivation.

In his preface Moisiodax describes the 'common style' as vivid and eloquent, claiming that its failings are entirely due to 'neglect or contempt'. He attacks the use of both Ancient Greek and the macaronic 'mixed-barbarian style' for practical use. Yet he was not satisfied with the spoken language as such, even though he recognized its relationship with 'the Hellenic' (i.e. Ancient Greek), which he calls its 'mother'. He argues that every regional variety of the common tongue contains an admixture of foreign words from the other languages spoken in the region (e.g. Turkish, Albanian, and Italian). He feels a duty to 'correct' it and make it more precise, and to exclude words of non-Greek origin, but its poverty also obliges him '*na lexopoiiso* [to coin new words]'. He seems to feel it unnecessary to comment on the fact that he used almost exclusively Ancient Greek morphology in his work. On the other hand, he refers explicitly to his use of some Ancient Greek vocabulary, and one of his excuses for using a slightly elevated language is that this would help readers to find Ancient Greek easier to understand. Because he uses some words from Ancient Greek, he seems to feel the need, with some exceptions, to make all his vocabulary inflect according to Ancient Greek morphological patterns; it does not seem to have occurred to him to adapt the ancient vocabulary to the morphological patterns of the spoken language.

In his *Treatise on the Education of Children* (1779), largely based on *Some Thoughts Concerning Education* (1693) by John Locke,[22] Moisiodax undertook the first thorough critique of contemporary Greek education, concentrating particularly on the teaching of Greek. He recalls with horror the way he was taught Ancient Greek vocabulary at school. The meaning of each word was taught by being placed together with a series of so-called synonyms in Ancient Greek, without distinguishing

[20] A. E. Megas 1927: 10.

[21] Yakovaki 2005: 176. The section of the 1761 prologue where Moisiodax defends the language of his translation is reproduced in Kitromilides 1985: 332–7.

[22] Kriaras 1939–43.

their meaning. Instead of this, he argued, it was better to teach a single word instead, with its *kyriolexía* [literal meaning].[23] By this he meant that the meaning of each Ancient Greek word should be taught by way of its equivalent in the spoken language.

In his *Theory of Geography* (1781) Moisiodax again defends the use of 'the simple style' in works of philosophy. Here his chief justification for using the common language is *safíneia* [clarity]. He specifically rebuts Voulgaris' 1766 attack, arguing, like Damodos before him, that 'the truth is common to all men..., and consequently in all dialects...; it is not attached by any means to a single dialect, Hellenic'.[24] He uses the precedent of European nations in support of the Greek vernacular, arguing that a writer should not hide behind the mask of language but should employ a readily comprehensible linguistic variety. Nevertheless, in the twenty years that had elapsed between his first book and this one, his own language had become increasingly archaic – a syndrome that was to affect many Greek linguistic compromisers and vernacularists.

Another cleric and teacher, Nikiforos Theotokis (1731–1800), born into an aristocratic family in Corfu, studied mathematics and natural philosophy at Padua and Bologna, taught for several years, and eventually succeeded Voulgaris as archbishop of Kherson (1779–86), after which he was transferred to the see of Astrakhan and Stavropol until 1792, when he retired to a monastery in Moscow. In his first book, *Elements of Physics* (published in two volumes in Leipzig in 1766–67, at the same time as Voulgaris' *Logic*) Theotokis chooses to write in the 'simple style', explicitly following the example of the 'modern writers of science' who aim at nothing but *to safés* [clarity]. Kitromilides comments that this concern succeeded in opening up education to a wider public.[25] Yet Theotokis, who was to remain a close associate of Voulgaris from the time when they met in Leipzig, went on to use a more archaized language in his later works: Konstantinos Sathas contrasts a passage from a funeral speech he gave in 1766, which is in a morphologically archaized version of the vernacular, with a passage from the book for which he became best known, the *Kyriakodromion*, a series of commentaries on the Gospel readings set for each Sunday in the Orthodox liturgy, published thirty

[23] The same complaint about the teaching of synonyms was made by Katartzis 1970: 31, and again by Vilaras 1995: 136 forty years later.

[24] The preface to Moisiodax 1781 reproduced in Kitromilides 1985: 357–68; the section that deals with language is on 361–5. For Damodos see note 6 above.

[25] Kitromilides 1996: 67–8.

years later (1796) at the expense of the Zosimas brothers to be distributed free of charge in churches.[26]

Rotolo points out that Theotokis' choice of language in the *Kyriakodromion* is the result of his realization that the faithful can no longer understand the Gospels.[27] In his preface to his book, he was the first to use the term *katharévousa* (albeit as an adjective modifying *glossa* [language]) to characterize his language. He writes that the 'dialect' he uses is 'not exactly that of our forefathers, which is no longer understood by all..., nor that spoken in the market-place and at the crossroads by the vulgar'. He succeeded in his effort to create a clear and elegant literary language that would not be far distant from the *koine* of the New Testament, yet would be comprehensible to 'the children of the Hellenes'.[28] He uses the ancient infinitive and the ancient negative particle *ou* instead of the vernacular *den*, and he avoids the use of the modern particles *na*, *tha*, and *pou*, whose ubiquitous presence in spoken Greek has always posed the greatest problem for archaists and purists. In 1870 Sathas claimed that Theotokis was 'the first to form today's written dialect understood by all', by which he meant *katharévousa*.[29] Later supporters of *katharévousa* such as Sathas and Megas were to point to the wide readership of the *Kyriakodromion* as evidence that people did not have to be highly educated in order to be able to read *katharévousa* without much difficulty. Yet, although Theotokis' language may have been comprehensible to all, it could only be written by members of a small and highly educated elite.

Though born in Athens, Panagiotis Kodrikas (Athens 1762–Paris 1827) became a member of the Fanariot circle, working first as secretary to the patriarch of Jerusalem in Constantinople and then to Michail Soutsos during the latter's three terms of office as hospodar of Wallachia and Moldavia. In the intervening periods he worked in the Dragomanate of the Ottoman fleet, eventually serving as First Secretary of the Ottoman Embassy in Paris (1797–1802).[30] Kodrikas translated Fontenelle's

---

[26] Sathas 1870: 131–5. The six Zosimas brothers, merchants from Epirus settled in Livorno, Nezhin, and Moscow, were later to fund the publication of Korais' *Hellenic Library*. A second volume of the *Kyriakodromion*, containing commentaries on the readings from the Acts and the Epistles, was published in Moscow in 1808. See K. Th. Dimaras 1985: 159–60 for the lexical problems faced by Theotokis in his attempt to translate Clémence's refutation of Voltaire from French into vernacular Greek in 1794.

[27] Rotolo 1965: 68.

[28] Theotokis 1796: 9–10, quoted in Ladas and Hatzidimou 1973: 30.

[29] Sathas 1870: 130.

[30] For Kodrikas' professional career see K. Th. Dimaras 1985: 348–53.

Entretiens sur la pluralité des mondes (1686) into 'purified Romaic [vernacular Greek]' at the behest and the expense of Soutsos in 1794. According to K. Th. Dimaras, the publication of Kodrikas' translation was an act of courage, given that in the previous year the Church had officially deplored modern philosophy. The translation seems to have provoked a published attack in Ancient Greek by Sergios Makraios (a friend of patriarch Grigorios V and a teacher at the Patriarchal Academy in Constantinople) against the followers of Copernicus.[31] Kodrikas also translated Alexander Pope's *Essay on Man* in 1795, though his translation remained unpublished.

In his introduction to his translation of Fontenelle, Kodrikas expressed his deep sorrow at the servitude under which the Greeks were living and which had adulterated their way of life, leading them to adopt foreign customs, foreign clothes, and foreign building styles, and resulting in 'that monstrous mixture of the so-called Romaic language'. In an implied riposte to Katartzis, whose ideas will be summarized and analysed in the next section, Kodrikas writes that the *Romaioi* cannot write in the spoken language of their capital city, since this is also the capital city of the *kratountes* [rulers], and the speech of the Constantinopolitan *Romaioi* is mixed with many foreign words because of their business and social dealings with the rulers.[32] This adulterated language can be cultivated and a 'common style' can be found in it, but the written use of the spoken language as it is at present, full of barbarous words, will leave 'that unfortunate nation to wallow in the mire of its thoughts and to wander about in the darkness of its unilluminated ideas'. The implication of this is that the language must be improved in order to improve the national character. 'By contrast,' he continues,

an idea that has been adorned with more florid words and nobler phrases sharpens the mind, delights the wit, pleases the intellect and arouses the imitative faculty of the soul to emulate, to learn more [words] or to invent similar ones, [with the result that] the *ethnos* [nation], led by the most glorious of expressions to the highest of concepts, will be able to take the first and most difficult step in the progress of learning.[33]

[31] Makraios 1797. Makraios bases himself on ancient Greek astronomical wisdom. His book was dedicated to Anthimos, patriarch of Jerusalem, author of the *Patrikí didaskalía* (1798). See K. Th. Dimaras 1985: 77, 351; Kitromilides 1996: 437.

[32] Rich examples of the 'uncorrected' Romaic of Constantinople can be found in Kodrikas' own journals, which he kept between 1786 and his arrival in France in 1797 and which he entitled *Efimerides*, detailing his everyday life and expressing a good deal of contempt for the Turks, their government, and their way of life. They are published as Kodrikas 1991.

[33] Kodrikas 1794: p. xxiv.

It is obvious that Kodrikas, like many other writers in the eighteenth century, confuses adornment and nobility of style with richness and precision of vocabulary and grammar.

Vernacularism: Dimitrios Katartzis, Daniil Filippidis, and Grigorios Konstantas

During the 1780s an enlightened proponent of the spoken language entered the scene. This was the Ottoman *philosophe* Dimitrios Katartzis (*c.* 1730–1807) from Constantinople, who served as Grand Logothetis [head of the princely chancellery] at the court of the Fanariot prince of Wallachia.[34] He planned a series of encyclopaedic works, which would be produced by himself and by various disciples of his. Inspired by the French *Encyclopédie* (1751–65), these works were intended to contain the sum of human knowledge and were all to be written in vernacular Greek.

Katartzis knew Ancient Greek, Latin, French, Turkish, Arabic, and Persian, among other languages. K. Th. Dimaras has stressed the importance of the knowledge of European languages – a phenomenon unknown before the early eighteenth century – for the emergence of the Greek Enlightenment, since this knowledge led not only to the reading and translation of modern European literature and thought but to comparisons between the Greek linguistic situation and that of advanced western nations which had abandoned Latin, even for most scholarly writing.[35]

Katartzis' correspondence with Lampros Fotiadis (d. 1805) from Yannina, the director of the Princely Academy at Bucharest, dating from 1789, is the first example of a written dialogue on the Greek language question, remarkable in that the two correspondents use completely different languages (spoken Modern Greek and Ancient Greek respectively). The fact that both men were living in Bucharest indicates that their correspondence was a formal exercise as much as a genuine exchange of views. The debate was probably broadened as the letters were copied and distributed to other interested parties. In this correspondence, Fotiadis argues that, just as the Venetians use their dialect in speech and verse but

---

[34] K. Th. Dimaras 1985: 177, 189. The happy coincidence that this Greek essayist held a post analogous to that of chancellor Francis Bacon was not lost on him; see Katartzis: 1970: 105 n. 3.

[35] The first modern European works published in Greek translation in the Ottoman period were Loredano's *Scherzi geniali* (1632; Greek translation 1711) and Fénelon's *Les Aventures de Télémaque* (1699; Greek translation 1742); see K. Th. Dimaras 1985: 136–7, 251, 266.

write their scholarly work in Tuscan, so the Greeks should write serious works in Ancient Greek. Katartzis justifiably counters that Fotiadis' analogy is false, since, unlike Ancient Greek, Tuscan is the living language of a contemporary community. 'In the whole world,' concludes Katartzis, 'except for the Great Khan of China, who . . . has authority over the words of his language, no one has the power to give a word a [phonological or morphological] form that it doesn't have in the mouth of the *laós* [people].'[36]

It is notable that Fotiadis does not reject Katartzis' theories out of hand, though he is not sure what other Greeks will make of Katartzis' Constantinople dialect. However, it seems that Fotiadis would not have objected to a purified version of the vernacular, and, like certain other intellectuals of the time, he looks forward to an academy of scholars that will lay down the rules for it.

None of Katartzis' writings in support of the use of spoken Greek was published in his lifetime, and his correspondence with Fotiadis, included in an edition of one of Neofytos Doukas' grammars in 1812, was the sum total of his writings to be published before Dimaras' edition at last brought Katartzis' complete works into the public domain in 1970.[37] Nevertheless, it seems that some of Katartzis' writings were known to others through copies of his manuscripts. His language theory was the most radical aspect of his educational reform programme. He believed that the cultivation of the common language would release creative energies that were being stifled by scholastic education in a dead language; this democratic outlook converted the language question into a political one.[38]

In his writings, Katartzis aimed at a faithful transcription of the common speech of Constantinople, which (as the seat of both the Sultan and the patriarch and the home of the Fanariots) he calls 'the *mitrópoli* [capital] of our *ethnos* [nation]'.[39] In fact, he writes, the ladies of Constantinople speak the best Romaic, because they do not mix it with school Greek.[40] He was not averse to using words borrowed by spoken Greek from other languages, though he did not hesitate to borrow Ancient Greek words for concepts that did not exist in the vernacular. His earliest work is entitled 'Essay, that the Romaic language, when it is spoken and written, has melody in its prose, rhythm in its poetry, and passion and

[36] Katartzis 1970: 432.
[37] Doukas 1812b: 53–84, reprinted in Sathas 1870: 154–76; extracts in Triantafyllidis 1938: 435–8.
[38] Kitromilides 1996: 219, 205–7.   [39] Katartzis 1970: 20, 208, 314.   [40] Ibid., 12.

persuasion in its rhetoric; that it is, like Hellenic, in all respects superior to the other languages; and that its cultivation and the writing of books in it are the general and total *agogí* [education/culture] of the nation'. Dating from 1783, this work is rightly said by K. Th. Dimaras to be Katartzis' manifesto.[41] Its title leaves no room for doubt that Katartzis feels proud to be a member of a nation – albeit a subject one – that possesses such an eloquent spoken language.[42] Dimaras suggests that Katartzis was 'the first to teach, with legal arguments, that, albeit under the yoke of slavery, the Greeks constituted a separate nationality with an independent existence'.[43]

Between 1784 and 1788 Katartzis wrote a descriptive 'Grammar of the Romaic or natural language' intended for children, and perhaps particularly for his beloved son Stefanos. He also wrote a grammar of Ancient Greek in Romaic. All previous grammars of Greek in Greek (with the exception of Sofianos' grammar, which was not published at that time) were grammars of Ancient Greek written in Ancient Greek.[44] Katartzis begins his grammar with the controversial proclamation: 'Hellenic and Romaic are two languages, not one.'[45] Elsewhere he claims that in order to write in Ancient Greek one has to translate from Romaic, a procedure that he felt to be intolerably artificial.[46]

The following passage sums up Katartzis' remarkably enlightened attitude to vernacular Greek:

Every language has by nature an unwritten or a written grammar... There is also a general grammar of all languages... Romaic, being a living language, has a grammar by nature, even though nobody has written it before, just as Peruvian and Lapp had a grammar, and it has only recently been written; ... its grammar is different from Hellenic, from which it is derived, just as French grammar is different from Latin, from which it is derived.[47]

We note here Katartzis' realization – rare among non-vernacularist participants in the Greek language question even up to the late twentieth century – that grammar is inherent in every natural language, even if it is not written.

---

[41] K. Th. Dimaras 1985: 203.

[42] Katartzis (1970: 201) refers at one point to the Bulgarians, Serbs, and Bosnians as *ethni* [nations] consisting of 'co-religionists and *sýndouloi* [fellow-slaves] of ours'.

[43] K. Th. Dimaras 1985: 18. For references to the subjection of the Romaic nation to the Ottoman nation see Katartzis 1970: 39, 44, 50, 104, 212.

[44] K. Th. Dimaras 1985: 190, 210, 229. For a critical survey of grammars of Modern Greek produced during the Greek Enlightenment see Kurelec 1999.

[45] Katartzis 1970: 217.   [46] K. Th. Dimaras 1985: 216.   [47] Katartzis 1970: 317.

He succinctly expresses his attitude to the various historical stages of Greek as follows:

[A]s for the common language of the free and autonomous Hellenes, I honour it to the point of idolatry, and I recommend its study with all my soul; I admire the language of the later Hellenes, who were renamed *Romaioi* [Romans], even though it is more deficient than the former; but I love, cherish and delight in the language of the *Romioí*, who are the descendants of the aforesaid two, as my *patria* [native] dialect.[48]

Contrary to the teaching of Voulgaris, Katartzis promoted Romaic as the instrument of expression for all branches of learning, seeing the use of Ancient Greek as an obstacle to the dissemination of knowledge: '[L]anguage was invented so that we can communicate our ideas', he wrote. Contrary to Korais' later promotion of the linguistic 'middle way', Katartzis wrote that we should not 'remain in the middle' by writing a neutral language which is understood neither by the Hellene nor by the *Romiós*.[49] But his ideas were not confined to Greek; he repeatedly argued that Wallachian children should be educated in their own language too.[50]

Katartzis wrote that Romaic is a derivative of Hellenic, which 'we' used to speak before, but that, like modern romance languages vis-à-vis Latin, Romaic possesses a separate sound system, morphology, syntax, and idiom from Hellenic.[51] As well as in language, 'we' are different from the ancient Hellenes in our polity, religion, customs and manners, behaviour, clothing, and utensils. Nevertheless, Katartzis considered Romaic to be the sixth dialect of Hellenic, the fifth being Hellenistic *koine*.[52] Similar claims were made by several proponents of spoken Greek before the War of Independence: instead of seeing Modern Greek as the latest phase in the historical development of Greek, they argued that it was a separate dialect of the timeless Greek language, thus giving the impression that the variety of Greek spoken in their time was in some way contemporaneous with the four chief dialects of Ancient Greek (Attic, Aeolic, Doric, and Ionic). This may have been a deliberate falsification with the aim of winning their argument, though it is more likely to have been due to ignorance of historical linguistics.

Katartzis acknowledged that the pronunciation of Greek had changed since Classical times. Having learned to pronounce Ancient Greek in the

---

[48] Ibid., 14.   [49] Ibid., 21, 12, 14.   [50] Ibid., 24–41.
[51] Ibid., 104; cf. ibid., 217.
[52] Ibid., 14, 17, 217. Probably the earliest reference to the Hellenistic *koine* as the fifth dialect of Greek is in Clement of Alexandria, *Stromateis*, 1.142 (thanks to Michael Silk).

modern way, he writes, educated Greeks transfer Ancient Greek words and grammatical features into the modern language without realizing that the two languages have different sound systems and that therefore ancient words need to be adapted to the modern sound system when they are introduced into the modern language. In this way, educated Greeks spoil the sound patterns of the modern language.[53] In the Greek context, Katartzis' linguistic ideas were way ahead of his time. Indeed, his rhetorical question, '[a] scientific law has no exceptions, so why do we make them?'[54] could equally have been posed by one of the German *Junggrammatiker* a century later.

What distinguishes Katartzis' language from that of every other writer of his time is that all of the vocabulary, irrespective of whether it is of ancient or modern origin, conforms to the phonological and morphological rules of the everyday spoken language. There are many archaic features, most of them set phrases and logical discourse markers such as 'therefore' and 'however', but these are fossilized expressions that do not affect the grammar as a whole. No Greek prose writer had ever applied the grammatical rules of the spoken language so systematically, and no one was to do so again, until Ioannis Vilaras and Athanasios Psalidas in the 1810s.

Katartzis' promotion of Greek education was not intended to lead to a Greek revolution; rather, his intellectual enterprise was meant to promote the well-being of the Greeks within the Ottoman empire by keeping them abreast of intellectual developments elsewhere in the world, in the hope that they might gain cultural and even political ascendancy within the empire. He pinned his hopes on the enlightened despotism of the Fanariot princes, who were justifiably alarmed by the outbreak of the French revolution. Dimaras points out that although the first signs of linguistic and intellectual freedom manifested themselves in the Danubian principalities, the deposition of Louis XVI in 1792 and his execution in 1793 put liberal ideas decidedly out of favour at the Danubian courts for the time being. From then on, the princes became more conservative and moved closer to the Church.[55] In 1791 Katartzis abandoned the use of the popular language; indeed, he even translated some of his essays (though not those specifically devoted to the language) into a version of the vernacular that archaized or 'corrected' the phonology and morphology but left the vocabulary and syntax intact.

---

[53] Ibid., 11.   [54] Ibid., 308.   [55] K. Th. Dimaras 1985: 312, 352.

Dimaras claims that Katartzis was the initiator of demoticism,[56] while Rotolo refers to Katartzis' 'complete linguistic system'. At the same time, Rotolo's strictures on Katartzis' language are just: it is 'certainly not easy. His style is tortuous, complicated, obscure, the syntax clumsy and laborious, the grammatical forms he adopts are not always convincing.... [H]e perhaps lacked that literary taste that is indispensable for anyone who aspires to become the creator of a language'.[57] Nonetheless, Katartzis' procedure of making Ancient Greek words conform to the morphological system of the spoken language was eventually adopted by the Standard Modern Greek that is in use today.

The only tangible fruit of Katartzis' encyclopaedic project was *Modern Geography* (1791) by Daniil Filippidis and Grigorios Konstantas from Milies on the Pelion peninsula. The title of their book is programmatic: *neorikí* means 'based on the work of the *neóteroi* [moderns]' as opposed to the ancients, and their material is based on their own observations as well as on the writings of other modern authors. The extensive sections devoted to Greece present practical information on the contemporary situation, such as topography, population, natural resources, and industries, as well as much historical material. The book is written in a very slightly 'purified' vernacular that is not at all archaic in style and syntax.

Their famous central argument on language is worth quoting in full:

The language we speak now bears a close relation to Hellenic, and it may justly be called the fifth dialect of Hellenic; a dialect, however, that is subdivided into others; this is a consequence of the great distance that separates the modern Hellenes from each other.... This difference is increased by our neglect and irrational contempt for our language, which prevents us from cultivating it and enriching it from Hellenic, and consequently by the shortage of books written with intelligence, with principles and linguistic rules, after the manner of the Italians, the French and the other nations of Europe.

Besides its other advantages, our language is very harmonious and poetic; this is admitted by all the foreign nations, while we alone do not know this. We seem to be an aged nation that suffers from the ailment of many old people: because of our long-sightedness we cannot see things close at hand and realize what a treasure we possess, whereas we look far away and see Hellenic, Italian and French verses without considering that Italian, and even French versification are nothing in comparison with our own.[58]

---

[56] K. Th. Dimaras 2000: 197.   [57] Rotolo 1965: 67.
[58] Filippidis and Konstantas 1988: 114.

In a later passage the authors display a modern attitude towards the function of grammar as being descriptive rather than prescriptive: '[T]he grammar of any language is nothing other than a description of the language, which paints its form, its characters and its idioms'. The context of this passage is an account of Athens, in which the authors take the opportunity to praise the ancient inhabitants of the city for cultivating their own spoken language for all written purposes. The authors argue that the best way for the modern Greeks to imitate their illustrious forefathers linguistically is to cultivate their own spoken language (which they call 'Romaic'), as the modern Europeans do too:

O descendants of those old and famous Hellenes, begin to imitate them by cultivating your language, and you will then be able to learn Hellenic better and more easily; for reading a grammar in his natural language, one learns it much more easily.... Then you can be sure that philosophy is returning again to its original nest; for she loves to speak with living people, and not with the bones of the dead.[59]

By contrast, 'the more we seek to bring [our language] closer to Hellenic, the further we remove it from its nature, and no sensible person can call this "cultivation"'.[60] The reference to 'nature' is reminiscent of Katartzis.

Filippidis and Konstantas challenge the idea that change in language means corruption; indeed, they see change as an inevitable process that affects all aspects of both the physical and the moral world.[61] They call for wider access to education through the use of simple language;[62] far from 'raising' their minds, the 'perfected' variety of the language excludes the mass of the people from education. The profound humanism that pervades their book is summed up in their statement that 'as long as a nation neglects and despises its natural language, it neglects and despises its humanity'.[63]

Modern Geography received a hostile reception on linguistic grounds – it was alleged that their book was written in the language 'of the grocers of Zagora'[64] – but was otherwise ignored. Perhaps discouraged by this, neither Konstantas nor Filippidis continued with their experiment of writing in a language as close to the spoken as possible. Filippidis' subsequent development was rather erratic. Nevertheless, although the language of most of his books after *Modern Geography* is slightly more archaized than he had used in that work, in most cases it is still simple Modern

---

[59] Ibid., 87–8.   [60] Ibid., 148–9.
[61] Ibid., 86, 147.   [62] Kitromilides 1996: 152–3.
[63] Filippidis and Konstantas 1988: 146.   [64] Sathas 1870: 185, but without references.

Greek. Because of the inconsistency in his choice of language variety from text to text (sometimes even within the same volume) and because of his sometimes obscure style, Filippidis has not gained the recognition that he deserves. However, Nasia Yakovaki has claimed that Filippidis' 1801 translation of *La Logique, ou Les Premiers développemens de l'art de penser* by Etienne de Condillac (1714–80), the original of which was published in 1780, is a major achievement, being both faithful and pioneering; before this, the book had been translated only into Spanish, and the original text was not introduced as a basic textbook in French schools until the year after the publication of Filippidis' translation.[65] Furthermore, Filippidis was a forerunner of the educational demoticists of the beginning of the twentieth century, in that he was genuinely trying to understand how children's minds work.

In his introduction to the *Logic*, Filippidis claims that there are two reasons why it is difficult to translate into what he calls, significantly, 'the spoken Hellenic dialect' (rather than Romaic or *graikikí*): first, because it is 'deprived of a grammar and a dictionary' and, second, because there are those who 'set themselves up as its arbiters' but are governed by *prolipseis* [preconceptions or erroneous beliefs]. In order to be understood by all, he continues, '[w]e are ... obliged to follow the nature of the language, to write as we express ourselves when we speak'.[66] The way Filippidis likens writing to speaking is highly significant. Despite this, he suggests that in most cases writers should preserve the morphological system of Ancient Greek and make newer words conform to it.[67]

Opposite the title page of his translation of the *Logic* Filippidis quotes the ancient exhortation, 'Know thyself' (previously the topic of one of Katartzis' essays), which he goes on to call a 'divine commandment'. This implies his belief that knowledge of the world is based on knowledge of the self, which in turn is founded on the knowledge of one's mother tongue. In his introduction Filippidis argues that children are shown the method of learning that will place them on the road to Parnassus and Helicon not by grammarians, rhetoricians, historians, physicists, or mathematicians, but by metaphysicians, i.e. those who have studied the human mind, namely Locke, Condillac, and Kant. He explains his reference to metaphysicians by arguing that 'the observation of the words of [the child's] spoken language ... is the metaphysics of language'.[68] He implies that he is following not Descartes' doctrine that children

---

[65] Yakovaki 2004: 416–19. [66] Filippidis 1801: pp. xxv–xxvi.
[67] Ibid., p. xxx. [68] Ibid., pp. xvi, xi, xv.

are born with innate ideas, but Locke's view that at birth the mind is a *tabula rasa*: children are born knowing nothing, and they learn through the senses.[69] His principle, based on that of Condillac, is to begin by teaching children what they have already experienced, and then go on from there to the unknown. The first thing that children should study after their language, he argues, is not geography or chronology or foreign languages but themselves, 'their intellectual and cognitive powers – in a word, their mind'. Under the present system, 'those children who displayed intelligence at the age of seven display imbecility at the age of seventeen'.[70]

The logical conclusion of the principles enunciated by Filippidis in this introduction is that, instead of learning to read through the medium of ecclesiastical and other archaic texts, children should first master their mother tongue and then be taught other subjects through the medium of that tongue. As he writes in the epilogue of his book, 'Our ideas are always more numerous than can be expressed in words...and we are richer in ideas than in words'.[71] The study of words, Filippidis implies, is not sufficient; one needs to study concepts, whether they refer to physical phenomena or abstractions.

Filippidis' co-author Konstantas too continued to campaign for the use of the vernacular. His translation of Giovanni Francesco Soave's handbook for high schools and universities, *Istituzioni di logica, etica e metafisica*, under the title *Elements of Philosophy* (1804), is preceded by a preface in which the translator begins by saying that 'we [i.e. the modern Greeks], the descendants of those who once enriched the world with writings on every subject, find ourselves poor and deprived of even the most essential'. Describing the education system, based on the learning of Ancient Greek, which prevailed in his time, he continues:

Pupils..., wasting the most appropriate time of their lives for progress by trying to master a foreign and long dead language and conversing with the Muses in it, after labouring ineffectually for five or ten years, finally wander off, leaving with nausea the road that they had set out upon with delight.[72]

'A *prólipsis* is deeply rooted in our *genos*', he continues, 'that our language is unsuitable for philosophy.' This, he says, is similar to the situation in Europe until recently, where Latin was held to be the only

---

[69] See also Filippidis 1818 (a work of Roman history translated into 'Aeolodoric dialect'); quoted in Sathas 1870: 203.

[70] Filippidis 1801: p. xxviii.   [71] Epilogue in Ancient Greek, ibid., 327.

[72] Konstantas 1804: 11.

language appropriate for philosophy; yet time and experience have shown that this is a delusion. The Muses like to converse in the spoken language, he argues, and we must do the same as the Europeans if we wish to recall the Muses to their homeland.[73]

As for the form of language he uses in his translation, Konstantas writes that he has used technical terms borrowed from the Hellenic language ('the mother of our own') or from Italian, or has created them according to 'the natural idiom of our own [language]'. As for the *yfos* [the grammar of the particular language variety], he preserves the morphology and orthography of Hellenic. In syntax, 'I followed the rules of the language I was writing'. In sum, he has drawn the grammar of his own language from 'use, which is the nature of language'. He wishes there were a grammar or dictionary of 'our language', 'a common rule', instead of everyone writing according to a different grammar; 'councils, lectures, debates, correspondences are needed' so that the language can be properly regularized.[74] He ends with a plea to his readers: 'Do not despise the book because it speaks our language'.[75] It is notable that Konstantas, like Filippidis, uses the concept of 'natural idiom' and likens writing to oral communication. As time went by, however, Konstantas became more of a linguistic compromiser, employing a variety similar to that of Korais.

---

[73] Ibid., quoted in Sathas 1870: 186–7.   [74] Sathas 1870: 187–9.
[75] Konstantas 1804: 23.

4

Adamantios Korais as language reformer

The writer who most systematically made the link between language and national identity in the pre-revolutionary period was the most important exponent of the Greek Enlightenment, Adamantios Korais (1748–1833). He was the first Greek in modern times to gain an international reputation as a Classical philologist. The fact that he was one of the earliest Greek cultural nationalists suggests that, despite his predominantly Enlightenment outlook, he underwent the influence of certain romantic ideas as well. According to Einar Haugen, Korais was also one of the first language reformers in modern Europe, and his 'restoration' of the Greek language was held up as a model for the Norwegians by P. A. Munch (1832).[1]

Adamantios (Diamantis) Korais was born and bred in Smyrna. His father was a silk merchant, dealing especially with Holland, who had moved to Smyrna from the island of Chios. His paternal uncle Sofronios became metropolitan of Belgrade,[2] while his mother, the daughter of a learned teacher, was probably the most educated Greek woman in Smyrna. The young Korais was taught Latin by Bernhard Keun, the Calvinist chaplain of the Dutch consulate in Smyrna, and it was through Keun that he began to come into contact with the Protestant ideas that were to influence him throughout his career. He worked unsuccessfully as a merchant in Amsterdam (1771–76), then in 1782 he decided to embark on medical studies at Montpellier, the oldest medical school in Europe. He translated Hippocrates into French (1800) and continued to retain an interest in medicine, which greatly influenced his views on what he perceived as the 'diseases' of language and thought, and on the measures that should be taken to cure them.[3] Having finally completed his studies at the age of forty, he settled in Paris on 24 May 1788, a little more than a

---

[1] Haugen 1965: 188.   [2] K. Th. Dimaras 1985: 107.
[3] See, for example, Korais 1984b: 36 [1804].

year before the outbreak of the French revolution, and he remained in the French capital for the rest of his long life. Korais was exceptional among the Greek intellectuals of his time in that he stayed in the same place for almost fifty years.[4]

According to Kitromilides, Korais 'could be considered the spiritual founder of the new nation'.[5] He opposed the idea that the Greeks should live under Russian 'protection', as occurred in the Danubian Principalities. While Napoleon's troops were in the Mediterranean (1797–1805), he published several anonymous polemical works in which he exhorted the Greeks to assist the French in their liberating mission.[6] In the brilliant lecture he gave in French in 1803 he memorably described the Greeks as 'a people that is preparing to become a nation'.[7] For him, as Kitromilides has pointed out, 'the reform of the language was an organic part of the more general effort aimed at the cultural rebirth of the nation'.[8]

Although he was entirely self-taught, Korais became a Classical scholar with a European reputation as a textual critic (i.e. an editor of Classical texts on the basis of manuscripts). He was decidedly a pedant, with little interest in the aesthetic aspects of literature and no appreciation of the imagery, sound, and connotative qualities of poetic language. As K. Th. Dimaras put it, Korais saw art as 'the handmaid of philosophy.'[9] Furthermore, his approach to the modern Greek language remained untouched by recent trends in linguistics, which were moving away from philosophical and psychological approaches to language towards the historical study of the grammatical (and especially phonological) structures of individual languages and language families. In fact, Korais was more of a moralist than a linguist, and he subscribed to the interconnection between language, thought, and morality proposed by Condillac. His chief aim was to educate the Greeks and improve their *ithi* [morals]. Although he does not define the term precisely, by 'morals' he means beliefs and opinions about the world, together with the behaviour that follows from them. His exhortations to his compatriots to love liberty, practise civic virtue, and prepare themselves to become good citizens of a free and democratic state were perhaps more significant than his purely linguistic work.

According to Korais, 'the barbarization of language, by perverting the true meanings of words, results in the perversion of morals'.[10] The faults

---

[4] Kitromilides 1996: 79.   [5] Kitromilides 1996: 426.   [6] Rotolo 1965: 30.
[7] Korais 1803: 44.   [8] Kitromilides 1996: 398.   [9] K. Th. Dimaras 1996: 92.
[10] Korais 1984b: 504 [1812].

that Korais diagnosed in the Greeks' moral character seemed to be manifested in the fact that, in his view, they thought and behaved more like Turks than like Parisians. In order to reverse the process of their moral decline, the language of the modern Greeks had to be brought closer to Ancient Greek. Korais consistently criticized the obscurantist church education prevailing in the Greek-speaking world and promoted what he called the 'rebirth of Hellas',[11] by which he meant the Greeks' cultural enlightenment through their re-connection with ancient Hellenic civilization and their engagement with modern European science and philosophy. Nevertheless, he argued that the modern language should be improved, taught, and used for all kinds of writing, including everyday commercial correspondence as well as philosophy and science.

His aim as a language reformer was utilitarian: to develop a standardized written prose language that was based on good sense, regulated according to simple rules, and close enough to spoken usage to be readily comprehensible, yet avoiding the unseemly vulgarity of everyday colloquial speech. This language was intended to be devised in accordance with rational principles rather than individual taste.

Korais did not encapsulate his ideas on language in a single book, nor did he ever publish a grammar or dictionary. Although he drafted a grammar of Modern Greek and a French–Greek dictionary, neither of these was included in the seventy volumes he published during his lifetime.[12] A five-volume collection of material entitled *Atakta* (1828–35) includes a critical edition of Byzantine vernacular poems and a total of more than 1500 pages containing lists of about 8000 Modern Greek words with comments on their etymology and usage.[13] He wrote that the dictionary of every language tends to precede the appearance of its classic authors, whereas the grammar of the language is written after the authors have written.[14] This was perhaps his justification for focusing his

---

[11] Korais 1984b: 221 [1807].

[12] The *Grammar of the Greek [Graikikís] Language*, which Korais was working on in 1800, first appeared in 1888 and has never been republished (Frankiskos 1984). It goes little further than noun morphology; most of the paradigms are of Ancient Greek words, with Modern Greek paradigms usually placed afterwards as 'anomalies'. The *Material for a French–Greek Dictionary* was published in 1881 (and again as Korais 1994); the material is a brief list, consisting mostly of words that Korais took from earlier dictionaries of vernacular Modern Greek, with the addition of a few suggested coinages of his own.

[13] For the word lists in the *Atakta* see Georgoudis 1984. According to Frankiskos 1984: 73, Korais was already compiling a 'dictionary of the common language' in 1791.

[14] Korais 1984b: 496 [1812]; Korais to Vasileiou, 12 April 1805, in Korais 1966: 255. For more on Korais' views concerning the writing of grammars see the section 'The "correction" of Modern Greek' below.

attention on the form and meaning of Modern Greek vocabulary rather than on the grammar of the language.

He propagated his views on the Greek language and his use of it by means of general precept and practical example, encouraging his disciples to imitate his use of vocabulary and grammar. His ideas on language were chiefly expounded in the prefaces to his editions of ancient Greek texts, beginning in 1804 and continuing with the *Precursor to the Hellenic Library* (1805) and the first six volumes of his series entitled *Hellenic Library*, published in Paris from 1807 to 1812; the whole sixteen-volume series was published from 1807 to 1826 and distributed to schools and libraries in Greece and outside, with the financial assistance of the Zosimas brothers. It is characteristic of the unsystematic nature of Korais' work that the prefaces to the volumes of the *Hellenic Library* bear the title 'Impromptu thoughts on Greek *paideia* [education/culture] and language'. Similarly, *Atakta*, the title he chose for his published collection of material on the history of the Medieval and Modern Greek vernacular, means 'miscellany' or 'things placed in a disorderly fashion'.[15]

His earliest statements about the language in his voluminous private correspondence date back to at least 1788, when he put forward the 'correction' of Modern Greek according to Ancient Greek rules as the ideal, adding, however, that this should be carried out only so far as *ethos* [custom or habit] permits.[16] His first public pronouncement on the subject came in an ideologically significant text entitled 'Letter to Alexandros Vasileiou on the new edition of Heliodorus... and, by way of digression, on the gradually barbarized Hellenic language and the language of the *Graikoí* [modern Greeks] which was born from it'. This appeared as a preface to his edition of the novel *Aethiopica* by Heliodorus (3rd–4th century AD), which was published in 1804 at the expense of his friend Vasileiou (d. 1818), a merchant who lived successively in Paris, Lyon, Genoa, Vienna, and Trieste (where he served as Ottoman consul) and who also assisted him in the financing, publication, and distribution of his books.[17] Like the 'Impromptu thoughts' that followed,

---

[15] Korais took the title *Atakta* from a work by the 4th- to 3rd-century BC lexicographer Philetas of Kos (Georgoudis 1984: 59). The subtitle of Korais' work is *Impromptu Collection of Various Impromptu Notes and Other Annotations on the Ancient and Modern Greek Language*. Nevertheless, in 1908 Hatzidakis was quoted as describing the *Atakta* as the only noteworthy attempt at a historical dictionary of Modern Greek until his time (Chronika 1908: 571). This judgement was repeated by Papadopoulos 1933.

[16] Korais to Lotos, 15 Jan. 1788, in Korais 1964: 94–5. For this same concept Katartzis and Psalidas use *exi* and *synítheia* respectively.

[17] Daskalakis 1966: 50.

the epistolary form of the 'Letter' allowed Korais to write in an informal style.

The tendentious title of the 'Letter' implies a whole theory of the historical development of the Greek language over the millennia: the language of the ancient Hellenes had gradually become barbarized as a result of foreign domination and had eventually given rise to the language of the *Graikoí*. For Korais, barbarization seems to have consisted of two chief components: impoverishment (the loss of many native vocabulary items, and of certain grammatical categories such as the infinitive), which allegedly prevented complete and precise expression, and adulteration (the presence of many words borrowed from foreign occupiers, which were perceived as shameful stains on the face of a once noble language).

In the absence of the relevant linguistic research, Korais, like most other Greek writers at the time, was unable to account for the phonological, morphological, and lexical changes in the Greek language that could not be readily attributed to foreign influence. He simply despised these changes, fitting them into a preconceived model of 'decline' and 'degeneration'. In this way he ended up throwing the baby out with the bathwater by rejecting a lot of native Greek grammatical features together with words of foreign origin.

In his 'Impromptu thoughts' Korais promoted the famous *mesi odós* [middle way], counselling his compatriots to steer a course between the extremes of archaism and vernacularism.[18] His criticisms were chiefly directed at the archaists and those who were linguistically and politically more conservative than himself – both those who argued for the use of Ancient Greek and those who assumed or even insisted that control over Greek education and culture should continue to be in the hands of the Church. It was these men who represented the *status quo* that he was seeking to overthrow. He did not openly attack the vernacularists, since they were a powerless minority.[19]

Although his statements about the language question and the Greek language itself are scattered about many of his books, the form of language that he used illustrates his doctrine: not only did he practise what he preached, but the variety of language he used remained remarkably consistent throughout his career, though by the 1820s he was using a greater

[18] Korais does not seem to have used the specific phrase *mesi odós* with reference to language in his early works, though he uses it later, e.g. in Korais 1984b: 498 [1812].

[19] He attacks the vernacularists in some of his private letters; however, since he does not name them, it is not clear which of their texts he had read.

number of vernacular features and fewer archaic ones than in 1800.[20] Since Korais' ideas on the language did not develop appreciably over the years, it is not difficult to summarize some of his basic tenets. These are his worship of Ancient Greek perfection; his defence of Modern Greek; and his correction of the modern language in the domains of vocabulary, morphology, and orthography. Before examining each of these tenets in turn, it would be as well to make some general observations about his linguistic theory.

Korais' linguistic theory

Like many eighteenth-century thinkers, Korais believed that the natural state of man (and of language) is barbarity and that there is a kind of entropy operating in human society that results in *parakmí* [decline]. Nevertheless, he also believed that it was possible to improve men's morals (and their language) by taking positive and decisive measures. In his view, the decline of the Greek language since ancient times was to be explained by the ignorance and obscurantism that had prevailed in the Greek world between the end of the Classical period and his own day, chiefly in consequence of the absence of democratic rule before and during the Roman conquest and the 'oriental despotism' of the successive Byzantine and Ottoman empires. In turn, the corrupted form of the Greek language that had resulted from these historical vicissitudes had had a deleterious effect on the thought patterns, belief system, and moral behaviour of the nation that spoke it.

Korais' view of Byzantine barbarism and obscurantism – typical of his time – was greatly influenced by Edward Gibbon's *The Decline and Fall of the Roman Empire* (1776–88).[21] As a representative of the progressive bourgeoisie, he was a republican who admired ancient Athenian democratic ideals, and he felt that in his own day these were represented in their finest form in post-revolutionary France.[22] He shared the view of the French language taken by the French revolution, that it was 'the language of freedom and enlightenment'.[23]

Korais, then, like Condillac, conceived of speech and thought as existing in a reciprocal relationship: 'He who thinks badly speaks badly,

[20] Rotolo 1965: 102; K. Th. Dimaras 1984: 20.

[21] Korais 1984b: 448 [1811] talks about 'the time of Byzantine barbarity'. Byzantium was not rediscovered and rehabilitated by Greek intellectuals as the 'missing link' in the tripartite 'continuity of Hellenism' (Classical–Byzantine–Modern) till the mid-nineteenth century; see Chapter 6.

[22] See, for example, K. Th. Dimaras 1996: 97.   [23] Ager 2001: 17.

and he who speaks badly prevents his mind from discovering the faculty of thinking, or even abolishes it completely.'[24] Korais believed that damaging changes to the linguistic mechanism of Greek had come about under external influence (subjection to tyrannical foreign rule), with the result that rectification had to be similarly imposed from outside, through the reintroduction of parts that had fallen out of it in the meantime. Like other Greek purists, Korais ignored the functional synchronic cohesiveness of spoken varieties of Greek in favour of an imaginary diachronic cohesiveness.

Condillac and other linguistic philosophers in the eighteenth century believed that language to a certain extent determines national character.[25] The logical consequence of Korais' assertion that 'the character of a whole nation is known by its language'[26] is that, if the Greeks of the present day have a barbarized language, then they too are barbaric. Conversely, if language determines national character, then to change a nation's language would be to change its character, which is precisely what Korais wanted to do with the Greeks. Given these ideas, it is not surprising that Korais' implicit assumption was that language – and certainly not religion – was the chief or sole marker of Greek national identity. 'The language is the nation itself,' he writes, referring to passages in the Old and New Testament where the word 'language' is used to mean 'nation'.[27] Korais saw language, in terms of the mother tongue, as the defining feature of the Greeks and ignored the fact that many people in the southern Balkans spoke a language other than Greek in the family. Korais seems never to have mentioned such languages in his published works, and perhaps only twice in his letters, where he asks Vasileiou about the use of Greek and Albanian in everyday situations in Epirus but fails to show any further interest in the matter.[28] Korais' view contrasts with that of Doukas, who believed one could become a Hellene by adopting Greek language and culture.

The worship of ancient Greek perfection

Little need be said about Korais' worship of ancient Greek perfection. His conception of ancient Greece was an idealized version of Periclean

---

[24] Korais 1984b: 492 [1812].   [25] Davies 1998: 34–5, 115.
[26] Korais 1984b: 52 [1804].   [27] Korais 1829: p. xxi.
[28] See Korais to Vasileiou (who was from Argyrokastron [Gjirokastër in modern Albania] and was clearly an Albanian speaker), 28 Oct. 1809 (Korais 1966: 536) and 4 Jan. 1810 (Korais 1979: 3). Thanks to Marjolijne Janssen for these references.

Athens, without slavery and without wars. In his view the ancient Greeks had reached the summit of freedom and moral perfection from which the modern Greeks had lamentably fallen. He believed that, after the Classical period, as the Greeks were deprived of the arts and sciences, so they were deprived of correct ideas, which were replaced by *prolipseis*, i.e. preconceived notions that are accepted without being based on empirical observation and without being subjected to the scrutiny of reason. Because of their enslavement to foreign rulers, the Modern Greeks were incapable of thinking properly and thus of speaking properly; the correction of language would, however, lead to the correction of both thought and behaviour. Only by eradicating 'vulgar' and 'erroneous' words, and replacing them with 'proper' and 'correct' (i.e. Ancient Greek) equivalents would the Greeks rid themselves of *prolipseis* and re-establish contact with truth and freedom.

'It is a rare thing,' he wrote, '... for someone to be enslaved like a bondsman to bodily pleasure if he has once managed to drink to the full the cup of that enchantress, the language of the Hellenes.'[29] For Korais, the teaching of Ancient Greek was necessary for the removal of 'the age-old filth with which barbarism has besmirched the most beautiful face of Hellas'.[30] He even went so far as to assert, with considerable exaggeration, that 'all the miseries of the nation' flow from 'the unmethodical teaching' of Ancient Greek.[31]

The defence of Modern Greek

Korais wrote that it was as feasible to revive Ancient Greek as it was to resurrect the dead. His defence of Modern Greek (which he regularly called 'our common language') must be stressed, since he tended to direct his attacks at the archaists, who refused to consider Modern Greek as the object of serious study, and at the macaronists, who confused Ancient Greek and Modern Greek without respect for either.[32] As he wrote

---

[29] Korais 1984b: 38 [1804].   [30] Ibid., 138 [1805].   [31] Ibid., 502 [1812].

[32] Only in his private correspondence did Korais acknowledge that his language too was macaronic: '[W]e are all more or less macaronists. The formation and the transition of one language to another are necessarily accompanied by macaronism at the beginning. When I ridiculed the macaronists, I meant those who macaronize deliberately and pretentiously, out of an idiotic revulsion against the commonly spoken language, not those who wisely and quietly seek its correction' (Korais to Vasileiou, July 1812, in Korais 1979: 208). Here Korais attempts to differentiate himself from the archaist Doukas, who however shared exactly the same attitude (see Chapter 5).

in 1804, the 'dye of liberty is so deep in the language of the Hellenes that the barbarization and misery of the Greeks over so many centuries have not washed it out completely even from our common dialect'.[33] 'The [modern] language,' he wrote twenty-five years later, 'much as it has been barbarized, is nonetheless a language spoken for very many centuries by all the common people of Hellas'.[34]

'Our modern language,' he proclaimed, 'is wholly Hellenic, with the exception of a very few Italian and Turkish words'.[35] All of the everyday modern words, he asserted, apart from those of foreign origin, go back to one of the dialects of Ancient Greek.[36] 'The language spoken today is neither Barbarous nor Hellenic, but the new language of a new nation, daughter and heir of a very rich old one, Hellenic', he wrote in 1832.[37] Here Korais uses the adjective 'Barbarous' in its ancient literal sense of 'non-Greek', though elsewhere he uses it in the purely pejorative sense in which it is used in modern languages.

The Greeks should read Ancient Greek but write in Modern Greek, he urged, and children should be taught how to read with the use of modern rather than ancient words and phrases.[38] Like Moisiodax before him, he criticized the archaists for their obscurantism: he pointed out, for instance, that Doukas used to publish translations or paraphrases of Ancient Greek texts into archaistic 'Modern Greek', in which perfectly comprehensible Ancient Greek words were rendered by rarer or more archaic ones.[39] Even though the variety of language Korais used and promoted was far from natural, he urged that everyone should write in a natural way: 'It is absolutely impossible to write correctly when one slavishly imitates others, and especially if the latter wrote in a language that has now ceased to be spoken.'[40] Finally, according to Korais, the advantages of Modern Greek over Ancient Greek for modern written use were that, while Ancient Greek was a 'foreign language',[41] Modern Greek was spoken by all, while at the same time it contained *leípsana* [relics] of Ancient Greek: the Modern Greeks could be proud that their natural language is the 'daughter' of Ancient Greek.

---

[33] Korais 1984b: 53.   [34] Korais 1829: p. xviii.   [35] Ibid., p. xxx.
[36] Korais 1832: p. vi.   [37] Ibid., p. viii.
[38] Korais 1984b: 239 [1807]; Ibid., 353–4 [1809].   [39] Ibid., 503 [1812].
[40] Ibid., 43–4.
[41] Ibid., 129 [1805]. As we have seen in Chapter 3, Konstantas too described Ancient Greek as a foreign language.

The 'correction' of Modern Greek

The fact that Korais, like many others, constantly talks about Modern Greek as the daughter of the ancient language shows that he conceived of two chronologically distinct varieties of Greek: the ancient language as recorded in texts, and the modern spoken language. Even though he published editions of medieval vernacular texts, he and his contemporaries possessed insufficient knowledge and understanding of the historical developments that had taken place in the Greek language between the Classical period and the present; it was Hatzidakis, more than half a century later, who first traced the history of Greek from antiquity to the present as a continuous process. One of the reasons why Korais thought Medieval and Modern Greek was in a dire state was that the chaotic state of the language used in medieval written vernacular texts – which contain many forms that are not found either in Ancient or in Modern Greek – blinded him to the systematic nature of spoken Greek.

Korais failed to treat Modern Greek as an autonomous system, and he constantly displayed a fetish for the written rather than the spoken word. He begins his unpublished grammar of Modern Greek with the words: 'Grammar is the art of speaking and writing correctly', and he ends it with the following: '[A] language in which there are no authors of any kind of *epistimi* [science/scholarship] cannot strictly possess a Grammar, since the rules for speaking and writing correctly are taken from the common usage of authors'.[42] Since he did not believe the language of any Greek writer during the preceding centuries was worthy of emulation, the implication of this statement is that Modern Greek is devoid of grammar. Elsewhere he asserts that the codification of the grammar of a living language is unnecessary until that language begins to decline; then grammar becomes 'a dam ... against the deluge of barbarism'.[43] It is clear that he confuses the grammar of a language (the description of how a language functions in practice) and the grammar book (which in his day tended to prescribe good usage). His attitude contrasts markedly with Katartzis' view that even languages that have not been written possess a natural grammar.

Korais once wrote that the fact that the Bible was heard every day in church was perhaps one of the reasons why the Greek language had not become totally barbarized.[44] In fact, it was the familiarity of all Greek Orthodox Christians with the language of the liturgy, whose texts were

---

[42] Korais 1888: 1, 111.   [43] Korais 1984b: 68 [1805].   [44] Korais 1829: p. xxx.

composed one and a half millennia earlier, that provided him with a tacit justification for his insistence on using the ancient morphological features that are found in the biblical and liturgical texts.

Korais asserted that the coexistence of two varieties of a language (one for the educated, the other for the uneducated) was a natural and universal situation, which had existed in ancient Greece too. He argued that every nation speaks a single language until it becomes civilized; from then on, the nation comes to be divided into two parties, the vulgar and the civilized or learned; the latter speak more elegantly than the others, while when they write they express their thoughts even more elegantly: 'Isocrates, Demosthenes, Plato and the other learned men of the nation spoke to the vulgar Athenians not as they wrote, but in a language similar to that spoken by the vulgar, which probably did not differ greatly from the usual language of today, although it was not exactly the same'.[45] This view, which betrays a lack of knowledge and understanding of linguistic history, is not far distant from the 'Aeolodoric theory' expounded by Christopoulos (see Chapter 5), in that it attempts to grant respectability to modern vernacular Greek by claiming that it goes back to ancient times.[46] It implies that it is not the vulgar tongue that has changed; what has changed is that the gap between the written language and the vulgar tongue has become progressively narrower; this gap must be widened so as to bring the modern written language closer to the ancient written variety, in which the great works of Classical antiquity were composed. Since the nation had reverted to its pre-Classical barbarism, it was as though the language that was spoken in his time consisted of the pristine words and forms that had existed before the Classical Greeks polished and refined them; thus the modern Greeks have to carry out the same process again.

It was Korais' notions of polishing and refining that gave rise to his theory and practice of 'correction', which had a far-reaching influence on the development of the Modern Greek language question and on the language itself. His outlook was utterly different from that of Katartzis, for whom the cultivation of Romaic entailed enriching its expressive potential while preserving its existing vocabulary and respecting its natural grammar.

[45] Ibid., pp. xxi, xxiv. This view was influenced by the prologue to Ilgen (1796: p. xxxiv), which includes an edition of Dimitrios Zinos' sixteenth-century 'vulgar' Modern Greek translation of the pseudo-Homeric *Batrachomyomachia*.

[46] Although he did not explicitly subscribe to the Aeolodoric theory or describe the spoken language as the 'fifth dialect' of Hellenic, Korais was not clear about the historical origins of Modern Greek. In his time most scholars were unaware that Modern Greek was descended from the *koine*.

By contrast, Korais' 'correction' entailed making radical changes to the vocabulary and grammar of spoken Greek. He defined the 'correction' of language in the following formulation, which clearly shows his concern for compromise: 'not only the transformation of various barbarously-formed words and constructions, but also the retention of many others, which those who have not carefully investigated the nature of the language seek to exile from it as being barbarous'.[47]

The enlightened men of the nation, he argued, have a duty to bring their national language to perfection by eradicating the stains of barbarity, especially foreign words, which are a matter for national shame and which impugn the national reputation:

To borrow from foreigners – or, to speak more clearly, to beg words and phrases, with which the storerooms of one's language are already replete – creates a reputation for complete ignorance [απαιδευσίας: lack of education/culture] or even idiocy as well as dishonour.[48]

Words such as 'reputation' and 'dishonour' reveal that Korais was constantly looking insecurely over his shoulder to gauge what western Europeans were thinking and saying about his fellow Greeks. Elsewhere he wrote:

If nothing else, it is good for us to appear, in the eyes of the enlightened nations of Europe, to be concerning ourselves with our own *paideia* [education/culture], and not to suffer them unjustly to snatch the honour of the rebirth of Hellas from our hands.[49]

We note here the importance of Greeks putting on a good outward show to enlightened Europe so that they can demonstrate that they are worthy of political freedom.

Nevertheless, Korais strenuously denied the charge levelled against him by his opponents, that he was trying to 'legislate' in matters of language. Emmanouil Frankiskos has suggested that the chief reason why Korais did not publish a grammar of Modern Greek was precisely that he wanted to avoid legislating on grammatical matters.[50] No one has the right to replace a nation's language, argues Korais; yet he clearly believed he had a right to change it. In order to convey his position, he used the analogy of parliamentary democracy: '[L]anguage is one of the most inalienable possessions of the nation. All the members of the nation share

---

[47] Korais 1984b: 36 [1804].   [48] Korais 1805b: p. lxxxv.
[49] Korais 1984b: 221 [1807].   [50] Frankiskos 1984: 82.

in this possession, as it were, with democratic equality'.[51] He stated that, in language as in politics, he was equally against tyranny or oligarchy (the imposition of a particular variety of language by dictatorial decree) and demagogy or mob rule (the imposition by the common rabble of their vulgar, incorrect speech).[52] He claimed that the true legislators in language are the poets and prose writers, but that it is for the *ethnos* as a whole to decide which authors are 'classical' (i.e. standards or models for imitation).[53] According to this analogy, authors are the democratically elected members of parliament, who will be voted in or out by their constituents according to majority vote. To become accepted as 'classics', authors must therefore write not for the intellectual elite alone, nor for the mob, but for the nation as a whole. We recall that in France Korais had experienced the transition from tyrannical monarchy to attempts at democracy, which were interrupted by mob rule; he saw language, like democratic politics, as based on a compromise between conflicting interests.

In Korais' view, one can correct and perfect one's language only once one has studied it closely; besides, he argued, a more thorough knowledge of the modern language can help the Greeks to understand Ancient Greek better. In order to name each concept, instead of simply ignoring the spoken language, one should try to find a word of Ancient Greek origin still living in some spoken dialect, which can then be used once the requisite correction – a process of phonological and morphological de-corruption – has taken place. He proposed that a team of scholars should tour the whole of Greece collecting words: '[H]ow are we to raise up our fallen language if we do not first excavate its ruins? . . . [H]ow can we cure it, if we do not know precisely what its ailment is, and which are its ailing parts?'[54]

What he aimed for, then, was a compromise between Modern Greek and Ancient Greek. As early as 1788 he wrote epigrammatically: '[O]ne must speak not only *sofós* [wisely], but *safós* [clearly]'.[55] Sixteen years later he asked: '[I]s it only the learned who need to condescend to the uneducated? Do not these too have a duty to rise slightly with

[51] Korais 1984b: 49 [1804].

[52] Korais to Vasileiou, 17 Aug. 1811, in Korais 1979: 129.

[53] Korais 1984b: 490–1 [1812]. He once wrote to Vasileiou that if a new Homer sang in the vulgar language, no power on earth would be able to prevent this language from prevailing (Korais to Vasileiou 28 May 1803, in Korais 1966: 90). It is significant that this claim is made only in a private letter.

[54] Korais 1984b: 503 [1812].

[55] Korais to Dimitris Lotos, 15 Jan. 1788, in Korais 1964: 94–5.

the learned?'[56] Here the concept of the 'middle way' is presented not horizontally but vertically, in hierarchical terms. There is no doubt that Korais wrote clearly, in terms of his thought processes and sentence structure; yet, from a purely communicative point of view, his clarity is compromised by his desire to write 'wisely', which in practice entailed the use of ancient morphological forms.

He urged teachers and their pupils to practise what he calls the *paráthesis* or *paravolí* [comparison through juxtaposition] of Ancient and Modern Greek. It should be emphasized that this was a progressive idea; all of the grammars of Ancient Greek that were used by Greek teachers and pupils until the early nineteenth century were written in Ancient Greek, whereas Korais urged that the ancient language should be taught through the medium of the modern, with the double purpose of helping them to teach and learn the ancient language and to 'correct and embellish the modern living language, spoken by living people, by rubbing and washing away the many unsightlinesses that have become attached to them as a result of the long misery of the Hellenic nation'.[57] The pairing of 'correction' and 'embellishment', as if these two theoretically distinct procedures are one and the same, indicates Korais' confusion between the communicative and aesthetic aspects of language. In his desire to show how little the language has changed since ancient times, when he provides examples of *paráthesis*, he succeeds in distorting both of the languages, misinterpreting not only the meanings of words but also the phonological rules.[58] Despite his defence of Modern Greek, he steadfastly refused to write down any modern word that did not already conform to an Ancient Greek pattern without first correcting it.[59] In addition, he concentrates on the similarities between individual words rather than on similarities between phonological and morphological systems. Furthermore, instead of adopting a truly historical approach to the continuous development of the language, his *paráthesis* compares and contrasts words or forms belonging to two discrete stages of its history.

In his discussion of individual vocabulary items, he is concerned to establish which Modern Greek words are the same as in Ancient Greek,

---

[56] Korais 1984b: 51 [1804]; cf. Korais 1829: p. xxv.

[57] Ibid., p. xviii. The two concepts had already been quoted as a pair in Korais 1984b: 50 [1804].

[58] Ibid., 330–41 [1809].

[59] For Korais' 'correction' of vocabulary Tsopanakis 1983: 33 aptly uses the term *ana-palaíosi*, a term used since the late twentieth century to refer to the restoration of old houses to their original form; an English rendering of this term might be 'reveteration' (i.e. the opposite of renovation).

which are derived from Ancient Greek, and which have come from foreign languages. He urges that words derived from Ancient Greek should be used as far as possible as they were used by Hellenic authors and poets; this means ancient Greek authors in general, not only those of the Classical period, but those of the Hellenistic and imperial Roman periods too; Korais was not an Atticist. Although in practice he used Greek words in their modern meanings, he urged his readers to trace words back to their 'original' meanings, which are closer to 'the nature of things'.[60] Whenever the meaning of a word in Modern Greek differs from its ancient meaning (e.g. καλός /kalós/, Ancient Greek 'beautiful', Modern Greek 'good'), Korais describes the modern meaning as a *katáchrisis* [misuse/abuse]. Where the form has changed since ancient times (e.g. ἐξηλόνω /eksilóno/; *sic*: the Modern Greek form is actually /ksilóno/ [dismantle; unstitch], from ancient ἐξηλόω), the modern form is a *diafthorá* [corruption].[61] Whereas the Ancient Greek ending of a word is 'genuine', the Modern Greek ending (if it is different) is 'barbarous'.[62] The moral overtones of these labels are obvious: linguistic 'corruption', as we have seen, accompanies the 'distortion' of moral character.

The piecemeal and gradualistic nature of Korais' 'correction' of Modern Greek can be summed up in the following extract from his 'Letter to Alexandros Vasiliou':

Root out from the language the weeds of vulgarity, yet not all at once by the forkful, but gradually with the hand, one after the other; sow Hellenic seeds in it, but these too by the handful and not by the sackful. You will be surprised how in a short while your words and phrases have passed from the book into the mouths of the people.[63]

The first word of this extract in Greek, *ekrízoson*, exemplifies Korais' correction of the modern language: he takes the modern vernacular form *kserízose* back to its ancient form by preserving the root and restoring the ancient prefix and suffix. On the other hand, in the phrase 'from the language', he constructs the preposition *apo* [from] with the accusative as in Modern Greek, rather than with the genitive as in the ancient language. The unsystematic nature of his procedure is illustrated by the fact that in a single word he can mix features of the ancient and modern language, as in *deíchnousin* [they show], in which the stem *deichn-* is modern, but

---

[60] Korais 1984b: 509 [1812], 1829: 129.   [61] Ibid., 339 [1809].

[62] Korais 1832: p. ix.

[63] Korais 1984b: 51–2 [1804]. The phrase 'sow by the handful and not by the sackful' became proverbial when the ancient poet Corinna criticized Pindar for putting too many mythological references into his poems.

the ending *-ousin* is ancient (or at least dialectal).[64] In a single line he may use two different forms for the same grammatical category, as in the third person plural forms *arpazoun* [they snatch] (with the modern ending) and *onomázousi* [they name] (with the ancient one).[65] Finally, Korais sometimes replaced forms that everyone used with forms that no one had ever used. It was this last category of corrections that opened him up to the greatest criticism and ridicule.

Assessment of Korais' contribution to the language question

Korais' secular attitude to Greek language, education, and culture was a break with the past. It was this attitude that ensured that the language controversy in the nineteenth and twentieth centuries became the struggle between different versions of Modern Greek rather than between Ancient and Modern Greek.

Yet, like many of his followers and many of his opponents, Korais often conceived of the Modern Greek language not primarily as a means of communication but as an object – a once elegant heirloom inherited from more glorious times, which had become tarnished and pockmarked through neglect and which needed to be restored and polished. There was no doubt that spoken Modern Greek was deficient in abstract and technical vocabulary in comparison with the written languages of ancient Greece and modern Europe. This deficiency meant that a large number of words had to be introduced into Modern Greek (whether borrowed or invented) in order to express the various concepts that were essential for the communicative needs of a modern nation; indeed, many of the neologisms that Korais himself coined have successfully passed into common usage (notably *politismós* [civilization]).[66] Korais' basic error was that these coinages – including borrowings from Ancient Greek – were not made to conform to the phonological and morphological systems of the spoken language. Far from making any such adaptations, Korais – like many Greek intellectuals before him – saw fit to adapt Modern Greek words to Ancient Greek phonological and morphological rules. Once the grammars of two languages (albeit two widely separated historical stages of the same language) have become mixed, there is no single system, no norm, and therefore no criterion of correctness. Korais was unaware that the most systematic form of a language is its natural spoken form.

[64] Ibid., 239 [1807].   [65] Ibid., 495 [1812].

[66] That he invented the Modern Greek word for 'civilization' in 1804 is not surprising, given the title of his 1803 lecture.

As soon as a single significant grammatical rule from an earlier form of the language is introduced, the system is in danger of becoming unstable.

Korais saw the absence of the infinitive in Modern Greek as 'the most frightful vulgarity of our language'.[67] It did not occur to him to study and analyse the ways in which Modern Greek expresses relations that are expressed in other languages by the infinitive; such a study would have shown him how extraordinarily versatile the particle *na* is. Instead, looking forward to the revival of the Ancient Greek infinitive, he used to write *thelo grapsein* [I will write], adding a final *-n* to the commonly used written future form of the time, *thelo grapsei*, in order to make it look more like an ancient infinitive.[68] He hoped that, through reading his work, people would gradually become accustomed to seeing the infinitive and would then begin to use it themselves in contexts where it was used in Ancient Greek.

Although Korais himself avoided the use of Ancient Greek categories such as the dative case and the single-word future and aorist middle forms, his exhortation to 'sow Hellenic seeds' and his great reputation were taken by later writers as a sanction for the wholesale introduction of such Ancient Greek grammatical categories into Modern Greek. He wrote to Vasileiou in 1807 that the modern language 'is still as unbent to the will of the author as an untanned hide', adding that 'the disgusting task of tanning' falls to the two of them, and it is up to them 'to prepare it [the language] and to hand it over to those around us in a form that is easier to bring to perfection'.[69] Modern readers of this statement, which alludes to the conversion of rigid hides into supple leather, may infer that the analogous work in language is a matter of using it for a variety of topics and for a variety of purposes; in other words, a matter of *stylistic* elaboration. Yet Korais and many of his followers and admirers in the following decades believed that further *grammatical* archaization of the modern written language was not only an indication of cultural progress but a way of rendering the language more flexible – whereas

---

[67] Quoted in Triantafyllidis 1938: 452. Fallmerayer expressed a similar view later when he contemptuously dismissed Modern Greek with the words, 'A language without an infinitive is no better than a human body without a hand' (Fallmerayer 1845: II 451–2, quoted in B. Joseph 1985: 90).

[68] The non-finite (impersonal) form *grapsei* used in the future and perfect tenses in Medieval and Modern Greek does indeed ultimately derive from an amalgamation between the ancient infinitive forms *graphein* (present) and *grapsai* (aorist).

[69] Korais 1966: 393. By 'the disgusting work' Korais means the steeping of hides in a liquid (euphemistically called 'pure' in English) made of canine or other faeces.

much of their work had the effect of making it stiffer and more difficult to handle.

Korais is a figure who has continued to divide Greek intellectuals until the present day. He has been appropriated by both liberal and conservative nationalists as the greatest founding father of Greek national independence, and he has been accused by exponents of demoticism, Marxism, and Orthodox Christianity alike as being the chief villain responsible for all the ills that have beset the Greek nation since his day. The fact that he has been seen by some as the founding father of modern Hellenism and by others as its enemy shows that these people are talking about quite different Hellenisms. In the last few decades he has become the object of analytical research, some of which appears to have been aimed at reclaiming him for the liberal centre and left. Yet his far from radical proposals on language reform have often been confused with his undoubtedly progressive and revolutionary political ideas. Filippos Iliou devoted a major study to the way that Korais was used as a straw man by his opponents in the twentieth century. However, in his desire to highlight Korais' liberal and radical political ideas, Iliou claims that Korais' language was 'learned demotic'[70] – a linguistically indefensible view that concentrates on features such as sentence structure while completely overlooking Korais' morphological archaization. There is no doubt that he left a positive legacy of political liberalism and civic virtue; yet his linguistic legacy – a national written language whose grammatical structure was artificial and highly unstable – was a confusing one.

Manolis Triantafyllidis' verdict on Korais was that the language that he strove to give to the Greek people

symbolizes the decision of modern Hellenism to create its position in life with greater confidence in its national strengths, judging more realistically what it can assimilate from the great past so as to proceed on life's way.[71]

Similarly, James Faubion defends Korais by claiming that, unlike the archaists, the language he constructed was 'the language of his contemporaries, "archaized" and "purified" enough to be able to enable its speakers to regain control of the past, to recover it without having to surrender to it.'[72] Alkis Angelou wrote that, in contrast to the blind imitation encouraged by the archaists, Korais was 'the first modern Greek who attempted to exploit the past in a creative manner'.[73] Paschalis

---

[70] Iliou 1984; for 'learned demotic' see ibid., 154.
[71] Triantafyllidis 1938: 168; see Bernal 2007a: 593.
[72] Faubion 1993: 151.   [73] Angelou 1998: 138*.

Kitromilides argues that Korais' 'purification' of the language allowed Greek speakers to approach ancient texts with greater naturalness and to read them with greater ease, seeing them as an organic part of their cultural heritage.[74]

Nevertheless, I believe that Vincenzo Rotolo's verdict on Korais' language remains just: it is impossible to reconstruct a linguistic system from Korais' oeuvre; his linguistic theory and practice have no organic unity; they present many contradictions at any one time and many oscillations over the course of the decades; in sum, they are a jumble: nebulous, uncertain, and confused.[75] Aside from vocabulary, the changes that Korais proposed were directed at the most structured parts of the language, namely phonology and morphology, which are the very features that most linguists since the early nineteenth century have seen as forming the basis of a language. It is in his dogma that the 'correction' (i.e. distortion) of the basic morphological features of Modern Greek is a positive and desirable undertaking that Korais' influence on the development of the language has been harmful: he gave his authoritative seal of approval to the continued practice of arbitrarily replacing any modern feature of vocabulary or grammar with an ancient equivalent.

It is instructive to compare Korais' work on Modern Greek with the elaboration of the French language since the Renaissance. The French language had deviated further from Latin by 1500 than Greek had from the ancient language by 1800. In terms of vocabulary and grammar, the French language reformers of the sixteenth and seventeenth centuries accepted their language more or less as they found it, enriching it with loanwords from Latin to fill semantic gaps, developing precise definitions of the meanings of words (definitions that came to be enshrined in the great Dictionary of the French Academy, first published in 1694), and borrowing some stylistic traits from Latin. Thus they refined their modern language into a precise and supple instrument of expression. No one in France thought of expelling (or 'correcting') 'corrupt' forms such as the negative particles *pas* and *rien*, or etymologically tautologous words such as *aujourd'hui* 'today' (where *hui* comes from Latin *hodie* [today]), or of etymologically simplistic words such as *beaucoup* [much, many] (literally 'fine blow', instead of Latin *multus*), or words of non-Latin origin such as *choisir* [choose] (from Gothic) and *guerre* (from Frankish) [war] (instead of Latin *bellum*) – not to mention the very names of the country and its people (France, Français). Strangely, neither Korais nor any of the other

74 Kitromilides 1996: 399.   75 Rotolo 1965: 151–3.

Greek non-vernacularists ever explicitly contrasted their procedure with the one that had been carried out in French. Despite the fact that he was living in France and using the French language on a daily basis, and despite the fact that in 1803 he wrote that the Greek language of his day was a new language, which was 'almost at the same stage as French was in the age of Montaigne',[76] Korais ignored the French example completely by tampering with some of the most basic elements of the vocabulary and grammar of Modern Greek.[77] This was because, as Rea Delveroudi has pointed out, the constitutive myth of the French language is clarity, which is predicated on its emancipation from Latin, whereas Korais and other Greek purists emphasized the continuity of the Greek language since antiquity.[78]

When a nation's civilization is killed off by slavery, writes Korais, 'the entire nation returns to its original barbarity'.[79] This is the converse of the Herderian and romantic belief that the language and songs of the folk encapsulate the soul of the nation. Korais showed no interest in folk culture, and remained silent about Claude Fauriel's collection of Greek folk songs, published in Paris in 1824–25, even though Fauriel was greatly assisted in his work by members of Korais' circle.[80] Similarly, Korais – who, it must be admitted, was an old man by this time – ignored the poetry of Andreas Kalvos and Dionysios Solomos, which began to be published in 1824–25 and which could be claimed to mark the beginning of Greek national literature. This poetry included Solomos' *Hymn to Liberty*, later to become Greece's National Anthem, which was published in the second volume of Fauriel's collection. According to Dimaras, Korais was suspicious of romanticism's turn towards religiosity and the Middle Ages.[81]

The ideological influence of the prestigious Ancient Greek language on the development of the Greek written language in the early nineteenth century can be seen in relief when we contrast the reform of the Serbian literary language undertaken by Vuk Karadžić (1787–1864), who was

---

[76] Coray 1803: 56.

[77] Korais may have been influenced by the Abbé Grégoire's *Rapport sur la nécessité et les moyens d'anéantir les patois et d'universaliser l'usage de la langue française*, which was sent, by order of the National Convention in Paris, to all authorities and all the communes of the Republic in 1792.

[78] Delveroudi 2008b.   [79] Korais 1829: p. xxiv.

[80] The core of Fauriel's collection came from the 1814 manuscript collection of songs compiled by Theodoros Manousis (later to become the first professor of history at Athens University), which was passed on to him by Korais himself (A. Politis 1974). It is possible that Korais had not even troubled to read it.

[81] Korais 1829: p. xxvii; K. Th. Dimaras 1985: 112.

a generation younger than Korais, had fought in the Serbian uprising (1804–13), and did not possess a universally adulated ancient language against which to measure the modern vernacular. Vuk succeeded in modernizing the Serbian written language and distancing it from both the Serbian and Russian versions of Church Slavonic. By the 1820s he had published a *Grammar of the Serbian Language* (1814), a *Dictionary of the Serbian language* (Serbian–German–Latin, 1818), two collections of Serbian folk songs (1814 and 1815), a collection of Serbian folk tales (1821), and the first part of a translation of the New Testament into Serbian (1824). In these works he laid the foundations for a new literary language whose roots lay in the speech of country folk rather than that of urban dwellers, working successfully to establish spoken usage as the basis for the written language of the southern Slavs. By contrast, few Greek writers before 1850 made a serious study of the songs and language of the uneducated folk.[82]

The impact of Korais' ideas

The 'Letter to Alexandros Vasileiou' (1804), which gained Korais both supporters and opponents, marked the beginning of an often vituperative dispute that lasted until the outbreak of the War of Independence in 1821, dividing Greek intellectuals into warring camps. Since Korais came from the bourgeois-mercantile class, it was to be expected that his views would gain widespread and enthusiastic acceptance among the influential Greek merchants of the diaspora. However, many other intellectuals who had hitherto differed from each other on linguistic matters came to see Korais as the common enemy. One of the reasons why the reaction against him was so indignant is that Korais tended to ignore or condemn both contemporary linguistic usage and the immediately preceding written tradition.

Criticism of Korais came from vernacularists, conservatives, and archaists alike, as we will see in Chapter 5. Dimaras has pointed out that the archaist Athanasios Stageiritis confused Korais' theories with the vernacularism of Katartzis, while the vernacularist Solomos identified them with Doukas' archaism. Korais himself lamented that he was

---

[82] Among the few exceptions is the Greek translation of Jernej Kopitar's review of Leake's *Researches in Greece*, which praises Vuk's collection of Serbian folk songs. The anonymous translator (probably Manousis) takes the opportunity to add a footnote in which he praises Herder and asserts the national importance of collecting Greek folk songs; see *Akolouthia* 1816: 401.

attacked from both sides: '[S]uch has always been the fate of those who counsel the middle way,' he wrote in 1812.[83] Many of the objections against his theory and practice were based on tiny details such as some of the more absurd of his 'corrections', in which he refused to use either the modern or the ancient form of certain common words, preferring hybrid forms of his own invention such as the future forms mentioned above. Others ridiculed Korais for some of his attempts to attribute Ancient Greek etymologies to certain modern words that are actually of foreign origin.[84]

Korais never became a member of the *Filikí Etaireía*, and he seems to have been unaware of the plans for the revolution.[85] When the revolution came, however, the leaders of the nation were keen to acknowledge Korais' status as its cultural precursor. For instance, the third national assembly, which took place at Troezen in April 1827, sent an official document to Korais expressing the respect and esteem of the nation for his ideas.[86] In the brief autobiography that he wrote in the same year, he recalled that in 1805 he had believed that the revolution would break out in the middle of the century, by which time his teaching and that of others would have filtered through to the Greeks more thoroughly, with the result that they would have acted and fought more like their ancient forebears.[87]

It is characteristic of his outlook that he advised a friend concerning the Souliots in 1803: '[I]f there was a way for you to teach some of their children the Hellenic language (that is, the language of liberty), you would give them an incomparably more useful gift than Prometheus' fire';[88] by 'Hellenic' he means Ancient Greek, and by 'Prometheus' fire' he is alluding to firearms. Less than a year before the outbreak of the war, he wrote: 'Only education [i.e. not arms] can liberate us from the insufferable yoke of the Scythian [i.e. Turkish] nation.'[89] In other words, for Korais, a moral and educational revolution was the prerequisite for a political revolution. His great fear was that if political independence were gained prematurely, the Ottomans would simply be replaced by Greek tyrants such as the Fanariots and the local Greek notables, who, in

---

[83] K. Th. Dimaras 1985: 487; 1984: 16; Korais 1984b: 519 [1812].

[84] Nevertheless, Korais was one of the first to discover the correct etymologies of a large number of Modern Greek words.

[85] Daskalakis 1966: 171–2.   [86] Kitromilides 1996: 422.

[87] Korais 1984b: pp. xxviii–xxix. For an English translation of Korais' autobiography see Clogg 1976b: 119–30.

[88] Korais to Idromenos, 27 Nov. 1803, in Korais 1966: 122.

[89] Korais to Tombazis, 14 June 1820, in Korais 1982: 238.

his view, had gained power, wealth, and prestige from their collaboration with the Ottoman regime. As Douglas Dakin put it, '[t]he Greek upper classes wanted Ottoman society without the Turks', as opposed to a democratic nation-state.[90] This succinctly sums up Korais' attitude; a text he wrote in 1830 is entitled, 'What is it profitable for Greece, liberated from the Turks, to do in order not to be enslaved to Turkified Christians?' In his correspondence Korais variously describes the Fanariots as 'un tas d'ignorants intrigants', 'those who slave for the Scythian [i.e. Turk]' and 'Scythian mannikins'.[91]

Korais' linguistic ideas became hugely influential, and his version of Greek was taken up by a number of writers before the War of Independence. His principle – though not the details of his practice – of linguistic correction was accepted by the majority of purists for a century and a half after his death. According to Sathas, Dimitrios Darvaris was the first to espouse Korais' ideas in his *Simple-Hellenic Grammar* (1806).[92] The theory and practice of his language were particularly disseminated by the first Greek scholarly journal, *Ermis o Logios* [*The Learned Hermes*], published in Vienna by some of his associates between 1811 and 1821. Some of Korais' opponents published their own magazines in which they attacked his views. After the outbreak of the War of Independence, however, no further attack on Korais' linguistic theory and practice was published.[93]

Before the War, Konstantinos Oikonomos and Konstantinos Koumas adopted Korais' teachings at the Philological Gymnasium in Smyrna, while Theofilos Kaïris put them into practice at Kydonies [Ayvali] and Korais' close friend and disciple Neofytos Vamvas applied them at the school in his native Chios, where he was headmaster from 1815 to 1821.[94]

[90] Dakin 1972: 44.
[91] Korais to Vasileiou, 5–12 Dec. 1811, in Korais 1979: 162; *c*.29 Sept. 1816, ibid., 505. In his correspondence Korais called Kodrikas the 'fratricide Cain' and the 'Turkish *andrápodon* [slave]' (Korais to Rotas, 31 Dec. 1818, in Korais 1982: 127; to Kokkinakis, 10 Apr. 1819, ibid., 158).
[92] Darvaris 1806: 396; Sathas 1870: 270–2.
[93] Daskalakis 1966: 188–9. *Ermis o Logios* was initially funded by the Philological Society of Bucharest, which was founded and run by metropolitan Ignatios during his culturally and educationally fruitful stay in the Wallachian capital (1810–12). In view of the erroneous claim that all the Fanariots were linguistic conservatives or even archaists, it is instructive that from 1818 to 1821 *Ermis o Logios* was subsidized by two successive princes of Moldavia, Skarlatos Kallimachis and Michail Soutsos (Camariano-Cioran 1975).
[94] See Oikonomos' speech of 4 September 1811 inaugurating the third year of operation of the Philological Gymnasium (Oikonomos 1811), which adopts many of Korais' ideas while preserving a traditional attitude towards religion; and the introduction to Koumas 1812, reprinted

Despite the reverence accorded to him by members of the political and intellectual elite during and after the War of Independence, however, the practical influence of his particular variety of written Modern Greek is not clearly perceptible. Early official documents, such as the declarations of the first national assemblies, are written in a moderately archaized version of the vernacular, but they do not use Korais' trademark linguistic forms. The *Grammar of Ancient and Modern Hellenic Language for Beginners* (1835) by Vamvas, which enshrines the older man's linguistic precepts and practice, including the juxtaposition and comparison between the (almost identical) morphology of Ancient and 'corrected' Modern Greek, could be described as the grammar that Korais never published.[95] However, the fashion during the period from the 1830s to the 1850s was to bring the contemporary written language gradually closer to Ancient Greek in form; Dimaras points out that few of Korais' followers remained faithful to his version of the language after his death, and even Vamvas eventually went with the archaic flow.[96]

in K. Th. Dimaras 1953: 347–60. Koumas remained Korais' most faithful and consistent follower (K. Th. Dimaras 1985: 106, 382–4).

[95] In keeping with Korais' Protestant connections, Vamvas' grammar (Vamvas 1835) was published '[a]t the Philhellenic Printing Press from America by the Reverend I. I. Robertson'. Vamvas was the chief Modern Greek translator of the Bible employed by the British and Foreign Bible Society.

[96] K. Th. Dimaras 1985: 115, 374.

5

Alternative proposals to Korais' project, 1804–1830

While a substantial number of intellectuals were prepared to follow Korais' precept and example, his proposed language reforms became the subject of heated debate in the years preceding the Greek revolution. Much of the reaction against Korais came from two groups: (a) archaists, some of whom were revivalists, in the sense that they believed that Ancient Greek could become the natural spoken language of the modern Greeks, and (b) political and linguistic conservatives who refused to countenance a change in the socio-political *status quo* and felt that Korais' campaign to persuade the Greeks to espouse his Enlightenment and secularist ideas was an unwarranted interference in Greek cultural affairs. The vernacularists too attacked Korais' linguistic ideas, but few of their writings were published at the time. The archaists and conservatives seem to have rarely thought it worthwhile to attack the vernacularists, since there seemed little likelihood that their views would carry the day. In this chapter I will summarize the arguments of each of these three groups (archaists, conservatives, and vernacularists) in turn.

Korais' publications gave rise to two chronologically overlapping language wars, one instigated by the archaist Doukas and the other by the conservative Kodrikas.[1] Much effort was invested in sometimes libellous attacks and counter-attacks emanating from each side, as the leaders of the differing factions jockeyed for the position of cultural leaders who would steer the Greeks towards the desired future. Korais' opponents, of whatever linguistic persuasion, were united in seeing him as an upstart from a mercantile background who had long been out of contact with the realities of Greek life and therefore had no right to claim cultural authority. In fact, mercantile circles were tending to supplant the Church in the cultural leadership of Greek society, as merchants provided funds

---

[1] Contrary to the commonly expressed view, going back to Kordatos 1927, that Kodrikas was a linguistic archaist, Rotolo 1965: 119 rightly describes him as a conservative in language.

for the foundation of schools both within Ottoman lands and in the diaspora,[2] and the dispute between Korais and Kodrikas was in effect a struggle between the champions of these two groups.

Archaists: Kommitas and Doukas

One of the leading archaists was the monk and schoolteacher Stefanos Kommitas (Thessaly, *c*.1770–*c*.1833), who in a grammar of Ancient Greek published in 1800 was the first to promote the use of Ancient Greek in writing with the aim that all Greeks (not just the learned) would become accustomed to its common use;[3] it was precisely such revivalism that Korais was reacting against. In the same grammar Kommitas attacks those who argue that grammars should be written in the vulgar dialect ('let us not willingly reach that extent of lunacy') and claims that the vulgar language is barbarous, uncultivated, and unregulated and that it would be futile to beautify it.[4]

He went on to publish a twelve-volume grammar of Ancient Greek, written in Ancient Greek (1812–14), which was too unwieldy to be of any practical use. In an article announcing the future publication of the first three volumes of this grammar, Kommitas holds it self-evident that 'the Hellenic language is the most praised, admired and desired by all nations, thought and said to be the language of the Gods and the Muses.... Our spoken language is a dialect of the whole Hellenic language and..., well formed and purged of the foreign words and idioms, it will become [Attic].'[5] Attic, he continues, is the most noble and most extensive dialect of the whole Hellenic language, just as Etruscan [i.e. Tuscan] is of Italian, Saxon is of German, and Parisian is of French. Kommitas here uses the same illogical and a-historical analogy that Lampros Fotiadis had done in his correspondence with Katartzis.[6] We consider our mother tongue to be none other than the Hellenic, he writes. It would be wrong to separate 'our dialect' from the 'whole Hellenic language'; it is precisely by avoiding doing so that we have been prevented from sinking into complete barbarity. The Church has assisted in this by preserving the only *agathón* [asset] that has remained in our possession (i.e. our language).[7]

---

[2] Kitromilides 1996: 78.   [3] Kommitas 1800, quoted in Daskalakis 1966: 10.

[4] Kommitas 1800: p. xvii.

[5] Even though Kommitas' 'purgation' makes him sound like Korais, it should be borne in mind that the latter was decidedly against taking the modern language back to ancient Attic.

[6] Even though the Fotiadis–Katartzis correspondence was not published until the following year, Kommitas may already have known it through Doukas.

[7] Kommitas 1811: 101–2.

Kommitas' views are markedly different from those of Korais, who, despite his archaization of Modern Greek, was keen to treat the modern language as a separate variety, and he gave the Church little credit for having preserved the Hellenic language. Some of Kommitas' attacks on Korais' linguistic views took the form of personal slanders. An example of this sort of vituperative language is to be found in a text written (though not published) in 1815 by Kommitas against what he called 'the heresy of the Koraists'. In this text (which, unusually for this author, is not written in Ancient Greek) Kommitas, having fulminated against the vernacularist doctrines of Katartzis, attacks Korais and his followers by using the language of religious fanaticism: Korais is 'impious', a 'heresiarch' and an 'atheist' as well as being *misellin* [anti-Greek], and he is motivated solely by *doxomanía* [lust for glory].[8] The accusation that Korais was leading a linguistic heresy was influenced by the fact that he kept his distance from the Orthodox hierarchy.

Korais' chief adversary among the archaists, however, was Neofytos Doukas, who accused him in various pamphlets of attempting to sabotage the 'rebirth of Hellas' by sowing division among its people, whereas in fact Korais was trying to bring them together by means of compromise.[9] Doukas' first publication was a grammar of Ancient Greek (1804), which was written in Ancient Greek and dedicated to his teacher Lampros Fotiadis, followed the next year by a practical educational programme for the teaching of the ancient language.[10] He also published Ancient Greek texts for use in schools, and his ambitious programme of editions – apparently published without subsidy – made him a serious rival to Korais. Between 1805 and 1814, while he was serving as Orthodox parish priest and teacher of Greek in Vienna, he published no fewer than thirty-six volumes containing editions of ancient authors; the first nineteen volumes include his translations of the ancient texts into somewhat archaic language. The texts that Doukas chose to edit are prose works by authors from Classical Athens and from the Atticist movement that flourished during the Roman period;[11] unlike Korais, Doukas saw Classical Attic prose as the model for imitation. In this phase of his publishing activity, Doukas avoided editing poetry, arguing that 'poetics has many other virtues, but it corrupts the language'. Between 1834 and his death in 1845,

---

[8] Skouvaras 1965: 278, 281–2, 304. Kodrikas too described Korais' ideas as 'heresy' (Kodrikas 1817).

[9] Doukas 1814: 310. As we have seen, Korais had already used the phrase 'the rebirth of Hellas' in 1807.

[10] Doukas 1804, 1805.   [11] For Doukas' editions of ancient texts see Charilaou 2007.

however, he edited almost the whole corpus of Classical Greek poetry – an undertaking that Neofytos Charilaou attributes to the 'romantic turn' in Greece after independence.[12]

Whereas Katartzis concentrated on the language that the Greeks actually speak, Doukas aimed to produce more Hellenes by propagating the Greek language.[13] Like Korais, he was a linguistic nationalist who normally defined the nation in terms of its language: '[T]he characteristic of a nation, more than anything else, is its language'.[14] Doukas was the prototype of a breed of selfless yet pedantic Greek schoolmasters who were so dazzled by the wonders of the Ancient Greek language that they were incapable of making any illuminating comments on the content of the texts. His colossal oeuvre is a monument to altruistic dedication and mental confusion. He asserted that, at least in some circumstances, the language of a text is more important than its content.[15] He seems to have confused knowledge of grammar with knowledge of words and concepts and to have believed that the former would automatically lead to the latter. His own style is rambling, repetitive, and convoluted, and his language is inconsistent. In 1804 he proclaimed that the language of the Greeks should be 'that of the documents issued by the Patriarchates, which, if cultivated, is capable of attaining its ancient distinction'.[16] Later, however, he declared himself in favour of the use of Ancient Greek as such.[17] Like Kommitas (and like Voulgaris earlier), he did not use Ancient Greek in all his writings: much later, in 1824, he contradicted his earlier statement by claiming that he used *archaia* [i.e. Ancient Greek] for philosophy and *neótera* [i.e. Modern Greek] for other subjects;[18] Doukas was one of the few Greeks of the pre-1830 period to use the adjectives *archaia* [original or ancient] and *neótera* [newer or modern] to refer to the Greek language. In whatever variety he wrote, his grammar presents a jumble of ancient and modern forms. This inconsistency, both in attitudes to language and in the actual language varieties used, was one of the greatest weaknesses in the archaists' armoury. Korais may have been inconsistent in his practical use of Greek morphology, but at least he wanted a single grammar to be used for all written purposes.

---

[12] Doukas 1808: xxiii; Charilaou 2007: 296.   [13] Sigalas 2004: 125.

[14] Doukas 1814: 300.   [15] Doukas 1834: p. xxix.

[16] This appears to bring Doukas close to the views later stated by Kodrikas, except that the latter believed that this variety of Greek was already sufficiently cultivated.

[17] Daskalakis 1966: 10.

[18] Doukas 1834: p. xxiii; this text is dated 1824. He also wrote some texts in the vernacular, notably an open letter addressed to the inhabitants of his native village (Doukas 1813c; slightly adapted extracts in Valetas 1947: 84–6).

Doukas argued that foreigners would continue to think the Greeks barbarous until they spoke Ancient Greek; the whole of Europe was awaiting the rebirth of Ancient Greek in its homeland, whereas Korais, he alleged, was doing his best to undermine this effort. Doukas was proud of having taught himself Ancient Greek without help from the 'enlightened Europeans', and was thus opposed to Korais' insistence that Greeks should be educated abroad: he claimed that, if young Greeks were taught at school to speak a language as close to Ancient Greek as possible, and if they taught it to their children as their first language, each generation would bring their spoken language closer to its mother, so that by the third generation it would be united with her – in other words, the Greeks would speak Ancient Greek as their natural language. He also predicted that Ancient Greek would become the language of universities and parliaments, and eventually of the common people, throughout Europe.[19]

Doukas' campaign against Korais' linguistic theory and practice began in 1808[20] and ended in 1815 when he moved from Vienna to take up an appointment as headmaster of the Princely Academy in Bucharest. In 1809 Korais' friend Alexandros Vasileiou published a personal counter-attack on Doukas' linguistic ideas and editorial practice,[21] which sparked off an exchange of polemical pamphlets that are characterized by the poverty of their ideas and the inconsistency of their arguments.[22] In 1812 Doukas divided contemporary Greek authors, according to their language, into *makaronistaí* [macaronists], *trakaristaí* [bunglers or bodgers], and *chydaïstaí* [vulgarists]. The 'bunglers' were Korais and his followers, whose 'middle way' was vividly described by Doukas, taking his metaphor from the philosophy of language, as 'the instantaneous present between the past and the future'[23] – the vulgar vernacular being, in his view, the past and Ancient Greek the future. In this text Doukas included himself among the exponents of macaronism, which he defined as 'the gradual progress of the language towards its ancient perfection'.[24] He does not seem to have been aware that, in the original sense of the word, macaronism (the mixing of Latin with modern Romance languages) was

---

[19] Doukas 1814: 339, 337.   [20] Doukas 1808: 1–181.

[21] Vasileiou (ed.) 1809, a critique of Doukas 1808. The texts contained in this pamphlet, presented as an exchange of letters between two friends, were written by Vasileiou and Konstantinos Koumas (Charilaou 2002: 314–15).

[22] Rotolo 1965: 105. For a thorough account of the Doukas–Korais dispute see Charilaou 2002: 297–501.

[23] Doukas 1812a: 24. My rendering of *trakaristís* as 'bungler' or 'bodger' is due to the interpretation 'poor craftsman' provided by Frankiskos 1995: 246.

[24] Doukas 1812a: 5–7.

intended to be comic. Macaronism was in essence the lazy option: even though the archaists promoted an archaic version of Greek, they did not always feel it necessary to follow all of the rules of the ancient language.

Unlike Korais, Doukas conceived of Ancient and Modern Greek as essentially the same language, though he was far more ignorant than his adversary about its historical development. In a text of 1814 entitled 'On the spoken language' and addressed 'To the wise correctors of the language', Doukas writes:

The language..., according to the doctrine of purging it of foreign [material], is, without contradiction, nearer to Attic than are all of the other dialects, indeed almost identical to it, since they, such as Doric, Aeolic and Ionic, differ from it in sounds and inflection.

By contrast, he maintains, this 'purged' language alone has preserved the sounds and forms unchanged. He goes on to ask the 'correctors' why they insist on importing forms that are due to the ignorance of the mob. 'It is beneficial, o Hellenes,' he writes, 'that we approach the Hellenes, because we are Hellenes.'[25]

In 1824, during the revolution, he wrote:

If foreigners ask us in what way we are superior to other nations, we cannot yet say in *evnomía* [good government] and riches; we can only say in the language of the forefathers: in this consists our Hellenic character; in other respects we are as we are, more naked than the proverbial pestle.

He seems to have lacked any sense that the Greeks could achieve anything new. In the same text he writes that 'we must learn the language of the ancestors more perfectly if we wish to remain Hellenes'. These sentiments have been frequently echoed by many Greek intellectual leaders since that time. 'If ancient authors are taught in translation in the poor common language,' he argued, 'the Greeks will remain Greeks and not Hellenes. How can they be called Hellenes if they do not use the Hellenic language?'[26] For the same reason, he steadfastly opposed Korais' insistence that Ancient Greek should be taught through the medium of the modern language.

As he put it himself, the current dispute was not between philosophy and poetry (as it had been in Plato), but between philosophy and grammar.[27] He sometimes implies, as he does here, that Ancient Greek

---

[25] Doukas 1814: 311, 342.   [26] Doukas 1834: pp. xx, xxvii, lxiii.
[27] Doukas 1813b: 11, 12. This battle between philosophy and grammar is reminiscent of 'the final victory of rhetoric in the long battle between rhetoric and philosophy for primacy in

grammar is all one needs in order to become educated, enlightened, and virtuous, though elsewhere he expresses himself in favour of 'philosophy' too. However, he explicitly stated that education in the physical sciences must only take place after a thorough grounding in Ancient Greek grammar.[28]

He once asserted that 'the common people, the unlettered mob' does not need demonstrations of electricity or Condillac's *Logic*, but grammar. In the light of this statement, it is curious that, according to Dimaras, Doukas appears to have been influenced by Condillac's philosophy of language. Quoting two passages from Doukas, Dimaras claims that a misinterpretation of Condillac's ideas led Doukas to believe that the speaking of Ancient Greek would automatically grant access to the ideas of the ancients and lead to similar intellectual achievements.[29] 'If we condescend, in the character of our discourse, to the capabilities of the vulgar folk,' he argues, implicitly criticizing Korais,[30] 'it will be impossible for us to go beyond their few ideas (since incomprehension of language is due to the conception of the thing rather than that of the word)'; conversely, 'if we imitate phrases, we also imitate the good [content] of discourse, and we have the imitation of our ancestors'.[31] This implies a mechanistic equation between a particular variety of language on the one hand, and specific moral behaviour and political ideas on the other. As so often, however, Doukas' convoluted thought processes fail to provide us with clear and unambiguous statements: in his writing he allows what he called 'ancient beauty' to take precedence over clarity.

As we have seen, Doukas' ideas were sometimes met with considerable hostility from the ecclesiastical hierarchy and from some of the Fanariots. By contrast, the fact that he was a revivalist did not stop Doukas from remaining on friendly terms with vernacularists such as his fellow Epirots Vilaras and Psalidas, who were equally opposed to Korais' 'middle way'.

[Greek] education' during the Roman period (Trypanis 1984: 33), Doukas' 'grammar' being equivalent to ancient rhetoric.

[28] Doukas 1813a: pp. viii–ix, quoted in Charilaou 2002: 401.

[29] K. Th. Dimaras 1985: 112.

[30] See Korais: '[I]s it only the learned who need to condescend to the uneducated?' (Chapter 4, p. 114).

[31] Doukas 1812a: 7 and *Ermou* 1813: 34. K. Th. Dimaras (1985: 17) notes that the first of these passages appears in a text that attempts to rebut the ideas of Korais rather than those of the vernacularists.

Conservatives: Kodrikas and the ecclesiastical and Fanariot establishment

A highly influential campaign against Korais was launched by Panagiotis Kodrikas, who had stayed on in the French capital as a translator and interpreter at the French Ministry of Foreign Affairs after the Ottoman Embassy closed down in 1802. From then on he became Korais' *bête noire*, as each of them – beginning with the publication of Korais' *Mémoire sur l'état actuel de la civilisation dans la Grèce* in 1803 and Kodrikas' *Observations sur l'opinion de quelques hellénistes touchant le grec moderne* in the following year[32] – competed with each other to be the most influential and respected Greek resident in Paris. Kodrikas' *Observations* aimed to defend the modern Greeks and their language against the calumnies of various European writers. As we have seen in Chapter 3, Kodrikas was by no means averse to modern philosophy; yet, as Dimaras points out, he shared with other Fanariots a remarkable facility for adapting to changing circumstances.[33]

Kodrikas must have been discomfited by the fact that, in his *Mémoire*, Korais described the Greek clergy as 'superstitious and ignorant' and castigated 'the self-styled notables of the nation, whose supposed nobility, nourished by the sweat of the people whom they oppressed, was even more laughable because, placed between the government and the people, they were forced to degrade themselves all the more before the idol of despotism'.[34] One of the texts contained in Vasileiou's 1809 pamphlet against Doukas must have increased Kodrikas' indignation, since it claimed that 'the few nobles of Constantinople' could not be seen as a model for language; rather, the pamphlet argued, it was the 'farmers of Hellas,... who constitute the majority of the nation' whose language should be corrected, purged of foreign elements, and adorned in such a way that it would be clear to them without being distasteful to the wise.[35] By contrast, in 1804 Kodrikas had promoted the 'universal language of the Greek nation' spoken by 'la partie saine de la nation', that is, by the 'distinguished class' of men who are marked out by the nation for their education and learning.[36] Korais and Kodrikas obviously had differing conceptions of the nation.

His quarrel with Korais – the most heated of those in which Korais became involved – had been brewing for many years. Kodrikas saw him as a threat to the control of the patriarchate and the Fanariots over

---

[32] Coray 1803; Codrika 1804.   [33] K. Th. Dimaras 1985: 352.   [34] Coray 1803: 7.
[35] Vasileiou 1809: 47–8.   [36] Codrika 1804: 15–16

Greek education and culture, while Korais saw Kodrikas as a traitor to his nation for having served as an Ottoman civil servant and diplomat and for having associated himself with the Fanariots, whom Korais despised as a throwback to Byzantium and as collaborators of the Turks in their barbaric occupation of Greece. Kodrikas' defence of the modern Greeks and their language against slanders uttered by Europeans suggested to Korais as early as 1804 that the younger man was attempting to challenge his monopoly over the dissemination of knowledge about modern Greece in France.[37] But, like a true Fanariot, Kodrikas knew how to bide his time. In 1816, after the restoration of the Bourbon monarchy following the hiatus of the revolution and the Napoleonic era,[38] and after the pamphlet war between Korais and Doukas had come to an end, Kodrikas came out into the open for the first time and attacked Korais, albeit not by name, in an open letter sent to the new editors of the Viennese journal *The Learned Hermes*, Theoklitos Farmakidis and Konstantinos Kokkinakis.[39] In his letter Kodrikas advised the editors to use the 'thoroughly refined and universally habitual style of the dialect' rather than that of the 'self-appointed correctors', which includes 'vulgar words' and the 'wittily ridiculed *korakistiká*',[40] which have been 'inelegantly extracted from the Greco-barbarian lexica of the writers of Turcograecia' and which 'are to be condemned as crimes of high treason against the public authority of the national dominion'.[41] In keeping with his use of the kind of political analogy that Korais himself was fond of using, Kodrikas connects the imposition of such usages with the rabble-rousers of the French revolution.[42] This text was Kodrikas' first bid for the leadership of the anti-Koraist camp.[43]

Kodrikas' first salvo was followed by a violent exchange of views with Korais in a series of pamphlets. In an anonymous and petulant pamphlet published in 1817 and again in 1818, Kodrikas accused Korais of dividing the nation into *Graikoí* and Hellenes, and into Koraists and anti-Koraists.[44] In another pamphlet, published anonymously in 1818,

---

[37] Korais' private expressions of his disapproval of Kodrikas' behaviour date from at least 1803; see his letter to Vasileiou, 23 Feb. 1803, in Korais 1966: 71, where he accuses Kodrikas of getting a reviewer of Korais' *Mémoire* to imply, falsely, that Korais praised Kodrikas' translation of Fontenelle.

[38] K. Th. Dimaras 1985: 358.

[39] This text was published as Kodrikas 1816, republished in Daskalakis 1966: 195–205.

[40] Here Kodrikas refers to Neroulos' comedy *Korakistika* (see below).

[41] Kodrikas in Daskalakis 1966: 195–7. Here Kodrikas quotes some of the more misguided of Korais' 'corrected' forms.

[42] Kodrikas, ibid., 200.   [43] Ibid., 61.   [44] Kodrikas 1817, in Dimaras 1953: 273.

Kodrikas alleged that Korais was undermining the language, the *genos* [nation] and religion.[45]

In the same year Kodrikas brought out his heavy artillery by setting out his ideas on Modern Greek in his *Study of the Common Hellenic Dialect*, which was the only full-length book devoted entirely to the Greek language question before 1821. The *Study*, presented in the form of a scholarly treatise, much of it covering the history of the Greek language since antiquity, aimed to refute the arguments put forward by Korais in his 'Impromptu Thoughts'.[46] Kodrikas had been planning the *Study* since before 1810,[47] but much of its argument can be traced back to his *Observations* of 1804. Its publication was financed by some Greek merchants, and it was printed in 1,000 copies and widely distributed. In this 400-page book, he set out to defend the attitudes and the language of what he saw as the Greek establishment, namely the patriarchate and the Fanariots, and to attack the 'correctors of the language', characteristically without ever once mentioning Korais' name.

Kodrikas' title was astutely chosen: he was studying the 'common' language, as opposed to the idiosyncratic 'corrected' language that Korais was allegedly concocting; this language was Hellenic (i.e. Modern Greek was not separate from Ancient Greek, but together they formed a single language); and 'dialect' because Kodrikas was specifying the particular kind or variety of language that should be used in writing. Kodrikas distinguishes between what he calls the 'common dialect' – the variety of Modern Greek written by the Fanariot princes and the prelates of the Orthodox Church, whose use he defends – and the 'demotic dialect' (the local colloquial language that differed from region to region);[48] in his view, Korais' language fits into neither of these categories. By 'common dialect', then, Kodrikas means a generally accepted variety of Modern Greek, in contrast to the ancient language, the local dialects, and Korais' 'corrected' version of the modern language.

In practice the language that Kodrikas uses in his book is very close in form to that of Korais, though perhaps less systematic in the application of rules. What was important was not so much the actual variety of language used, as the rationale one employed in its support. As Emmanouil Moschonas writes, 'the distinctive features are to be found more in

---

[45] Daskalakis 1966: 84.

[46] Iliou 1997: 552. The volume of the *Study* published in 1818 was announced as being volume 1, but Kodrikas was prevented by the outbreak of the revolution from completing the planned second volume.

[47] Daskalakis 1966: 110.   [48] Kodrikas 1988: 132.

their consciousness of what they believed each particular version of the language to represent than in the actual result'.[49]

Like Korais, Kodrikas argued that only language – by which he means mother tongue – can truly distinguish between nations, for it is the surest marker of *ethnikí ýparxis* [national existence].[50] What he has to say about an earlier language reformer, Iosipos Moisiodax, whom he knew in Bucharest, is illuminating. According to Kodrikas, Moisiodax was

foreign by birth to the *Genos* [Nation] of the Hellenes, and consequently not having tasted the milk of Hellenic nurture. Furthermore, he learned the Hellenic language through study and not through habit and natural use from infancy. His eyesight and his mind were exercised in the reading of the old [i.e. ancient] authors, but his hearing was not accustomed to the harmony of the dialect of the New Hellenes. Therefore it was not easy for him either to imitate the sophisticated *frasis* [language variety] of the Authors, or to express himself genuinely in the simple demotic dialect. Thus he too resorted to the trite refuge of half-learned teachers, that the common language of the New Hellenes is corrupt and requires correction.

As soon as it made its appearance, continues Kodrikas, the arbitrarily corrected language of Moisiodax was, by common consent, declared to be *pakkálikon yfos* [grocers' style].[51] This is one of the very few instances where an author writing in Greek criticizes the written Greek of another author on the grounds that he is not of Greek origin. Kodrikas' pride in being an Athenian rather than an inhabitant of more northerly Balkan regions overlooks the significant proportion of Albanian speakers among the inhabitants of Athens and Attica in his time.

Kodrikas begins his book with the words already quoted in the first epigraph to my book. Elsewhere he writes that what is at stake is 'not simply two or three little Graecobarbarian words', but 'the chiefest *éthima* [manifestations of culture] of our *Genos*'.[52] Kodrikas' worship of Ancient Greek was equal to Korais': he talks of 'the celestial Hellenic Language, that archetypal construct of preternatural inventiveness'.[53] Although he sometimes distinguishes, as Korais does, between 'the old and the new language',[54] he talks about the *akeraiotis* [integrity, unity] of the Greek language from ancient to modern times, and one of his criticisms of Korais is that he disconnects the modern language from Ancient Greek.

---

[49] Moschonas 1981: p. xxix.   [50] Kodrikas 1988: p. iii.   [51] Ibid., p. xxv.
[52] Ibid., p. lii.   [53] Ibid., 204.   [54] Ibid., 234, 241.

Kodrikas argued that the language of the *spoudaioi* [learned] has rejected foreign words such as are to be found, in his erroneous view, in the seventeenth-century Cretan romance *Erotokritos*;[55] yet it is not to be confused with *mixovárvara*, the mixture of 'barbarized' Modern Greek with Classical Attic on which (like all other Greek authors of his time) he showers contempt. He also politely chides archaists such as Doukas.[56] He takes a sympathetic view of 'the ingenious system of Katartzis concerning the *Romaic Language*' – probably because Katartzis too was a member of the Fanariot circle – but he considers it to be impracticable because this 'vulgar' variety represents only the language of Constantinople, while writers should be aiming at a common (i.e. universal) variety of Greek, based on the whole language rather than on a single local dialect.[57] Interestingly, Kodrikas calls Katartzis' language 'poetic', suggesting that because the unadulterated vernacular had hitherto only been cultivated in poetry, it was bound to have a certain lyrical undertone.[58] He could envisage Athanasios Christopoulos' version of the vernacular being used for poetry and drama, but not for scholarly writing.[59] Apparently following Christopoulos, whose views we shall discuss below, Kodrikas states that Modern Greek is a mixture of features derived from various Ancient Greek dialects.[60] He does not mention the more recent vernacular programme of Vilaras and Psalidas.[61] In sum, Kodrikas opposed those who used ancient Attic, those who used a regional variety, and those who tried to purify the language by correcting it.[62]

'The Hellenic *Genos*, amid the direst calamities, has preserved its national integrity, because it has preserved the language of its ancestors', writes Kodrikas. He particularly objects to Korais' allegation that Modern Greek has been 'corrupted', since this implies that 'the national existence of the Hellenic *Genos* is unfounded and problematic'.[63] He argues that the traditional written language used by the Church hierarchy and the nobles (i.e. the Fanariots), among whom he includes himself, originated in the *koine* of the New Testament and the Byzantine liturgy. This form of the language, he claims, which has been handed down from generation to generation and has no need of self-appointed 'correctors' or 'legislators',

---

[55] Kodrikas shows that he is unfamiliar with the *Erotokritos*: while it is written in a literary version of spoken Cretan dialect, it contains very few words of foreign origin. The younger Constantinopolitan Stefanos Kanelos similarly criticizes the *Erotokritos* for the numerous Italian loanwords it allegedly contains; see Iken 1825: I 164–9, mentioned in Lauxtermann 2007: 135.

[56] Kodrikas 1988: pp. lxxii–lxxiii.   [57] Ibid., pp. xxvi–xxxiv.

[58] Ibid., 174; K. Th. Dimaras 1985: 212.   [59] Kodrikas 1988: pp. xliv–xlv.

[60] See e.g. ibid., 241.   [61] Angelou 1998: 111.   [62] Rotolo 1965: 124.

[63] Kodrikas 1988: p. iii.

is the best kind of written Greek available today and is accepted by the whole nation (hence it is 'common'). The adjective 'self-appointed' is intended to contrast the upstart Korais with the patriarchs, princes, and their civil servants, who, according to Kodrikas, have been elected to public office – though this kind of election is far from the truly democratic election that Korais had in mind. Kodrikas implies that Korais, by contrast, is an anarchist, opposed to all hierarchies, and particularly that of the Orthodox Church and the patriarchate, with which Kodrikas clearly wanted to identify himself.

Most of all, Kodrikas' quarrel with Korais was based on the determination of a powerful traditional aristocracy to defend its cultural, moral, and political authority over the Greeks against the challenge presented by the liberal mercantile bourgeoisie.[64] Kodrikas' elitist objections to Korais' revolutionary, egalitarian, and democratic convictions and his new proposals for the future are obvious in his use of phrases such as 'demagogic teaching', 'rabble-rousing philosophy', and 'mob-rule ideology', through which, as in his earlier pamphlet, he associated his opponent with the breakdown of law and order during and after the French revolution.[65] Moreover, by suggesting that some of Korais' 'corrections' were based on the usage of a foreign language (i.e. French), Kodrikas was alleging that Korais was unpatriotic. According to Kodrikas' schema of recent Greek history, when Orthodox Christians began to be appointed to high secular positions in the Ottoman empire from the seventeenth century onwards, the Nation ceased to be *aichmáloton* [captive], and became instead *ypíkoon* [subject]; for Kodrikas, this marked 'the first phase of the rebirth of our *Genos* since its capture'.[66] He implies that the present political order in Greece needs to be preserved; in his vision of an independent Greece, the existing Orthodox establishment, consisting of the hierarchs and the princes, would simply take over the areas of authority currently controlled by the Ottomans. This is exactly what Korais feared might happen.

[64] Compare Kodrikas' contemptuous dismissal of the language of Moisiodax as 'grocers' style'.

[65] Kodrikas 1817, in K. Th. Dimaras 1953: 274, 282. These charges are unjust: Korais, who (unlike Kodrikas) had witnessed the excesses of the revolution in Paris, was always at pains to distance himself from them.

[66] Kodrikas 1988: xvi, 154–5. Kodrikas' view of the Greek nation as 'subject' rather than 'captive' is similar to that of Katartzis (see Chapter 3). Kodrikas uses the term *aichmálotos* [prisoner of war] to refer to the legal status of the Ottoman Christians under Islamic law, as having been enslaved through capture in war.

Angelou rightly claims that Korais' views on the language were always expressed in connection with education, whereas Kodrikas never once mentions education, with the result that his arguments are unfocused.[67] The linguistic preoccupations of Katartzis and Doukas too were part of their general concern for what the young should learn, and how they could best learn it. Kodrikas' lack of interest in education is an indication of his aristocratic and conservative stance.

One of the aspects of the *Study* that Korais found especially infuriating was the fact that, in some of the copies of his book, Kodrikas included a dedication to the Russian Tsar Alexander I. Amid the anti-revolutionary climate of post-Napoleonic Europe, Kodrikas' dedication of his book to one of the chief representatives of absolutism seemed to Korais to be a betrayal of the cause of Greek liberation. In his dedication Kodrikas claims that the tsar's policies are founded in the Christian religion and that he is destined to fulfil the decrees of divine providence; since Christian doctrine was spread through the world by means of the Greek language ('cette Langue divine, qui unit l'homme à Dieu'), the tsar must protect it. The object of his work, he concludes, is to demonstrate the origin of today's language and its identity with Ancient Greek.[68] In this way Kodrikas appeared to be internationalizing the dispute between the two rival Parisian Greeks.

The publication of Kodrikas' *Study* sparked off a new conflagration in the polemic between him and Korais, beginning with an anonymous 150-page riposte, written under Korais' guidance and published in *The Learned Hermes* in June 1819.[69] The authors claim that for thirty years now (since the time of Moisiodax, Katartzis, Filippidis and Konstantas, and Christopoulos) all the learned – not just Kodrikas – have accepted that 'the spoken language', 'the modern language of the Nation', is Hellenic, whereas previously it had been thought of as barbaric. The same year saw the publication of two anti-Korais journals, *Kalliopi* in Vienna and

---

[67] Angelou 1998: 35.

[68] 'A sa majesté l'empéreur et autocrate de toutes les Russies, Alexandre Ier', in Kodrikas 1818 (unnumbered pages). Apparently Korais learned with relief that Kodrikas' dedication had been inserted without the tsar's permission. K. Th. Dimaras 1996: 53 says that the dedication was subsequently removed from all available copies, but the fact that it was printed as a separate signature (as in the two copies in the Bodleian Library at Oxford) suggests that it was always intended to be insertable or removable at will.

[69] Filologia 1819. Angelou (1998: 24) states that this text was by Stefanos Kanelos and Athanasios Vogoridis, while Iliou (1997: 552) claims it was by the journal's editors, Farmakidis and Kokkinakis.

Athina in Paris. These magazines were well funded, possibly by virtue of the editors' close contacts with the patriarchate.

Korais was also incensed by the fact that Kodrikas managed to obtain letters from patriarch Grigorios V of Constantinople and his predecessor Kyrillos VI, as well as patriarch Polykarpos of Jerusalem, congratulating him on the publication of his book and proclaiming that 'the teachings about language of those who publicly profess philosophy have fallen into the void'.[70] The patriarchs' congratulation of Kodrikas came later in the same year as an encyclical issued in March 1819 by patriarch Grigorios and the Holy Synod, which condemned the exclusive teaching of mathematics and physics, allegedly proposed by certain 'unordained teachers', on the grounds that the study of such subjects impedes the progress of the young to the happiness of true education.[71] The authors demanded either that teaching be confined to the proper learning of the ancient language or that perfection in the latter, together with training in logic and rhetoric, be a prerequisite for the study of 'philosophy'. The encyclical asserted that the Hellenic language ('the language of the ancestors') is admired by all the wise Europeans and 'has been preserved as our only valuable treasure and the sole heirloom that is the characteristic/distinctive mark of our ancestral nobility'.[72] To what avail will the young learn arithmetic, geometry, and physics, ask the encyclical's authors, if they speak barbarically and write solecistically? In an elegant and suggestive formulation, which adumbrates the later Greek nationalist 'Helleno-Christian' ideology, the encyclical urges teachers to make their students into 'Christians who Hellenize in their phrases, and Hellenes who Christianize in their doctrines, their morals and their manners'. Some of the encyclical reads like an attack on Korais based on the false allegations made by Kodrikas and Doukas that Korais and his like were trying to dissuade the young from learning Ancient Greek. At the same time the encyclical condemns the fashion for giving Ancient Greek names (as opposed to the names of saints recognized and celebrated by the Church) to infants as showing 'contempt for Christian nomenclature'.

According to Alexis Politis, in order to rebut the innovative tendencies of Korais and his like, Grigorios was barricading himself behind

---

[70] Kodrikas proudly had these letters published in the journal *Kalliopi* 2 (1820) 186–8 (Daskalakis 1966: 124); the text of Grigorios' letter is reproduced in Triantafyllidis 1938: 376.

[71] For the text of the encyclical, which was published in the pro-Korais magazine *Melissa* 2 (1820) 219–29, see Dimaras 1953: 299–304; for the quotations see ibid., 301, 303, 304. For a partial English translation see Clogg 1976b: 86–8.

[72] Cf. Kommitas' description, already mentioned, of the Greek language as 'the only asset that has remained in our possession'.

Ancient Greek grammar.[73] The concern of the Church hierarchy with
the dissemination of Ancient Greek is also shown by the publication in
1819, at the patriarchal press in Constantinople, of the first volume of the
Ark of the Hellenic Language, a huge dictionary of Ancient Greek, with
interpretations in the modern language, that aimed to compile material
from all existing dictionaries of the language into a homogeneous whole.
The first volume contained words beginning with the first four letters of
the Greek alphabet. The editors' choice, in the dictionary's title, of a term
with Old Testament connotations, not otherwise used in Ancient Greek,
is highly significant. In a preface to the volume that is scattered with
verses quoted from Ancient Greek poetry, Ilarion Sinaitis, the censor
and superintendent of the patriarchal press, writes that, just as Noah's
ark gathered together all manner of animals, brought them to safety, and
filled the whole earth with them, so this volume includes every word
of the forebears, which will fill the whole of Greece – 'though not in
the way that the Hellene-hating Hellenes believe', he concludes, with a
swipe at Korais and his like.[74] Here we see the Orthodox Church bidding
to monopolize not only the study of Ancient Greek but also the use of the
name 'Hellene'.[75] The continued publication of the *Ark* was prevented by
the outbreak of the Greek revolution in March 1821. Ilarion also wrote
an encomium of Sultan Mahmud II as part of an invitation to learned
men to submit their writings for publication by the patriarchal press;
this has been seen as an attempt by the patriarchate to neutralize the
Enlightenment.[76]

The polemic between Korais and Kodrikas lasted right up to April
1821. *Kalliopi* ceased publication a few weeks after the outbreak of the

[73] A. Politis 2007: 472.

[74] Ilarion in Kivotos 1819: iv. For the history of the compilation of the *Ark* see Marcellus
1851: 315–56. The story that the *Ark* was compiled on the advice or even under the direction of
Korais (see Neroulos 1827: 108 and Marcellus 1851: 352) is implausible. Marcellus claims he
was told this story by Ioannis Kolettis.

[75] As an indication of the low interest that the *Ark* provoked in monastic circles, Iliou 2005:
209–16 points out that only thirty-three copies were bought by subscription by the Athonite
monasteries, whereas they subscribed to more than 400 copies of each of three posthumous
works by Nikodimos of the Holy Mountain published in the same year.

[76] Kitromilides 1996: 452–3. Ilarion's 'Prosklisis' was published in *Kalliopi* 2 (1820) 145–
51 and *Melissa* 3 (1821) 250–62. In the latter, it was preceded by a sarcastic introduction and
followed by a critique. In 1818 Ilarion had begun translating the New Testament into Modern
Greek for the British and Foreign Bible Society, which published the translation in 1828. He
later served as metropolitan of Trnovo in Bulgaria (1821–27 and 1830–38), where he is reputed
to have made efforts to suppress Slavonic culture, although the story that he set fire to the library
at Trnovo has apparently been proved groundless (Sfyroeras 1969–70). For the concerted efforts
of the patriarchate in 1819–21 to combat the Greek Enlightenment see Iliou 1988.

War of Independence, while *The Learned Hermes* was closed down by the Austrian authorities, though not before being obliged to publish the patriarch's condemnation of Alexandros Ypsilantis' revolutionary movement in its final issue; one of its editors, Kokkinakis, was arrested for being a member of a secret society.[77] Yet the armed civil strife that took place in Greece during the revolution was not accompanied by civil strife over the language. Even before the revolution broke out, some learned Greeks who had publicly taken sides in the language dispute came to realize that the Korais–Kodrikas polemic was dividing the nation and decided to seek reconciliation. Doukas published articles calling for peace and concord among the learned 'for the common weal'. One of these concludes with the statement that such a reconciliation would be 'worthy of the *Patrís* [fatherland], worthy of the descendants of Thrasyboulos, worthy of the New Hellenes'.[78] After the outbreak of the war Doukas even addressed a deferential letter to Korais.[79]

The dispute between Korais and Doukas was important enough, since it revolved around the nature of the relationship between the modern Greeks and the ancients. But in the dispute between Korais and Kodrikas the stakes were even higher: what was at issue was whether the Greeks would be governed democratically or oligarchically once their independence was won. Korais' model represented a radical break in tradition and a return to the political ideals of Classical Athens, whereas Kodrikas' model represented the continuity of a political and linguistic tradition that went back to Byzantine times.

Vernacularists

Christopoulos, Vilaras and Psalidas

Meanwhile, the proponents of the written use of the spoken language were defending their views. This is where the history of the language controversy becomes deeply involved with the history of Modern Greek literature, since some of these men were poets. As Horrocks has put it, '[g]iven that education rather than fiction was still seen [e.g. by Korais] as the central task of prose writers, it was this poetic revival which first

---

[77] The two letters from patriarch Grigorios V to metropolitan Veniamin of Moldavia, dated March 1821, condemning the revolt and excommunicating Ypsilantis and his collaborators were published in a supplement to the last issue of *Ermis o Logios*, 1 May 1821, 303–10. For a partial English translation see Clogg 1976b: 203–5.

[78] Doukas 1820; his text is dated Bucharest, 1 Sept. 1819.

[79] Doukas to Korais, undated (1821), in Korais 1984a: 305–6.

sought to give Greece an identity in terms of its contemporary history and culture'.[80]

Two poets (Athanasios Christopoulos and Ioannis Vilaras) had been demonstrating in practice that the vernacular, in its uncorrected form, was an expressive and subtle medium of poetic expression. Although their poetry was soon to be justly overshadowed by the work of Dionysios Solomos, theirs was perhaps the best poetry to be written in Greek since the *Erotokritos* in the early seventeenth century. Vilaras (who was born on the Venetian-ruled island of Kythera in 1771 but lived most of his life in Yannina and died in 1823) wrote simple love poems, satires, and fables in an uncompromising vernacular with the decidedly rural flavour of Epirus. Christopoulos (Kastoria 1772–Bucharest 1847) published a collection of poems, *Lyrics*, in 1811, although the contents had apparently been written considerably earlier. His charming poems in praise of love and wine are quintessentially neoclassical, written in the tradition of imitations of the ancient Greek poet Anacreon that was revived during the Italian Renaissance. The amorous and bibulous subjects of these poems were not intended to be anything other than frivolous. They are exercises in a variety of metres and rhyme schemes and in a sophisticated urban spoken language. Christopoulos claimed that he wrote them 'simply in order to show the harmony of our tongue', and that their language, which he calls *polítiki* [Constantinopolitan] or *fanariótiki*, hardly differs from 'our own' (i.e. the dialects of northern Greece);[81] in fact, it is not significantly different from the language spoken in Athens today. His *Lyrics* were prefaced by a contribution to the language controversy in the form of an anonymous tale entitled 'Dream' (perhaps by the editor of the volume, the young Constantinopolitan Stefanos Kanelos), in which the narrator recalls dreaming of two monstrously ugly creatures named 'Mixed-Barbarian Language' and 'Orthography'. The narrator calls Korais' language *korakistiká*,[82] a comic term soon to be taken up by Neroulos, as we shall see below. The popularity and importance of Christopoulos' collection of poems are indicated by the fact that it was frequently republished and that its sixth edition (1825) was the first book ever to be printed in Athens.

Christopoulos was a member of the Fanariot circle, though his ideas were considerably less conservative than those of Kodrikas, who was ten years older. He worked as a doctor and jurist in Bucharest. Later, in

---

[80] Horrocks 1997: 348.
[81] Christopoulos to Psalidas, 10 Nov. 1811, in Moschonas 1981: 6.
[82] See Moschonas 1981: 65 for this passage.

1817, as we have seen, he drew up the Civil Code of Wallachia. But it was his experience of writing poetry that led him to make his foray into amateur linguistics in his grammar of Modern Greek, entitled *Grammar of Aeolodoric, or The Language of the Hellenes Spoken Today* (1805). The title is programmatic: this is a grammar of the Aeolodoric dialect of Hellenic, and those who speak it today are Hellenes. The morphology of the language he uses and describes in his grammar is slightly archaized in comparison with the language of his poems.

Christopoulos knew Konstantas, and it seems that he learned about Katartzis' theories through him.[83] In his grammar he follows Filippidis and Konstantas (1791) in calling present-day Greek the 'fifth dialect' of Hellenic, but he differs from them in naming it Aeolodoric rather than Romaic, because, he claims, the differences between the Ancient Greek we know from texts and the Greek that is spoken today can be explained by the fact that, unlike standard Ancient Greek (Attic or *koine*), Modern Greek is the product of a combination between the ancient Aeolic and Doric dialects. He fails to provide any historical evidence or explanation for this hypothesis; he simply provides lists of individual similarities between Aeolic or Doric forms and their equivalents in spoken Modern Greek, which, he claims, correspond precisely to the differences between Aeolic–Doric and Attic. He argues that the linguistic features that characterize modern spoken Greek have always existed since ancient times, and that it is only by chance that some of them have failed to be preserved in ancient texts.

The basis of Christopoulos' Aeolodoric theory is completely erroneous. The similarities he adduced between spoken Modern Greek and Aeolic–Doric are due to coincidence: there is no systematic correspondence between them. Like Filippidis and Konstantas, Christopoulos failed to see the spoken Greek of his time as being the result of developments in the language over a period of two millennia; he preferred to see the whole of the Greek language as in some way timeless. He clearly felt the need to justify the written use of the spoken language by giving it a noble ancient pedigree. It seemed to him to be permissible to employ any feature from the spoken language in writing only if that feature could be traced to some variety of Ancient Greek. The fact that Christopoulos' grammar was written in two months[84] did not prevent the Aeolodoric theory

---

[83] Ibid., p. xlvi.

[84] Christopoulos 1805: 164. He tells Psalidas in 1811 that in his grammar he was 'forced to reconcile *prólipsi* [preconception] with truth' (Moschonas 1981: 6); by this he was presumably referring to the compromises with archaic language that he felt compelled to make in order for his linguistic ideas to gain general acceptance.

from becoming so influential that G. N. Hatzidakis, the first professor of linguistics at Athens University, felt the need, even towards the end of the nineteenth century, to refute it in his first published article.[85]

Around 1811, a new development was taking place for the first time in what was later to become part of the Greek state. This was a radical new educational and linguistic reform project, which has come down to us in the form of unpublished correspondence between a number of enlightened men, though their letters were copied and sent or read out to a larger circle.[86] The reforms were proposed chiefly by two men in Yannina, the capital of the increasingly independent province of the Ottoman empire governed by Ali Pasha from Tepelenë in Albania. These were Athanasios Psalidas (Yannina 1767–1829), the headmaster of one of the local Greek schools, and Vilaras, whose travels on campaign to various parts of Greece as personal physician to Ali's son Muhtar Pasha had brought him into close contact with the popular culture of rural Greece. As Katherine Fleming has pointed out, Ali used Greek as his court language:

His use of Greek as the official language of his government... kept the predominantly Greek population of his territories connected to the governmental elite in a way alien to other provinces of the Ottoman Empire... Ali's territories provide the interesting example of a non-Greek, non-Christian ruler who made significant contributions to the language of Hellenism and of Christianity.[87]

Psalidas had studied medicine and philosophy in Russia and in Vienna, and in 1791 had published a book in Greek and Latin entitled *True Happiness, or The Basis of Every Religion*, whose title betrays a distance from Orthodox Christian dogma. In 1794 he published a translation from Latin of an arithmetic book for schools into 'a middle *yfos*, that is neither so simple as to provoke offence, nor so Hellenic as to be incapable of being interpreted in the Schools of Hellas'.[88] In 1795 he produced a poorly written pamphlet in which he addresses his readers as 'Hellenes' and attacks Voulgaris on a number of counts: for serving up theology in

---

[85] Hatzidakis 1881. Hatzidakis' argument that the chief characteristics of the Modern Greek language were already being formed during Hellenistic times enabled him to discount the possibility of significant influence from Slavonic, Italian, and Turkish. Well before Hatzidakis, the Aeolodoric theory had already been rejected by J. M. Heilmaier, who in 1834 argued correctly that Modern Greek is descended from Hellenistic and Byzantine Greek; see Kapsomenos 1985: 11–12 and Delveroudi 1996: 226. Later Christopoulos himself implicitly rejected the Aeolodoric theory by stating that 'our language' is a mixture of Attic, Doric, Aeolic, and Ionic (Christopoulos 1853: pp. ccii–iii; probably written in the 1840s); he still failed to see that Medieval and Modern Greek are derived from the Hellenistic *koine*.

[86] Now published in Moschonas 1981.   [87] Fleming 1999: 65–6.

[88] Psalidas 1794, in Ladas and Hatzidimou 1970: 280–2.

the guise of philosophy (teaching in his *Logic* that the Creator, through Revelation, is the first source of ideas), for criticizing Moisiodax and others for philosophizing in the modern language, for translating Virgil into Ancient Greek language and Homeric hexameters instead of the 'simple dialect' and fifteen-syllable verses, and for pinning his hopes for Greece's future on Russia. Instead of admiring Voulgaris, Psalidas urged his compatriots to wake from their deep sleep, open their eyes and follow the Europeans, so as to attain the 'first glory of our ancestors'.[89] His language in these early works is a jumble of ancient and modern features.

Vilaras had studied medicine in Italy, where he had taken part in revolutionary activities. An indication of his originality is that his earliest known work, dating from 1801, is a grammar of Albanian, written in Greek though not published until recently.[90] The later writings of the two men bear witness to their remarkably enlightened broadmindedness. In their official capacities they could not afford to write openly about revolution in Greece, but both of them seem to have been in favour of a movement for autonomy from the Ottoman empire. Vilaras probably saw Ali as the best hope for securing secession.[91] In their correspondence, Psalidas constantly talks of autonomy as a prerequisite for the development of the arts and sciences in Greece, and he may have envisaged complete political independence, but he no doubt saw autonomy from the cultural hegemony of antiquity as being equally necessary.

Either through personal contact or by way of correspondence, Psalidas and Vilaras were in touch with a number of like-minded individuals in other parts of Greece. Acutely aware of the dire social, economic, and cultural state of Greece, they saw the urgent need for a practical and secular education, which they believed could only be based on the spoken language. To this end some of these men employed the Greek alphabet to devise a system of phonetic transcription of the spoken language, which was no doubt partly inspired by Vilaras' experience, during his studies in Italy, of the virtually one-to-one correspondence between pronunciation and spelling in Italian. Another doctor, Georgios Kalaras of Corinth, who had also studied in Italy, had already been developing his own version of a

[89] Psalidas 1795. Psalidas had revised his ideas since *True Happiness*, which he had dedicated to Catherine II of Russia and in which he had written that reason cannot lead to knowledge without divine revelation. For extracts from Psalidas 1791 see Ladas and Hatzidimou 1970: 5–16.

[90] Now published in Vilaras 1985.

[91] See, for instance, his epigram on Souli, praising Ali, in Vranousis 1955: 274.

phonetic script, which he had used in an unpublished grammar of spoken Greek that he had written in 1804, before he came in contact with Vilaras and Psalidas.[92] Vilaras' phonetic system had two aims: to make it easier to learn to write, and, more importantly, to separate the modern language from Ancient Greek, thus granting the modern spoken language its own autonomy and at the same time discouraging the constant temptation to archaize experienced by almost every learned Greek writer. While Psalidas and Vilaras seem to have had no direct contact with the work of Katartzis, they were in touch with Christopoulos, who – at least for a time – was converted to their view. In return Psalidas accepted that 'the present language of our *genos* is Aeolodoric, not Attic',[93] though he did not make this into a major component of his argument.

Christopoulos claims in a letter to Psalidas that he intended his *Lyrics* to be printed in this phonetic orthography (as opposed to the traditional *stravografía* [wrong-writing], as he calls it), but that his wishes were ignored by his publishers. In the same letter, Christopoulos attacks *The Learned Hermes* and claims that both the nobility (i.e the Fanariot princes at whose courts he served) and the populace are of one mind in supporting the spoken language: no doubt he saw the language of Korais as a bourgeois construct. He adds that Prince Nikolaos Mourouzis approves of Psalidas' language and says it is exactly like the language of Constantinople.[94] In a later letter he even urges Psalidas, who acted as an adviser to Ali Pasha, to see to it that Vilaras' language is used in the official documents issued by Ali's administration.[95]

As was often the case with the vernacularists, the labours of Psalidas and Vilaras bore little immediate fruit. In 1814 Vilaras published a little book in Corfu entitled *The Romaic Language* and dedicated to Psalidas, which contained samples of prose and verse to illustrate his linguistic ideas. This was the only book to be printed in their phonetic orthography, which dispensed with all accents and breathings and cleverly distinguished the vowel /i/ from the semi-vowel /j/, as in βιολη /vjolí/ [violin]; these two sounds are not distinguished in the traditional Greek orthography used both at that time and today. *The Romaic Language* includes a translation of Pericles' funeral speech from Thucydides – an

---

[92] For Kalaras' own account of how he came to write his 'Dokimi gramatikis tis glosas mas [Attempt at a grammar of our language]' under the influence of the more or less phonetic spelling of Italian, see his letter to Vilaras, 1 Apr. 1815, in Moschonas 1981: 202–3. For his career see Patrinelis 1997.

[93] Psalidas to Doukas, 5 October 1815, in Moschonas 1981: 97–8.

[94] Christopoulos to Psalidas, 10 Nov. 1811, ibid., 5–6.

[95] Christopoulos to Psalidas, 7 July 1815, ibid., 7.

ideologically significant choice[96] – and Plato's *Crito*; these were among the first Classical Greek texts to be published in demotic translation.

In 1820 Psalidas and Vilaras were preparing a collaborative publication which would have constituted a more reasoned argument for their ideas – a kind of vernacularist manifesto. Vilaras gave this planned book the provisional title 'Writings of a *Romiós* to a *Romiós* about their language': the dialogic character of the text is typical of writings by Vilaras and Psalidas on the language question, suggesting that they are not the work of one man but the outcome of debate. The manuscript of this book is in Psalidas' hand, with emendations by Vilaras, but it is difficult if not impossible to distinguish between the contributions of each. This was one of the very few truly collaborative contributions to the Greek language controversy before the twentieth century. As Moschonas pointed out, when Vilaras and the members of his group criticized alternative varieties of language, they generally did so impersonally and on grounds of principle;[97] this was a striking contrast with the personal attacks of Doukas and Kodrikas. However, their project came to nothing, since in August 1820 they were obliged to flee Yannina (which was being besieged by the Sultan's troops, who assassinated Ali and burned the town in 1822), leaving their mission unfulfilled.

Vilaras' romantic tendencies are indicated in an allegorical story included in *The Romaic Language*, where the playing of two violinists is constrasted: the one who has learned by ear plays with greater expression and feeling than the one who has learned by reading a musical score. The parallels between music and language in Vilaras' text are unspoken but obvious. In another story by Vilaras, 'The *logiótatos* [erudite] traveller', eight *lógioi* [learned men] (as many as there are parts of speech) gather at Fanatasiopoli [Fantasyville], capital of the empire of Prolipsi [Preconception], and are sent all over Greece to study the state of the language and to correct it by bringing it closer to Ancient Greek.[98] The plot of this story may have been inspired by Korais' proposal to send scholars all over Greece in search of modern words that are derived from Ancient Greek. Most of the story consists of a dialogue between one of the scholars and a wise and implausibly learned old peasant, who, in keeping with the tone of the story of the violinists, speaks in allegory rather than using logical argument. He insists that everything in life is subject to

---

[96] Kitromilides 1996: 112–13.   [97] Moschonas 1981: pp. lxxvii–lxxviii.
[98] Rotolo 1965: 76. The story was first published in Vilaras 1827: 211–23; reprinted in Vranousis 1955: 296–30.

change, and that you can as easily make a language revert to an earlier stage as you can bring back to life the people who spoke it. Echoing Filippidis and Konstantas, the old man compares writing to painting: just as the painter reproduces a visual image exactly from nature, so a writer should precisely represent the sounds of speech; here we have a view of language (and perhaps of literature) as being a mirror held up to nature. The recurrent exhortation expressed by the wise old peasant in this story, and by Vilaras elsewhere, is to shed *prólipses* (preconceived ideas, beliefs that are accepted without being subjected to logical analysis and without being tested against experience). One of these *prólipses* is the fear of being ridiculed by those who might think you uneducated and uncouth because you use the vernacular – a fear that has beset many Greeks over the centuries.

Elsewhere Vilaras uses other colourful analogies, for instance that Ancient Greek resembles an old woman, who was certainly beautiful in her youth, but whom it is useless to try to doll up now; Modern Greek is her daughter, and is still in her swaddling clothes, but will gradually reach maturity and beauty; Modern Greek may borrow words from Ancient Greek, just as a daughter borrows her mother's finery, but she must adapt them to suit her own appearance.[99] Another example is a utilitarian analogy with currency: he appreciates Ancient Greek as he appreciates his collection of Ancient Greek coins; but it would be foolish to go to market to try and buy merchandise with them.[100]

Vilaras' three basic axioms are that the purpose of language is the practical one of communicating ideas; that the more usual and comprehensible the form of a written language is, the more useful it is; and that the most usual and the most readily comprehensible language is that which is written and read exactly as it is spoken.[101] The 'general language' of the Modern Greeks is not that which the few write but that which everyone speaks.[102] At one point, in a statement that echoes Katartzis and anticipates Noam Chomsky, Vilaras writes that grammar is not in the hand, but in the mind. He argues, in addition, that the learned and the vulgar follow the same grammatical rules; the former simply use additional words and different 'modes of expression' (i.e. different

---

[99] Vilaras to Psalidas 11 May 1812, in Moschonas 1981: 150.

[100] Vilaras to Melas, 17 May 1815, ibid., 169. Solomos makes a slightly different analogy between the currency of language and the currency of coins (Solomos 1955: 12).

[101] Vilaras to Genovelis, 4 March 1815, in Moschonas 1981: 161.

[102] Vilaras to Melas, 17 May 1815, ibid., 167.

styles).[103] One of Vilaras' objections to Korais' language was that it could be written but not spoken.[104] Vilaras' linguistic message to his fellow Greeks could be summed up in the exhortation: have the courage to be what you are and write in your mother tongue.

As for Psalidas, he laid out his linguistic views in their most comprehensive form in an important letter that he wrote to his fellow Epirot Doukas in 1815. There he argues that, in order to behave like the ancient Greeks, one should write in one's own local dialect as they did, since there is no real problem of communication between speakers of different regional varieties of the modern spoken language. He points to the example of the Cretan Renaissance poets Chortatsis and Kornaros, who used their dialect to creative effect; this was perhaps the first time for a century that Cretan Renaissance literature had been discussed by a learned Greek writer in unreservedly positive terms. Psalidas argues that a common language would develop naturally and gradually. He claims there is no need for a grammar and a dictionary to be written until after the language has been enriched and standardized by learned writers: the only legislator in language, he argues, is *synítheia* [custom or habit]. He makes extensive use of an organic metaphor which was to be used by later demoticists: the archaists (whom he calls *nekrómyaloi* [brain-dead]) wish to graft dead Attic branches on to the living tree of the spoken language.[105] Here Psalidas expresses a clear preference for 'nature' over 'art' and 'culture', suggesting that, like Vilaras, he was influenced by the Romantic movement, in contrast to the Enlightenment neoclassicism of Korais.

Neroulos

One of the most successful satires on Korais' proposed reforms and on his use of Modern Greek was the comedy by Iakovos [Iakovakis] Rizos Neroulos (1778–1850), *Korakistika, or the Correction of the Romaic Language*, which was written in 1811, partly inspired by the 'Dream' prefaced to Christopoulos' *Lyrics*, and first published in 1813. Born into a Fanariot family in Constantinople, Neroulos served in the interpreting service of the Sublime Porte and as Grand Postelnic at the princely courts of Wallachia and Moldavia.

---

[103] Vilaras to Psalidas, 15 July 1812, ibid., 156. By 'modes of expression' Vilaras means style as opposed grammar; as we have seen (Chapter 3, note 2), Kodrikas used the same formulation.

[104] Vilaras to Psalidas, 11 May 1812, ibid., 149.

[105] Psalidas to Doukas, 5 October 1815, ibid., 91, 106–7, 97, 93, 101. Charilaou 2002: 295 points out that Doukas is unlikely to have received Psalidas' letter, because he had already left Vienna for Bucharest.

The title of Neroulos' comedy (meaning 'the language of the ravens') is the name of a secret language used by Greek children, but it is also a pun on Korais' surname.[106] The central character against whom the satire is directed is a pedant who is ridiculed by other members of his household for insisting on speaking in Korais' language. During dinner one evening an enormous polysyllabic archaic compound word that the pedant has invented to denote cabbage salad (*eladioxidioalatolachanokarýkevma*) gets stuck in his gullet and almost chokes him to death. Only when he is persuaded to pronounce the 'vulgar' word *lachanosalata* is he cured. Thereupon he recants his ideas, and common sense prevails. The comedy was not intended to be performed, but Neroulos seems to have considered the dialogue form of drama to be appropriate for disputes on the language.

The *Korakistika* also presents characters from Lesbos, Yannina, Chios, and Cyprus who speak in their local dialects. The preface, written in colloquial language by another Fanariot, Theodoros Negris, states that the chief target of the play is *Koraïsmós* [Koraism], since it is 'most epidemic. among our learned men', but that the author 'does not prefer any of the various local idioms of our language'. It is significant that the young enlightened characters who seem to enjoy the author's sympathy and support speak in the vernacular, using very few archaic forms.[107]

Neroulos also wrote an unfinished mock-heroic poem, *The Rape of the Turkey-Hen* (1816). This charming but unashamedly frivolous poem is composed in fifteen-syllable rhymed couplets, and its vernacular language is lively and racy, with relatively little archaization.[108] In addition, he wrote two dull and earnest tragedies on ancient Greek themes, *Aspasia* (2nd edn 1823) and *Polyxeni* (1814), the first about the wife of Pericles and the second about the daughter of Priam; these are written in an archaized version of Modern Greek, quite different from the language of his satirical poem. It seems that for him the use of the spoken language was only appropriate for comic themes.[109]

Not long after the *Korakistika* appeared in print, Neroulos, no doubt seeing where his true interests lay, felt obliged to declare that he was an admirer of Korais and to renounce his play as a frivolous *jeu d'esprit* which had been published without his knowledge. He went on to write

---

[106] The children's language is in fact called *korakístika*, with the stress on the third syllable, whereas the title of Neroulos' play has the stress on the final vowel.

[107] Negris, in Neroulos 1813: 3. It is an indication of the influence of Korais' linguistic ideas that he had an -ism named after him. For an analysis of the *Korakistika* see Puchner 2001: 23–92.

[108] Neroulos 1816.

[109] Neroulos knew of Katartzis' theories though Filippidis (Moschonas 1981: xlvii).

patriotic poetry during the War of Independence.[110] In 1827, when it had become politically correct for Fanariots to be patriotic Hellenes, Neroulos wrote in a series of lectures on modern Greek literature:

Moi aussi j'ai été un des Grecs jadis appelés Fanariotes; mais je me crois assez supérieur aux préjugés de la naissance, pour parler avec impartialité d'hommes auxquels j'ai été attaché par tant de rapport... [J]e ne me suis jamais considéré comme Fanariote, j'ai toujours été Grec, et je le serai jusqu'au tombeau.[111]

Neroulos, like Kodrikas, was successful at adapting himself to changing political circumstances.

Filippidis in the 1810s

The linguistic inconsistency of the times is illustrated by the case of Daniil Filippidis during the 1810s. Within two years he published two books in widely different language varieties. Because the second of these books was supposedly in Christopoulos' Aeolodoric, it is appropriate to mention Filippidis at this point. The first of these two books, however, *Geography of Romania* (1816), has an epilogue justifying the fact that he has written his book in 'the so-called old Hellenic language [i.e. Ancient Greek] and not the one now commonly in use'.[112] He claims that he wants to avoid the horrors of the forms proposed by Korais, together with 'the rest of that nausea', and he attacks those who lay down linguistic rules from afar with endless 'repulsive advice and exhortations'. In sum, he says, 'Hellas needs not words but deeds'. His argument against linguistic regulators is accompanied by a nice visual joke: his book includes a map of Asia, which shows a people called the 'Koraïkoi' (presumably Korais and his followers) living in the extreme north-east corner of Siberia, to the south of the river Anadyr.

The following year Filippidis published the *Philippica* by the Roman historian Pompeius Trogus, 'translated into the Aeolodoric Hellenic dialect'. Again the translator appends an epilogue justifying the language he uses. It is significant that this epilogue is addressed to a friend and reads like an oral conversation, with loose sentence structures and explicit references to speaking:

---

[110] Neroulos expressed his admiration for Korais in a letter he sent to Vamvas shortly after the publication of *Korakistika*. Later he published a letter explaining that he was not responsible for the publication of his comedy (*Ellinikos tilegrafos* 4 (1815) 256; see Dimaras 1996: 153, 235).

[111] Neroulos 1827: 69, 86–7.   [112] Filippidis 1816: 3, 5, 6.

I'm publishing this book in the language I speak; it would have been easier for me to write in Attic; . . . in the language . . . I speak, not in a motley language as others do, mixing one with the other and thus covering up their ignorance of both, but in pure Aeolodoric, as far as I can. I say Aeolodoric because, if we're sensible, it's inevitable and essential to provide a name defining the Hellenic that we speak; for this is, indubitably and incontrovertibly, a Hellenic dialect, and perhaps the oldest. . . . I confess that I find myself limping and in difficulty when writing the language as I should; there are no books written in it or dictionaries with its principles and its idiom according to its nature; of those who write, each one writes according to his imagination; they despise the common principles as being barbarous, even though they use them when speaking.[113]

Our language is similar to Attic, he continues, yet 'similarity is not identity'.[114] This language must have a name, as the other Hellenic dialects do, but 'both the words Romaic and *Graikikí* are foreign and shameful to us, and we provoke confusion when we use them'. Unwittingly echoing Korais, he continues:

Come, my friend, and condescend to the many, so that the many will ascend to us learned men; otherwise we're fighting with shadows or fighting with air, and we manage to do nothing except appear futile and freakish. . . . Our Aeolodoric language, perhaps the oldest in Europe after Slavic and Cimmerian, is the sister of Attic, and in a sense is identical to it, the only difference being that it's easier. . . . Whoever knows the Aeolodoric language knows five sixths of Attic.[115]

The mistaken idea that Aeolodoric is older than Attic is put forward as a justification for using a version of the modern vernacular, while the references to Slavic and Cimmerian are pure nonsense. Despite Filippidis' claim, and despite the informality of its syntax, most of the morphological features of the language used in this book have been 'corrected' according to Ancient Greek grammar. Since the language variety he uses here is less radical than that of Katartzis in this respect, Filippidis' implication that he is a pioneer in the use of the vernacular is not justified; nevertheless, this variety is far closer to the genuine vernacular than is the variety promoted by Korais.

Children should start their education by studying Aeolodoric, writes Filippidis, and by applying this study to the study of things. He stresses the importance of practical knowledge: children should not start by learning the alphabet but by studying the familiar objects that surround them. 'The Attic Hellenic dialect must not be the beginning of study,

---

[113] Filippidis 1817: 1–2.   [114] Ibid., 6.
[115] Ibid., 9, 11, 15. For the similarity with Korais see Chapter 4, pp. 114–15.

nor the common study,' he contends.[116] There is thus a fundamental difference between Filippidis and Doukas: for Doukas, knowledge begins from language, and therefore one must teach the 'best' language from the outset, whereas for Filippidis knowledge begins from pre-school experience, and the function of language is to express knowledge.

Solomos

In 1824, having completed his *Hymn to Liberty*, the young Italian-educated aristocratic poet Dionysios Solomos (1798–1857), living in the safety of British-protected Zakynthos rather than in the Ottoman-occupied areas of insurgent Greece, wrote a 'Dialogue' on the language, which was not, however, published until after his death. By this time, the language controversialists had largely fallen silent, except in the United States of the Ionian Islands. As Mario Vitti has argued, there was not such a radical sense of diglossia in the Ionian Islands as there was in other parts of the Greek world, since the elites were content to use Italian rather than Greek for official purposes. Vitti also points out that, like the Italian language question in Solomos' time, his attitude to the Greek language had two orientations, one aesthetic and the other patriotic. His chief influence from contemporary Italy was the writings of his friend Giuseppe Montani, who upheld the use of everyday speech in poetry against the arguments of Vincenzo Monti, who argued in favour of the use of a common national language based on the written poetic tradition going back to the Trecento. Montani and others presented this dispute in terms of nature versus art.[117]

Solomos, who had the advantage of being fifty years younger than Korais, was in a position to receive the Romantic message that the language and songs of the folk express the soul of the nation. By the time he wrote the 'Dialogue', Fauriel had already published the first volume of his collection of Greek folk songs, together with an introduction in which he extolled the expressive qualities of the Greek vernacular. As a poet, Solomos never doubted that the spoken language was the only form of Greek suitable for poetry, and in the 'Dialogue', influenced by Dante's *De vulgari eloquentia*, he confines his arguments to the language of poetry. He shows he has studied the Greek folk songs and the work of Christopoulos and Vilaras, but he also brings forward parallels with the situation in other modern languages. The speakers in the 'Dialogue' are the Poet, his Friend and a *Sofologiótatos*; this last word (literally 'most

[116] Ibid., 25.   [117] Vitti 1959: 80.

wise and learned'), originally an honorific title used when addressing a teacher or other learned man, had come by that time to mean a pedant.

The Pedant, with whom the Poet argues, supports the 'correction' of the vernacular language, and Korais is the only named target of the Poet's attack, even though Solomos seems to know Korais' work only by repute. It is telling that the Pedant speaks in exactly the same variety of the language as the Poet – an indication that Solomos' knowledge of Greek was more or less confined to the vernacular. The Poet asserts that 'it's not the writer who teaches words; in fact, he learns them from the mouth of the *laós* [common people]'.[118] He also argues – perhaps under the influence of Fauriel – that there is a common spoken language that transcends the differences among the dialects; he claims that he has employed servants from various parts of the Greek-speaking world, and he has never had difficulty understanding them.[119]

One of the most effective passages in the 'Dialogue' is the one in which the Poet demonstrates the futility of any attempt at the grammatical 'correction' of the vernacular by taking the first line of Dante's *Inferno* and 'translating' it word for word by fitting the Italian vocabulary into Latin grammatical structures. Thus, in order to be 'corrected', Dante's 'barbarous' verse, 'Nel mezzo del cammin di nostra vita', must become 'In medio cammini nostrae vitae' – which is neither Latin nor Italian.[120] Fully aware of the intentionally comic nature of macaronic writing in Italy, Solomos realized that this was precisely what Korais' correction consisted of. He argues that the creativity and nobility of the writer are manifested in the way he puts words together: only thoughts, rather than words, can be base or noble.[121]

'One of the wisest of our nation wrote that to write with the words of the people we must also think with the thoughts of the people', argues the Pedant, to which the Poet retorts: 'These [ideas] are deformed children of a handsome father', and he goes on to refer to Condillac.[122] Dimaras has convincingly argued that here the Pedant is paraphrasing Doukas, and that Solomos is aware that Doukas' assertion that the form of a word reflects the ideas of the person who uses it is a distortion of Condillac's theory.[123]

Most of the Poet's arguments in the 'Dialogue', however, are passionate rather than logical: as Dimaras points out, Solomos, realizing that words have not only cognitive but also emotional content, injects

---

[118] Solomos 1955: 14.   [119] Ibid., 22.   [120] Ibid., 17.   [121] Ibid., 20–1.
[122] Ibid., 14.   [123] K. Th. Dimaras 1982: 138; 1985: 217, 345.

[handwritten manuscript text in Greek cursive — The beginning of the first draft of the poem]

The beginning of the first draft of the poem 'The Free Besieged' by Dionysios Solomos, dating from the late 1820s, in the poet's own manuscript version.

'Ετότες εταραχτήκανε τὰ σωθικά μου, καὶ ἔλεγα πῶς ἦρθε ὥρα νὰ ξεψυχήσω· κ' εὑρέθηκα 'σὲ σκοτεινὸ τόπο καὶ βροντερό, 'ποῦ ἐσκιρτοῦσε 'σὰν κλωνὶ στάρι 'ς τὸ μύλο 'ποῦ ἀλέθει ὀγλήγορα, ὡσὰν τὸ χοχλὸ 'ς τὸ νερὸ 'ποῦ ἀναβράζει· ἐτότες ἐκατάλαβα πῶς ἐκεῖνο ἤτανε τὸ Μισολόγγι· (Solomos 1964: 299).

Then my bowels shuddered within me and I told myself that my time had come to give up the ghost: I found myself in a dark and thunderous place, which was leaping like an ear of corn in a mill grinding at speed, like a bubble in furiously boiling water; then I realised that that was Missolonghi. (Translation by Peter Thompson, in Solomos 2000: 13.)

Solomos' poem (parts of which, like this one, are in prose) was inspired by the closing stages of the siege of Mesolongi by Ottoman forces in April 1826. Solomos used an unsystematic phonetic script with few diacritics, but when his work was published it was printed with traditional orthography and diacritics. The typographical transcription beneath Solomos' manuscript version shows how this passage was printed in the first edition of the poet's works in 1859, using the orthographic conventions of the period. In this passage he writes every /e/ sound as ε, every /i/ as ι and every /o/ as o, whereas the printed version uses αι besides ε for /e/, η, υ, and ει besides ι for /i/, and ω besides o for /o/, following conventions that go back to the pronunciation of Classical Greek of the fifth century BC. He also represents /ev/ as εβ instead of ευ. In Standard Modern Greek the passage would mostly be spelled like the printed version above, except for the diacritics. Solomos' use of diacritics is more or less confined to the use of a grave accent, as in Italian, to indicate that a word is stressed on the final syllable. By contrast, the printed version employs three accents and two breathings; it also uses the apostrophe to indicate a vowel that has been deleted since ancient times. In Standard Modern Greek the diacritics would be slightly different, even if the polytonic system were used. Using the monotonic system, none of the initial vowels would be written with breathings, and an acute accent would be written over the stressed vowel in words of more than one syllable. Almost all of the apostrophes would be dispensed with in Standard Modern Greek.

poetic passion into the dry, abstract arguments of his predecessors.[124] The romantic Poet stresses the importance of expressing true and profound emotion, which cannot be achieved in an artificial language. Conscious of his vocation as a national poet, Solomos argues, through the persona of the fictional Poet, that poets must be allowed to celebrate the glories of the revolution in a language that the warriors themselves can understand: the warriors' self-sacrifice has sanctified the spoken tongue, and a language that is good enough for the liberators of the nation should be good enough for the liberated nation. He argues that the revolution is a struggle for liberation not only from the Turks but also from the pedants, whose high social prestige, he believes, is a consequence of the obscurantism brought about by servitude. 'Do you think I have anything in my mind except liberty and language?', he asks. 'The first of these has begun to trample on the Turkish heads, the second will soon trample *ta sofologiotístika* [the language, arguments and actions of the pedants], and then they will walk the path of glory arm in arm, without looking back if a pedant croaks or a Turk barks, since for me they are one and the same.'[125]

Solomos' close friend Antonios Matesis (1794–1873), also from Zakynthos, wrote (but did not publish) a 'Treatise on language' in 1823, in which he echoes Kodrikas by attacking the 'self-elected legislators' of the new language (whom he calls *kainourgioglossites* [new-languagists]) for their insistence on abandoning the spoken language in favour of a macaronic concoction of their own making.[126] Like Kodrikas, Matesis saw himself as a conservative, preserving the established usage of his aristocratic circle against the linguistic innovations of the bourgeois former merchant Korais. Unlike Kodrikas, however, the established language that Matesis was defending was based on the everyday spoken language that the aristocrats of the Ionian Islands shared with the common people. Matesis went on to write an important drama, *The Basil Plant* (1830) in a refined demotic, which was not published until 1859.

However, the aristocrats Solomos and Matesis, like Kodrikas, ignored the practical arena of education, and Solomos' prediction that the pedants' language would soon be trampled underfoot turned out to be wrong: poetry was overcome by pedantry. The outbreak of the War of Independence had already ensured that the vernacularists' aspirations would

[124] K. Th. Dimaras 1982: 138.   [125] Solomos 1955: 12.
[126] Matesis 1953.

not be fulfilled, and the romantic-classical ideology of the new state that
emerged from it could not condone the use of 'vulgar' spoken Greek;
instead it installed the linguistic compromise solution advocated by
Korais as a provisional measure until such time as Ancient Greek could
be fully revived. What was perhaps intended to be a temporary stop-gap,
however, eventually became firmly entrenched as the established form of
Greek in official use.

In January 1824, around the same time that Solomos and Matesis
were drafting their defences of the vernacular, Psalidas wrote to the
revolutionary leader Alexandros Mavrokordatos (apparently a supporter
of the spoken language, at least in his younger days[127]), calling upon
him to ensure that 'the *yfos* [language variety] of the *Genos* [Nation]
and not that of Korais' was used in the semi-official newspaper *Hellenic
Chronicle*, published at Mesolongi from 1824 to 1826. 'The national style
charms the ears of the *Genos*,' argued Psalidas, 'because it understands
it.'[128] But Psalidas' exhortation was of no avail. The newspaper reports of
military operations, disdaining the language of the often illiterate Greek
warriors, translated their defiant words and heroic deeds into inflated
archaic rhetoric.[129] In 1826 Psalidas' application for the directorship
of the Greek community school in Trieste was rejected because of his
linguistic views:[130] the tide was by now definitely against the use of the
vernacular for official and educational purposes.

[127] Some verses by Mavrokordatos in praise of Neroulos' *Korakistika* are published in the
volume containing this comedy (Neroulos 1813: 5).

[128] Psalidas to Mavrokordatos, 18 Jan. 1824, in Angelou 1971: 96, quoted from Vranousis
1952: 131.

[129] For samples of the reports in the *Hellenic Chronicle* see Simopoulos 1971: 49–60.

[130] Moschonas 1981: p. lxxxi.

6

Language in the two Greek states, 1830–1880

According to K. Th. Dimaras, the Greek revolution of 1821 marks a radical cultural break: the polemics cease, the production of books slows down, magazines stop being published, and theatres fall silent. 'From this war, which lasted ten years, Greece emerged free and ruined.' The business of the erudite was no longer to follow the correct road towards the creation of the nation but to constitute and consolidate the state and to set up a new education system. 'The liberal wind no longer had any reason to blow,' Dimaras concludes caustically, 'since the country had been liberated.'[1]

In 1830, at the very outset of the Greeks' existence as an independent nation, the Austrian historian J. P. Fallmerayer published the following words:

Thus not a drop of genuine and unmixed Hellenic blood flows in the veins of the present Christian population of Greece. A storm, the like of which our race has only rarely encountered, has poured out, over the entire region between the Danube and the innermost recess of the Peloponnesian peninsula, a new race of cultivators, related to the great race of the Slavs. And a second, perhaps no less important, revolution, through the incursion of the Albanians into Greece, has completed this scene of annihilation. Scythian Slavs, Illyrian Albanians, children of the most northerly lands, blood relations of the Serbs and the Bulgarians, the Dalmatians and the Muscovites – these are the peoples whom today we call Hellenes, and whom, to their own amazement, we elevate to the pedigree of a Pericles and a Philopoimen.[2]

The prevalence of the ethnological notions of 'blood' and 'race' in this passage is all the more striking because they are absent from the Greek discourse on national identity before and during this time. While many

[1] K. Th. Dimaras 1985: 168–9, 388.
[2] Fallmerayer 1830: iv (my translation). Thanks to Constanze Güthenke for locating the original passage and for advice on the translation.

European authors talked about the 'degeneration' of the Greeks since Classical antiquity, Fallmerayer went further by claiming that a complete replacement of the country's racial stock had taken place. This claim that the modern inhabitants of Hellas were not racially Hellenes wounded Greek intellectuals deeply, and made them determined to demonstrate not only that the Modern Greeks were at least culturally – if not racially – descended from the ancients but that they were fully worthy of their forebears.

Dimaras remarks that, after Fallmerayer, '[t]he old spirit of daring... was replaced by a fretful tendency towards the display of national virtues'; 'the exquisite realism of Korais' gave way to 'the rejuvenated watchword of Doukas'.[3] Nevertheless, Fallmerayer unwittingly provided the Greeks with an incentive to study the medieval history and culture of their country and to see the Middle Ages not as marking a break between ancient and modern Hellas but as the link between them. The results of these investigations were, in the long term, to bring about radical changes in the Greek national identity.

For the time being, however, one of the chief methods used by Greek intellectuals to achieve their goal was the continuation of Korais' attempt to reverse what was perceived to be the process of corruption and degeneration that had occurred in the Greek language since antiquity. During the period 1833–53 there was a gradual turn of written Modern Greek towards greater archaism, to the extent that it was possible to write in 1857 that 'the language has progressed so much that even Korais himself has long been out of date'.[4] For instance, authors employed the dative case (not found in any of the traditional spoken dialects of Modern Greek and not used by Korais) and constructed *apo* [from] with the genitive (as in Ancient Greek) rather than the accusative (as in spoken Modern Greek and in Korais). The arguments supporting this trend were no longer theoretical, as they were with Doukas, but political: the use of the ancient language would reveal the ancient descent of the modern Greeks.[5]

Those who devised, developed, and wrote in *katharévousa* were driven by the conflicting impulses of utilitarianism and utopianism. The utilitarian impulse sought to enrich and modernize the language by importing the concepts that it lacked from western European languages; the utopian impulse sought to make the modern language look as much like Ancient

---

[3] K. Th. Dimaras 1985: 388.   [4] G. G. Pappadopoulos, quoted ibid., 373.
[5] Ibid., 115.

Greek as possible, so that these new concepts were expressed with the use of Ancient Greek morphemes rather than foreign words. Hardly any writer appears to have been aware that these two impulses – the one ideological, the other practical – were not necessarily related to each other. While Korais managed to strike a balance between them, later writers tended to let the utopian impulse predominate.

This chapter sketches out developments in the discourse on language and national identity articulated in the two nominally independent Greek states, namely the Kingdom of Greece and the United States of the Ionian Islands, during the first half-century after 1830 (the two states were united in 1864 after the replacement of King Otto by King George I).

Spoken and written language in the Greek capital in the 1830s

The makings of a common spoken language, used in speech by moderately educated Greeks from various areas, must have existed before independence, but its precise nature is unknown and the history of its development remains unclear. In fact, the very existence of a common spoken language was frequently denied by those who insisted on the use of an archaized version of the modern language.

After the revolution, the development of the common spoken language in the capital of the new Greek state (Nafplion from 1827, then Athens from 1834) increased in pace. It has conventionally been assumed that this common language was chiefly based on Peloponnesian dialects, since the Peloponnese formed the bulk of the territory included in the new Greek state. Peloponnesian varieties also happened to be phonologically closer to the norms of written Greek than the other chief native varieties, namely dialects of the northern group, such as Rumeliot, which are characterized by a radical divergence from written norms in their treatment of vowels, and those of islands such as Cyprus, which differ from these norms in their treatment of consonants. Nevertheless, recent research suggests that the morphology of the common language spoken by Greeks today differs markedly in many respects from Peloponnesian varieties.[6] Constantinople too must have acted as a melting-pot for the multifarious varieties of Greek spoken by the Orthodox Christians who lived there. After 1821 a large number of influential Constantinopolitans and Heptanesians settled in the capital, and the speech of the regions

[6] See Pantelidis 2001.

from which they came happened to be close to Peloponnesian varieties in many respects. At all events, with notable exceptions such as the comedy *Babel, or the Local Corruption of the Hellenic Language* (1836)[7] by D. K. Vyzantios and the arguments used by certain purists to support the use of *katharévousa*, the issue of the mutual incomprehensibility of the Modern Greek dialects – in contrast to Italy, for instance – rarely played a major role in Greeks' consciousness of their own language.

Vyzantios (Dimitrios Konstantinou Hatzi-Aslanis) was born in Constantinople about 1790 and died in Patra in 1853. *Babel* is a rumbustious comedy set in a coffee house in the new capital, Nafplion, in 1827, amid the excitement following the destruction of the Ottoman and Egyptian fleet by the British, French, and Russian navies at Navarino. Each of the characters is a newcomer from a different part of the Greek world, and the rudimentary plot revolves around an incident in which an Albanian feels deeply insulted when he misunderstands an innocuous expression uttered by a Cretan, and the ensuing fracas has to be halted by the police. Ideologically speaking, the whole play, which is lively and amusing enough to be performed even today, is an argument in favour of *katharévousa*: the uneducated characters are able to speak only their own local dialect (seven of which are represented), while the pedant speaks in Ancient Greek, with the result that nobody can understand anybody else. As the author makes clear in his introduction to the first edition, this shows the need for a supradialectal language variety, in which the 'corruption' of the spoken language is rectified by the introduction of Ancient Greek vocabulary, phonology, and morphology.[8] The fact that the misunderstanding in the fictional plot is due entirely to regional differences in vocabulary rather than grammar seems to have escaped the author's notice.

Dimaras sees the year of Korais' death (1833) as marking the beginning of a new phase in the language question.[9] In that year a collection of Korais' prefaces to his editions of ancient texts was published in a new edition, thus making it easier to gain an overall view of his opinions and proposals, which had been scattered in his various 'Impromptu thoughts'.[10] Nevertheless, the educational law of 1834, which remained in force until 1880 and established seven-year compulsory schooling in Greece, specified that Ancient Greek, rather than the variety of Modern Greek used and promoted by Korais, was to be the language of school

---

[7] The play was probably written about 1831.   [8] D. K. Vyzantios 1972: 79–80.
[9] K. Th. Dimaras 1985: 371.   [10] Korais 1833.

readers and other textbooks, beginning from the first year of primary school.[11] Thus, just as they had done before the revolution, children continued to learn reading by means of words and phrases in Ancient rather than Modern Greek.

As Elli Skopetea writes, despite the absence of a linguistic academy and despite the fact that '*katharévousa* was not taught as a language (nor was demotic, naturally) during the first, linguistically crucial, half-century in the history of the Greek state', a written language was nevertheless created.[12] One factor contributing to this situation is that the ability to use *katharévousa* became a valuable cultural, social, and symbolic asset in which people were willing to invest a tremendous amount of time and effort. Purism met with an enthusiastic reception from the bourgeois and petty bourgeois public. Greek shopkeepers eagerly erected signs in *katharévousa*, archaistically proclaiming their shops to be παντοπωλείον [grocer's], ιχθυοπωλείον [fishmonger's], and ζυθοπωλείον [ale-house] and thus making them seem superior to what they would have been if they had been called μπακάλικο (ultimately from Turkish *bakkal*), ψαράδικο (a Greek vernacular word), and μπιραρία (cf. Standard Italian *birreria* and dialect *biraria*).

Another factor favouring the establishment of *katharévousa* is that the romantic ideologues who dominated the discourse of Greek national identity in the period 1840–60 did not wish to restrict membership of Hellenism to those who spoke Greek as their mother tongue. As Socrates Petmezas puts it,

[v]ery few scholars felt the need to turn their attention to the spoken vernacular or to celebrate the Greek demotic language as a product of the national genius, thus clearly differentiating the Greeks from the other Balkan Christians. . . . Language was used as a measure of value, but only in the sense that a more pure and classical form could better reveal the unaltered Greek genius. . . . Language in its vernacular form could thus never be upgraded to become the nucleus of the national attributes, because this would endanger the conscious project of nation formation in incorporating all other Greek-Orthodox Christian groups in the Hellenic nation. Hellenism was associated with a common religious and cultural tradition, open to all Greek-Orthodox Christians in the Balkans.[13]

---

[11] Hatzistefanidis 1986: 49–50; Vagenas 1992: 58. Bien 1972: 63 states erroneously that 'Korais' *koine* [was] recognized in King Otho's educational laws of 1834 and 1836 as in effect the language of the Greek state'. This is a misreading of Chourmouzios 1939: 1442, who states that 'the educational laws of 1834 and 1836 essentially recognized the archaizing language as the official language'.

[12] Skopetea 1988: 108.   [13] Petmezas 2009.

The adoption of vernacular Greek as the national written language would have privileged mother-tongue Greek speakers over other Balkan Christians, thus undermining the hegemonic project of Greek romantic nationalists, which depended upon the use of religion and culture rather than spoken language as the prime identity marker of the 'Greeks beyond the frontier'.

During the first half-century of the Greek state, the language controversy lay comparatively dormant, seeming to have been definitively resolved, at least in practice, in favour of what later came to be called *katharévousa*. As Anna Frangoudaki points out, from the 1830s onwards *katharévousa* was an 'ingenious compromise that... made it possible for the newly formed Greek state to opt for the living, spoken language, even if in purified form, instead of Ancient Greek'. The adoption of *katharévousa*, she argues, 'represented the triumph of Enlightenment intellectuals over the Ancient Greek resurrection proposal'.[14]

This language was very quickly developed by literary figures, teachers, politicians, journalists, civil servants, and others and was enthusiastically espoused by most members of the cultural and political elite and the bourgeoisie in the nineteenth century. It is characteristic of the Greek case that, while language reforms in other new states were undertaken with the help of official and semi-official bodies, *katharévousa* was developed in an empirical and unsystematic fashion, without congresses, commissions, and academies, and with little official support. Nevertheless, administrative, juridical and military terminology was created, and relevant vocabularies issued, at the invitation of the state, by various academics and professionals during the first thirty years of the Greek state.[15] This terminology tended to be particularly archaic, Ancient Greek nautical terms, for instance, being officially introduced into the Royal Hellenic Navy, while the traditional terms (many of Italian origin, while others were purely Greek) continued to be used in civilian seamanship.[16] This effort contrasted with the introduction of neologisms into the Greek language during the Ottoman period, when most of the words added to the word stock of the Greek language were loanwords from foreign languages.

Grammars and bilingual dictionaries were compiled by individuals, generally without state sponsorship. According to Marianna Ditsa, lexicographers were perhaps the prime inventors of neologisms in nineteenth-century Greece, lexicography being seen not only as a matter

[14] Frangoudaki 1992: 367.   [15] C. Dimaras 1975: 32.
[16] Triantafyllidis 1938: 563–69.

of collecting material but of invention. The authors of bilingual dictionaries were really producing dictionaries of Greek, using the foreign language as an alibi that protected them from involvement in the language controversy.[17] It was not until 1933 that there appeared a monolingual dictionary of Modern Greek, that is, one in which both the language defined and the defining language were neither Ancient Greek, nor a foreign language, nor a modern regional dialect.

Those who developed *katharévousa* were highly successful in the domain of vocabulary, where they either coined new words on the basis of morphemes and derivational rules of Ancient Greek, or else revived words from the ancient language. Where there was no existing word for some modern concept, most of their proposals have become established and are used today by all Greeks. Examples include πανεπιστήμιον [university] (used by Korais in 1810), ὑπουργεῖον [ministry] (1824), δημοσιογράφος [journalist] (1826), λεωφορεῖον '[(omni)bus] (1863), and ποδήλατον [bicycle] (1889).[18] As for their proposals for replacing already existing words of foreign origin with ancient Greek words (mostly in new meanings) or with new words based on ancient Greek morphemes, many of these have also been accepted. For example, κυβέρνησις replaced γκουβέρνο (Italian *governo*) [government] and κράτος superseded ντοβλέτι (Turkish *devlet*) [state]. Others, however, were not accepted; for example, Ancient Greek ἐσθής did not displace the indigenous φόρεμα [woman's dress], and the new coinage λαιμοδέτης (1871) failed to supplant γραβάτα (Italian *cravatta*) [necktie]. The archaic words that were successfully transplanted into the modern language were generally those denoting concepts used in formal registers, while those that failed to establish themselves typically denoted physical objects encountered in everyday life.

What the spoken language lacked was a rich resource of vocabulary for expressing the more abstract concepts of modern culture. The purists believed that the introduction of ancient words and new coinages based on Ancient Greek morphemes had to be accompanied by the introduction of the greater part of the morphological system of the Hellenistic *koine* rather than by the adaptation of archaic vocabulary to the morphological system of the modern spoken language, as happened, for instance, in the case of words borrowed from Latin into modern Italian.

[17] Ditsa 1988: 65, 70.
[18] The words ending in -ν are used without the final ν in demotic and consequently in today's Standard Modern Greek. The dates given here and in the following examples are taken from Koumanoudis 1980.

Just as the autocephalous Church of Greece was established in 1833 with its seat in Athens, so the national written language was chiefly elaborated in the new capital of independent Greece. From the 1830s to the 1850s, with little resistance from practical or theoretical vernacularists, the archaized written language was gradually enriched through its use in a variety of influential works, most of them published in Athens. In the 1830s alone, these influential works included grammars of Modern Greek and a dictionary, as well as novels and poetry.

Apart from the one by Vamvas mentioned at the end of Chapter 4, grammars included Venthylos' *Grammar of the Modern Hellenic Language* (1832)[19] and Chrysovergis' *Grammar of our Hellenic Language in Comparison with the Ancient* and *Grammar of the Neo-Hellenic Language* (1839a and 1839b). The first of Chrysovergis' two grammars is a description – very rare at this time – of the spoken language; the term *paráthesis* [comparison through juxtaposition] in the title indicates that he is following Korais' methodology, namely the parallel teaching of the modern and ancient languages. The second is a grammar of the written language and is therefore more prescriptive than descriptive; 'neo-Hellenic language' here means what later came to be called *katharévousa*, the spoken varieties being termed 'spoken language', 'demotic language', and 'demotic style'.[20]

Skarlatos Vyzantios' *Dictionary of our Hellenic Dialect Interpreted into Ancient Greek and French* (1835) was the first dictionary of genuine spoken Modern Greek to be compiled by a Greek for almost two centuries.[21] Vyzantios shows the influence of Korais in his preface when he refers to 'the people' as 'the first and *par excellence* the legislator of every language'. He claims to have attempted to find words that are common to all the dialects. On the other hand, he asserts, it would be ridiculous to express scientific and scholarly ideas 'in grocers' style'; for this reason, in order to be written down, our spoken language must be corrected according to that of our ancient forebears: the gap between Ancient and Modern Greek must be eliminated by writing in a more archaic language than that which is spoken, so that readers will familiarize themselves with

---

[19] Venthylos was professor of Greek philology at the University of Athens. His grammar was, significantly, published at the expense of the 'American Philhellenic Printing House' in Athens.

[20] Chrysovergis 1839a: 9. Chrysovergis was a schoolteacher.

[21] The previous one was the *Tetraglot Thesaurus* (1659) by the Cretan Gerasimos Vlachos, metropolitan of Philadelphia (with his seat in Venice), which interpreted Modern Greek words into Latin, Italian, and Ancient Greek. Vyzantios states in his prologue that he started compiling his list of entries on the basis of Vlachos' dictionary, adding and removing words as he saw fit.

the ancient forms. He expresses the belief that poets and other writers will control the future development of the language, and he urges them to use Attic words and phrases.[22]

The fact that Vyzantios felt the need to define the meanings of Modern Greek words by using Ancient Greek and French shows that he considered the ancient language, like French, to be one whose words and their meanings could be taken as given, whereas the words of the modern language required interpretation – even, it seems, for its own speakers. At the end of his dictionary he included a list of words of foreign origin that were to be expelled from the language. It is illuminating to see how multifarious were the words of Turkish origin in use in his time; it is also interesting to observe which of these have survived in the common spoken language in more recent times, and which ones dropped out of it fairly soon afterwards. Vyzantios' dictionary, as well as subsequent Greek dictionaries up to the present day, illustrates the truth of Sue Wright's assertion that 'dictionaries are part of nation building'.[23]

The first Greek novels – *Leander* (1834) by Panagiotis Soutsos (Constantinople 1806–Athens 1868) and *The Exile of 1831* (1835) by his brother Alexandros (Constantinople 1803–Athens 1863) – were written in a moderately archaized language, while the early poetry produced in the capital (Nafplion and Athens) – also beginning with the Soutsos brothers in the 1830s (for example, Panagiotis' dramatic poem 'The Wayfarer' [1831], which is usually credited with inaugurating Athenian romanticism) – used a large amount of vernacular vocabulary and grammar. However, the written language became progressively more archaized as the decades went by. Some authors archaized their language yet more in each successive edition of their works. 'The Wayfarer', for instance, was reissued in 1842 and 1853, each time with its language radically revised in order to reflect Soutsos' more archaistic linguistic ideology.[24] Such archaization was clearly motivated by a view of the language as a noble edifice requiring restoration rather than as a practical and efficient vehicle of communication. In addition, the publication of Greek newspapers, in Athens and in other towns in Greece and abroad, ensured that far more material in 'corrected' Modern Greek was being written and that far more people were becoming accustomed to reading it than ever before.

[22] S. Vyzantios 1835: pp. v, vii, xx.

[23] Wright 2004: 58. For examples of words of Turkish origin that have disappeared from Greek since Vyzantios' time see Chapter 2, p. 73.

[24] For the linguistic history of 'The Wayfarer' see K. Th. Dimaras 2000: 367.

Literary production and the language debate in the British-protected Ionian Islands (Heptanese) to 1864

Meanwhile, in the Ionian Islands, which had been under British rule ('protection') since shortly before the final defeat of Napoleon in 1815, Solomos continued to write in an uncompromising variety of the vernacular deeply infused by the rhythms of folk poetry, which he elevated to a supreme instrument of poetic creativity. Members of the intellectual circle that revolved around him also contributed to this process, both in theory and in practice.

There were in effect two rival romantic movements in Greece, one based in Athens and the other centred in (or originating from) the Ionian Islands. The different intellectual outlooks of both movements – the Classicizing romanticism of Athens orientated towards the consolidation of the Greek state, and the more European romanticism of the Ionian Islands oriented towards liberation – went together with their tendency to use different versions of Greek: *katharévousa* in Athens, demotic in the Heptanese. After *katharévousa* became established in Athens, the 'language of freedom' continued to be used for poetry in the Ionian Islands, where the vernacular continued to be cultivated for literary use until such time as it could be handed over to the Athenian Generation of 1880.

Among the friends and admirers of Solomos (who was generally ignored in Athens) was the Zakynthian Georgios Tertsetis (1800–74), who, like him, wrote both in vernacular Greek and in Italian.[25] In a letter written in 1826 to the young Dimitris Botsaris after the death of the latter's father Markos in battle, Tertsetis, successfully imitating the style of a simple, uneducated person, uses the word *Romiosyni* to refer to the Greek people as a whole; although this letter remained unpublished until 1952, it is one the earliest attestations of the word.[26]

In the late 1820s, however, while continuing to write poetry in the vernacular, Tertsetis switched to *katharévousa* in his prose writing, much of which consisted of patriotic speeches. In 1833 his friend Solomos, having read the text of some lectures that Tertsetis had given at the officer cadets' school in Nafplion, wrote to him chiding him for using

[25] Other Heptanesians, such as Typaldos and Laskaratos, also wrote in both Greek and Italian.

[26] Konomos 1984: 210. It is curious that this term, which is intimately connected to Orthodox Christianity, was used by Tertsetis, who was a Roman Catholic. Palamas n.d.: VI 278 pointed to the occurrence of the term in the vernacular 'Song of Daskalogiannis', which refers to a revolt by Christians against the Ottomans in Crete in 1770; however, the date of the text (first published in the late 1880s) is uncertain.

'quella lingua babelica' [that language of Babel], by which he meant *katharévousa*. In the same letter, Solomos bewailed 'il mare della rea usanza' [the sea of guilty usage], accusing those who used 'purified' language of being 'coloro che uccidono la civiltà della Grecia' [those who are killing the civilization of Greece].[27] In 1832 and 1833, Tertsetis published his first two (not altogether successful) attempts at composing poems in fifteen-syllable verse, each of which he described as 'an essay in national poetry'.[28] By 'national poetry' he meant poetry whose language and metre were modelled on those of the folk songs, although in practice the language of his poems is a clumsy mixture of oral and learned features, with more echoes of Solomos' poetry than of the folk songs.

Tertsetis consolidated his patriotic credentials, which he had established through his role in the revolution, by publishing fairly faithful transcriptions of memoirs dictated to him by heroes of the independence struggle, most notably those of Theodoros Kolokotronis (transcribed in 1836 and published in 1846): this oral history complemented his friend Spyridon Trikoupis' written account of events, about which I shall say more below. Later he published a book with the indicative title *Simple Language* (1847), containing poems and prose by himself together with poems by Solomos. Like Solomos, Tertsetis saw the popular language as being sacred, since it was the language of the heroic men and women who had liberated the Greek nation. For this reason, he felt, it was blasphemous to belittle it. However, his case is symptomatic of the fact that, as some of the early proponents of the vernacular took up leading positions in the administration of the Greek state, they gradually espoused its language when writing in prose.[29]

In 1848 the Ionian Parliament instituted freedom of the press in the United States of the Ionian Islands, and in 1849 it decreed that from 1852 onwards Greek should be the sole official language of the state. However, the official gazette continued to include material in Italian and English, and the variety of Greek that was used there and in most other publications was usually a 'corrected' version of the modern language. Looking back over a number of decades in the 1880s, the aristocrat Andreas Laskaratos (1811–1901) made a comparison between the use of Italian in the Ionian Islands and the use of *katharévousa* in Greece itself.

[27] Solomos to Tertsetis, 1 June 1833, in Solomos 1991: 252–3. Matesis too had described Korais' language as the 'language of Babel' (Matesis 1953: 324).

[28] Konomos 1984: 71, 76.

[29] Bouchard 1970: 50. Tertsetis was employed by the Greek state as (successively) a teacher, judge, and archivist.

He recalled that, in the Ionian Islands thirty years previously, all proceedings in parliament and the law courts, as well as official documents, were in Italian, and gentlemen spoke and wrote in the same language except when communicating with servants and peasants. Laskaratos relates that, when he began his career as a barrister in 1840, he would pretend not to know Italian and would ask the judge to explain what was being said. During one session, another lawyer became so irritated by Lasakaratos' behaviour that he said to him: 'Non vi vergognate di parlare in greco? Parlate in italiano, che è la lingua Signorile [Aren't you ashamed to talk in Greek? Talk in Italian, which is the gentlemanly language].' 'In 1884,' noted Laskaratos, 'only we old people understand Italian, whereas our language is the language of the Nation.' He concluded by predicting that *katharévousa* would be replaced by the 'language of the people' in Greece as a whole just as quickly as Italian had been replaced by Greek in the Ionian Islands.[30]

In the 1850s there was a resurgence in expressions of support by Ionian Islanders for the written use of the spoken language. The first collection of Greek folk songs published by a Greek in Greek lands was the work of a Heptanesian, Antonios Manousos.[31] Manousos' collection, significantly entitled *National Songs* (1850), is prefaced by a fictional dialogue whose chief characters – in tacit homage to Solomos – are the Editor and a pedant. The difference from Solomos is that here the pedant's interlocutor is not a poet, but a scholar who has gathered together the poetry of the nation. The Editor, who speaks in the vernacular, defends his decision to publish the songs against the criticisms of the pedant, who fulminates, in highly archaized Greek, against their language. The Editor asks:

How can I change or deny a language I have received from my father, just as he received it from my grandfather, and he from my great-grandfather, and so on and so on – a language I have nurtured for so many years, which I have always used to express my ideas, my will, my pain and my joy, to my friends and my compatriots...?

To the Editor's emphasis on the emotional connotations of the spoken language the pedant retorts that

---

[30] Laskaratos 1959: III 523.

[31] Manousos' collection was preceded by a collection published by Georgios Evlampios in St Petersburg under the poetic and symbolic title *The Amaranth, or, The Roses of Resurrected Hellas: Demotic Poems of the Modern Hellenes...* (Evlampios 1843).

the true language...was raised resplendent to the summit of glory, not from the bosom of the Nation, not from the soul of the Mob, but from ancient papyri, from libraries, from grammars and dictionaries.

The pedant goes on to let the cat out of the bag by asserting: 'To write, my dear friend, and not to be understood: behold! the problem is solved.' Significantly, the Editor brings the dialogue to an end by quoting a long passage from Vilaras in support of the written use of the spoken language.[32] In this way, no doubt influenced by Herderian notions that the language and songs of the folk embody and express the soul of the nation, Manousos explicitly links himself to the radical vernacularist tradition that had been interrupted by the revolution. Manousos himself uses the vernacular in his introductions to and commentaries on the individual songs in his collection, thereby implying that the vernacular is appropriate not only for poetry but also for expository prose.

In 1855 Solomos' disciple Iakovos Polylas (1825–96) published a translation of Shakespeare's 'The Tempest' in vernacular prose, together with a study of the play, also in a language approaching the spoken. The following year Laskaratos published a satire on social life on his home island, *The Mysteries of Cephalonia, or Thoughts on Family, Religion and Politics in Cephalonia* (1856), written in a racy language heavily tinged by local speech – a work for which he was excommunicated by the Church. Ioulios Typaldos (1814–83), in the epilogue to a collection of his poems (also published in 1856), entitled simply 'The language', states that the 'demotic language' is 'the present-day language of the Greeks'. Perhaps influenced by Spyridon Zampelios, about whom I shall have more to say later, Typaldos argued that 'the question of the language' was a social and national matter rather than a purely literary one. He claimed that the superior culture of ancient and modern Greece had waged a perpetual struggle against the East: Achilles and Alexander had united Greece politically and, like the warriors of 1821, had taken part in 'a duel between immobility and progress, past and future'. The language question was about writing for the whole nation, with the aim that Greece would become sufficiently powerful to be unified again.[33] This argument was based on the Athenian ideology of the *Megali Idea* (for which see below), but it was also influenced by a sense that Greeks living outside the Greek state were being ignored by the language policies of Athens.

[32] Manousos 1850: 8–9, 11, 12–14.   [33] Typaldos 1953: 324–9.

In Zakynthos in 1859, two years after Solomos' death in Corfu, Polylas published an edition of his master's works, preceded by a prologue on the poet's life and oeuvre written in a very slightly archaized vernacular. In his prologue, using organic imagery characteristic of romanticism, Polylas argued for the use of the vernacular in prose as well as in poetry:

Poetry, which cannot breathe except in the embrace of nature, does not accept any medium but the living voice with its [grammatical] forms, which is nothing other than the palpitating heart of the whole of society; nor should prose accept any other, unless it wishes to be reduced to a dry logical mechanism, capable, like mathematical formulae, of serving the mind, but voiceless and fruitless for the society to which it is called upon to grant the benefits of enlightenment.[34]

Polylas' emphasis on the oral, living and natural character of the vernacular is typical of the arguments adduced in its favour. For Polylas, the fact that Solomos' *Hymn to Liberty* was written by 'an author almost unlearned in Ancient Greek demonstrates the correctness of the theory that our literary language can be formed not through the mechanical approximation of the ancient, but through the organic development of the modern'.[35]

To many readers (especially in Athens), the eagerly awaited first edition of Solomos' extant works came as a grave disappointment. As early as 1825, two years after its composition, Spyridon Trikoupis had described the *Hymn to Liberty* as the 'national anthem'.[36] (Set to music by the poet's friend Nikolaos Mantzaros in 1828, it became the official Greek National Anthem in 1864, after the union of the Ionian Islands with the Greek state, much to the chagrin of certain purists who objected to its 'vulgar' language.[37]) Yet the man whom Polylas called the 'national poet' had published very little after the *Hymn*, and the Greek reading public were impatient to read what Solomos had been busily writing since then. Most of what they found in Polylas' edition was the editor's brilliant attempt to piece together a more or less coherent oeuvre out of a jumble of successively reworked fragments. Few readers at that time were in a position to appreciate Solomos' heroic struggle to express his transcendent romantic vision in the demotic language and in the metre of the Greek folk song. Modern readers may be thrilled and fascinated by the

[34] Polylas, in Solomos 1961: 15.   [35] Polylas, in Solomos 1961: 28.

[36] *Geniki Efimeris tis Ellados* 5 (21 Oct. 1825), quoted in Polychronakis 2006: 44n.

[37] In 1891, for instance, A. R. Rangavis called for the first two stanzas, which are the only ones normally sung, to be translated into *katharévousa*; see Triantafyllidis 1938: 496; Triantafyllidis 1963c: 232–3; and A. Dimaras (ed.) n.d.: 11–12.

extraordinary flashes of brilliance in Solomos' work, but what the Greek reading public wanted in 1859 was a solid body of poetry that would consolidate and flatter their national pride. For such people, Solomos' poetry was an abject failure – and so was his demotic language. By the 1850s, however, the writings of some of the Heptanesians (particularly Polylas) show that the thirty years that had elapsed since Solomos' 'Dialogue' had brought a good deal of compromise with the Athenian written language.

From the Ionian Islands to Athens

Now the agenda was definitely being set in Athens, which was the seat of national political and cultural power. One of the books that greatly influenced the codification of simple *katharévousa* was the *History of the Greek Revolution* (1853–57) by Spyridon Trikoupis (1788–1873). Trikoupis, born in Mesolongi, had begun his literary career with *Dimos: a Kleftic Poem* (1821), one of the earliest literary imitations of Greek folk song in language and metre – though not in theme, despite its title.[38] Much later, in 1859, Trikoupis claimed that the time he had spent with Solomos in Zakynthos in 1823 had had a decisive effect on the poet's career, since Trikoupis had urged him to study the folk songs and the poetry of Vilaras and Christopoulos and to put his obvious poetic talents in the service of the Greek revolution; furthermore, Trikoupis claimed that his efforts to help Solomos to learn to write in Greek had been so successful that he was soon able to write the *Hymn to Liberty*.[39]

In the introduction to his *History* Trikoupis attacked the archaizers and promoted Korais' 'middle way', which he followed in practice in his book, albeit with some deviations towards both the spoken and the ancient. He expressed the hope that the spoken and written language would eventually become one and the same, arguing that the spoken language could not be properly cultivated if it was so widely separated from the written variety that mutual influence between the two became impossible. He claimed that he employed certain vernacular words and forms where necessary for the sake of clarity and euphony, and that he avoided showing off by using ancient forms and words that were not in common written use in his time. He recognized that certain excessively

[38] At that time, the adjective 'kleftic', properly used for folk songs about the klefts (patriotic brigands during the Ottoman period), was often applied to Greek folk songs in general.

[39] In an early draft of Solomos' 'Dialogue', the third participant in the discussion was called Trikoupis, but the author later removed the name and replaced it with 'The Friend'.

archaic forms were not feasible when pronounced in the modern way because they sounded ridiculous.[40] This care for 'euphony' is clearly subjective and unsystematic, and it indicates Trikoupis' conflation of grammar with aesthetics. Like other moderate purists of his time, he still tacitly subscribed to the erroneous theory that the modern spoken language was a continuation of ancient dialects other than Attic, and that the only kind of archaism that should not be permitted was the use of features peculiar to Attic.

As the codification of *katharévousa* proceeded, many writers gradually introduced more and more Ancient Greek forms into their writing, with the ultimate aim of making the modern written language as close as possible to Ancient, or at least Hellenistic, Greek. It is interesting to observe how Korais' ideas were later developed by purists who no doubt believed they were improving on his legacy. In 1852, for instance, Ioannis Zampelios from Lefkada (1787–1856) wrote a 'Dissertation on the Neo-Hellenic language', in which he presented the tripartite nature of the Greek language in the following way:

The literary language of modern Greece [i.e. *katharévousa*], intermediate... between the ancient language and the vulgar language [αγοραία, literally 'of the market place'], has on her right, as mother and mistress [δέσποινα], the ancient, from whence she certainly expects more assistance, and on her left, as handmaid and servant [θεράπαινα], the vulgar language, because of the venerable relics that the vulgar language has still preserved from the ancient; hence she affords to some the opportunity to accept her and provide her with Hellenic garments, and to others to dress her in penurious rags.

This *filologikí glossa* [literary language], Zampelios continues, is 'a girl still in her infancy, hitherto wrapped in swaddling clothes'.[41] We may note Zampelios' use of Korais' idea of the valuable 'relics' that Modern Greek has retained from Ancient Greek; yet, whereas Korais was claiming to correct Modern Greek according to Ancient Greek rules, Zampelios seems now to be adhering as closely as possible to Ancient Greek while allowing some features of Modern Greek to contribute to the mixture.

Five years later, Zampelios' son Spyridon (1815–81) argued that the Greek language of his time had defied the laws of philology, since it was both modern and ancient at the same time. What Zampelios *fils* means

---

[40] The author's comments on the Greek language and his justification for his choice of language variety are to be found in Trikoupis 1853: 9–13, 355–8.

[41] I. Zampelios: 1860: 502. The same image was used, coincidentally, by Vilaras in 1812 (see Chapter 5, p. 149).

by this is that Greek is exceptional in that its history runs counter to the dogma that had been preached by the science of historical linguistics during the previous three decades, namely that all languages are subject to inexorable change over time. In fact, Zampelios continues, if one omitted ten or twenty words of Latin or Turkish origin, the modern language is pure Ancient Greek.[42] Nevertheless, while he himself used strikingly archaic features (including the connecting particles *oun* [therefore] and *gar* [for], which had disappeared from spoken Greek almost two millennia previously), he warned against 'Atticizing', which was one of the ways in which Byzantine obscurantism had kept people in ignorance. One can only conclude that he and his like kept their ears closed to what was being spoken around them, and even to their own mode of speech. The example of Zampelios *père et fils* shows that by no means all of the intellectuals from the Ionian Islands were vernacularists. However, unlike many purists, Spyridon Zampelios claimed that all Greeks possessed a common spoken language with a common accent and common idioms.[43]

Athens again: the historically crucial decade of the 1850s and its cultural and linguistic repercussions

By 1853 the ideological climate had changed. The struggle for political independence from the Ottoman empire had been superseded by the *Megali Idea* [Great Idea], first enunciated by Ioannis Kolettis in 1844. When the new Greek state gained its independence around 1830, its population was about 800,000, a figure that represented only a quarter of the total Greek population of the Near East, the remainder living either in the Ottoman empire or in the British-protected Ionian Islands.[44] The goal of the national struggle was now to consolidate the state and expand it by incorporating the 'unredeemed Greeks' within it.

The *Megali Idea* originated from the co-existence, within the Greek state, of 'autochthons' (Greeks from within the borders of the state) and 'heterochthons' (Greeks from elsewhere). There was considerable public feeling that those Greeks who had arrived in the country from elsewhere after the War of Independence should be excluded from Greek citizenship and barred from holding public office. Following a successful revolution calling for constitutional rule in 1843, the debates in the assembly charged with drafting the constitution included a prolonged discussion as to whether the members of the future parliament should be natives

[42] S. Zampelios 1857: 646.   [43] Ibid., 649–50.   [44] Petropulos 1968: 23.

of the constituencies that they represented. The ensuing dispute has been described as an 'identity crisis' in Greek society.[45] Those members of the assembly who stood to be excluded by this provision included Kolettis, a doctor of Aromanian origin from Syrrako in Epirus, who had served as physician to Ali Pasha of Yannina and subsequently as Greek ambassador in Paris. The provision was accepted, although an exception was made for Kolettis and a few other heterochthons. The debate highlighted the conflict between two opposing views of Greek identity, namely state identity and ethnic identity.

In his maiden speech to the constitutional assembly on 14 January 1844, Kolettis summed up the 'Great Idea' in his statement that Greece was destined to enlighten the West with its fall (i.e. in 1453) and the [Near] East with its rebirth: '[T]he first was fulfilled by our forefathers, while we are entrusted with the second; it is in the spirit... of this great idea that I have always seen the representatives of the nation assemble to decide not on the fate of Greece but of the Greek race'. He contrasted the fall of Classical Hellas, which was due to the fact that it was divided into separate states, with the Hellas of the future, which would be united in a single state. He went on to argue that those who had fought in the War of Independence – like Rigas Velestinlis before them – had taken up arms for 'that great idea of the fatherland' and for the whole of Christendom (by which he particularly meant Orthodoxy), not, he implied, for the temporary rump state of Greece that existed in his time. He concluded his speech by calling upon the other delegates to 'embrace the great destiny of our homeland'.[46] Dimaras argues that the Greek discourse on the national 'destiny' and 'mission' fitted well with *katharévousa*: both lacked a grounding in reality, and each fed off the other.[47]

The problem of the written language became most acute in the realm of literature. In 1851 an annual national competition for a poem or poems 'on a moral subject' was inaugurated and funded by Amvrosios (Amprouzis) Rallis, a rich Chiot merchant in Trieste and a cousin of the famous Ralli Brothers, whose company remained for many years the biggest and wealthiest Greek trading firm in the world. The competition was adjudicated by Athens University professors, and the reading of the adjudication and the announcement of the winner, which took place each year on Greek Independence Day, 25 March, became an occasion

[45] Dimakis 1991: 8.

[46] Details of Kolettis' speech and its background are taken from K. Th. Dimaras 1982: 405–12, Dimakis 1991: 7–49, and Dimitrakopoulos 1996: 171.

[47] K. Th. Dimaras 1985: 386–7.

for national celebration, the winner often being carried triumphantly at shoulder height through the streets of the capital amid crowds of admirers.[48]

The rules for the competition, drafted by Rallis himself, specified that the language of the entries must be 'appropriate to the theme, but always seemly and eloquent' – which clearly implied *katharévousa*.[49] The Rallis competition consolidated the hold of *katharévousa* over literary verse in Athens, marking the official recognition of the so-called Old Athenian School, whose tone had already been set by the epico-lyric poem *Hellas against the Turks* by Alexandros Soutsos (1850), written in archaistic language. Entries to the competition tended to be epico-lyric in form and patriotic in tone, and their diction was characterized by rhetorical vapidity. Some writers submitted poems in demotic, but the judges refused to award the prize to any of them. In fact, the adjudicators made it clear that the aim of the competition was the promotion of a more archaized variety of *katharévousa* as much as the promotion of poetry.

Not all university professors were happy with Rallis' language stipulation. The recipient of Rallis' letter in his capacity as vice-chancellor of the university, Spyridon Pilikas, a native of Zakynthos and a friend of Solomos, took a different view. In the speech he gave when handing over the vice-chancellorship to his successor, he stated that 'in modern poetry the archaeological dress of words and phrases seems contradictory; the breath of the cemetery dries up the tenderness of feeling'.[50] Reading the reports of the adjudicators, however, one is struck by the plethora of grammatical errors they felt obliged to point out. The fate of poetry and poets in Athens for the next twenty-five years came to be decided by university professors.[51] Some of those who were considered the best poets were themselves professors: grammatical 'correctness' seemed to be the chief criterion of poetic excellence, and it seemed that only pedants could write 'correctly'.

The first Rallis competition was won by Georgios Zalokostas (formerly Tsalakostas, 1805–58), a poet of Aromanian origin (from Syrrako in Epirus, like Kolettis) and an admirer of Solomos. Zalokostas wrote in both *katharévousa* and demotic. His prize entry in 1851 was an epico-lyric poem entitled *Mesolongi* recounting the Ottoman siege of that town in 1826, in which he had fought. *Mesolongi* stands in contrast to 'The Free

---

[48] For a full account of the national poetry competitions see Moullas 1989.
[49] For the text of the rules see Moullas 1989: 34–5.
[50] Pilikas, speech on 28 Sept. 1852, quoted in K. Th. Dimaras 1986: 191.
[51] Koutrianou 2003: 67.

Besieged', the ambitious and transcendent poem in demotic on which Solomos worked for almost twenty years but failed to complete. Solomos' poem was inspired by the same historical event, of which he knew only at second hand; the drafts of his composition were not published until eight years after Zalokostas' poem. Zalokostas won the prize again in 1853 with another epico-lyric poem, *Armatoles and Klefts.* His ambitious and bombastic patriotic poems on national historical themes also contrast starkly in quality with his tender, moving poem written in demotic in 1848 and inspired by the death of his son – one of seven out of his nine children who died in childhood – entitled 'The North wind that stifles the lambs', which was justly described at the time as being 'full of simplicity and passion';[52] yet even this poem is composed in anapaestic metre, which is a far cry from Greek folk poetry.

Zalokostas' attitude to the demotic language is clear from the following passage, which he wrote, in *katharévousa,* in 1852:

The demotic language..., first-born daughter of Ancient Hellenic..., has been corrupted today in the cities, but is preserved chaste and virginal where the shepherd's pipe sounds, where the plough tears the earth, where the solitary cottage rises. But civilization has penetrated the innermost depths of Greece, accompanied by luxury, which effeminates our life, by fashion, which uproots our customs, and behold! the people of the cities forget their ancestral language and distort it in the belief that they are Hellenizing.[53]

Here Zalokostas prefigures the view of many later demoticists, who wished to turn the clock back by promoting the language spoken by the traditional rural folk rather than that of the urban populace who had been influenced by *katharévousa.* What is also interesting about this passage is the use of *patrios* [ancestral] to refer to demotic, at a time when other writers were using the same adjective to refer to Ancient Greek.[54] Everyone claimed that they wanted to use their ancestral language; it depended how many generations one wanted to go back.

In the 1853 competition, honourable mention was awarded to a poem on an ancient theme ('Corinna and Pindar') by Georgios Tertsetis, which was ineligible for the prize because it was written in demotic. In his prologue to the poem, Tertsetis explains that the poet Corinna defeated Pindar in a poetry competition because he used old Doric, while she sang

---

[52] G. Paraschos, quoted in L. Politis 1966: 229.
[53] Zalokostas, quoted in Skopetea 1988: 103.
[54] See, for instance, the quotation dating from 1870, ibid., 102–3.

'simply, in the language of the people'.[55] Quite apart from the clever device of embedding the story of one poetry competition within a poem submitted for another, it is especially significant that in Tertsetis' poem it is a female character, Corinna, who is depicted positively as speaking in support of the 'language of the people'. What impressed the adjudicators in this poem (much of which is frankly doggerel, with clumsy handling of language and versification) is the fact that, for the first time, the demotic language, together with stylistic echoes of the folk songs, was being used in an ambitious poem that aimed to bring the ancient world to life.

In his adjudication speech the poet, novelist, diplomat, and archaeology professor Alexandros Rizos Rangavis (1809–92), who had by this time turned his back on the romanticism of his youth,[56] pointed out the incongruity of the fact that in Tertsetis' poem the ancient poets Pindar and Corinna speak in demotic, while in Zalokostas' entry the illiterate armatoles and klefts speak in *katharévousa*.[57] Nevertheless, Rangavis asserted that 'we must not dissipate our forces in the specific development of dialects, but concentrate them on the dignified formation of the Panhellenic language'. In the following year the same adjudicator claimed that the competition aimed to ensure 'the return [of the language] to its ancient forms'.[58] Rangavis' reference to dialects and 'Panhellenic language' reflects the view expressed by many leading Greek figures in the mid-nineteenth century that the reason for the decline of Classical Greece had been that the Greeks were split into different states speaking different dialects, and that for the modern Greeks to be strong they must be a united nation with a unified language. Such people tended to argue that the spoken language was split into dialects and was therefore nationally divisive. This militated against the use of the vernacular in literature.

Tertsetis was probably the first to use the word *katharévousa* as a noun in print – to describe the language in which he wrote an explanatory note appended to 'Corinna and Pindar' when he published the poem in 1856.[59] In a satirical poem he submitted (with no hope of winning) to the 1858 competition and rashly entitled 'The triumph of the 1858 poetry competition', a modern Athenian woman understands instinctively what her brother became aware of only by travelling round the Greek countryside,

[55] Konomos 1984: 422.

[56] His narrative poem *Dimos and Eleni* (1831) has been seen as one of the earliest manifestations of Athenian romanticism, while his prologue to his drama *Frosyni* (1837) has been described as the manifesto of that movement. For Rangavis as a romantic poet see Güthenke 2008: 149–62.

[57] Rangavis, quoted in Skopetea 1988: 112n.   [58] Moullas 2006: 16.

[59] Konomos 1984: 109. For the history of the noun *katharévousa* see Delveroudi 2008a.

observing Greek country folk dancing and singing and participating in weddings and funerals, namely the beauty of the everyday spoken language. Tertsetis even has the recently deceased Solomos appear in a dream to the heroine, telling her that her brother should finish writing a poem on a patriotic historical theme that he has left incomplete, and that he should enter it for the competition. The brother claims that to accuse a nation of not possessing a language reduces it to the level of savages.[60] In this poem, Tertsetis, like other vernacularists, points out that the pedants confuse style with grammar.[61]

In 1850 relations between the autocephalous Church of Greece and the patriarchate of Constantinople were normalized after almost two decades of estrangement. This gave the impression that the patriarchate condoned Greek nationalist policies[62] and encouraged citizens of Greece to look beyond the confines of their small kingdom and to think of their co-religionists in the Ottoman empire as unredeemed brothers and sisters waiting to be liberated by being incorporated into the Greek state. According to Elli Skopetea, the regularization of relations between the Greek Church and the patriarchate also freed Greek historians to legitimize Byzantium as an integral part of the Hellenic tradition.[63] It is notable that Kolettis' speech had not made a single direct reference to Byzantium.

The 1850s was a time of nationalist mania and religious fervour in Greece. One of the reasons was that 1853 was exactly four hundred years after the fall of Constantinople to the Turks. In the Crimean War (1853–56), France and Britain sided with Turkey in order to forestall any Russian attempt to take over the Ottoman empire. Not content with this, they imposed a blockade on Greek ports for the duration of the war to prevent Greece from offering assistance to Russia. Many Greek intellectuals, who had hitherto been content to see Greece as being part of western Europe, came to realize that the most important component of their national identity, apart from language, was Orthodox Christianity, and that Protestant England and Catholic France had formed an unholy alliance with the Muslim Ottomans to combat the Orthodox Russians. At the same time, the two historical poles of Greek identity, namely the Orthodox tradition moulded by Byzantium and the Ancient Greek heritage promoted by the Enlightenment, which had previously been

---

[60] Konomos 1984: 160.   [61] Ibid., 150.   [62] Koubourlis 2005: 328.
[63] Skopetea 1988: 178. For the gradual discovery of Byzantium by Greeks in the period 1830s–1850s see K. Th. Dimaras 1985: 394–410.

viewed as mutually exclusive, came to be seen as being the twin sources of modern Greece's legitimate national existence.[64]

In 1851 Skarlatos Vyzantios began the prologue to his book entitled *Constantinople* by referring to the Byzantine period as 'an inseparable and essential part of our overall Hellenic history'.[65] The following year Spyridon Zampelios coined the term 'Helleno-Christian civilization' to imply the unbroken continuity of Hellenic culture from ancient to modern times by way of Byzantium.[66] Zampelios founded and inspired the Greek school of national historiography by attempting to discover the philosophical meaning and the political direction of Greek history since ancient times. Since antiquity, he proclaimed, the Greek people had had a divinely sanctioned civilizing mission and that it now possessed a unique historical destiny: to reclaim the throne of the Emperor Constantine.[67] In his *Byzantine Studies: on the Sources of Neohellenic Nationality* (1857), the first study of Byzantine history to be published by a Greek, Zampelios took the argument of Kolettis' *Megali Idea* speech a stage further by claiming that under Alexander the Great the Greek *genos* (the Greeks by lineage), who had been divided into separate states in Classical antiquity, became a united Greek *ethnos* (a Greek polity) and that the Byzantines had preserved this political unity.[68] He argued that it was time to put an end to modern Greeks' exclusive orientation towards antiquity and to rehabilitate and appropriate the Byzantine Christian Middle Ages, which was when the Greeks were united in a single Christian state.

Konstantinos Paparrigopoulos (1815–91), professor of the history of ancient nations at Athens University since 1851, succeeded in converting Zampelios' inchoate and clumsily expressed vision into a coherent narrative. In 1853 Paparrigopoulos published the first version of his *History of the Greek Nation*, which, although it included only a few pages on Byzantine history, contributed to the retrospective Hellenization and nationalization of Byzantium.[69] As Thanos Veremis points out,

---

[64] See, for instance, Dimitrakopoulos 1996: 52.

[65] S. D. Vyzantios 1851: i. Vyzantios was from Constantinople – hence his surname ('Byzantine').

[66] S. Zampelios 1852: 464. Following a Hegelian dialectic, Zampelios no doubt conceived of the 'Helleno-Christian' synthesis as being superior to either the Hellenic or the Christian alone.

[67] Koubourlis 2005: 34, 112, 128, 136, 140, 158. Koubourlis points out that Jules Michelet expressed similar ideas about the French as a chosen people with a divinely sanctioned mission to save the world (ibid., 178–80). He also notes that the concept of Greece's 'civilizing mission' is already present in Kolettis' *Megali Idea* speech of 1844 (ibid., 28).

[68] S. Zampelios 1857: 47–8, quoted and discussed in Koubourlis 2005: 189–90.

[69] For Paparrigopoulos' gradual progress towards acceptance of the Byzantines as 'medieval Hellenes' see Kourboulis 2009.

Paparrigopoulos managed to express in historical terms the unity of the Hellenic nation that Kolettis had expressed geographically.[70] The same period that saw the rehabilitation of Byzantium in the Greek national narrative (1830s to 1850s) also saw ancient Macedonia gradually being fitted into the discourse of Greek national continuity; this move went hand in hand with the desire to incorporate modern Macedonia within the Greek national territory.[71]

On 29 May 1853, the anniversary of the fall of Constantinople, Panagiotis Soutsos published a newspaper article prophesying that the Ottoman empire would be defeated by Russia in the imminent war and that the Greeks would recover their empire.[72] Soutsos, who came from a Fanariot family, was anti-Enlightenment, anti-Western, and anti-Heptanesian, orientated towards Russia, Byzantium (his birthplace), and Orthodox Christianity. He was probably the author of an anonymous newspaper article that had already attacked Tertsetis for his poem 'Corinna and Pindar'; it was inappropriate, the anonymous author argued, for the Heptanesians, who possess a 'poor Greek dialect', to impose it on 'the language of the free Hellenes'.[73]

Up to now the general linguistic tendency in Athens had been that, while expressing their respect for Korais, writers felt it necessary to 'improve' on it, following his example by introducing into the written language more and more lexical and grammatical features of Ancient Greek. Soutsos announced a break with this tradition in a pamphlet entitled *New School of the Written Word, or Resurrection of the Ancient Greek Language Understood by All* (1853), which has been described by K. Th. Dimaras as being, in its time, 'the most important linguistic manifestation since the foundation of the [Greek] state'.[74]

In the *New School*, Soutsos broke the taboo on criticizing Korais, accusing him of ignoring the language written by the prelates of the Church, the Danubian princes, and the local elders – a reprise of Kodrikas' attack on Korais in 1818. Soutsos alleged that Korais had imported French political and philosophical ideas wholesale into Greece, filling the language with Gallicisms and creating a 'meagre Frankish

---

[70] Veremis 1997: 29–30.

[71] For changing Greek views on Macedonia in the 1840s see A. Politis 1993: 39–45.

[72] P. Soutsos, 'I Eikosti Ennati Maïou', *Aion*, 29 May 1853, quoted in Moullas 1993: 265. Soutsos' brother Alexandros had already talked in 1845 about 'the Hellenic nation having reigned imperially in Constantinople' (K. Th. Dimaras 1985: 339).

[73] I. S., 'Filologia', *Aion*, 15 April 1853, quoted in Moullas 1993: 268–9.

[74] C. Dimaras 1975: 34.

edifice', a '*Neograikikí glossa* [Neo-Greek language]',[75] which was now used by all academics, journalists, authors, and translators, and which was to Ancient Hellenic what the English plaster cast of the Erechtheum Caryatid was to the original marble sculpture. Soutsos claims that Boeotian shepherds speak purer Greek than university professors, who use literally translated French.[76] He asserts that the hearts and minds of the modern Greeks will be elevated by writing Ancient Greek, and that they will thereby learn Truth and Freedom.[77] These sentiments are similar to those of Korais, with the crucial difference that Korais claimed that one would obtain these results from studying Ancient Greek rather than writing it. In this respect, as in others, Soutsos was following the example of Doukas.

Soutsos' message, which is full of imperatives, is addressed to the younger generation: 'O youths, throw down the walls separating our language from the ancestral one!'[78] He urges his fellow writers to use a simplified version of the ancient language, rooting out all literal Greek translations of foreign phrases. He claims to be raising 'the Hellenic language of the ancestors, formerly called *koine*, from the tomb' – something that Korais had said was as impossible as raising the dead themselves. 'The language of the ancients and of us the moderns,' Soutsos continued, 'shall be one and the same; their grammar and ours shall be one and the same. Their words and phrases alone shall be acceptable.'[79] All of the ancient prepositions, pronouns, conjunctions, declensions, and conjugations should be revived, including the infinitive, the optative mood, the aorist middle, the ancient future and perfect tenses, and the participles, most of which had died out of the spoken language more than a millennium previously. However, he made an exception for the dual number, on the grounds that the ancient Aeolians did not possess it and therefore the modern Greeks were justified in not using it.[80] He had reservations about certain other forms too; for example, he felt that for the time being it would be better to avoid ancient logical connectors such as *gar* [for] and *oun* [therefore], and that the negative particle *ou* was 'as yet

---

[75] P. Soutsos 1853: 4–5. His term *Neograikikí glossa* was a dig at Korais, who usually called the modern Greeks *Graikoí*; by coining the adjective *Neograikikós* (based on the French *néo-grec*), Soutsos was suggesting, with some justification, that Korais had viewed his compatriots through western eyes.

[76] Ibid., 42.

[77] Ibid., 26. The reference is to the statue that was shipped to England by Lord Elgin in 1809–10 and sold to the British Museum and to the plaster cast that was later erected in its place in the Erechtheum on the Acropolis at Athens.

[78] Ibid., 16.   [79] Ibid., 5.   [80] Ibid., 16.

alien and harsh to our hearing', though given time it would cease to be so; in the meantime, he advised his readers to try to avoid the modern negative particle *den* as much as possible.[81] In practice this entailed the ludicrously difficult feat of avoiding the use of negative indicative clauses.

Soutsos ends his little book with a call to arms addressed to his fellow Greeks, in which he eagerly claims that the Russians are trying to force the British to hand over the Ionian Islands 'to the future Emperor of the Greek *genos* [nation]'.[82] It is clear that the hoped-for resurrection of the 'Greek [= Byzantine] empire' and that of the ancient Greek language were indissolubly connected in Soutsos' mind.

Some of Soutsos' criticisms of Korais are sound (particularly his allegation that Korais introduced forms that belonged neither to the learned written language nor to colloquial speech); some of the passages he quotes from the writings of university professors are truly horrendous; and some of his recommendations are even in use today. But his knowledge of Ancient Greek was shaky, and he did not always practise what he preached; these two faults were commonly found in the linguistic arguments of the archaists and purists in the nineteenth century. At all events, it is perhaps not coincidental that Soutsos (fortunately) produced no more poetry after this.

Soutsos' views and modes of expression show how Doukas' messianic Hellenism, which had been overshadowed by Enlightenment ideas, re-emerged in the 1850s.[83] Soutsos was not the only Greek of his time to entertain such utopian ideals; Skarlatos Vyzantios, for instance, wrote in 1862 that '[t]he resurrection from the dead of our paternal language is our sweetest dream'.[84] The chief cause of this utopianism was an intense frustration at the smallness and the economic, political, and cultural poverty of modern Greece compared with both ancient Greece and modern European nations, which led to a desire to transcend the narrow physical limitations presented by contemporary Greek life – a desperate desire for Greece, held tightly in the economic and political grip of Britain and France, to expand its frontiers, to 'liberate the enslaved brethren', to become the centre of learning and culture for the whole of the Near East, and in general to become great again. We also have to take into account the continuing reaction to the ethnological theories of Fallmerayer.

---

[81] Ibid., 19.   [82] Ibid., 86–92.
[83] Kitromilides 1984: 36 talks of Greek 'national messianism' in the 1850s.
[84] S. Vyzantios 1862: p. xiii.

The most significant riposte to Soutsos' manifesto came from Konstantinos Asopios (1785–1872), who held a university chair in Classics that Soutsos considered should have been his own and who is frequently criticized by name in Soutsos' book. Asopios responded to Soutsos' assertions and criticisms in an anonymous, longwinded, and pedantic diatribe, *The Soutseia, or Mr Panagiotis Soutsos Scrutinized as a Grammarian, Philologist, Schoolmaster, Metrician and Poet* (1853), in which he proclaimed himself proud to be called a follower of Korais, though he believed he had improved on Korais' language by making it more archaic. Asopios went on to point out errors and solecisms in Soutsos' own language – a habitual tactic used in the squabbles among the pedants of the time.

Asopios' view, like that of Korais, was that Modern Greek had been forcibly (i.e. unnaturally) barbarized by *apaidefsía* [lack of education and culture]: only remnants of Ancient Greek shine brightly through the 'dirt', the 'ugliness', and the foreign elements. As for the written language, however, Asopios argued that one should not revive any ancient features that are totally absent from Modern Greek. Where, for instance, an ancient preposition is used in some fossilized expression (e.g. the *ex* and the *en* in the fossilized expressions *ex aitias* [because of] and *en toutois* [nevertheless]), its use could be generalized to other phrases according to Ancient Greek grammar, while other Ancient Greek prepositions that do not appear at all in Modern Greek usage (e.g. *amphi* 'round, about') should not be revived. Like other supporters of *katharévousa*, Asopios had to walk a tightrope between the use of too few and too many features of Ancient Greek in the modern language. His proposal to generalize the employment of Ancient Greek features that happened to be used in fossilized expressions was a totally haphazard and unsystematic approach to language. Asopios subscribed to the frequently expressed argument that as long as the *laós* [common people] could passively comprehend a certain usage, then this was sufficient justification for adopting it; the question whether the *laós* could *actively* handle such a usage was usually ignored.

In his weighty tome – almost three times as long as Soutsos' pamphlet – Asopios intended to demolish Soutsos and all his works, as the title of his book indicates. But it is obvious that Asopios' motivation – and Soutsos' for that matter – went beyond matters of vocabulary and grammar, and even beyond personal rivalries. As so often happened in the Greek language controversy, what was at stake was nothing less than a struggle to control Greek culture. The dispute between Asopios and

Soutsos – like the dispute between Korais and Kodrikas a generation earlier – was a war between two world-views: the liberal humanist view of the Enlightenment, represented by Asopios, which ignored or despised Byzantium, and the chauvinistic view of romantic religious nationalism, represented by Soutsos, which considered Byzantium to be the hitherto missing link in the continuity of Hellenism from antiquity to the present. It is precisely because both pagan antiquity and Christian Byzantium employed Ancient Greek (or, to put it another way, the Ancient Greek language belonged to both antiquity and Byzantium) that the two camps were equally fixated on the relationship between the ancient and the modern languages. It is also for this reason that the combatants on both sides often employed linguistic varieties that were scarcely distinguishable from each other, yet each writer constantly found fault with the language used by his detractors, pointing out, with gleeful indignation, literal translations from French phrases and grammatical errors. Yet, since *katharévousa* was, almost by definition, a chimerical jumble of heteroclite linguistic features, it was impossible to agree on a common standard of correctness by which a text could be judged.

Asopios' book provoked a series of attacks and counterattacks from other pedants in the form of pamphlets, each author priding himself on his dispassionateness, impartiality, and clemency – qualities that his opponents allegedly lacked – while in reality each was equally impassioned, biased, and determined to find fault.[85]

During the period 1830–70 few writers in Athens argued in favour of using demotic: the Soutsos–Asopios controversy was one of a series of pamphlet wars in which each member of the *katharévousa* clique would criticize others, often trying to score points against them for purely personal reasons. Each tried to outdo the other in their ability to adduce Classical examples in support of their arguments, while attempting to perform the impossible balancing act of writing in as archaic a language as possible without actually writing Ancient Greek. All these learned men were in favour of a mixture of Modern Greek and Ancient Greek, but they disagreed on precisely which ingredients from each language should make up the mixture. The basic (though unstated) principle was: 'I'm right and you're all wrong: what I write is elegant, correct, learned, but readily comprehensible Greek, while what you write is macaronic, arbitrary, solecistic, and incomprehensible.' Nevertheless, there is a good

---

[85] On the Soutsos-Asopios controversy see Moullas 1993.

deal of wit in the best of these polemics, and some of them still make amusing reading.

In 1856 a royal decree was issued with regard to the language used in Greek primary schools: 'As the Grammar of the Greek language..., that of the ancient language alone is prescribed.'[86] It is unlikely that this decree was influenced by Soutsos' book, but it is indicative of the backward-looking ideology of the times. It is ironic that, in the very year that the term *katharévousa* was first used in print as a noun denoting the officially sanctioned written language, the Greek state specifically reiterated that pupils were to be taught Ancient Greek, rather than *katharévousa*, from the outset of their school careers.

Greeks and others once more

In 1821, given the choice between continuing to live in the Ottoman empire and helping to create an independent Greek state, Orthodox Christians speaking various languages had thrown in their lot with the Greek national cause. Thirty years later Spyridon Zampelios wavered between language (Hellenism) and religion (Orthodoxy) as the defining factor of the Hellenic nation and praised the Bulgarians, 'the adopted children of Orthodoxy', for their contribution to the Greek revolution of 1821.[87] Similarly, he expected the other Orthodox Christian peoples to continue to become assimilated to Hellenism and to further its cause.

In the introduction to the 1853 version of his *History of the Greek Nation*, Paparrigopoulos writes: 'All those who speak Greek as their own language are called the Greek nation.'[88] Nevertheless, it is instructive to look at Paparrigopoulos' attitudes to Slavs, Aromanians, and Albanians in the same book. Since the Slavs who settled in the Peloponnese in the early Middle Ages were far fewer than the Greeks, he writes, they received Christianity and the Greek language from them. He predicted that the same would happen in the more northerly Greek lands where Slavs had preserved their language until recently because they were more numerous than those who moved south. In his view, the Aromanians arrived in Greek lands in the later Middle Ages not to pillage but to settle. They consisted of a mixture of various nations, including descendants of Greeks, and therefore they immediately began to learn the Greek language, to

---

[86] Triantafyllidis 1938: 492.

[87] Koubourlis 2005: 321–7. For Bulgarians who took part in the Greek insurrections see Todorov 1964.

[88] Paparrigopoulos 1970: 33.

see the Greeks as brothers and, by practising various peaceful and useful trades, increased the strength of the Greek nation. As for the Albanians who arrived in Greece in the late Byzantine period, Paparrigopoulos continues, they are descended from the ancient Illyrians, who were a nation related to the most ancient of the Greeks (by which he probably means the Pelasgians). Their spoken language, he writes, is a mixture of the most ancient Greek with many later Greek words, together with Italian and Turkish words; for this reason, those Albanians who were not forced later by the Turks to espouse Islam always thought of themselves as being *omogeneís* [members of the same race or nation] with the Greeks.[89] Thus Paparrigopoulos variously incorporated these groups of incomers into the Greek nation by way of religion, descent, language, and culture and looked forward to their imminent assimilation. In fact, since the Albanians, like the Greeks but unlike the Slavs and the Aromanians, were considered to have been indigenous to the Balkans since the earliest antiquity, they were often considered by Greek nationalists to be the closest relations, both racially and culturally, of the Greeks.

The University of Athens, which was founded in 1837, was the only university to be established in the Balkans until the foundation of the University of Bucharest in 1864. For this reason it attracted a number of Orthodox Christian students from non-Greek backgrounds. However, the rise of Greek nationalism, which carried along with it many speakers of other languages, eventually led to rival nationalisms in the Balkans, which emerged both under the influence of Greek nationalism and in reaction against it. As the nineteenth century progressed, it became increasingly obvious that many Orthodox Christians in the Balkans did not feel themselves to be Greek; indeed, they felt themselves to be dominated as much by Greek culture as by the Ottoman political system. Intellectuals began to 'discover' that they were not really Greeks at all but Romanians, Bulgarians, Albanians, or Macedonians, and they began to spread this new 'discovery' with quasi-religious zeal among large masses of those they considered to be their people. The story of the Bulgarian national movement, in particular, is about the struggle for emancipation from Greek cultural hegemony as well as liberation from Ottoman rule. According to Giuseppe dell'Agata, the leaders of the Bulgarian national movement were educated in Greek schools, and it was precisely their Greek education that awakened their Bulgarian national consciousness. Most of the Bulgarian intellectuals who debated the proper nature of the

---

[89] Ibid., 104–5, 107, 112.

written Bulgarian national language in the 1830s and early 1840s wrote to each other in Greek.[90]

In many Balkan towns north of the predominantly Greek-speaking regions, Greek had become the common language of education and commerce used by people of Aromanian-, Slav-, and Albanian-speaking origin; indeed, it was spoken as their home language by the families of high-profile figures such as merchants, doctors, and teachers. The career of Grigor Parlichev (1830–93) is typical of the kind of metamorphosis of identities that was beginning to take place in those regions. Parlichev was born and bred near Ohrid in what later became the Yugoslav Republic of Macedonia. As his autobiography shows, to learn to read and write in the Ottoman Balkans in his time still meant to read and write Greek, which was the language of the Church. At school in Ohrid in the 1830s Parlichev was taught Orthodox liturgical texts rather than Greek nationalist ones, and he went on to teach these same texts to his pupils. In 1860 he won the Greek national poetry prize as 'a pro-Greek Bulgarian' under the name Grigorios Stavridis, sparking off a controversy that culminated in the discontinuation of the Rallis competition.[91]

A few years later, however, Parlichev espoused the Bulgarian national cause and proceeded to teach Bulgarian at Ohrid and to agitate for the introduction of Church Slavonic in the churches there, in an ultimately successful attempt to reverse the process of Hellenization that he had been previously involved in.[92] What made Parlichev adopt the Bulgarian nationalist cause was the fate of the Miladinov brothers, one of whom had been his Greek teacher at school in Ohrid. In 1861 the brothers had published a collection of Bulgarian Macedonian songs in Zagreb, dedicated to Joseph Strossmayer, Catholic bishop of Diakovár [Djakovo], who was an active supporter of the pan-Slavist movement. The brothers were imprisoned by the Ottomans on the grounds that they were working for the Catholic Church, and they died in prison of typhus in 1862.[93] Horrified by the fate of his beloved teacher and suspecting that the arrest and ill-treatment of the brothers was due to a plot by the local Greek bishop, Parlichev abandoned the Greek cause. It is probable that, if Parlichev had been born a generation earlier, he would have remained

---

[90] Dell'Agata 1984: 174.

[91] For the circumstances surrounding the award of the prize see Moullas 1989: 151–8.

[92] For his autobiography see Parlichev 1927, and Parlitsef 2000. A few years before this, Michail Perdikaris had written that his poem *Ermilos* (written 1806, published 1817) 'was completed in utterly Bulgarian Ohrid'.

[93] Roudometof 2002: 91.

an active propagandizer of Greek culture rather than simply retaining an emotional attachment to Ancient Greek poetry; yet if he had been born two generations later, he might have become a Macedonian nationalist. Today Bulgarians consider Parlichev to be a Bulgarian and Macedonians consider him to be a Macedonian, while some Greeks still consider him to be a Greek poet.[94]

In 1870 an event took place that radically changed the religious and national make-up of the Balkans. After a campaign beginning in the late 1830s,[95] which was originally aimed at ensuring that Bulgarians were appointed as bishops and that the liturgy was celebrated in Slavonic in areas inhabited by Bulgarians, and partly in reaction to what they saw as the increasingly cosy relationship between the patriarchate of Constantinople and Greek national aspirations, Bulgarian nationalists managed to persuade the Sublime Porte to allow the establishment of a Bulgarian church, based in Constantinople. The Bulgarian exarchate, as it was known, was granted jurisdiction over large areas of Bulgaria, Thrace, and Macedonia and was given the right to acquire further territories provided that two-thirds of their inhabitants wished to join.[96] This was perhaps the first time that the Ottoman government had recognized a community's freedom to choose which *millet* it wished to belong to. This decision served its own interests, since it succeeded in dividing its Orthodox subjects into separate communities that were in opposition to each other. As a result of this development, the *Millet-i Rum*, which since 1767 had included all the Orthodox Christians of the Balkans in a single flock, lost a large number of its members, and it suddenly seemed likely to lose even more. Up to this point, Greek nationalists had generally assumed that all the Orthodox Christians who lived in the regions they claimed as Greek were willing to support the Greek national cause. From now on, they realized that the other non-Greek-speaking Christians in the Balkans were in danger of following the Bulgarians towards ecclesiastical (and ultimately political) independence. One of the effects of these developments was that the Ecumenical Patriarchate of Constantinople, so called because it was supposed to be universal, without distinction of race or language, came to be seen by Greek nationalists (and eventually to see itself) as a specifically Greek institution that should support Greek national aspirations.

---

[94] In Bulgarian his surname is written Пърличев, in Macedonian Прличев, and in Greek Σταυρίδης.

[95] Todorov 1975: 127.   [96] Hupchick 2001: 245.

Dimitris Livanios points out that, during the course of the nineteenth century, language fought a long and painful war with religion for the coveted position of the main criterion for being a Greek. After the establishment of the Bulgarian exarchate,

[t]he dilemma of how to approach the position of the Slavs in relation to the Greek nation became...quite acute, for if 'Greekness' was allowed to be confined to the Greek-speakers only, then 'Greece' itself would have to be cut down to its linguistic size and could not make much headway in Macedonia. Consequently, the power of language to determine ethnicity had to be somehow tempered. A solution to such a problem came through the application to the Slavs of two relatively novel terms: 'national descent' [εθνική καταγωγή], and 'national sentiment' or, perhaps, 'national consciousness' [φρόνημα]: the Slavs of Macedonia and beyond were Greeks, not by virtue of their language but because of their Greek descent.... After all, it was argued, if the Alsatians can be both German-speaking and French, why should the Slavs of Macedonia be prevented from doing the same with regard to Greece?[97]

The teaching of Greek to non-native-speakers came to be seen as a matter of national urgency. In 1869, a few months before the Bulgarian exarchate was established, a Society for the Dissemination of Greek Letters was founded in Athens, while around the same time the Greek state began encouraging the establishment of Greek schools north of the border (which still ran from the Gulf of Arta to the Gulf of Volos, as it had done since 1832), and especially in Macedonia, Bulgaria, and Romania.

The schools set up by Greek, Romanian, and Bulgarian authorities in regions of the Ottoman Balkans on which each of these authorities had territorial claims became major channels for the dissemination of the competing nationalisms and national identities. While Greek teachers tried to persuade all of the local Orthodox Christians that they were Greeks, Romanian teachers tried to persuade Aromanian speakers that they were Romanians, and Bulgarian teachers tried to persuade Slav speakers that they were Bulgarians. As is clear from this, the criterion for being Bulgarian or Romanian was based on language, while the criterion for being Greek was 'consciousness' and ideology. However, as Ioannis Koliopoulos points out, the foundation of schools in towns beyond the Greek borders by the Church and private individuals before 1870 was efficiacious because there were socio-economic incentives for learning Greek, whereas the Greek state's policy of establishing schools

---

[97] Livanios 2006: 59–60. The theory that the Slav speakers of Macedonia were the descendants of Greeks who had lost their language seems to date from the 1870s, immediately after the establishment of the Bulgarian exarchate (see Gounaris 2007: 339).

in villages from 1870 onwards was less successful, since inculcating 'national consciousness' was seen by the various authorities as a higher priority than the teaching of the language.[98] As Karakasidou argues,

> Bulgarian propaganda in Macedonia enjoyed far greater success than its Greek counterpart, owing largely to the central use Bulgarian activists made of the language issue.... This was particularly true of liturgical language, since it meant that finally rural inhabitants could hear mass and other rituals conducted in a language they could understand.

The standardized Bulgarian language used in churches, she continues, was far closer to the spoken Slavonic vernaculars than the liturgical Greek used by patriarchist priests was to spoken Greek.[99]

The Heptanese strikes back: continuing arguments in favour of the written use of the spoken language in the 1870s

In the 1870s, some chinks began to show in *katharévousa*'s armour, though it is indicative that most of the few proponents of demotic were Heptanesians, and that they tended to promote its use in poetry. Since 1864 the Heptanese had been part of the Greek kingdom, and some of these men were living and working in Athens, bringing the literary and linguistic legacy of Solomos with them to the nation's capital. One of the voices raised to defend the use of the spoken language in poetry was that of the teacher and translator Antonios Fatseas (Kythera, 1821–72), who in 1870 published a pamphlet 'On the language and culture of the modern Greeks'.[100] This was a riposte to the adjudicators' criticisms of his entry to the national poetry competition, which, he claimed, was much liked by the audience. In this pamphlet he accepts the situation that there is one language for poetry, the 'national language, the language of everyday life', which is under the jurisdiction of the *laós*, and another for science and scholarship, which is the domain of university professors. He attacks the professors for presuming to lay down the law for poetic language; this can be seen as a modern manifestation of the ancient quarrel between poetry and philosophy, although Fatseas does not present it as such. Significantly, he asserts that the natural, common language is not only 'the language of life and truth' but also 'the continuation of Hellenic, the distinguishing feature of the nation', whereas scientific language is international. In keeping with his explicit

[98] Koliopoulos 2003: 87–8.   [99] Karakasidou 1997: 99–101.
[100] Fatseas 1952: 123–43.

references to Herder, Fatseas claims that the common language, like a mother, preserved the Greeks' nationality during the years of their slavery by means of her folk tales, her songs, her myths, and her proverbs. Although Fatseas' pamphlet is written in simple *katharévousa*, he claims that when he writes poetry the mother tongue tells him: '[I]n me is found your poetic treasury, the metaphors, the proverbs, the allegories, the images, the myths, the commonplaces', in a word, 'modern Greek *vios* [life, culture]'. He expresses the hope that 'the masterpieces of art' will decide on the language of the Greeks. In this hope he was no doubt influenced by the widespread assumption that the works of Dante and other poets decided the outcome of the Italian language question in favour of the vernacular. He expresses his contempt for Byzantium and alleges that it is the reactionary and pedantic 'Byzantine spirit' that is responsible for the dire political and cultural state of Greece in his own time. '[T]he sense of our own insignificance is deeply rooted in our souls,' he adds, 'yet with such principles, with such feelings we want to capture Constantinople.' He ends by calling for the recognition and cultivation of 'our language', which up to now has been deadened by being kept subservient to Hellenic, so that the patriotism of the ancient Greeks can be resurrected.

In 1872 Gerasimos Markoras (born in Cephalonia, 1826–1911) composed a poem entitled 'Simple [language] and *katharévousa*', in which he wrote that, ceaselessly seeking out the language in the mountainous regions of Epirus and Macedonia – 'in those parts / where the air resounds / with kleftic verses' – he fancied he had found 'unlettered Tyrtaioses / wearing kilts' and had fallen in love with their 'poor, free Muse'.[101] Tyrtaios was an ancient Spartan poet of patriotic war songs; the language and poetry of the kleftic songs may have been 'poor', the poet implies, but it was the language of the free.

A Heptanesian who exerted significant influence on the acceptance of demotic in poetry in Athens was Aristotelis Valaoritis (born in Lefkada, 1824–79). As a member of the Ionian Parliament in Corfu, he had consistently argued for the union of the Ionian Islands with the kingdom of Greece and, after this took place in 1864, he settled in Athens as a member of the national assembly. Valaoritis wrote lively, patriotic epico-lyric poems on historical subjects in vigorous demotic, notably *Kyra Frosyni* (1859), which recounts the story of a Greek woman who was drowned in Yannina lake on the orders of Ali Pasha in or around 1801,

---

[101] Markoras 1988.

and *Athanasis Diakos* (1867), which dramatizes the capture and execution by the Turks of one of the heroes of the revolution. Nevertheless, the voluminous historical material in prose that accompanied Valaoritis' poems when he published them was written in *katharévousa*. Valaoritis was firmly convinced that 'the language of the people' was appropriate for poetry, if not for erudite prose: 'Born automatically, it is not the work of art, unlike the one that is being devised at present [i.e. *katharévousa*],' he wrote in 1857; 'it is the sole remaining shoot on the venerable old tree of our nationality.' In the same text, countering the allegations of Rangavis and others that the spoken language was split into dialects, he asserted: 'The language of the *laós* is one. The language of the *lógioi* [learned] is heterogeneous.'[102]

Valaoritis' passionately patriotic poems, with their linguistic and metrical echoes of the Greek folk song and their dramatic use of dialogue, made such an intense impression on the Athenian establishment that in 1872, shortly after the fiftieth anniversary of the outbreak of the revolution, he was commissioned by the university to write a poem to mark the unveiling, on 25 March, of the statue of patriarch Grigorios V, who had been executed by the Ottomans in 1821.[103] This commission was tantamount to an official sanction for the use of demotic in poetry; indeed, the text of the university's invitation to the poet describes his language as 'sweetly spoken and entirely national'.[104] But it was also a manifestation of a new and specifically Greek popular patriotism (or patriotic populism): the remains of the martyred Ecumenical Patriarch of Constantinople, who had been the spiritual leader of all the Orthodox Christians of the Ottoman empire, irrespective of ethnicity and language, had recently been transported from Odessa to Athens, where he was now being celebrated in demotic Greek rather than in the supposedly supranational language of the Church. It is significant that two months after the public recitation of Valaoritis' poem, Paparrigopoulos referred to him as the 'national poet'.[105]

Back in the Ionian Islands, Laskaratos published a collection of poems entitled *Various Versifications* (1872) and dedicated to Tertsetis. In the prologue, Laskaratos writes that 'the *logiótatoi* [pedants], the enemies of the nation, while pretending to speak to the nation in a language better

[102] Valaoritis 1857: 9–11.

[103] This statue, together with that of Rigas Velestinlis, erected in 1871, was paid for by Georgios Averof, a Greek benefactor of Aromanian origin (Kefallinaiou 1995: 459–60). Both statues still stand in front of the University building in Panepistimiou Street.

[104] Valaoritis 1907: 195.   [105] K. Th. Dimaras 1970: 31–2n.

than its own, are speaking and writing in a language that the nation doesn't understand, [with the result that] it remains untutored, ignorant and barbarous, and consequently betrayed by them'.[106]

In 1873 Nikolaos Konemenos (1832–1907), born in Preveza (Epirus), brought up in Lefkada and Corfu and resident of Patra in the Peloponnese, where he served as Ottoman consul, published a book entitled *The Question of the Language*. Writing in fluent demotic with some Heptanesian features, but unafraid to use *katharévousa* words and forms where appropriate, Konemenos argues that the spoken language, in which dialect differences are minimal, should become the basis of the national written language. He asserts that it has an inner coherence that does not appear on the surface because it has not been adequately studied. 'Language . . . is a means, not an end,' he writes, and its purpose is to transmit thoughts and emotions to others.[107] He points out the paradox that the *lógioi* have accepted demotic as the medium of poetry,[108] yet still persist in calling it a 'jargon', or a 'vulgar idiom': how can this be, he asks, when it is used in poetry, and is therefore capable of expressing the noblest and most sublime concepts? 'I believe,' he continues, 'that our modern language is a perfection of the ancient.'[109] As for its alleged vulgarity, he writes (echoing Solomos): 'Vulgarity and impropriety do not exist in any language. Vulgarity and impropriety may exist only in the idea and in the manner in which the idea is expressed.'[110] 'All other nations have a present,' he argues; 'we do not. . . . By despising and renouncing our language, we are despising and renouncing our present.'[111] Finally, Konemenos moves well beyond the confines of the language question when he claims that adherence to ancient models 'keeps us static . . . and sickly. . . . We need to get out of the tombs, to get out from under the yoke, to breathe, to live, to seek a new world, to create a new civilization of our own.'[112]

Konemenos' views are a sign of a new turn in Greek national ideology, which looks forward to the emergence of the demoticist movement. Two years later he published a second book, *Once More on Language* (1875), in which he defended the language he used in his earlier book against those who claimed that it was not pure spoken Greek. In fact, as he points out, he had made great efforts to write a de-regionalized vernacular. With his experience of the regional language of various parts of the

---

[106] Laskaratos 1959: II 390.   [107] Konemenos 1873: 6.

[108] This cannot be an allusion to Mistriotis' adjudication speech, which was delivered in May 1873 (see below), because Konemenos' text is dated January of that year.

[109] Konemenos 1993: 81n.   [110] Konemenos 1873: 15.

[111] Ibid., 22.   [112] Ibid., 55.

Greek-speaking world, Konemenos was able to discover its common features. 'There is a single common language,' he argues; 'we don't have dialects, but we have idioms.'[113] 'We are alien to antiquity,' he asserts; 'we have our own independent language, we have our own grammar.'[114] In his writings, Konemenos too shows that he understands the distinction between grammar and style.[115] As for the pedants, he claims, instead of adjusting technical terms borrowed from Ancient Greek so as to conform to the rest of the language, they have made the whole of the language conform to the technical terms. This, he says, is like chopping and squeezing the body to fit the clothes rather than cutting and adjusting the clothes to fit the body.[116] Finally he provides a translation into the 'simple language' of a text on international law written in archaic *katharévousa*: this was one of the earliest attempts to translate a complex legal text into spoken Greek.

In a second series of national poetry competitions (the Voutsinaios competition, 1862–77), the language stipulation was omitted.[117] In the event, however, very few poems were submitted in demotic. The continuing difficulty of finding a balance between archaism and vernacularism is illustrated in the adjudication speech delivered by Rangavis at the 1867 poetry competition. He criticizes one entry because its language is 'tinged not with genuine Hellenic colours, [that is] ancient ones, but with modern ones'. It is significant that, in linguistic discourse, the adjective 'genuine' is still being used here to refer exclusively to Ancient Greek. However, in the same speech, Rangavis criticizes the use of archaic vocabulary in two entries and praises the author of another for avoiding, 'with very few exceptions, everything that is excessively antiquated and, so to speak, *glossimatikón* [unusual or obsolete]'.[118] Opinions about what was 'excessively antiquated' necessarily differed according to the extent of the individual author's puristic tendencies.

In 1873, for the first time, the national poetry prize was awarded to a collection of poems in demotic by an Athenian university student named Dimitrios Kampouroglou (1852–1942), who later became an eminent historian and a member of the Academy of Athens. The collection

---

[113] Konemenos 1875: 12.   [114] Ibid., 50.

[115] Konemenos 1873: 42 points out that S. Vyzantios makes the same confusion in the prologue to his dictionary.

[116] Konemenos 1875: 14.

[117] Moullas 1989: 173 attributes this to the fact that Ioannis Voutsinas, who founded and funded the competition, was from Cephalonia.

[118] *Krisis* 1867: 7, 19, 25, 46.

bore the symbolic title *The Voice of My Heart*, which could be taken to apply as much to the demotic language of the poems as to their content. These poems have since come to be seen as heralding the new poetry of the 1880s: reminiscent of Christopoulos' poems in their urban demotic and their intimate and sometimes playful tone,[119] they stand far from the patriotic bombast of the public poetry written in *katharévousa* that had hitherto won national prizes. In his adjudication speech, a newly-appointed young professor of Classics, Georgios Mistriotis, later to become one of the most intransigent opponents of the demoticist movement, praised the connotative quality of the demotic language and the absence of such qualities in *katharévousa*.

It is indicative of the changing climate that the 1876 poetry prize was awarded to a collection by Georgios Vizyinos containing some poems written in demotic and inspired by Greek folk poetry, while the chairman of the adjudicators, Professor Theodoros Orfanidis, himself a poet, dismissed a collection of poems entirely in *katharévousa* submitted by the seventeen-year-old student Kostis Palamas, later to become the leader of the demoticist movement in Greek literature, as 'the ice-cold versification exercises of a learned grammarian'.[120]

The careers of the poets and fiction writers of the so-called Generation of 1880, of which Palamas was to be the most important representative, were greatly facilitated by the death of a number of established poets of the old school – some of them at quite an early age – during the 1870s. These include Ioannis Karasoutsas (formerly Karatsoutsas), who committed suicide in 1873 aged 50, Dimitrios Paparrigopoulos (son of the historian), who committed suicide the following day aged 30, Spyridon Vasileiadis, who died of consumption in 1874 aged 32, and Valaoritis, who died of a heart attack in 1879 aged 55. With the exception of Valaoritis, these poets wrote all or most of their work in *katharévousa*.

With hindsight, the commission to Valaoritis to write the poem on Grigorios V and the award of the national poetry prize to Kampouroglou's collection of poems can be interpreted as (conscious or subconscious) reactions to the Bulgarian schism of 1870. Following the realization that non-Greek-speaking Balkan Christians could no longer be expected to become automatically assimilated into Hellenism, some Greek intellectuals shifted the focus of national identity to what they felt to be naturally and quintessentially Greek, namely the spoken language

[119] The comparison with Christopoulos is made by Moullas 1989: 315–17.
[120] See, for instance, Koutrianou 2003: 180.

and folklore. Thus Kampouroglou's title can be seen as referring not only to the emotions of the individual but to the true expression of the national soul.

National history, national folklore, and the history of Greek language and literature

The definitive version of Paparrigopoulos' *History of the Greek Nation* (1860–74) set out to demonstrate the historical continuity of the Greek nation from mythological times to the present. Paparrigopoulos argued that there had never been a break in historical and cultural continuity among the Greeks as there had been in the West, where the fall of Rome had made it necessary, a thousand years later, to create a Renaissance. At the same time, he continued his campaign to elevate the position of Byzantium in the Greek historical consciousness: whereas the first complete edition of his history gave more or less equal space to ancient and Byzantine history, the definitive version devoted about half of its total pages to what he variously termed 'Byzantine Hellenism', 'Our medieval kingdom', and 'the empire of medieval Hellenism'.[121] Paschalis Kitromilides has characterized Paparrigopoulos' vast project as 'the most important intellectual achievement of nineteenth-century Greece'.[122] Through this monumental work by the man who is known as Greece's 'national historian', Greek national history and culture came to be presented as diachronically unitary and uninterrupted 'from Agamemnon to George I', as G. N. Hatzidakis aptly expressed it.[123]

The ideology of the continuity of Hellenic culture was especially desirable at a time when the geographical boundaries of the Greek state were so narrow that they excluded more than half of those who could be classified as being ethnically and culturally Greek. In this way the idea of diachronic unity both compensated for the lack of synchronic unity and encouraged the desire and hope for the geographical unification of all the lands inhabited by Greeks, a unification analogous to those that took place in 1870–71 in Germany and Italy.

In order to justify the maximalist aspirations of the Greek state, the importance of Greek as a written language and as the language of the Orthodox Church had been seen as counterbalancing the numerical weakness of the vernacular Greek-speaking element in parts of the Balkans.[124]

---

[121] Paparrigopoulos 1860–74; Paparrigopoulos 1886.   [122] Kitromilides 1998: 28.
[123] Hatzidakis 1905a: 699.   [124] Sigalas 2004: 148.

This was one of the factors that had encouraged the use of *katharévousa*. As a large proportion of the non-Greek-speaking populations of the Balkans began to adopt a non-Greek (and often anti-Greek) national identity, it seemed sensible to some Greek scholars and literary figures to turn their attention towards the study of the culture of the Greek-speaking rural population.

In a lecture given in Serres in Greek Macedonia in 1953 (the quincentenary of the fall of Constantinople) and entitled 'The significance of folklore studies for the national struggle', Stilpon Kyriakidis, professor of folklore at Salonica University, stated that Greek folklore studies were 'the product of a national struggle, and specifically a struggle not against the conquerors, the Turks, but against the Slavs'. In the face of Fallmerayer's assertion that the modern Greeks were for the most part racially Slavs and the later claims by Bulgarians on territory that the Greeks considered their own, Kyriakidis continued, it had been necessary for Greek scholars to demonstrate the unbroken continuity of the language and culture of the Greek people from antiquity to the present.[125]

As Fotis Dimitrakopoulos writes, the language question and national identity are prevalent and interconnected themes in the prologues of collections of Greek folk songs published by Greeks, from Evlampios (1843) onwards. Most of the editors of these collections are keen to argue that the language, themes, and ethos of the modern Greek folk songs demonstrate the survival of ancient Greek culture into the present day.[126] As early as 1857 the minister of Ecclesiastical Affairs and Public Education addressed a circular to teachers encouraging them to collect words, phrases, proverbs, songs, narratives, and all kinds of traditions.[127] But the systematic and scholarly study of folklore was initiated in Greece by Nikolaos Politis (1852–1921), whose precocious *Study of the Culture of the Modern Greeks* (1871–74) was based on his own collections of folk songs, tales, proverbs, sayings, and details of customs.[128] Politis' study was his entry to a competition organized by the University of

---

[125] Kyriakidis 1953: 34–7 pointed out that Paparrigopoulos' first published book (Paparrigopoulos 1843) was an attempt to refute Fallmerayer's claims about Slav settlements in the Peloponnese.

[126] Dimitrakopoulos 1996: 87–9 refers to the prologues to twelve of these collections, published between 1843 and 1902.

[127] A. Politis 1993: 52.

[128] Although Politis' *Study* was published in two separate parts, it was designated as 'Volume 1' and given the programmatic subtitle 'Modern Greek Mythology', which implied that the folk beliefs of the modern Greeks were both the equivalent and the continuation of those of the ancients.

Athens for the description of modern Greek customs and manners and their comparison with their ancient counterparts.[129] This was a novel way of both defining modern Greekness and establishing the *cultural* continuity of the Greeks since antiquity; Politis' project ran parallel to that of Paparrigopoulos, which traced the *historical* continuity of the Greek nation by way of Byzantium.[130] Both these projects were ways of countering Fallmerayer's reading of Greek history.

Though Politis himself wrote exclusively in *katharévousa*, this new respect for Greek traditional popular culture as the natural survival of ancient Greek culture led inevitably to the recognition of the popular spoken tongue as the natural development of the Ancient Greek language. For the adherents of this attitude, arguments based on cultural survival came to be seen as more convincing than those based on cultural revival. The natural survival of the spoken Greek dialects and all other aspects of traditional rural life was emphasized by what came to be called the demoticist movement, which started in earnest in the 1880s. Adherence to *katharévousa* entailed a view of language as an instrument, as a means of understanding the liturgy, as a means of communicating with the culture of ancient Greece, as a means of demonstrating one's racial and/or cultural descent from the ancient Greeks, and as a means by which non-Greek speakers could be Hellenized. Adherence to demotic, on the other hand, entailed a view of language as the spontaneous expression of the national soul. From this time onwards it became increasingly frequent to refer to the Greek folk songs as *dimotiká tragoudia* 'demotic songs', thus implying that they had an indissoluble bond with the demotic language.[131]

The Greek *laografía* [folklore] movement shows how ideologies 'attempt...to render otherwise incomprehensible social situations meaningful'.[132] Politis and others interpreted traditional Greek rural culture for the urban intellectual elite, elevating and idealizing it as the repository of texts, beliefs, and practices that demonstrated the cultural continuity of the Greek nation from ancient times to the present day.

---

[129] K. Th. Dimaras 1982: 384. This was the sixth biennial Rodokanakeios Agon, named after Theodoros Rodokanakis, a Greek merchant and benefactor in Odessa, who provided the prize money.

[130] For the contribution of folklore to the development of Greek national identity see Kyriakidis 1953 and Herzfeld 1982; for its contribution to the demoticist movement see Kyriakidis 1939.

[131] Rangavis (1837) had already published a group of his own folk-song imitations under the title 'Demotic songs' (Güthenke 2008: 151), while the title of the collection of songs by Evlampios (1843) includes the phrase 'demotic poems'.

[132] Geertz, quoted in Jaffrelot 2005: 37.

The elevation and idealization of Greek rural culture led inevitably to the elevation and idealization of the language in which this culture was expressed, that is, the language of the rural Greek folk.

German romantic nationalists had found national unity in the German language; as Jacob Grimm wrote: 'unsere sprache ist auch unsere geschichte'.[133] They also found unity in a common German folk culture.[134] These ideas were taken up by the Greek demoticists, who, like Zampelios, faced up to – indeed extolled – the realities of medieval and modern Greek history, which Korais had found almost too shameful to contemplate. Looking back in 1926, the poet Kostis Palamas was to claim that Politis' folklore studies had sought out and discovered 'the fragmented face of the national soul under the masks that [changing] times have forced it to wear'.[135] This is a revealing statement of a romantic nationalist belief that there is an integral and unalterable essential national core, which it is the task of historians, folklorists, and literary writers to discover and reassemble.

During this period, a small number of books were published on the medieval and modern history of the Greek language and the Greek language question. Dimitrios Mavrofrydis (1828–66) published the first and only volume of his *Selection of Monuments of the Modern Greek Language* (1866), containing editions of certain long poems written in the vernacular during the late Byzantine period (eleventh to fifteenth centuries), some of which had never been published before. In his introduction, he forestalls objections to 'the publication of these wretched stammerings of the wretched vulgar Muse of those grim centuries' by asserting that these texts are 'monuments, testimonies, of the ... condition of the language of the Greek nation in its modern phase, the Romaic or neo-Hellenic'. 'Our forefathers in those times,' he continues, 'albeit ignorant, unfortunate and wretched, but nonetheless our forefathers ... , had a demotic literature of their own, separate from the pedantic Atticizing and in general archaizing literature of the lettered of their time.'[136] He ends by claiming that it is the sacred duty of every Greek to save these texts from oblivion and subject them to the light of science, so that Greek history and language will be illuminated. In his efforts to study the history of the vernacular language during the medieval period, which were hampered by

---

[133] Grimm 1851: 46 (*sic*, without capitals).   [134] Dimitrakopoulos 1996: 86.

[135] Palamas n.d.: XIII 57.

[136] Mavrofrydis 1866: xiii–xiv. Mavrofrydis, who was born in Cappadocia, changed his surname from Karakasoglou by translating the first component (Turkish *karakaş* 'black eyebrow') literally into vernacular Greek (Petropoulou 1988–9: 184).

serious illness and ultimately cut short by his untimely death, Mavrofrydis constituted a link between Korais and Georgios Hatzidakis.

Mavrofrydis' 700-page *Essay on the History of the Greek Language*
(1871) was published posthumously. This was his prizewinning submission to a competition announced by the University of Athens in 1856
for the writing of a history of the modern Greek language. The value
of the *Essay* is seriously vitiated by the fact that Mavrofrydis traced
the history of each phonological and morphological change individually
instead of viewing each stage of the language as a system, and that he
continued to subscribe to Christopoulos' erroneous Aeolodoric theory
concerning the origin of spoken Modern Greek – a theory later demol-
ished by Hatzidakis. In addition, the *Essay* contained insufficient material
on the medieval period. Nevertheless, both of his books helped Greek
intellectuals become more aware of and interested in the history of their
language since ancient times.

In 1870 Konstantinos Sathas published a *History of the Question of
the Neohellenic Language*. This was chiefly an anthology of writings
about the language from the sixteenth to the nineteenth centuries, with
introductions and comments. Sathas declares himself to be a supporter of
'the present-day *katharévousa* Neohellenic language' and talks of Korais
as an enemy of the 'purifying idiom' that was defended by Kodrikas.
At first, Sathas continues, Kodrikas seemed to have been defeated, but
after the revolution 'the *Graikiká* of Korais were forgotten'.[137] While he
made it plain that he sided with the purists who had re-routed Korais'
'middle way' in the direction of archaism, he brought a lot of little-
known texts to public attention and impressed on his readers the national
importance of the language question.

At the same time, Emile Legrand's series *Collection de monuments
pour server à l'étude de la langue néo-hellénique*, published in Athens
and Paris in 1869–71 and 1874–75, brought texts of vernacular literature dating from the fourteenth to the early nineteenth centuries to the
attention of the Greek public. The latter series included a version of
the Byzantine heroic poem *Digenis Akritis*, which Politis was later to
dub 'the national epic of the modern Greeks'. In fact, three versions
of this poem were published in the period 1875–81. Thus, when they
began to write, the demoticists of the 1880s onwards – both poets and
scholars – had at their disposal a wealth of linguistic and literary material
in vernacular Greek from earlier centuries.

[137] Sathas 1870: 211.

7

The beginning of the demoticist campaign, 1880–1897

Developments in literature

In the nineteenth century, literature was often thought of as the highest form of linguistic expression and as one of the most important manifestations of national culture. In Greece, poetry was the first area in which writers felt no linguistic inhibitions. This was because the influence of Romanticism encouraged the view that literature was a vehicle for expressing genuine personal emotion. The result of this was that poets did not feel constrained by any obligation to be on their best linguistic behaviour.

A contributory factor to the definitive victory of demotic in Greek literature around 1900 was the influence of literary trends from late nineteenth-century Europe, such as realism and the emphasis on the immediacy of experience. Such trends inevitably led to the virtual abandonment of *katharévousa*, first in poetry and subsequently in fiction. Writers in demotic at this time, however, found that the existence of *katharévousa* was something of an advantage, since they had the exhilarating sense that they were expressing new feelings in a language that was not weighed down by bourgeois convention and not littered with dead metaphors inherited from Ancient Greek or French.

The poets of the Generation of 1880, sometimes known as the New Athenian School, firmly established demotic as the language of poetry. The year 1880 saw the publication of the first collections of poems by two young representatives of this generation, Nikos Kampas (1857–1932) and Georgios Drosinis (1859–1951). About half of the poems in Kampas' collection are in *katharévousa*, while the rest are in demotic. It is striking that his *katharévousa* poems are sculptural, cold, and pallid, and the subject matter is viewed from an emotional distance, while in his demotic poems the poet's emotional involvement in his subject matter is directly expressed. Drosinis, who published three collections of poetry within four years, displayed a remarkably rapid career development. All but one of the poems in his first collection (*Spider's Webs*) are in demotic; most of them are light, urbane, and humorous love poems, showing the influence of the French poet François Coppée (the so-called 'poète des humbles') but also looking back to the Anacreontic tradition of Christopoulos. His third collection, however, characteristically entitled *Idylls* (1884), consists almost entirely of poems inspired by Greek folk songs, folk tales, and legends, in which the humorous element is largely absent. These poems indicate Drosinis' espousal of the national folklorist project initiated by his friend Nikolaos Politis.

Drosinis' and Kampas' close friend Kostis Palamas (1859–1943), who later became the leading figure of the Generation of 1880, published his first collection of poems, *The Songs of my Homeland*, in 1886; all of these are in demotic, the earliest dating from 1878. The first noun in Palamas' programmatic title, *tragoudia*, both indicates his belief that poetry is closer to song than to the written word, and suggests a connection with folk song.[1] As for the second noun, the poems make it clear that by *patrida* he means not only his national homeland, namely Greece, but in particular the places where he was born and grew up (Patra and Mesolongi). As Pantelis Voutouris argues, in Palamas' collection the concept of the *patrida*, which is 'vague and lifeless' in the poetry of the Old Athenian School, takes on an 'earthy, experiential, confessional and partly realistic existence: specific locations are interwoven with personal memories and with the history, legends and traditions of the people that inhabit it'.[2]

A number of journals, including the prestigious family magazine *Estia* (1876–95) and the satirical and political newspapers *Rampagas* (1878–89) and *Mi chanesai* (1880–83) and the latter's successor, the newspaper *Akropolis*, opened their pages to poetry in demotic from 1880 onwards, followed by prose fiction a few years later. Palamas was among the leading contributors of such poems; in 1882–83 he and Drosinis published more poems in *Estia* than all the other contributors put together. From 1889 onwards, *Estia*, under the editorship first of Drosinis and Politis together, then Drosinis alone, then Grigorios Xenopoulos (1867–1951), became the chief organ of the demotic movement; from 1894 it became a daily newspaper.[3]

---

[1] Tziovas 1986: 232–3 contrasts the demoticists, who promoted speech (including singing and recitation) as being more 'real', 'natural', 'immediate', 'authentic', and 'springing from the soul', with the purists, who favoured writing as being more 'permanent' and 'authoritative'.
[2] Voutouris 2006b: 85.   [3] Fletcher 1984: 32–4, 39, 41, 85.

Nevertheless, literary prose continued to be written almost entirely in *katharévousa* for some years, a notable exception being *Behold the Man* (1886), a humorous attempt at a typology of human characteristics in the tradition of Theophrastus by the Cephalonian satirist and moralist Laskaratos. In fact, the three finest and most prestigious fiction writers of modern Greece wrote in *katharévousa*: Emmanouil Roïdis (1836–1904), Georgios Vizyinos (1849–96) and Alexandros Papadiamantis (1851–1911). Roïdis, born in Syros into a cosmopolitan mercantile family with its roots in Chios and brought up partly in Genoa, was never in contact with the language and culture of the rural Greek folk. Especially in his satirical novel *Pope Joan* (1866), Roïdis writes *katharévousa* in such a way that, although he takes few lexical and grammatical liberties with it, he seems to be using it ironically, with tongue in cheek. His ice-cold precision and delicious Voltairean irony mock both religious superstition and literary Romanticism.

Vizyinos was born in the small town of Vizyi (Vize) in Ottoman Thrace, not far from Constantinople. His family was so poor that after attending primary school he was apprenticed to a tailor in Constantinople. While there, he came to the attention of two benefactors, who enabled him to continue his education in Cyprus and, at the age of twenty-five, to finish high school in Athens, eventually gaining a doctorate from the University of Göttingen with a thesis on the psychology of children's play. After 1877 he decided to abandon the use of *katharévousa* altogether in his poetry. He had already begun exploiting motifs from Greek folk songs and folk legends in some of his poems, but he was using a language far removed from the rural spoken tongue; from then on he overcame the discrepancy between language and content.[4]

Vizyinos began publishing short stories in *Estia* in 1883. Most of these tales, written in the first person, are set in his native Thrace. There is a contrast between the fairly strict *katharévousa* of the narrative passages, which are written in a complex style that is readily translatable into western European languages, and the dialogues involving other members of the narrator's family, which are colloquial, idiomatic, and more specifically Balkan in both feeling and expression.

In one of the stories there is a reference to the adult narrator's change of name: his mother knows him only as Georgi, son of Michalios, and she cannot remember the new highfalutin surname by which he is known to the outside world (presumably Georgios M. Vizyinos, with which the

---

[4] For Vizyinos' abandonment of *katharévousa* in poetry see Koutrianou 2003: 52–3, 80–4.

author signed his published works).[5] In view of his change of name, it is ironic that, in a now famous newspaper article dating from 1885, Vizyinos recalls his schoolmaster instructing his fellow pupils to call him not by his normal name but by that of the ancient philosopher Gorgias. Vizyinos goes on to relate his confusion and dismay at being taught that an apple tree should properly be called by the ancient and *katharévousa* word *miléa* rather than by the demotic *miliá*. Instead of answering his question as to what kind of 'thing' an apple tree is (i.e. its essence), the teacher insists that the boy call it by a different name. Having been mercilessly beaten by the teacher, he decides he can accept the *katharévousa* name for apple trees in general, but not for the one in his own family garden, which he knows and loves through intimate personal experience. Vizyinos ends his text by arguing that

the mania of those who want to teach not the nature of things... but unfamiliar words... renders Greek education a Sisyphean labour and condemns the nation to the worst possible death from spiritual starvation! For this reason the question concerning the Greek language is, in my view,... more vital than the Eastern Question.[6]

The fact that Vizyinos relates the language question to its effect on the mind and emotions of the child prefigures the psychological concerns of the educational demoticists (see Chapter 8). As for Vizyinos' contrast between the language question and the Eastern Question (the question as to which nations were to gain which territory from the collapse of the Ottoman empire), they were to be firmly yoked together by Psycharis as being both interrelated and of equal importance.

In some of Papadiamantis' finest and most moving stories too, the narrator relates his experiences as a child in a confusing and hostile world, and their effects on his adult self. Again the adult narrator uses *katharévousa*, albeit subtly infiltrated and infused with features of the spoken language as well as pre-Christian and ecclesiastical texts, while the child speaks in the vernacular, although the discrepancy is never referred to explicitly. In some stories Papadiamantis even uses local dialect in the dialogue; such texts thus display three different linguistic varieties: *katharévousa*, common demotic, and dialect. Papadiamantis' Orthodox Christian piety – and his respect for that of his characters – led him to use numerous words and phrases from religious texts, namely the Septuagint and the New Testament, and liturgical texts dating from the

[5] Vizyinos 1991: 147–8, quoted and discussed in Koutrianou 2003: 13.
[6] Vizyinos 1991: 320–6.

early Byzantine period. His unique brand of *katharévousa*, which in its morphology differed little from liturgical Greek, is perhaps an indication of his insistence on the timeless continuity of traditional Greek culture and his resistance to certain aspects of modernity.

Vizyinos' and Papadiamantis' displays of textual knowledge and rhetorical virtuosity were only feasible in *katharévousa*. The rich texture of their writing would have been impossible to achieve in the demotic of their time, and even in modern translations of Papadiamantis' work into demotic his style and language lose much of their poetry. Papadiamantis never expressed any doubt about the appropriateness of writing fiction in *katharévousa*; indeed, when he was once prevailed upon to write a story in demotic, he failed to achieve the complexity of his best stories in *katharévousa*. In this particular story, the author's linguistic self-denial seems to be literally cramping his style, prohibiting him from exploiting his creative gifts to the full.[7]

Demotic was finding its way not only into the dialogue but into other areas of narrative fiction too. Vizyinos started a trend towards placing as much of the narrative as possible in the mouths of uneducated characters: this spoken narrative (sometimes taking up almost the entire text) could then be in demotic. Writers such as Papadiamantis who were interested in exploring the psychological make-up and the inner life of their characters also made use of free indirect discourse (the literary rendering of characters' thoughts and speech without the use of tags such as 'he thought to himself' or 'she said'), which again afforded them the opportunity to write as though in the characters' own words.[8]

Younger fiction writers did not feel so happy about writing in *katharévousa*. Grigorios Xenopoulos, born in Constantinople but brought up on his father's native island of Zakynthos, prefaced the serial publication of his first novel, *The Miracles of the Devil* (1883) with a prologue in which he writes that 'the Greek language, or rather that monstrous mixture which the Greeks of today call a language, is an abyss' that causes such difficulties for anyone who wishes to use it that it actually discourages writing altogether. In the first novel he published in book form, *Nikolas Sigalos* (1888), whose narrative is written in rigid *katharévousa*, Xenopoulos has a fictional writer say to himself:

---

[7] The story is published in Papadiamantis 1985: 367–80.

[8] For the gradual entry of demotic into otherwise *katharévousa* discourse in the fiction of this period see Vitti 1991: 76–83. For Papadiamantis' use of free indirect discourse see Farinou-Malamatari 1987: 210–37.

'The devil!...Call this a language? Is this writing or translating? What have I been doing all this time? Translating into so-called *katharévousa* what I am thinking in the vernacular, in my mother tongue. *Katharévousa*!...a monstrosity...!'

As Amalia Amilitou points out, Xenopoulos wrote this novel in *katharévousa* 'because there were no rules of demotic on which he could base himself, while after the publication of Psycharis' *My Journey* in 1888 [for which see below] he was discouraged by the furore it provoked'.[9]

It was Politis who encouraged Drosinis to write his series of non-fictional *Agricultural Letters*, which he published in *Estia* from 1882 onwards and in which he reported to his fellow townspeople on the life of the villagers who lived near his country house at Gouves on the large island of Euboea (Evia).[10] His own discourse is in *katharévousa*, but he quotes the villagers' narratives in demotic, and he includes numerous local technical terms in italics. In this and in his fictional works, which followed soon afterwards, the discrepancy between the language of the author's or narrator's discourse and that of the dialogue contributes, more than in Vizyinos and Papadiamantis, to an ironical (and sometimes patronizing) attitude towards the characters. By writing in *katharévousa* for his bourgeois reader and by peppering his narrative with the occasional vernacular term to show his knowledge of popular terminology, the bourgeois author/narrator of Drosinis' prose works shows himself to be detached from (and possibly superior to) his peasant characters: class distinctions are preserved, and the peasants are kept at a distance. By contrast, in the first-person stories of Vizyinos and Papadiamantis, the distinction between the language of the narrator and the language of the characters often emphasizes the distinction between the child hero and the adult narrator, showing not only what he has gained through his later experiences but also the alienation of the adult intellectual from the time, place, and culture in which he grew up.

In 1883 the magazine *Estia* organized a competition for the composition of a short story on a Greek theme consisting of 'scenes from history or social life'. The adjudicator was Politis, who awarded the prize to a 'charming rural idyll' by Drosinis.[11] The competition provided a boost to the fashion for writing short stories set in the Greek provinces and depicting characters from traditional backgrounds, including sometimes

---

[9] The information in this paragraph is based on Amilitou 2002: 24–6. Xenopoulos published his first novel in demotic in 1891, but this was aimed at children.

[10] For Politis' encouragement see Kyriakidis 1939: 1486.

[11] The call for entries to the competition, drafted by Politis, is reproduced in Kyriakidis 1939: 1486–7. For a discussion of the competition see Vitti 1991: 63–8.

their difficulties in coming to terms with modernity. Such writing, which came to be known as *ithografía* [the study of manners], collaborated with *laografía* [the academic study of folklore] by providing vivid depictions of traditional Greek customs and manners,[12] thereby preserving, by means of language, the fast-disappearing indigenous Greek rural culture.

In 1881 provision was officially made for the teaching of the Modern Greek language in primary education for the first time. In the relevant document the word used for the specific language variety to be taught was *kathomilimeni* [literally, 'generally spoken'], but in practice it meant *katharévousa*.[13] In 1884 Greek literary texts dating from the seventeenth to the nineteenth centuries were introduced into school readers, albeit in learned language and only at primary level, at the instigation of Politis.[14] As far as secondary education is concerned, no Modern Greek of any sort was taught till 1909, and then only *katharévousa*. While creative writers were exploring and exploiting what they regarded as the bases of their national culture, namely the demotic language and the songs, tales, beliefs, and legends of the Greek rural population, the education system continued to display an almost total disregard for modern Greek culture.

The resurgence of the language controversy: the Kontos debate

During the 1880s the controversy between the proponents of *katharévousa* and demotic, which had lain comparatively dormant since the end of the War of Independence, broke out again. This resurgence of the language controversy was perhaps connected with a greater political stability and national confidence in Greece during the premierships of the liberal reformist Charilaos Trikoupis (son of Spyridon) in 1882–85, 1886–89, and 1892–95. Trikoupis' practical policies greatly encouraged the dominance of the bourgeoisie and initiated an ambitious programme of public works that enabled considerable industrial and economic development. Another factor that contributed to the resurgence of the language

---

[12] On the relationship between *ithografía* and *laografía* see Beaton 1982–83.

[13] I am grateful to Anna Frangoudaki for this information. The form of the term used in the relevant document, καθωμιλημένη, differs slightly from the form καθομιλουμένη (*kathomilouméni*), which was later used to denote a slightly archaized variant of the vernacular.

[14] For details of these texts see A. Dimaras 1973: 256 ff.

controversy was the dissension over how best to face the challenge posed by the Bulgarian national movement.

Coming shortly after the establishment of the Bulgarian exarchate, the establishment of an autonomous Bulgaria under Russian control by the Congress of Berlin (1878) sent shivers down the collective spine of Greek nationalists, who realized that Bulgaria might imminently try to seize control over Macedonia, which they thought of as rightfully Greek. As a result of the Congress, the Powers had decided that the Ottomans should cede the province of Thessaly to Greece in 1881, thus bringing the Greek frontier up to the southern edge of Macedonia.[15] The combined effect of Greece's expansion to the north and the new Bulgarian threat to further Greek territorial aspirations led more Greek intellectuals to argue in favour of the introduction of vernacular Greek into education and other areas of public life.[16]

The linguistic archaism preached by the classical philologist Konstantinos Kontos (1834–1909), a professor at Athens University, in his book *Linguistic Observations Regarding Modern Greek* (1882) gave a boost to the demoticist movement by unwittingly showing up the impossibility of perfecting *katharévousa*. Constantine Trypanis has described this book as 'a unique monument of erudition and utopianism';[17] its ideas were the logical conclusion of the gradual archaization of *katharévousa*. The preface to Kontos' book is illuminating:

> The advent of liberty and its attendant culture could not be satisfied with a language that had been created in slavery and barbarism. Thus *i kath' imas glossa* [our modern language], urged on by necessity, leaped beyond its earlier narrow boundaries; yet it did so without restraint, and for this reason we observe that it has been infiltrated with foreign and incongruous phrases and sayings and a discordant style and a general lack of harmony and regularity.[18]

It is these failings, Kontos' preface concludes, that he has set out to remedy in his book. He did not present his arguments in a systematic and coherent fashion – let alone in the form of a systematic grammar – but preferred to present two hundred separate 'observations' on individual 'errors' perpetrated by writers of *katharévousa*; he declared these usages

---

[15] Clogg 1992: 69–70.

[16] See Drettas 1981: 73 for 'the demoticist current' that gained force after the Congress of Berlin.

[17] Trypanis 1984: 51.

[18] Kontos 1882: unnumbered page (preface signed by the publisher but probably written by Kontos himself).

to be erroneous on the grounds that they did not conform to the rules of Ancient Greek grammar. Kontos acknowledged the importance of Korais' contribution to the written language but claimed that the language had advanced since then, by which he meant that the modern written language had become closer to Ancient Greek. Kontos went on to criticize the leading theorists and practitioners of written Greek since the eighteenth century, pointing out errors in the usage of Voulgaris, Korais, Doukas, and Asopios, and showing how even the most learned Greeks continually infringed the most basic rules of Ancient Greek grammar.

Kontos' own knowledge of Ancient Greek was phenomenal, and some of his strictures have been vindicated by later usage. In particular, he attacked semantic sloppiness in the use of words and promoted *kyriolexía* [literalness]. However, aside from his pedantic hair-splitting, the chief drawback of his 'observations' was precisely that they relied totally on Ancient Greek usage and ignored the changes that had taken place in spoken and written Greek since Classical times. He never used the term *katharévousa* and did not regard the modern written language as an autonomous, rule-governed variety of Greek. He opposed all compromise solutions and thrust aside the tradition of mixed language that had developed during the previous two millennia. He was a true purist: for him, the form and meaning of each word had to be either purely Ancient Greek or purely demotic. Yet he failed to provide any statement of the general principles underlying his specific observations.

Kontos' provocative attacks on earlier and contemporary authors and scholars brought a counterattack from another professor (and romantic dramatist), Dimitrios Vernardakis (Lesbos, 1833–1907), who had resigned his university post in 1869 after quarrelling with Kontos and others and had been reappointed in 1882. In a long, rambling book entitled *A Censure of Pseudo-Atticism* (1884), Vernardakis condemned Kontos for his 'linguistic anarchy' (which is precisely what he practised himself) and for his attacks on 'erroneous' usages of his own devising instead of addressing the problem of the language of Greek education. Like the participants in the Soutsos controversy during the 1850s, Vernardakis was not a demoticist. While he expressed his admiration for the 'language of the people' and the language of Cretan Renaissance poetry, he criticized the version of the vernacular used by younger poets as not being true to the genuine spoken language of the rural folk. Vernardakis took a dim view of this new poetic 'demotic', which for him consisted of *katharévousa* words with their heads and tails chopped off, and he saw a danger that this language might corrupt the 'language of the people'.[19] This was an argument frequently used by supporters of *katharévousa*: that demotic was essentially the language of peasants, and that attempts should not be made to enrich it with abstract vocabulary and cultivate it for written use. In this respect, for all his own use of a mixed language, Vernardakis was ideologically a linguistic separatist, arguing that the two varieties of Modern Greek, *katharévousa* and demotic, should be kept distinct.

Unlike the reactionary Kontos, the conservative Vernardakis recognized that there was a learned tradition of writing in Greek that had existed for centuries and was different from pure Classical Attic. Kontos wanted to eradicate any form that had never been spoken, either in ancient or in modern times, whereas Vernardakis accepted conventional written *katharévousa* as he found it, albeit he would have liked it to be somewhat simplified; indeed, he actually uses the term *katharévousa*, which Kontos avoids. According to Vernardakis, in order to enrich Modern Greek, one should not confine oneself to Attic words and usages but should feel free to exploit the resources of the whole history of the Greek language. In his view the Attic dialect of Ancient Greek enjoyed high prestige not because of any intrinsic superiority but because of the excellence of those who wrote in it; they based themselves on the language of the people, but used it with greater clarity and precision. Vernardakis saw language as a reflection of society, and he held out little hope of any improvement in Modern Greek until there was a general improvement in moral standards in Greece. In contrast to Kontos, he called for the written language to be moulded according to the spirit rather than the letter of Classical Attic, and showed that the language written in his time, which purported to be the language of Plato, was really French thought and locution served up in pseudo-Attic dress with the addition of the modern particles *tha* and *na*. Similar attacks on the Gallicisms of *katharévousa* had already been made by Soutsos and Kontos, and they were soon to be made again by Psycharis.

Vernardakis continued to write dramas in *katharévousa* on mythical and patriotic historical subjects, some of which gained a certain popularity, but he played no further role in the language controversy after Psycharis appeared on the scene. In the same year (1884) Kleon

---

[19] Vernardakis 1884: 461. Only the general conclusions of this voluminous tome, from p. 406 onwards, are worth reading today. The title of his book refers to a work by the Atticist writer Eratosthenes (3rd–2nd century BC) against what he calls the 'pseudo-Atticists' (Trypanis 1984: 24).

Rangavis, the son of A. R. Rangavis, a diplomat and one of the last archaists in Greek literature, proudly boasted that in his dramatic poem *Theodora* he had written four hundred pages without a single instance of the modern particles *na*, *tha*, or *den*, and without a single ancient infinitive.[20] This entailed the avoidance of negative statements and all expressions of volition and futurity – an achievement as remarkable and futile as Soutsos' *New School* (1853).

Vernardakis' book provoked a riposte from the young Cretan linguist Georgios Hatzidakis (1848–1941), who had been appointed assistant professor of linguistics at Athens University in 1881. In his very first published article, on the history of Greek, which appeared in the year of his appointment, Hatzidakis had written the following:

> I can assure [my readers] that a far greater regularity and order are observable by careful examiners in the language of the peasant who has never read a book or left his village, than in the language spoken by us in Athens. If anyone should doubt this . . . , let him attempt to teach the language spoken in Athens, if he knows it as he should, to a foreigner, and he will immediately observe the truth of what I have said.

The 'regularity and order' of the spoken language had already been used as an argument in its favour by Konemenos eight years previously, yet it was ignored by those who despised the 'vulgar tongue'. Hatzidakis hastens to add, however, that he is not calling for the abandonment of the written language, which has been cultivated for many years: 'I do not fear that any generation will ever reach such madness', he writes.[21]

Before turning to Hatzidakis' defence of Kontos, it is worth looking at another article that he had published a few months earlier in the magazine *Estia*, entitled 'Why do the modern Greeks not cultivate the vernacular Greek language?' Here he criticizes the trend toward increasing archaism in the written language and expresses his regret that the vernacular language has not been cultivated. 'In our struggle to render the written language more noble,' he writes, 'we are allowing the Greek people to become more uncouth.' This acknowledgement that the overdevelopment of *katharévousa* has entailed the underdevelopment of the vernacular, thus widening the gap between the educated and the uneducated, is remarkable coming from a supporter of *katharévousa*. Nevertheless, in the same article he was still able to write, somewhat contradictorily, that it is the written language of his time that unites the nation.

---

[20] K. Rangavis 1884: p. vii.   [21] Hatzidakis 1881: 14.

Regarding the history of Greek, Hatzidakis writes in the same article: 'No sane person doubts that Modern Greek is a phase of a single Greek language, just as the language of Homer and the *koine* were other phases of the same Greek language.' For this reason, he argues, it is erroneous to claim that Modern Greek is the daughter or niece of Ancient Greek, since it is all one and the same language. He criticizes those who have contented themselves (as those in Korais' time had done) with searching for individual similarities between Ancient and Modern Greek, and urges scholars to search for *differences* between these two phases and to discover the laws that connect these differences. In effect, he is calling for something that had hardly been attempted before: a study of the history of Modern Greek from a synchronic perspective. Many of the statements Hatzidakis makes in this article could have been uttered by moderate demoticists of a later generation; however, in order to avoid misunderstandings he makes it clear that he is not urging his readers to jettison today's written language and to write in 'the tattered *Romaic language*, which is not sufficient for anything'.[22]

It seems that Kontos' intransigence led to a hardening of Hatzidakis' own attitudes. In his *Study on Modern Greek, or Trial of the Censure of Pseudo-Atticism* (1884), he defends Kontos against Vernardakis' attack, arguing that, since the Modern Greek written language is an artificial one, a *Kunstsprache*, it should be used correctly, and it should be constantly adjusted in accordance with Ancient Greek rules.[23] He looks forward to the adoption of demotic for all written purposes, but only once its laws have been discovered and a Shakespeare or Dante has come to erect an 'outstanding linguistic edifice'. So far, he argues, contrary to Vernardakis' assertion, it has been impossible to discover the common features of the Modern Greek dialects, since they have not been sufficiently studied.[24] While Hatzidakis devoted most of his career to studying the medieval and modern history of the Greek language, thereby ensuring that the first of his two preconditions was met, from 1888 onwards he steadfastly opposed the written use of the vernacular and stubbornly ignored the output of poetry and literary prose in demotic.

---

[22] Hatzidakis 1883. This article was not republished in his collected writings in its full and original form and under its original title. He writes the phrase '*Romeiki glosa [Romaic language]*' in italics, using Vilaras' phonetic spelling.

[23] Hatzidakis 1884: 36, 55.

[24] Ibid., 96, 80–1.

Psycharis

Background

The language controversy might have subsided again had it not been for a bombshell that burst on the Athenian cultural scene in 1888, in the form of a book entitled *My Journey* by Psycharis (1854–1929).[25] Psycharis, who became, together with Hatzidakis, one of the two leading Greek linguists of his time, was born into a well-to-do Greek mercantile family in Odessa. His paternal grandfather had served as Ottoman governor of Chios. The young Psycharis grew up in Constantinople (from the age of six) and in France; he never lived in Greece. When he was a child, his home languages were Russian and French; his mother spoke to him in Russian, but she died when he was only two years old, while he spoke French with his father, and he continued to correspond with his family in that language as an adult. As was the case with Korais, Psycharis' father's family came from Chios, and, like Korais, he lived most of his life in Paris. He settled there with his grandmother at the age of thirteen and studied law in Bonn and then Latin literature back in Paris. In 1882 he married the daughter of one of the leading intellectuals of nineteenth-century France, the orientalist, historian, moralist, and (non-believing) theologian Ernest Renan, who encouraged him in his work and brought him into contact with other important French intellectuals. In 1884 Psycharis published his first book, a small pamphlet about the formation of the future tense in Modern Greek. In the following year he took up a teaching post in Byzantine and Modern Greek literature at the Ecole Pratique des Hautes Etudes and published the first volume of his *Essais de grammaire historique néo-grecque*, on the history of Modern Greek noun declension; the second volume, published in 1889, was devoted to the history of Greek in medieval times. In 1887 he was appointed at the Ecole des Langues Orientales as the assistant to Emile Legrand, whom he succeeded as professor of Modern Greek in 1904; he held this post until his death.

Psycharis lived between two cultures, French (in which he was known as Jean Psichari) and Greek (in which he preferred to be known only by his surname). He aspired to become famous in both of his cultures, not only as a scholar but also a creative writer, and he published a number of novels in French and in Greek. He loved both of his *patrides*, he wrote,

---

[25] 'You threw the bomb of Truth into our midst': Eftaliotis 1901: 4,

'Frenchman and *Romiós* as I am'.[26] He believed that he possessed two identities, perhaps even two souls, a French one and a Greek one.

Psycharis' correspondence with his fellow scholars Konstantinos Sathas (between 1881 and 1884) and Nikolaos Politis (beginning in 1883) was at first in *katharévousa* and sometimes in French, until he first wrote a letter in a rather clumsy and uncertain demotic in 1885. His knowledge of *katharévousa* was limited, and he handled it in an idiosyncratic way.[27] In 1886 he travelled to Constantinople, where he had been invited to give a paper at a conference to celebrate the twenty-fifth anniversary of the founding of the Greek Philological Society in the Ottoman capital. When he arrived, he was informed that the conference had been cancelled by the Ottoman authorities at the request of the German ambassador. Psycharis took advantage of his trip to spend some time in Constantinople and then to make his first visit to Greece, where he carried out linguistic fieldwork. He travelled to Athens as well as to Chios, which was still under Ottoman rule.

The first extended text he wrote in demotic was the paper that he wrote on the eve of his journey to Greece and Turkey, with the intention of reading it in Constantinople.[28] Fifteen years later he claimed, with reference to this paper, that 'nobody had yet written [demotic] for philological, artistic or scholarly purposes. And I came out and spoke to them in a kind of academic style.'[29] It is remarkable how quickly he had mastered the art of writing in demotic Greek and had devised his own fully-fledged language variety and style, to which, with some exceptions, he adhered for the rest of his career. Kriaras likens Psycharis' struggle to attain Modern Greek to the struggle of the whole Greek nation to do so; in this way Kriaras suggests, perhaps misleadingly, that Psycharis had no political agenda at the outset, and that *My Journey* is largely a projection of his own personal difficulties with the Modern Greek language.[30]

In his 1886 paper and in the first edition of *My Journey* he normally used the terms *Graikoí* and *graikiká* to refer to the modern Greeks and their language, but he changed these to *Romioí* and *romaíika* in

---

[26] Psycharis to Eftaliotis, 4 June 1899, in Karatzas 1988: 138.

[27] Psycharis' early correspondence with Sathas and Politis is published in Vertsoni-Kokoli 1980 and discussed in Kriaras 1981. In 1888–93, after the publication of *My Journey*, Psycharis corresponded with Emmanouil Roïdis in French; for the correspondence see Roïdis 1913: 29–57.

[28] The text was first published as Psichari 1888.

[29] Psycharis 1902: 54. Psycharis appears to have forgotten that he did not deliver his paper orally.

[30] Kriaras 1981: 794–5.

subsequent editions of his book, from 1905 onwards.[31] In his 1902 introduction to the reprint of his 1886 paper he claims that '*Romiós*, in those days, didn't strike the ear beautifully'.[32] It is ironic that he used two different terms for each of these unique concepts. One of the problems faced by Psycharis and his chief confederates, Argyris Eftaliotis (1849–1923) and Alexandros Pallis (1851–1935), who were Greeks of the diaspora and whose homelands were in the Ottoman empire, was that most educated people (and many others) in Greece itself did not want to be *Romioí*, but aspired to be Hellenes. In contrast to the *Romioí* and *Graikoí* who became Hellenes in 1821, Psycharis struggled to transform himself from a *Graikós*, which implies a member of the Greek diaspora, into a *Romiós*, that is, a true and complete native-born Greek. His early writings in demotic, including the first edition of *My Journey*, contain a number of Constantinopolitan morphological and syntactical features.[33] He reduced these (without effacing them completely) in his subsequent work in an effort to avoid regionalisms and present a common language, but he occasionally justified his use of them as being a contribution towards the political union of the two Greek capitals, Athens and Constantinople. He refused to make concessions to Heptanesian usage on the grounds that the Ionian Islands were already part of the Greek state.[34]

In parallel (or rather in conflict) with Hatzidakis, Psycharis produced a large number of articles and books (the more scholarly ones in French, the more polemical ones in Greek and intended for a more popular readership) on the history of Medieval and Modern Greek, on Modern Greek grammar, and on the language controversy. Unlike Hatzidakis, his conclusions led him to argue for the use of demotic for all written purposes, not only for literary prose but also for scholarly writing. While Hatzidakis, living in Athens, vehemently supported the *status quo*, Psycharis was able to take an outsider's view, looking at the contemporary Greek cultural situation without the presuppositions that were fostered by Greek education. Like other participants in the Greek language controversy living abroad at that time, Psycharis was a nationalist who felt frustrated by Greece's failure to expand its boundaries and assume its apparently destined role as the leading power in the Near East. Horrocks remarks

---

[31] In the first edition he uses *Romiós* only three times, plus 'i glossa mas i *roméiki*' (his italics; 1971: 146 [=1888: 170]) and 'ta romaíika' (1971: 165 [= 1888: 200]) once each; note the fact that he wavers between two different spellings. His decision to change to *Romiós* and *romaíika* in the 1905 edition may have been encouraged by the publication of Eftaliotis' *History of Romiosyni* in 1901.

[32] Psycharis 1902: 55.   [33] For a brief analysis of these see Horrocks 1997: 352–3.

[34] Psycharis 1906: 172, 177–8.

that in *My Journey* Psycharis adapts the 'conservative [i.e. nationalist] rhetoric to the demoticist cause'.[35] Like certain other participants in the language controversy both before and after him, Psycharis believed that the language question was not just about vocabulary and grammar but about the identity and the destiny of the Greek nation. In his view, the wholesale replacement of *katharévousa* by demotic would be the most effective step towards solving Greece's political, social, and economic problems; it would demonstrate that the Greek establishment was at last adopting a practical approach to the problems of the nation instead of living in a cloud-cuckoo-land of wishful thinking.

Psycharis was an obstinate and opinionated man, with a passion for grandiose schemes and a psychological need to impose his personality and his views on others. He felt he was practically the only person to have a clear understanding of Greece's problems and a mission to solve them more or less single-handed. He was a romantic idealist who felt he was fighting for a better future. It is not surprising that Psycharis was one of Emile Zola's closest collaborators in his campaign to clear the name of Captain Alfred Dreyfus; Psycharis himself compared the language controversy with the Dreyfus affair, and in his engagement in both of these campaigns he showed himself determined to expose evildoers in his fight for 'truth and justice'.[36] He saw the language struggle as total war, in which the most effective defence was attack and any compromise or concession was a sign of weakness that would inevitably lead to defeat. He categorized people as either allies or enemies, and was ruthless in his attacks. Whenever his views were politely questioned by his allies or directly challenged by his enemies, he dug his heels in and consistently refused to acknowledge that any alternative view might have an iota of justification. This did not stop him from accusing even his allies of being megalomaniacs and trying to control others.[37] Once, when Hatzidakis falsely accused Psycharis of paying a pupil to write a linguistic article for him, Psycharis challenged him to a duel.[38] This symbolizes the fact that each of these men was determined to monopolize the discourse on the Modern Greek language.

Psycharis had a love–hate relationship with the *Romioí* in general, about whom he often makes sweeping generalizations, as he does about other peoples: 'Even the Romaic language doesn't possess words to

[35] Horrocks 1997: 351.
[36] Psycharis to Eftaliotis, 20 Sept. 1898 and 26 July 1899, in Karatzas 1988: 104, 170.
[37] See Psycharis to Eftaliotis, 19 Nov. 1906, ibid., 576–7, referring to Pallis.
[38] Andriotis 1976: 479.

express how much I'm disgusted by *Romiosyni*', he writes at one point. Not only does he express his contempt for almost all the intellectuals in Athens but he describes Greeks in general as ungrateful and envious children; he tells Eftaliotis that between them they will make the Greeks into *ánthropoi* [human beings].[39]

The contradictory nature of Psycharis' personality and ideas is manifested in the fact that in his publications he claims to be the ultimate authority on vocabulary, grammar, and usage, yet in his private correspondence he shows himself to be ignorant of many commonly used words and idioms. For example, he wants to begin using the popular Modern Greek names for the months (which are of Greek origin, unlike the Latin names that are normally used), but he has to ask Eftaliotis which is which because he confuses them.[40] At one point he cannot think of the colloquial word for the Adam's apple, while at another he confesses, with some exaggeration, 'I've forgotten my Romaic', and he tells his friend, 'You really must teach me Romaic – it's high time.'[41] He lives in Paris, where he rubs shoulders with the nobility as well as with leading intellectuals, while he consults Eftaliotis (who is living in Liverpool) on what is said and not said by the Greek *laós* [folk]. He praises and envies Eftaliotis for having remained a *Romiós* despite living abroad and because Romaic words and phrases come to him naturally.[42] He once wrote to Eftaliotis that it was a thousand times easier for him to write in French than in Romaic.[43] To the same correspondent he wrote revealingly about his sense of rhythm and metre: 'I have an ear in French – and a very fine one to boot.... In Romaic, as luck would have it, I haven't.'[44]

He was not sufficiently conversant with idiomatic usage, while he disdained to read anything written in *katharévousa*, which was one of the two sources that were feeding Modern Greek. He constantly problematized Modern Greek, encountering a word or form from the learned tradition that was in normal use but which he did not like, then racking his brains to invent an alternative, thereby ignoring the history of recent usage and trying to turn the clock back in search of some supposed 'purity' or 'correctness' in the more distant (and usually imagined) past.

---

[39] Psycharis to Eftaliotis, 5 Sept. 1896 and 15 Feb. 1895, in Karatzas 1988: 75, 53.

[40] Psycharis to Eftaliotis, 23 July 1897, ibid., 85. Psycharis started to use the traditional popular names for the months regularly from 1900 onwards.

[41] Psycharis to Eftaliotis, 14 Sept. 1901, 23 July 1899, and 11 Apr. 1905, ibid., 383, 162, 555.

[42] Psycharis to Eftaliotis, 27 Dec. 1891 and 29 July 1899, ibid., 32, 173.

[43] Psycharis to Eftaliotis, 15 July 1897, ibid., 83.

[44] Psycharis to Eftaliotis, 3 Aug. 1899, ibid., 195.

Rather than use a *katharévousa* word, he would often prefer either to use an existing word that was only approximately synonymous or to coin a new one. He mentions in one of his letters that some of his correspondents who were not part of his close circle did not understand some of the words he used. In a letter to Eftaliotis in 1899, he wrote: 'Papadiamantis. Never heard of him. What and where has he written?'[45] Given that Papadiamantis is considered by many Greeks to be the greatest fiction writer in their modern literature, and even given the possibility that Psycharis deliberately ignored his work because it was not written in demotic, this quotation shows how distant Psycharis was from the cultural reality of Greece.

Psycharis told Eftaliotis not to translate foreign books on the grounds that each *laós* has a different way of thinking and therefore needs different books;[46] this is the opposite of Korais' concept of the transfusion of European knowledge into Greek. 'Our language is untranslatable and inimitable', writes Psycharis.[47] Indeed, it is as if the Modern Greek language needs to be untranslatable so as to be able to express and foster the uniqueness of the Greek people; translation is imitation, whereas, in order to progress, Greece needs to cultivate its own unique genius. Like Korais before him, Psycharis believed that Greek culture needed prose rather than poetry in order to show that it had passed beyond its childhood stage. He claimed that in his novels he was revealing the true soul of the *Romiós* and that he was the leading Greek fiction writer of his time.

My Journey

The extreme position to which Kontos had taken linguistic archaism perhaps made it inevitable that the pendulum would swing back in the other direction. The dismissal of the whole of the modern Greek written tradition by such an eminent philologist left Psycharis free to impose his own doctrine in *My Journey*. While most of the previous participants in the controversy had proposed just another version of the mixture between Ancient and Modern Greek, Psycharis proposed a variety of Greek based on the common features of the modern spoken dialects and excluding any compromise with the phonology and morphology of Ancient Greek and *katharévousa*.

---

[45] Psycharis to Eftaliotis, 12 Nov. 1899, ibid., 222. See below for Papadiamantis' assessment of Psycharis.

[46] Psycharis to Eftaliotis, 11 Nov. 1890, ibid., 9.

[47] Psycharis to Eftaliotis, 18 Dec. 1891, ibid., 30.

My Journey was the first novel-length prose work written entirely in demotic. Apart from the fact that it was written in a lively vernacular, what made Psycharis' book particularly effective was that it had both literary and scholarly pretensions: it was a combination of a travelogue, a novel, and a work of philological scholarship and polemic written in a chatty, colloquial, and often humorous style, with abundant use of the first and second persons. This established a personal, oral-like rapport between author and reader that had normally been avoided by writers of *katharévousa*. At the time of its publication it was the longest prose work ever to have been written in demotic, and its grammar was more systematic and uncompromising than any variety of demotic that had been used in prose since the days of Psalidas and Vilaras seventy years earlier. *My Journey* extended the use of demotic in two dimensions: from poetry to prose and from literary to scholarly discourse.

My Journey is a fictionalized account of Psycharis' visit to Constantinople, Chios, and Athens in 1886, conveying his impressions of the people and their culture. On the way, it sets out his views on the language question, which he was able to approach with all the advantages of an outsider observing unfamiliar phenomena through the eyes of what appeared to be common sense. In his view, the natural linguistic sensibilities of the Greeks – and therefore the Greek national character – had been distorted by *katharévousa*, which was either literally translated French or bureaucratic gibberish. In a striking passage about his visit to the reading room of a club in Constantinople, he describes his impressions while reading Greek newspapers: the *katharévousa* in which they are written strikes his French eye as being literally translated from French, to such an extent that he fancies he can glimpse the French original showing through the gaps between the Greek letters. As an example he quotes the Greek phrase ἐλάμβανε τὸν κόπον 'he took the trouble' and, realizing that it is a word-for-word translation of the French expression *il prenait la peine*, he sees the French phrase peeping through from behind its Greek equivalent as follows:

ἐΙλLάPμRβEαNvAεIτTὸLvAκPόEπIoNvE[48]

Thus he vividly presents *katharévousa* – and the Greek culture that surrounds it – as the product of a double imitation, of Ancient Greek form and French content.

[48] Psycharis 1971: 71–2 [=Psycharis 1888: 50].

In the language of modern Greece and in its culture as a whole Psycharis diagnosed a blind worship of the ancients that had led to an excessive reliance on Classical Greek language and culture. He contrasted the way the Italians had been able to avoid dependence on ancient Rome by striving, since the time of Dante, to produce a culture as sublime as (but different from) that of Rome. He himself had no doubt that the modern Greeks were descended from the ancients. Whatever they did, however, they should not imitate; instead, they should discover the essence of their national character and strive to be themselves.

His pupil and academic successor, André Mirambel, summed up the basic tenets of Psycharis' doctrine, as he presented it in *My Journey* and elsewhere, as follows: a belief in the continuous development of the Greek language since antiquity; a belief in the absolute rigour of its phonetic laws; and a belief in the need to develop and institutionalize a common, unified written language on the basis of living spoken usage.[49]

Psycharis believed that Greece could not discover and express its true self until it had adopted demotic for all purposes; this was the converse of the views of the archaists and purists, who were seeking elsewhere for Greece's true self. As Tziovas has pointed out, Psycharis believed, like Herder, that a national language is the expression of the national soul; his identification of language and soul resulted in an emphasis on speech, and consequently on demotic.[50] For him, then, demotic was the natural expression of the soul of the Greek individual and the Greek community, the outward manifestation of the inner essence of Greekness, while *katharévousa* was purely a matter of external form.

Psycharis was deeply influenced by those of the so-called *Junggrammatiker* [Young Grammarians] in Germany who viewed phonetic laws as dominant and exceptionless within the history and the present state of a given language and who claimed that only spoken languages were real and natural.[51] For such linguists, language consisted primarily of sounds, and the writing system was secondary. Psycharis argued that *katharévousa* employs the phonological system (i.e. the pronunciation) of Modern Greek but the orthography of Ancient Greek; it is therefore inconsistent and artificial, since it mixes the synchronic with the diachronic.[52] He saw the fact that *katharévousa* was a compromise between Ancient and Modern Greek as a symptom of the half-measures

---

[49] Mirambel 1957: 93.   [50] Tziovas 1986: 121 ff.

[51] For a nuanced account of the influence of the *Junggrammatiker* on Psycharis see De Boel 1999.

[52] Philippaki-Warburton 1988.

that characterized the whole of Greek culture that had been developed since independence.

Unlike most of those who opposed the written use of the vernacular, Psycharis explicitly acknowledged that the pronunciation of Greek had changed since Classical times.[53] In a striking passage in *My Journey*, he uses the Greek word for 'compromise' in order to illustrate a brilliant lesson in Young-Grammarian linguistics.[54] He points out that the consonant cluster /mv/ found in the word συμβιβασμός, pronounced /simvivazmós/ in Modern Greek, did not occur in Classical Greek and does not occur in any of the dialects of Modern Greek, but is only found in *katharévousa*: in the modern dialects, the ancient cluster μβ (pronounced /mb/ in Classical Greek), is manifested as either /mb/ (spelled μπ) or /v/. The first of these two pronunciations is exactly the same as in Ancient Greek, and for this reason Psycharis is able to argue that the spoken language is essentially (i.e. phonologically) closer to Ancient Greek than *katharévousa* is. In fact, he argues, *katharévousa* is not genuine Greek at all, because it contains clusters of sounds such as /mv/ that have never been uttered naturally by Greek lips.[55] This is because *katharévousa* has been erroneously developed on the basis of historical orthography rather than on the basis of the historical development of the pronunciation.

In a later text Psycharis argues that linguistic science has progressed since Korais, and we are now aware of the mistakes in *katharévousa* that he could not see. For example, Psycharis shows how in Ancient Greek *graphsō, the underlying aorist subjunctive form of *graphō* 'I write', becomes *grapsō*. Similarly, in demotic the subjunctive of *paidevo* 'I punish' is *paidepso*, while *katharévousa* forms the subjunctive of *paidevo* 'I educate' as *paidefso*. Here again, he argues, demotic behaves phonologically in the same way as Ancient Greek, whereas *katharévousa* does not. Thus demotic *is* Ancient Greek: '[T]here's no point in searching for our linguistic unity anywhere but in our demotic', he concludes, countering Hatzidakis' argument that only *katharévousa* can unite the

---

[53] See, for instance, Psycharis 1971: 193–7 [=Psycharis 1888: 245–53]. Hatzidakis too supported the view that the pronunciation of Greek had changed since Classical times. For the influence of the *Junggrammatiker* on Psycharis' view that *katharévousa* lacked the internal structural coherence of a 'real' language see Horrocks 1997: 352.

[54] Psycharis 1971: 142–57 [=Psycharis 1888: 163–88] (Chapter 21).

[55] Much later, Psycharis was to connect the phonological laws of demotic with the Greek national character, explaining that the reason for the Modern Greek treatment of certain consonant clusters was that '[t]he speech and the mind of the *Romiós* need air and broad horizons' (Psycharis 1935: 51).

nation.[56] This sums up Psycharis' view of the relationship between language and national identity.

Psycharis claimed that, in the unsystematic jumble of ancient and modern features that constitute *katharévousa*, the purists had produced a travesty of Greek, a variety that was neither ancient nor modern – a *misí glossa* [half-language] which could not be spoken but could only exist in written form. Psycharis viewed Modern Greek as a synchronic system, whereas many other Greek writers have seen it in terms of individual words and grammatical phenomena, any of which may be altered at will. In his writings, he aimed to give the Greeks a *sostí glossa*, in the double sense of a 'complete language' and a 'correct language'.

In Psycharis' view, language is subject to immutable laws, and it is the duty of the linguist to discover them, not to make them. These laws are dictated by natural and historical evolution. It was post-Classical and post-Hellenistic history that had dictated the laws of Modern Greek; this was ignored by the archaists and the purists. Psycharis claimed that the variety of Greek that he used in *My Journey* had been arrived at scientifically: it had been purged of all features that contravene the historical laws of Greek linguistics. By criticizing *katharévousa* for not being proper Ancient Greek and by trying to purge the modern language of all the archaic features that are found in *katharévousa*, Psycharis showed himself, in his own way, to be very much a purist too.

However, although it was in theory possible to have a structurally pure demotic (though not a structurally pure *katharévousa*), even Psycharis realized that in practice everyone writing in Greek had to make some compromises with *katharévousa* (or at least Ancient Greek), and he was not always consistent in his application of his 'immutable' rules. He claimed to want a systematic language in contrast to the arbitrary mixture that is *katharévousa*, yet he often chose forms quite arbitrarily, simply because he happened to like them.[57] The suspicion that, to some extent, he was laying down his own personal choices is borne out by the Constantinopolitan morphological and syntactical features that he used in *My Journey*. He paid tribute to 'the immortal Vilaras', whom he acknowledged as a 'father' and 'guide',[58] yet in his desire to be totally original he failed to give due credit to the work of the post-Solomos writers from the Ionian Islands, whom he no doubt felt to be rivals.

---

[56] Psycharis 1903: 6–11.
[57] See e.g. Psycharis to Eftaliotis, 27 Oct. 1901, in Karatzas 1988: 410.
[58] Psycharis 1903: 33–4 and in several other places; see Kriaras 1973: 30.

Indeed, in *My Journey* he actually claimed to be the first person to be writing 'a language that is the child and only daughter of the old Hellenic, our new *graikikí* [Greek] language'.[59]

Like the work of Korais, Kodrikas, Zampelios, and others before him, Psycharis emphasized that the language question was a matter of national and political importance, and, in a sign of the increasing public awareness of the problem, the phrase *glossikón zítima* [language question] came to be far more widely used in Greece from 1888 onwards. *My Journey* was written very much in the spirit of the *Megali Idea*: it was a call to arms, urging the Greeks to regain the heroic spirit of 1821 and to unify and consolidate their nation by expelling the Turks from the ancestral Greek lands at a time when Greek education was diverting people's minds from this urgent task by filling them with Ancient Greek grammar. This call to arms turned out to be an early prelude to the victorious Balkan wars of 1912–13.

In the very first paragraph of the introduction to *My Journey* Psycharis calls demotic the 'national language': 'Language and *patrida* [homeland] are the same thing. To fight for the homeland or for the national language is one and the same struggle',[60] he writes, recalling the passage in Solomos' 'Dialogue' beginning, 'Do you think I have anything in my mind except liberty and language?'[61] Near the end of his book Psycharis writes: 'The language question is a political one; what the army is fighting to do for the physical frontiers, the language wants to do for the intellectual frontiers; both [kinds of frontier] must go much further and take up more space.'[62] In his view, a fully independent nation with its own particular character needs a fully independent language. He saw demotic as an instrument of modernization that would lead to Greek territorial gains. Instead of trying to rid the language of Turkish words, the Greeks should be expelling the Turks from ancestral Greek territory. With reference to the word *toufeki* 'gun', from Turkish *tüfek*, he writes: 'It's impossible to expel *toufeki* from our language, because it kills Turks; it would be far more sensible to expel the Turk from the islands and the provinces, because the Turk may kill Christians.'[63]

[59] Psycharis 1971: 59 [=Psycharis 1888: 31]. The adjective *graikikí* is omitted from the second edition (Psycharis 1905: 51).

[60] Psycharis 1971: 37 [=Psycharis 1888: i]. The first sentence of this quotation is repeated near the end of the book (1971: 201 [= 1888: 260]).

[61] Solomos 1955: 12. The Solomos passage is quoted in Psycharis 1971: 200 [=Psycharis 1888: 258].

[62] Psycharis 1971: 201 [=Psycharis 1888: 259–60].

[63] Psycharis 1971: 181 [=Psycharis 1888: 227].

Assessment of Psycharis' contribution to the language question

Although Psycharis tends to present the national struggle as being one between Greeks and Turks, it is likely, as I have already suggested, that the development of rival nationalisms in the Balkans also influenced his attitude to the language question, leading him to identify the Greek nation with the native speakers of the Greek language. In his writings Psycharis, like Korais, appears to be unaware of or indifferent to the fact that many people who might be classified as Greek actually spoke a different language at home. In fact, one of the weaknesses of Psycharis' approach to the Greek language question was precisely that he narrowed it down to a two-way conflict between demotic and *katharévousa*. By contrast, one of the great theoretical and practical advantages of the approach adopted by the Athenian demoticists from the first decade of the twentieth century onwards was that it placed the Greek language question firmly within the context of the multilingual reality of the Balkans.

While *My Journey* was perhaps what was needed to awaken Greek intellectual leaders from their torpor, Psycharis' persistence in his uncompromising attitude towards the specific language variety he proposed, as well as to the language question in general, provoked an extreme reaction that delayed the resolution of the *katharévousa*–demotic conflict for several decades. One of the chief practical drawbacks of Psycharis' formalistically rigid view of the Greek language was the assumption that a single language variety should be used for all purposes, both oral and written, allowing little leeway for variation according to linguistic register.[64] It is difficult to know in what style Psycharis expected, for instance, newspapers to be written: was the written expression of Romaic culture condemned to remain forever tied to the oral? And was translation from western European languages to be denied to the Greeks? Georgia Pateridou points out that most of the characters in his novels tend to speak in the same language variety; in his desire to present a uniform national identity based on language, he makes little attempt to convey his characters' class origin or social status through their speech.[65]

In a sense, Psycharis was too much of a grammarian and not enough of a sociolinguist, and he did not possess a high degree of aesthetic sensitivity to language. Strangely, however, he never produced a complete grammar of Modern Greek.[66] His justification for not doing so was that

---

[64] Browning 1982: 58.   [65] Pateridou 2004: 53.

[66] For his *Great Romaic Scientific Grammar* (1929–37), which does not proceed further than phonology, see Chapter 9, p. 298.

'I wrote the grammar with every word, every [grammatical] form of *My Journey*':[67] for Psycharis, as for other demoticists, the grammar book should not precede practical writing but follow it.

Horrocks has rightly stated that Psycharis attempted to create a common language 'by an act of individual will'.[68] It is worth quoting two assessments of Psycharis' contribution by linguists who stand in opposing camps on the post-1976 language question. The veteran demoticist Emmanouil Kriaras, professor of medieval Greek literature at the University of Salonica, has written about *My Journey*: 'The appearance of this book on the intellectual horizon of our country constituted, after Solomos, the first basic landmark in the renewal of our literary life'.[69] Georgios Babiniotis, a professor of linguistics at Athens University known for his conservative linguistic views, has written that 'without the scholarly linguistic support, the struggles, and the publications of Giannis Psycharis . . . , and chiefly without *My Journey*, which marked the beginning of the Modern Greek linguistic revolution, we would perhaps not have reached, ninety years after *My Journey*, in 1976, the recognition of demotic (common Modern Greek) as the official language'.[70]

However, most educated Greeks were not prepared to accept Psycharis' exhortation to 'take the boatman as our teacher . . . , and run and study our language at the feet of the tailor and cobbler'.[71] Many authors who were disposed to write in demotic but whose linguistic sense had been partly shaped by *katharévousa* were alienated by the dogmatic purism of Psycharis' orthodox demoticism, which included the imposition of exceptionless phonological rules on words from the learned tradition that had already become universally accepted, not only in written discourse in *katharévousa* but in the everyday spoken usage of moderately educated people. As Horrocks puts it, whereas the archaizers 'antiqued the modern', Psycharis 'modernized the antique'.[72] Examples in *My Journey* include ἀρφάβητο for ἀλφάβητον 'alphabet', συθῆκες for συνθῆκαι 'conditions', λάψη for λάμψις 'flash of light', χερόγραφο for χειρόγραφον 'manuscript', and φτυχισμένος for εὐτυχισμένος 'happy'. Psycharis' versions sounded like mispronunciations of learned words by uneducated people, who would be unlikely to be familiar with many of these words in the first place. In the version of demotic that was later to be codified and promoted by Triantafyllidis

---

[67] Psycharis 1905: 9–10.   [68] Horrocks 1997: 353.   [69] Kriaras 2004: 54.
[70] Babiniotis, quoted in Kriaras 1998: 197.
[71] Psycharis 1971: 171 [=Psycharis 1888: 210–11].   [72] Horrocks 1997: 352.

and others, and which has become standard today, these words, in the monotonic system, have taken on the forms αλφάβητο, συνθήκες, λάμψη, χειρόγραφο, and ευτυχισμένος. Examples such as the first four are compromises: the phonology and spelling of the stems preserve their ancient and *katharévousa* forms, while the inflectional suffixes conform to demotic morphology.

Another feature of Psycharis' language that alienated many educated people was his passion for inventing technical terms made up of demotic morphemes to replace already existing terms that had either been borrowed from Ancient Greek or coined in *katharévousa* with the use of ancient morphemes. The fact that Psycharis coined new terms particularly in his writings on linguistics gave rise to a set of rather ludicrous words such as ἀβγάτισμα for αὔξησις 'augment', which were as unfamiliar to linguists as they were to the lay public and thus had little hope of imposing themselves in place of the existing terms. Also Psycharis himself did not always succeed in avoiding what he would have decried as *gallikoures* [Gallicisms] if he had found them in texts written in *katharévousa*.[73]

Psycharis was to become indignant when a later generation of demoticists came to 'adulterate' what he felt to be the only legitimate written variety of the Greek language. Contrary to Psycharis' predictions, the phonology of the spoken language – which he claimed to be unchangeable – has altered, and forms such as *symvivasmós* have come to be standard in Greek today. Indeed, Triantafyllidis explicitly acknowledged that the language variety that he himself promoted was a compromise, and that compromise, which Psycharis detested, was both desirable and necessary.[74] By contrast, in most respects the morphology of demotic has established itself as standard, albeit supplemented with a number of learned forms (e.g. *prágmatos* as the genitive singular of *pragma* 'thing') and even whole paradigms (e.g. *akrivís* 'precise', *proïón* 'product').

The reception and aftermath of My Journey

My Journey soon came to be seen as the manifesto of demoticism. This was a movement that set out to demolish the shaky Greek ideological, cultural, and educational edifice based on an unreflective reliance on the

[73] For example, 'Μην του ρωτάς να στο ξηγήση' (Psycharis 1971: 153) 'Don't ask him to explain it to you', in which he uses the verb ρωτάω 'ask [what, whether, etc.]' instead of ζητάω 'ask [someone to do something]', confusing the two Greek verbs because their distinct meanings are both expressed by a single verb, *demander*, in French (cf. 'Ne lui demande pas de te l'expliquer').
[74] Triantafyllidis 1965a: 297 [1933].

ancient past and to rebuild modern Greek culture on the foundations of rural popular tradition. Its supporters hoped that this new Greek culture would re-establish what they saw as the natural and genuine Greek identity and enable their compatriots to engage critically and creatively with the ancient tradition. The advent of demoticism marked a paradigm shift in Greek intellectual life. It was both a response and an encouragement to social changes, which included increasing urbanization and industrialization, the need for more widespread literacy, the aspiration for greater democratization, and the desire to prepare for wars of territorial expansion in which men would be prepared to sacrifice themselves for their fatherland.[75]

Demoticism saw language and nation as living organisms rather than static entities.[76] It was based on the belief that the language and culture of the Greek rural population were the natural modern continuation of ancient Greek language and culture and that the common features of the dialects spoken by the Greek people should form the basis of the written language used in literature, education, government, and indeed all walks of life except church ritual. In particular, the study of Modern Greek language, folk songs, folk tales, proverbs, and other manifestations of traditional Greek rural life should play a leading role in education. The ultimate aim was to bind the nation together, both geographically (the Greeks of the kingdom and those of the Ottoman empire) and historically, into a single, unified, and homogeneous imagined community. Demoticism was a neo-romantic movement, adopting Herderian and Humboldtian beliefs that the language and songs of the traditional rural folk express the national soul. At the same time, it aimed to be an anti-elitist, modernizing movement. Also, although this was not stated explicitly, it was essentially a secular movement. Demoticism has many similarities with national-liberation movements, including the desire to replace one elite by another – except that in this case both of the elites shared the same ethnicity and nationality. Demoticism, then, was a social revolution articulated in terms of national liberation.

Although demoticism became the focus of intensely political dissentions, no particular Greek political party was ever committed to demoticism as part of a 'counterhegemonic project', unlike, say, the Labour Party in Norway.[77] In Greece, as in Norway, the language reform movements were top-down; yet in Greece, unlike Norway, the initiatives

---

[75] For demoticism as the second of three stages in the 'invention of Greece' see Bien 2005.
[76] Tziovas 1986: 115–17.   [77] Cf. Bucken-Knapp 2003: 9.

and the decisive actions were carried out not so much by political elites as by cultural elites. As Tziovas points out, the demoticists believed that by seizing literature they would be able to take control of the language and the literary and historical past of Greece.[78] It is therefore not surprising that the manifesto of demoticism aspired to be a work of literature.

In *My Journey* Psycharis made little pretence that the first-person narrator was anyone but the author himself. This removed the linguistic inhibitions of many writers, who decided to abandon *katharévousa* in favour of demotic in their literary work. Psycharis' book encouraged Kleanthis Michailidis to become a writer of prose fiction, and also to write poetry in demotic rather than *katharévousa*. At the same time Michailidis adopted the folksy *nom de plume* Argyris Eftaliotis in place of the archaic name that was given him at birth.[79] His *Island Stories*, set in his native Lesbos – still part of the Ottoman empire until 1912 – and published as a volume in 1894, are written in colloquial language and in chatty style. The first of these stories appeared in *Estia* the year after *My Journey* and was probably its first literary fruit. This story, entitled 'A True Tale', presents the portrait of a cultural hybrid, a man who has taken on a 'Frankish' (western European) air, Frankish manners, and even a Frankish walk through having lived in Europe for twenty years. This is his first visit back to his native island, and he is shocked to find that foreign innovations have been introduced into his small town: the inhabitants have been corrupted by a rootless international culture emanating from Europe via Constantinople and Syros, and even his own house has been filled with Frankish furniture. The story is unashamedly autobiographical: Michailidis, who had been living in Manchester and Liverpool since the age of eighteen, visited his native island in 1887 for the first time in twenty years while on his way to a posting at the Ralli Brothers' branch in Bombay, where he lived until 1891.[80]

Throughout Eftaliotis' collection of stories, the narrator gives the impression that he has retained the memory of aspects of traditional Greek life that people still living in Greece, under the twin influences of European modernity and the culture of *katharévousa*, have forgotten. After the appearance of *Island Stories*, Psycharis wrote to Eftaliotis

---

[78] Tziovas 1986: 7.

[79] The name Eftaliotis means 'man from Eftalou', the name of a seaside location in Lesbos known for its medicinal springs.

[80] For biographical information on Eftaliotis see Stavrou 1966. It is ironic that some of the earliest stories aiming at a realistic depiction of Greek rural characters and manners should have been written in India.

that the latter's book had revealed 'the soul of the *Romiós*'.[81] Shortly
afterwards Psycharis wrote to him: 'After so many centuries during which
the soul of *Romiosyni* has been silent, it must now speak and appear. We
must produce novels so as to give it voice.'[82] Psycharis' words express
his belief in the crucial role of literature, and particularly prose fiction,
in rendering the true Greek national character audible (through language)
and visible (through writing).

The novel *The Slender Maiden* by Andreas Karkavitsas (1865–1922),
published in instalments in *Estia* in 1890, was written in *katharévousa*,
but when it was issued in book form in 1896 it was prefaced by an
apology from its author concerning its linguistic form. In the same year
Karkavitsas published *The Beggar*, the first novel to appear in demotic,
which was well received.[83] The 'words' of his collection of short stories
Words of the Prow (1899) are the yarns the narrator has heard while
sitting with the sailors in the prow of the steamer on which he works.
These yarns include encounters with supernatural spirits and the kinds
of popular legend – about Alexander the Great and his sister the Gorgon,
about the fall of Constantinople, and prophecies foretelling its recapture –
that Politis later published in his collection of folk legends entitled
Paradoseis (1904).

Each writer of *ithografía*, setting his stories and novels in those parts
of free and Ottoman-occupied Greece that he knew best, contributed to
a mosaic that represented Greek culture as a rich, age-old and colourful
organism that had preserved many features from ancient times yet did
not depend on Classical antiquity for its existence. The advantages of
writing about rural life in demotic were obvious: in particular, authors
could demonstrate their solidarity with the peasants and imply that there
was a unified Greek nation. The folklore demoticists saw the rural folk
as the living representative of the ancient forebears and therefore argued
that their language should not only be respected but should become the
language of the whole nation.

Despite setting their fictions in various regions, the authors of
ithografía used few regional dialect features.[84] They normally tried to

---

[81] Psycharis to Eftaliotis, 6 Jan. 1892, in Karatzas 1988: 36.
[82] Psycharis to Eftaliotis, 10 Aug. 1892, ibid., 43.
[83] Serialized in 1896 and published in book form as Karkavitsas 1897.
[84] Exceptions include Konstantinos Hatzopoulos (1868–1920) from Agrinio, who often has
his characters speak in northern dialect (see especially the ironically titled *Love in the Village*:
K. Hatzopoulos 1910), and Ioannis Kondylakis (1861–1920), whose characters speak in Cretan
dialect in that rare comic masterpiece, *Patouchas* (1892).

use a common demotic in both narrative and dialogue, though they might give the dialogue a slight local coloration. Demoticists in general played down divergences between the dialects, both as an argument against the supporters of *katharévousa* and in an attempt to forge a unified Modern Greek literary language which would help to cement the Greek nation into a unified whole. Walter Puchner notes that dialects disappear from the stage too at the end of the nineteenth century as 'theatre undertakes an increasingly more "national" mission, in which the unity of the nation is reflected in the unity of the language'.[85]

Demotic did not begin to dominate non-fictional prose until later. Palamas, for instance, while writing some of his critical work in demotic from about 1894 onwards, continued to write in parallel in *katharévousa* until 1907, then again from 1914 onwards, adopting *katharévousa* if this was demanded by the newspaper or other publication where the article was to appear.

My Journey polarized Greek intellectuals, and many of them declared themselves either for or against it. Emmanouil Roïdis published a favourable review of the book soon after its publication. Some of Psycharis' arguments against *katharévousa* also found support in a book-length study by Roïdis entitled *The Idols* (1893). Roïdis had announced the future publication of his book as early as 1885, when he had argued that it had become impossible to write in Modern Greek without being obliged to choose between words and grammatical forms that were 'either exiled from our written discourse on the grounds that they are vulgar, or archaic and therefore alien to spoken usage'.[86] *The Idols* was almost complete by the time *My Journey* was published, which accounts for the fact that Roïdis does not refer to Psycharis' book until the epilogue. The title of Roïdis' study refers to the 'linguistic fallacies' of the purists[87] – that spoken Modern Greek is corrupt, poor in vocabulary, and split into regional dialects – and he set about demolishing each of these shibboleths in turn with the help of judicious quotations from an impressive range of German, French, British, and American linguists. As a creative writer himself, Roïdis claimed, in his usual lively style – and in *katharévousa* – that because it was impossible to write about objects such as food, clothes, furniture, and utensils in *katharévousa*, it was unsuitable for either poetry or realistic prose, which was why there were no good creative writers in *katharévousa*.[88] By quoting folk songs from various parts of Greece, he

---

[85] Puchner 2001: 373.   [86] Roïdis 1885: pp. xi, xxiii   [87] Roïdis 1893: p. xii.
[88] Roïdis was ignoring the realistic aspects of Vizyinos' and Papadiamantis' writing.

challenged the argument that spoken Modern Greek is divided into mutually incomprehensible dialects and asserted that it is a single language.
He rightly argued that whereas all nations have different styles (we
might say registers) for spoken and written usage, most learned Greeks
have confused this stylistic distinction with a difference of grammars.
Nevertheless, he recommended gradual change, for which he used the
vague and unhelpful term *katharismós tis katharevousis* [purification of
katharévousa].[89]

In 1889, the year after the publication of *My Journey*, Palamas was
awarded the first annual Filadelfeios national poetry prize, organized
by the Greek Olympic committee. The rules for the competition stated
that entries could be in either *katharévousa* or demotic. Palamas' prize
entry was an ambitious poem in demotic language and folk-song-type
fifteen-syllable unrhymed lines entitled *Hymn to Athena*. The poem's
title indicates Palamas' ambition to rival Homer (compare the so-called
Homeric hymns to various deities composed between the eighth and the
sixth centuries BC) and to become the poet laureate of modern Athens by
relating the story of how the ancient Athenians came to choose Athena
as the patron goddess of their city. In his adjudication speech, Nikolaos
Politis said that the poet 'renders archaic feelings familiar to the audience,
as it were renewing and enlivening them through popular language' and
through the verse form that is modelled on the folk songs.[90] By winning
this nationally prestigious poetry prize for a poem in demotic on an
ancient theme, Palamas had achieved what Tertsetis had failed to do in
1853. He won the prize again in 1890 with a collection of poems entitled
The Eyes of my Soul.[91] By this time the use of demotic in poetry had
clearly gained a high degree of public acceptability.

Nevertheless, the purists closed ranks to oppose the burgeoning
demoticist movement that was manifesting itself in both literature and
linguistics. In particular, Hatzidakis published a series of polemics on
the language controversy between 1890 and 1895.[92] It is indicative that
from this time onwards they increasingly used the term *katharévousa* to
refer to the form of language they supported. The adjudicator appointed
for the third Filadelfeios prize (1891), Angelos Vlachos (1838–1920), a
diplomat, poet, playwright, and critic writing in *katharévousa* who had
won the 1866 and 1868 Voutsinaios competitions with a collection of
light lyrical poems and a verse comedy, reversed the trend set during the

---

[89] Roïdis 1893: p. x.   [90] Quoted in Kasinis 1982–84: 338.   [91] Palamas 1892.
[92] Hatzidakis 1890–95.

first two years of the new competition. He awarded the prize to a poem by an unknown writer named Damianos[93] because of its 'pure demotic language' but shunned the entries submitted by Eftaliotis, which consisted of one long poem and a collection of sonnets displaying Shakespearian influence in their form and diction;[94] the long poem received honourable mention, but the sonnets did not. In his adjudication speech Vlachos argued that demotic was only capable of being used for simple subjects – a view similar to that of Vernardakis. Vlachos only accepted the 'pure popular language, rendered immortal by the folk songs'.[95] It is ironic that 'immortal' here essentially means 'dead': Panagiotis Moullas remarks that the 'popular language', which such figures associated with the folk songs, was regarded not as a living language capable of evolution but as a fixed object of imitation.[96] Vlachos criticized young poets for creating new words 'according to unprecedented and unheard-of etymological rules', by which he meant the derivational rules of demotic rather than Ancient Greek; poets should 'content themselves with creating ideas and stop trying to create a language', since 'languages are only created and moulded by peoples'.[97]

Vlachos' speech provoked a flurry of indignant comments from writers and critics who were sympathetic to demotic.[98] Palamas wrote a series of long articles (also in *katharévousa*) inspired by Vlachos' adjudication, in which he claims that demotic is not the language of the folk songs but that of the people who sing them, and that the poet is part of the people. It is the right and duty of the poet to use linguistic material taken from the people, even if this is not preserved in the songs that have been recorded so far. '[I]f the People is the Creator that gives life, the Poet is, chiefly, the Mind that adorns', he declares. Aware that a language is characterized not by its vocabulary (in which it may be rich or poor) but by its grammar, Palamas challenges Vlachos by arguing that writers of demotic should be allowed to borrow words from Ancient Greek and *katharévousa*. Like the ancients, he writes, the young Greek poets of his day use 'poetic words' taken from the dialects or earlier stages of the language, or else coined by themselves, thus contributing to the 'pan-harmonious unity of

---

[93] Fletcher 1984: 64.

[94] The title of Eftaliotis' set of sonnets, *Agapis logia*, was probably intended to stand in contrast to the title of Palamas' entry to the 1876 Voutsinaios competition, which had been criticized for its coldness; both of the titles mean 'Words of Love', but while Palamas' was in archaic Greek, Eftaliotis' was in demotic.

[95] Moullas 1989: 172.   [96] Ibid., 172–3.   [97] Quoted in Palamas n.d.: II 238–9.

[98] Vlachos' adjudication was published in *Estia* 1891b, 265, 281 (see L. Politis 1949).

the poetic language'. It is precisely at this time that demoticists began to use the word *glossoplastis* [creator of language] as a term of praise for poets who were expanding the expressive range of the demotic language, especially by demonstrating its remarkable capacity for forming new words.[99] Palamas concludes his articles by supporting the right of every poet to write in his own style and by asserting that style is not the same as language variety, as Vlachos had alleged.[100] Despite the force of Palamas' arguments, the rules of the Filadelfeios competition were changed in 1892 to specify that entries were to be in either *katharévousa* or 'the pure language of the folk songs' – a retrograde step, as he pointed out in another article.[101]

A venerable representative of the Heptanesian school, Iakovos Polylas, published an attack on Vlachos' adjudication in a booklet entitled *Our Literary Language* (1892), in which he also expressed strong disagreement with Psycharis' views. Polylas had already made a significant contribution to the public acceptability of demotic through his edition of Solomos' works, together with his prologue to it, and, more recently, through his demotic translation of Homer's *Odyssey*, which he published in four instalments between 1875 and 1881. This was the first time that one of the Homeric poems had been translated into demotic. By means of his translation Polylas demonstrated in practice that demotic Greek was adequate for re-embodying the founding texts of ancient Greek culture and conveying them to a modern audience.

By the 1890s, however, having lived in Athens for some years as a member of parliament, he was using simple *katharévousa* in prose, although he himself, as Dimitris Polychronakis argues, conceived of it as 'refined demotic'.[102] Polylas argued that the written language had influenced even the speech of the uneducated, and that it was a mistake to ignore this influence, as Psycharis had done. Nevertheless, Polylas claimed that he did not support *katharévousa*: on the contrary, he

---

[99] Koumanoudis 1980 gives 1890 as the date of his first sighting of the word *glossoplastis*.

[100] Palamas' long critique of Vlachos' adjudication was published in the newspaper *Efimeris* in the same year and is reprinted in Palamas n.d.: II 233–98. Individual passages referred to and quoted here are from ibid., 288, 291, 245, 286–7, 282, and 293.

[101] Palamas n.d. II 301.

[102] Polychronakis 2002: 297. For Polylas' linguistic philosophy and practice (the former deeply influenced by Humboldt) see ibid., 245–99. Polychronakis argues that Polylas' linguistic practice did not change appreciably through his career. He quotes the Corfiot author writing in 1860 that the 'elevation of language' does not mean 'the arbitrary emendation of its morphological and syntactic forms' (Polylas 1860: 15); yet such 'emendation' is precisely what characterizes his writing in the 1890s.

attempted to show that it was bankrupt by pointing out inconsistencies, solecisms, and incomprehensible syntax in the works of purist writers. Arguing that the mission of the writer was 'to contribute to the organic development of the national language', Polylas described *katharévousa* as a 'makeshift archaic construct' and contrasted it with 'the marvellous organism of the ancient language', implying that *katharévousa* lacked the organic quality that characterizes properly cultivated natural languages.[103] Faithful as always to his idealism, he called upon writers to carry out the '*pnevmatopoíisis* [spiritualization] of the national language', by which he meant the vernacular. Polylas ends by quoting Vlachos' negative description of Eftaliotis' language: '[I]t is not that of folk poetry, it is not that which is commonly spoken by the Greek people, it is not some specific dialect of Greece, yet it is all these things together and something more.' The same, Polylas concludes, could equally be said of the literary languages of France, Germany, England, and Italy, and is precisely what is needed in Greece.[104]

In a critical review of Roïdis' book *The Idols*, Polylas maintained that the science of linguistics was valid only for the study of spoken dialects but not written languages. Contrary to the teaching of his master Solomos, he claimed that the Modern Greek dialects differ appreciably from one another, and he challenged the evidence for a common spoken language that Roïdis adduced from folk songs, claiming (with some justification) that the editors of most of the folk-song collections had tacitly adjusted their language to what they considered to be a common standard. 'For the sake of linguistic science,' he cautions, 'we should not appear to be more popular than the people.' He argued that since literary languages are formed through collaboration between the *laós* [folk] and the *lógioi* [learned], writers should inflect words of ancient origin according to Ancient Greek grammar and words from the oral tradition according to the grammar of Modern Greek – a peaceful co-existence of ancient and modern features that challenged Psycharis' imposition of grammatical uniformity.[105]

It would not have been feasible to follow Polylas' proposal to the letter, since speakers and writers would have to know which declinable words originated from the popular tradition and which from the

---

[103] Polylas 1892, in Polylas 1959: 272. See the comments by Tziovas 1986: 133 on this passage.

[104] Polylas 1892: 75, in Polylas 1959: 304.

[105] Polylas 1893. He makes the same argument against the formal demoticization of learned words more clearly in another article (Polylas 1894).

learned tradition. There has been a certain degree of merging between the two morphological systems of demotic and Ancient Greek/*katharévousa* in what has become Standard Modern Greek today. Yet, with certain exceptions, the morphological adaptation of learned words to demotic morphology (though not demotic phonology) eventually became the norm in the twentieth century.

In 1895 Nikolaos Konemenos published an article rejecting the imposition of exceptionless phonological and morphological rules as proposed by Psycharis. He points out that 'the common people' pronounces a number of words (e.g. *ámvonas* [not *ámbonas* or *ávonas*] 'pulpit') in the *katharévousa* manner. He writes that he does not accept that 'only the unlettered peasant or some other common craftsman has the right and the competence to destroy and create [the language] and that I haven't some small right myself'. While Psycharis accepts the unlettered as his teachers, Konemenos accepts them as his colleagues. He shares the language with them on an equal basis, refusing to be either their master or their slave. Psycharis, he implies with his usual good sense, is first subjecting himself to the language of the uneducated, then foisting forms on them that theoretically conform to the rules of their language but in practice differ from the forms they actually use.[106]

In interviews published in 1893 two established authors of fiction expressed their unease about Psycharis' theory and practice in terms that came to be frequently used by creative writers. Karkavitsas declared that Psycharis 'looks at language from a scientific point of view and thus he writes demotic without feeling it',[107] while Papadiamantis is reported as stating that Psycharis' 'monomania' to impose demotic has become a 'psychosis' and alleging that, despite being 'a Levantine,... a Chiot, almost a foreigner, an aristocrat, a Fanariot' who has not had sufficient contact with the demotic language, Psycharis is attempting single-handed to impose himself as 'the creator and teacher of whole nation'.[108]

Psycharis' cousin Dimitrios Vikelas (1835–1908) was a representative of those linguistic compromisers who realized that much of *katharévousa* was impossibly complex and contradictory, yet could not

[106] Konemenos 1895.
[107] Karkavitsas, interview given to Bohème [Mitsos Hatzopoulos], *To Asty*, 9 Apr. 1893, reprinted in Karkavitsas 1973: 311.
[108] Papadiamantis, interview given to Bohème, *To Asty*, 26 Feb./7 March 1893, reprinted in *Nea Estia*, Christmas 1941, 113–14. An anonymous footnote relating to Papadiamantis' interview warns that the interviewer may have spiced up Papadiamantis' views. The pun on Psycharis' surname and 'psychosis' became recurrent, e.g. during the Gospel riots (see Chapter 8).

bring themselves to cut themselves free from Ancient Greek vocabulary and morphology. Vikelas, a member of a cosmopolitan mercantile family who spent most of his life outside Greece and who remained on friendly terms with some of the demoticists, wrote in 1893 that

books are written and published to be read, while the speakers of genuine unmixed demotic did not study at school and do not know how to read. Therefore writers do not address themselves to these people, but to those who have studied at school. Such people have been unable to avoid the influence of school, nor will they avoid it as long as the Greek nation is and remains such as past centuries have made it.[109]

Such circular arguments, which were liable to encourage the indefinite continuation of the linguistic *status quo*, were vehemently resisted by Psicharis.

The fact that the language controversy did not seriously become a nationally divisive issue until after the military defeat by Turkey in 1897 is shown by the fact that a lecture given by Psicharis in demotic to the prestigious Parnassos literary society in Athens in early November 1893 was attended by the king, the queen, and two princes. Psicharis commented later that the audience were surprised that he spoke just like them (he implies that some of them expected him to use some unnatural and outlandish linguistic construct), though they were rather perplexed when they read the text of the lecture in the newspaper, since they were unaccustomed to seeing demotic in print.[110] His lecture, entitled 'The kiss', is one of the finest things he ever wrote: it is learned, witty, charming (and very French), and without the belligerence that tended to characterize his later writings. Psicharis regaled his audience with a history of the demotic word *filí* [kiss] since Homeric times and a history of the kiss in ancient and medieval European literature. He claims that Dante was the first to mention the affectionate kiss on the (closed) lips, in contrast to the 'deep kiss' of erotic love, and that the Greek folk songs depict precisely the same kind of kiss. Psicharis' emphasis on the mouth implies the primarily oral nature of language. Psicharis concludes that Greek folk poetry 'is like an anonymous Dante' and that there is no need, as Hatzidakis had argued, for a Greek Dante to come and impose the demotic language through the force of his poetic genius, since the

[109] Vikelas 1997: 15.

[110] Psicharis 1903: 48. He was invited to give his lecture by Nikolaos Politis, who was the chairman of the Parnassos society. The text of the lecture was published in *Estia*, 7 Nov. 1893 and is reprinted in Psicharis 1903: 43–92.

only thing that modern poets need to do is draw their inspiration from the folk songs.[111] His closing words express the wish and the hope for national reconciliation and national unity, which will be brought about through a combination of language, literature, and love: '[T]he greatest achievement [of the poet] would be . . . if everyone in Greece could kiss each other with the demotic kiss, the national kiss.'[112] Psycharis plays here on the double meaning of the adjective *dimotikós*, which can apply equally to the folk song and to the demotic language.

In 1890 there appeared in London a book entitled *Dante's Inferno, Purgatorio and Paradiso, Translated into Greek Verse by Musurus Pasha, D.C.L.* Like Psycharis, Konstantinos Mousouros was a *Romiós* from Constantinople, but the two men had quite opposite ideological outlooks: Mousouros was a member of the 'Fanar after the Fanar', that group of Orthodox Christians who rose to high office in the Ottoman public service after the Greek War of Independence. He had been Ottoman ambassador in London since 1851, having previously served as governor of Samos and as Ottoman ambassador to Athens and Vienna. His translation – a far cry from Psycharis' image of Dante – is in very archaic Greek, and it is not clear who it was aimed at and who read it; rather like Voulgaris' translations of Virgil a century earlier, it seems to have been a feat of learning intended more to be admired than to be read.[113] Mousouros was probably unaware that, in *My Journey*, Psycharis had mocked those Orthodox Christians who served the Ottoman government in an official capacity: 'You become a civil servant and then you can sit and talk wisely and calmly about the nobility of the language, about Xenophon; you can scatter dative cases, talk as much as you like about the rebirth of Greece, and everyone is amazed at your powers of rhetoric.'[114]

A Turkish historian has written that '[w]hen Mousouros pasha, an Ottoman bureaucrat *par excellence*, stood at the apex of Ottoman bureaucracy, he was also a devout Orthodox Christian, and very much a proud member of his *Rum* community'.[115] Musurus Pasha did not possess

---

[111] Ibid., 89–90.

[112] Ibid., 92.

[113] Dante 1890. This was the second edition of a work that had been published in three volumes in 1882–85, but it is probable that Musurus had given away all the copies of the first edition rather than sold them.

[114] Psycharis 1971: 103 [=Psycharis 1888: 101–2]. Psycharis is careful to distinguish the type of Ottoman Greek he is satirizing here from his own grandfather, who served the Ottomans only so as to help his own people.

[115] Birtek 2005: 44.

a Greek national identity in the modern sense; he represented an old world in which national, religious, and ethnic identities could be highly complex – a world that would almost entirely come to an end with the exchange of minorities between Greece and Turkey in 1923.[116]

[116] I say 'almost', because a century later, in 1988, one of the Turkish participants in Greek–Turkish negotiations was a Greek-speaking member of the Orthodox Christian community in Istanbul named Niko Maksimiyadis. For a Greek journalist's indignant reaction to Maksimiyadis' patriotic Turkish attitude and his denial that he was a Hellene, see Chasapopoulos 1988.

8

Educational demoticism and political reform, 1897–1922

Historical background

In 1897 Greece embarked on an ill-conceived territorial war with Turkey. Having invaded Ottoman territory, Greek troops were decisively pushed back, and the war ended with Ottoman troops occupying part of the territory in Thessaly that Greece had peacefully annexed in 1881. Although the international borders were soon re-established by treaty, the catastrophic national humiliation of 1897 shook the Greek establishment to its foundations. As Anna Frangoudaki has pointed out, it revealed the utopian nature of a policy that promised the extension of Greece's frontiers to the north and east, yet was incapable of defending already acquired Greek territory from Turkish incursions.[1] Greece's military defeat made many Greek intellectuals feel the need to rethink the ideological and linguistic basis of their national education and written culture, and it provided a boost to the demoticists and their sympathizers, who argued that the time was ripe for the now dilapidated archaistic edifice to be replaced by a new, realistic Greek national ideology based on practical education and genuine popular tradition rather than on revivalism.

The period 1897–1912 marked a significant change in the morale of Greek public culture. Much of the literature produced during the early years after the defeat expresses a national depression and self-criticism coupled with a desire to escape from the real world. Yet by the end of this period literature was embodying the more positive nationalistic outlook that led to the military putsch of 1909, the first appointment of the Cretan liberal statesman Eleftherios Venizelos as prime minister in 1910, and ultimately the victorious Balkan wars of 1912–13 against Turkey and Bulgaria. As a result of these wars the geographical area of the Greek

---

[1] Frangoudaki 1977b: 117.

state increased by 70 per cent, while its population doubled between 1910 and 1920.

During this period the language controversy well and truly entered the public sphere, provoking riots in the streets of Athens in 1901 and 1903, while in 1907–08 it became irrevocably attached to partisan politics with a long-running debate over the relationship between the demoticist movement and the conflicting ideologies of nationalism and socialism.

Developments in the language question till 1901

By the end of the nineteenth century, puristic language nationalism in Greece, which had been so dynamic during the time of Korais, had become backward-looking and conservative. Instead of offering a vision of the future, the Greek nationalist outlook that was wedded to *katharévousa* had become a slave to nostalgia. As we have seen, Psycharis and other demoticists saw *katharévousa* as a barrier to the modernization of the Greek state, which, they hoped, would lead to what they sometimes called 'national self-realization' and the 'fulfilment of the national destiny', that is, the acquisition of more lands that were inhabited by Greeks.

Athenian newspapers had been publishing occasional articles by Psycharis in demotic since 1893.[2] By 1900 a significant amount of literature was being written and published in demotic. Poetry, short stories and serialized novels in demotic were being published in magazines with a relatively wide circulation. Palamas' 'Olympic Hymn', written in demotic, and set to music by Spyros Samaras at the behest of Dimitrios Vikelas, the first president of the International Olympic Committee, had been heard by thousands of people at the opening ceremony of the first modern Olympic Games in Athens in 1896. It was around 1898 that Palamas began to campaign, through articles in the press, in favour of the written use of demotic. Palamas, who was the dominant Greek poet of the period from the 1890s to the 1920s, reached the peak of his poetic output in the first decade of the twentieth century. His poetry of this period is particularly rich in the kind of demotic neologisms whose ideological purpose was to demonstrate the creativity of demotic.[3]

---

[2] With few exceptions, however, articles by Psycharis stopped being published in newspapers after the Gospel riots of 1901.

[3] Charalampakis (2006) has counted more than four hundred coined words in two collections published by Palamas in 1904 and 1907.

As we have seen, the first novel in demotic, Karkavitsas' *The Beggar*, had appeared in 1896. Giannis Kampysis (1872–1901) published dramas in demotic from 1896 onwards, though no drama in demotic was performed publicly on stage till 1901, when Konstantinos Christomanos founded the *Nea Skiní* [New Stage] company. Dramas in demotic were even staged at the recently inaugurated Royal Theatre from 1902 onwards.

The 1897 defeat was soon followed by the publication of the first literary magazine to be written entirely in demotic: this was *I techni* [*Art*], which was published by Konstantinos Hatzopoulos (later to become a socialist) and whose first issue appeared in November 1898.[4] *I techni* took for granted that demotic was the appropriate language for literary discourse, and it avoided any involvement in disputes over the language.[5] Although the publication of *I techni* has traditionally been hailed as beginning a new era in the history of the demoticist movement, the fact is that most of its contributors, for all their allegiance to the use of the vernacular in literature, adopted a markedly aristocratic stance towards modern Greek culture. As Moschonas put it, after the 1897 defeat the intelligentsia lost faith in the *laós* [folk] and turned to superhuman Nietzschean ideals, using the popular language without its social content.[6] *I techni* was practically Palamas' mouthpiece, and he became its most regular contributor, while Psycharis and Eftaliotis attacked the magazine because of its German and Nietzschean orientation.[7] Hatzopoulos was so stung by attacks on *I techni* that he closed it down less than a year after it had begun publication; a year later he was to call it 'that most lamentable magazine'.[8]

When the Athens daily newspaper *Akropolis* carried out an opinion poll among its readers in 1900 as to 'what language the Greek people want', the majority voted for *katharévousa* rather than demotic. Palamas had refused an invitation to serve as a member of the committee organizing the poll. 'What we need to know,' he wrote, 'is not what language the Greek people *want* but what language they have.... The Greek people are the worst advisers for the job in hand'.[9] Palamas' words reveal a strikingly elitist attitude towards the language question.

---

[4] For more on the ideological background to the magazines *I techni* and *O Dionysos* see Voutouris 2006a: 205–71. The newspaper *Estia* playfully dubbed the magazine *Mastorosyni* [*Artisanship*] on the grounds that those writers who espoused extreme demoticism cannot aspire to high art (*Estia*, 9 Nov. 1898, quoted in Petrounias 1997: 548).
[5] Gounelas 1984: 39.   [6] Moschonas 1975: xvii.   [7] Voutouris 2006a: 247.
[8] Voutouris 2006a: 255.
[9] Palamas to editor of *Akropolis*, 3 Oct. 1900, in Palamas 1975: 62.

Establishment approval was granted to demotic as a vehicle for literary expression when an edition of Dionysios Solomos' works was published in Athens in 1901 in a prestigious series of seventy-four publications funded by the great benefactor Grigorios Maraslis, who was heir to a commercial fortune made by his father in Odessa and who served as mayor of that city for seventeen years in the late nineteenth century. The editorial committee of the Maraslis Library series included at least nine professors at the University of Athens, including the folklorist Nikolaos Politis and even Georgios Hatzidakis, the professor of linguistics and implacable defender of *katharévousa*. Not only were all of Solomos' Greek works written in demotic but the editors of the series invited Palamas – a poet rather than a literary scholar – to write the prologue. This prologue, also written in demotic, turned out to be one of the lengthiest and finest critical introductions to Solomos' life and work ever written, and it helped to confirm the status of Solomos as Greece's national poet. The Maraslis Library also published Politis' monumental collections of modern Greek proverbs and traditions in six volumes, which invited educated readers to value the language and traditions of the uneducated rural Greek folk as a national treasure.[10]

The controversy intensifies: riots in Athens

The publication of much of the demoticist literary and scholarly output from 1900 until the First World War was subsidized by Alexandros Pallis (1851–1935), who had lived in Manchester from 1869 to 1875, in India from 1875 to 1894, then in Liverpool until his death. In all of these places he was working for the Ralli Brothers trading firm, of which he became a partner and director; he became a British citizen in 1897.[11] In 1892 Pallis had begun publishing his own uncompromisingly demotic translation of the *Iliad*[12] – making fewer concessions to the learned language than Polylas had done in his *Odyssey* – which he published not under Homer's name but as if it was the creation of the anonymous ancient Greek folk.

Aware that market forces could not be trusted to disseminate literary works in demotic, Pallis contributed all or part of the publication costs of Palamas' chief books of poetry during this period and a collection of

---

[10] N. G. Politis 1899–1902, 1904.   [11] Stavrou 1966.

[12] Incomplete edn in 2 vols, 1892–1900, complete edn 1904, dedicated to Psycharis. In 1905 the Association pour l'Encouragement des Etudes Grecques in Paris awarded the Zappeion prize to Pallis for his *Iliad* translation; see Palamas 1975: 284.

his short stories,[13] as well as the second edition of the stories of Pallis' close friend Eftaliotis, a novel by Karkavitsas and one by Grigorios Xenopoulos.[14] Among other publications funded by Pallis were Elisaios Gianidis' brilliant polemical defence of demotic, *Language and Life* (1908), and what was to become the classic collection of Greek folk songs published by Nikolaos Politis in 1914. Pallis was also the largest contributor to the costs of publishing the demoticist magazine *Noumas* for its first ten years (1903–13).[15] In 1900–01 he sent a subvention to the Athens newspaper *Akropolis* to carry articles supporting the demoticist cause, and he paid Palamas to write a series of articles in the newspaper *To Asty*, including a favourable review of the first and only volume of Eftaliotis' *History of Romiosyni* (1901), whose publication he had also subsidized.

Eftaliotis' book, which was written in response to the 1897 defeat, pro-voked articles by Politis and the archaeologist Georgios Sotiriadis chal-lenging the appropriateness of the word *Romioí* as opposed to 'Hellenes' as a label for the medieval and modern Greeks.[16] The ideological outlook of Eftaliotis' book, which focused on the early Byzantine period from Constantine I to Justinian (fourth to sixth centuries AD), was based on that of Paparrigopoulos' nationalistic *History of the Greek Nation*.[17] The controversy it sparked off was an indication that both the use of demotic and the controversy over its use were spreading beyond the boundaries of literature and into the debate about modern Greek history and identity. Sotiriadis claimed that *Romiós* had come to mean 'a base, vulgar person', to which Palamas retorted that in the word *Romiosyni* he found 'something poetically and musically coloured, something winged, heroic and ethereal, which I don't think *Ellinismós* possesses, with its

[13] Palamas 1901, 1904, 1907, 1910.

[14] Eftaliotis 1911; Karkavitsas 1904; Xenopoulos 1915. Xenopoulos' novel had originally been published in instalments in the magazine *Panathinaia* in 1905. It was Xenopoulos' first novel for adults in demotic. In the 1906 preface to the first edition of a novel he had published in instalments in 1893, Xenopoulos talks of its 'miserable hyper-*katharévousa*...', which persistently translates the most everyday objects', and tells his readers they will have to translate it back as they read (Xenopoulos 1906: p. xv).

[15] As an indication of the limited influence of the demoticist movement at the time, *Noumas* was only selling a hundred copies of each issue in its first year (Pallis to Vlastos, 7 Jan. 1903, in Karatzas 1985: 309). Even by 1906 it had only two hundred and fifty-five subscribers and was selling another hundred copies on the street (Pallis to Vlastos, 26 Dec. 1906, ibid., 162).

[16] For Eftaliotis' purpose in writing the book see Eftaliotis 1901: 3. On the debate see Kasinis 1982–84. Only one volume of Eftaliotis' *History* was completed; he appears to have abandoned work on the second volume because of the poor reception accorded to the first.

[17] The 'Introduction' to Eftaliotis' history briefly covers the Roman period, while the main body of the text covers the history of the Greeks from 323 to 565 AD.

heavy and immobile magnificence'.[18] In 1895 Palamas had already written in a poem that '[h]idden within much-afflicted *Romiosyni* / I seem to discern Queen Hellas', and in 1897 that '[t]he ancient soul lives within us, / unwittingly hidden'.[19] These passages stress Palamas' belief in the unconscious survival of ancient Greek civilization in the popular culture of modern Greece, in contrast to the exaggeratedly self-conscious imitation of antiquity offered by the official *katharévousa* tradition. Nevertheless, the demoticists were fighting a losing battle on this front: the dispute over the use of the terms *Romiós* and *Ellin* was eventually won by *Ellinismós* rather than *Romiosyni*.[20]

Pallis was not the only demoticist domiciled abroad to subsidize the publication of works in demotic. Psycharis too had contributed financially to the publication of *Noumas*, though usually on condition that the magazine serialize his novels – a constant source of irritation for Pallis, who found Psycharis' fiction so dull that, in his view, it threatened to harm the demoticist cause. In 1901 Psycharis instituted an annual competition for the best literary or linguistic prose work to be written in demotic. The first prize in the first year was shared between the author of a collection of short stories and by Menos Filintas, the self-taught author of the first scholarly grammar of Modern Greek to be written by a Greek in the vernacular, entitled *Grammar of the Romaic Language*, which was published in an incomplete version in 1902 with a long prologue about the language question.[21]

Filintas (1870–1934), from Artaki [Erdek] on the Sea of Marmara, worked as a schoolteacher in Constantinople and Asia Minor, but several times lost his job because of the patriarchate's opposition to the employment of demoticists in the schools under its control. In his prologue Filintas claims that the demoticists are defending Truth against *prólipsi*

---

[18] Palamas n.d.: VI 279. It is probably not a coincidence that Palamas' article was published on 12 Oct. 1901, while the publication of Pallis' translation of the New Testament was in progress.

[19] Palamas n.d: III 19; I 368. In 1945–47, during the crucial period immediately after the German Occupation, when the political future of Greece was in the balance, the left-wing poet Giannis Ritsos wrote in his poem with the programmatic title 'Romiosyni', '[t]here's no need to remember; we know' (Ritsos 1984: 63).

[20] Ironically, it may be that the modern Greek meaning of *Ellinismós* (often translated misleadingly as 'Hellenism'), which denotes the totality of the Greeks as bearers of a common cultural tradition, was originally based on the meaning of the vernacular word *Romiosyni*, which corresponds semantically to Turkish *Rumluk*. For a more recent impassioned defence of *Romiosyni* as a word and a concept see Valetas 1982: 13–50.

[21] Pallis contributed to the publication costs of the first version of Filintas' grammar (1902) and at least the first volume of the complete version (1907).

[preconception], that demotic is the legitimate daughter of the noble Ancient Greek, while *katharévousa* is illegitimate, and that the consonant clusters of *katharévousa* (such as the /fθ/ and /ns/ in the word *diéfthynsis* [direction; address], which extreme demoticists altered to *diéftisi*) are damaging the Greeks' vocal organs. He describes the Greek folk as 'the great *glossoplastis*' and praises the folk songs as the summit of modern Greek literature, likening them to the Homeric poems.[22] He goes on to express his belief that, just as the Greeks of the past had assimilated neighbouring peoples through their spoken language, so – but for *katharévousa* – the Greeks of the present would have assimilated 'all the neighbouring Christian *ethnoulakia* [nationlets] that are baring their teeth at us today', by which he particularly means the Bulgarians.[23] Despite expressions of nationalistic sentiment such as these, the fact that the most radical demoticist statements came from abroad provided conservatives with opportunities to condemn the demoticists as unpatriotic.

In 1901, the same year as the *Romiosyni* debate, a controversy was sparked off by a translation of the New Testament into a moderately archaized version of Modern Greek. This translation was commissioned by Queen Olga from her private secretary, Ioulia Somaki (later Karolou). The queen was the daughter of the Russian Grand Duke Constantine, who was one of the leading figures in the pan-Slavist movement. While visiting a military hospital during the 1897 war, the queen had been shocked to find that poor people could not understand the New Testament in its original Greek form. The queen and Somaki decided to proceed with the publication of the translation despite the refusal of the patriarch of Constantinople, Konstantinos V, to grant his permission.[24] The fact that this translation was the work of two women may have been one of the factors that contributed to the furore that greeted its publication.

Before the controversy surrounding Somaki's translation had died down, the Athens newspaper *Akropolis* began serializing a demotic translation of the Gospels by Pallis. Pallis was a devout Christian who, living in a Protestant country, had developed anti-clerical leanings and had come to believe that the sacred texts of Christianity should be available to all people in their own language for their own private study. Another purpose of his translations was to show that demotic was capable of embodying the spirit of the founding texts (and the highest peaks) of

---

[22] Filintas 1907: 33, 11–12.   [23] Ibid., 9.

[24] Stamatopoulos 2007: 287. An account of the events leading up to the publication of the Olga-Somaki translation is given in Karolou n.d.: 125–77; for the Gospel riots in general see Carabott 1993.

FIGURE 8.1 The front page of the Athens newspaper *Akropolis*, Sunday, 9 September 1901. The right-hand column contains the first instalment of the translation of St Matthew's Gospel into demotic by Alexandros Pallis. The translation is headed with St Paul's words: 'So likewise ye, except ye utter by the tongue words easy to understand, how shall it be known what is spoken?' (I Corinthians 14.9). The headline reads 'THE GOSPEL IN THE LANGUAGE OF THE PEOPLE'. The editorial, written by the paper's owner, Vlasis Gavriilidis,

pagan and Christian Greek literature, namely the Homeric epics and the four Gospels. Most of all, his translation of the Gospels aimed to foster national moral and political regeneration after the 1897 defeat, both by enhancing the prestige of the colloquial modern language and by democratizing and modernizing national culture and opening it up to the broad masses of the population.

On Sunday, 9 September 1901, *Akropolis* published the first instalment of Pallis' translation of St Matthew's Gospel on its front page, preceded by a provocative editorial by the newspaper's owner, Vlasis Gavriilidis, which placed Pallis' initiative within the context of the effort in Europe, initiated by the French revolution, to 'raise the lower classes'. The editorial claimed that all the social reforms that had taken place during the previous century had been inspired by the Bible. It continued,

Who amongst the peasants and the workers, who even among the merchants and the clerks and all those who have not completed secondary education can understand the language of the Gospels? No one.

What was perhaps even more provocative was that Gavriilidis explicitly dissociated the Bible from *filopatría* [love of one's country] and misleadingly associated Pallis' translation with that of Queen Olga. He ended by claiming:

Rarely, perhaps for the first time, has the vernacular language taken on such a godlike gentleness and sweetness and harmoniousness as in the language of Mr Pallis. It is as though one is listening to the tinkling of the bells of a distant flock, such as those that first greeted the Birth of Christ.[25]

[25] Gavriilidis 1901a.

FIGURE 8.1 (CONTINUED) is headed: '*Akropolis* is continuing the Queen's work'. This refers to the translation of the New Testament which had been commissioned by Queen Olga and had been published earlier that year. This translation, into a rather conservative variety of Modern Greek, had already caused controversy. The translation of the Bible into Modern Greek implied that the modern language was sufficiently different from the ancient language that uneducated people could not read Holy Writ. This was an implication that conservative nationalists strenuously opposed. Moreover, Queen Olga was Russian, and Russia was supporting a pan-Slavist policy that supported Bulgarian claims over Macedonia, over which Greece believed it had an exclusive historical and ethnological claim. The publication of Pallis' translation in a newspaper was felt by conservatives to be a further attempt to undermine Greece's national identity and territorial ambitions. It led to the Gospel riots of November 1901, in which about eight protestors were killed by the security forces.

In the face of protests, publication of Pallis' translation was discontinued after the last instalment of St Matthew's Gospel, which appeared on 20 October. Nevertheless, the matter continued to be debated. In an editorial entitled 'Sacrilege', published on 26 October, *Akropolis* defended itself by arguing that the Orthodox Church had recently authorized translations of the Gospels into Turkish and Bulgarian for the benefit of Christians who spoke those languages, and asked whether the Greeks were to be the only people not to be allowed to have a translation in their own tongue.[26] The next day, however, the editor of *Akropolis* admitted that he had reservations about some details of the language used by Pallis in his translation, attributing these to the fact that Pallis lived outside Greece and was influenced by 'the linguistic psychosis' – a pun frequently used to mock the variety of Greek proposed by Psycharis.[27] Soon two separate issues were becoming confused: whether the Gospels should be translated into Modern Greek at all, and whether Pallis' variety of demotic was appropriate for this purpose. Many readers were shocked by the sheer novelty of seeing a familiar text in the unfamiliar guise of a highly colloquial and sometimes idiosyncratic variety of their language. Protestors objected, for example, to the rendering of 'Mount of Olives' by the folksy-sounding 'Ελαιοβούνι' instead of the original ''Ορος των Ελαιών'.

On 29 October, as protests continued to increase, the Theology Faculty of Athens University condemned all 'paraphrases' of the New Testament, and on 3 November it approved a memorandum addressed in the same spirit to the Ministry of Education and the Holy Synod of the Church of Greece. On 5 November a number of students broke into the offices of *Akropolis* demanding that publication of the translation should cease, which it had already done. They then went to the residence of the Archbishop of Athens to demand a ban on translations. Despite the fact that both the patriarchate and the Holy Synod had recently approved a translation of the Gospels into simple *katharévousa*,[28] the Holy Synod proceeded on 8 November to condemn all translations of the Bible into Modern Greek. In the meantime, patriarch Ioakeim III had already condemned Pallis' translation as vulgar.[29] But these announcements came too late to avert the violence that had been building up for weeks and eventually erupted on 7–8 November.

[26] Gavriilidis 1901b.   [27] Gavriilidis 1901c.

[28] This was a translation published by the Anaplasis association in 1900, following approval by the Patriarchate (1896) and the Holy Synod (1897); see *Akropolis*, 7 Nov. 1901.

[29] *Akropolis*, ibid.

On 7 November, after an all-night sit-in at the university, a large number of students, accompanied by non-members of the student body who were motivated by party-political rivalries and with history professor Pavlos Karolidis at their head, marched to the archbishop's residence, where Karolidis delivered the students' demand that all translations of the Bible be not merely condemned but anathematized.[30] The next day, following the archbishop's refusal to accede to the demands, members of the artisan guilds held a meeting, together with the students, to demand the excommunication of the culprits, a ban on tampering with the original text of the Gospels, and the confiscation and destruction of all copies. About eight demonstrators were killed in clashes with the police and military forces that were attempting to prevent them from reaching the archbishop's residence again. The archbishop resigned two days later, followed by the government.

With the *Evangeliká* [Gospel events], the demotic movement had irrevocably entered the political arena. Demonstrators alleged that Pallis' translation represented a mockery of the Scriptures, Hellenism, and 'the sublime language of the Greeks'. In the Greek parliament a former minister of Religious Affairs and Education, Konstantinos Papamichalopoulos, likened the demonstrations to the national insurrection of 1821: the demonstrators, he asserted, driven by 'divine inspiration', had risen up in defence of the 'divine language', which was no less sacred than religion itself.[31] The Holy Synod of the Ecumenical Patriarchate in Constantinople issued an encyclical condemning the translation of Holy Writ into an 'abortive and monstrous idiom' as 'an unforgivable crime and a repugnant and atrocious act'; the encyclical went on to ban the publication of Bible translations into any variety of Modern Greek and to forbid the employment of demoticist teachers in the Ottoman empire.[32] Since the patriarchate controlled the education of the Orthodox Christians in the empire, leading figures in the demoticist movement such as Gianidis and Filintas were several times suspended or dismissed from their teaching posts, as we have seen.

The publication of Pallis' translation of the New Testament – not only into extreme demotic but in the profane context of a daily newspaper – changed the language question for ever; indeed, it probably held back the official adoption of demotic for several decades. Psycharis was sensible enough to leave religion alone, and he had advised Pallis to do the

---

[30] *Akropolis*, 8 Nov. 1901.   [31] Hatzidakis 1905a: 810–14.

[32] The patriarchal encyclical was published in *Ekklisiastiki Alithia*, Constantinople, 21 December 1901 (Papakostas 1989: 19).

same, arguing that it was provocative enough for the demoticists to be challenging the secular authority of *katharévousa* without challenging the Orthodox Church as well. The action of Pallis and those who encouraged the publication of his translation ensured that the demoticist movement – and indeed the demotic language itself – could henceforth be associated with attacks on Orthodox Christianity. At the same time, the Gospel riots succeeded in bringing the Greek language question to the world's attention, since reports and comments on the events in Athens were published in newspapers and magazines in Europe and America.

The riots also enabled anti-demoticist wags to fabricate and circulate comic expressions that they falsely claimed to have found in Pallis' translation. Among these was the following. Where the robber crucified with Christ says to him, 'Lord, remember me when thou comest into thy kingdom' (Luke 23.4) the original Greek has: 'Μνήσθητί μου, Κύριε, ὅταν ἔλθῃς ἐν τῇ βασιλείᾳ σου.' It was alleged that Pallis had written 'Θυμήσου με, αφεντικό, όταν έρθεις στα πράματα', which could be rendered as 'Remember me, boss, when you get in' – the kind of phrase that an uncouth constituent might use when asking a parliamentary candidate for a future favour in return for helping him to get elected. This phrase was not merely a travesty of Pallis' translation;[33] it was also intended to be a wickedly humorous summing up of what was allegedly the 'Romaic' (as opposed to the 'Hellenic') attitude to the democratic process.

An ancient drama (Euripides' *Alcestis*) had already been staged in demotic, without adverse reaction, by Christomanos' *Nea Skiní* in 1902. But riots broke out in streets of Athens again in 1903 after the Royal Theatre staged a production of Georgios Sotiriadis' translation of a German adaptation of Aeschylus' *Oresteia* trilogy.[34] Georgios Mistriotis (1839–1916), the professor of Classics at Athens University who had awarded a prize to a collection of poems in demotic thirty years previously, now described the demoticists as anti-Greek, alleging that they were receiving Russian roubles to further a pan-Slavist conspiracy with the aim of weakening the Greek nation by splitting the Greek language into dialects and cutting the Greeks off from their ancestral culture. He stirred up

[33] Pallis translates this passage as 'Ιησού, θυμήσου με όταν πας στη βασιλεία σου' (*Nea* 1910: 194).

[34] The Greek performance text prepared by Sotiriadis, later to become a professor of history at Athens University, was a translation of an abridged German version of the trilogy by the theatre director Paul Schlenther, which was based on Ulrich von Wilamowitz' German translation of the *Oresteia* and was first performed in Vienna in 1900 (Andrianou 2005; Siouzouli 2005).

students to demonstrate and to call upon the king to ban 'travesties' of the 'national heirlooms' and to punish any civil servant who plotted against the national language. This last attack was directed against Palamas, who had been working as general secretary of the University of Athens since 1897 and who had been commissioned to compose a poem to be recited before the first performance of Aeschylus' tragedies. This time two people were killed in riots; the *Oresteiaká* (as these events came to be known) constituted a second political crisis occasioned by the language controversy within two years.

It was not so much the variety of Greek used in this version of the *Oresteia* that was controversial: it was not in demotic but in a haphazard mixture of features from various varieties of Greek. However, the fact that the Royal Theatre had staged a translation rather than the original text implied that it had the blessing of the royal family itself.[35] Similarly, one of the reasons why protests had been sparked by the publication of Pallis' translation was that it was mistakenly linked with the initiative of Queen Olga. Mistriotis was motivated to mobilize the students to demonstrate against the *Oresteia* production by both personal and ideological factors. He felt himself marginalized because he had been organizing amateur performances of ancient drama in the original language by his students. In his view, to translate ancient texts into Modern Greek implied that Ancient and Modern Greek were two different languages and that therefore the ancient and modern Greeks were two different peoples. Mistriotis was tried for incitement to violence, though he was not found guilty.

On 11 November 1903 the newspaper *Estia* was published entirely in Ancient Greek as an ironic comment on Mistriotis' attacks on the *Oresteia* translation.[36] However, so great was the trauma caused by the *Oresteiaká* that, although performances of Sotiriadis' version of the *Oresteia* were repeated, the Royal Theatre did not stage a production of an ancient Greek tragedy in demotic translation until 1911.

The 1901 and 1903 riots broke out partly because there had been no real public dialogue on the language in the 1890s and 1900s: amid the swirl of misunderstanding and misinformation about the relevant issues, violence came to be seen by some as the only way to protect their interests. In the last analysis, neither the *Evangeliká* nor the *Oresteiaká* were purely about language. Anta Dialla has recently argued that the

---

[35] Stavridi-Patrikiou 2005: 19–20. Spathis 2005.
[36] Tangopoulos to Pallis, 10 Nov. 1903, in Karatzas 1985: 375.

Evangeliká were primarily a demonstration of anti-Slav sentiment, driven by the fact that Russia had been supporting Bulgaria rather than Greece since the end of the Crimean War.[37] The perceived threat of pan-Slavism in Greece at the time should not be underestimated: if pan-Slavism had been established, it would have spread from Vladivostok to the southern borders of Serbia and Bulgaria – wherever these might have been – and there would have been little to stop Slav irredentists from trying to complete the job by taking over regions that Greeks believed to be theirs. Evidence of a Slav threat could also be found in the fact that there had been an influx of Russian monks into the monasteries of Mount Athos in the latter half of the nineteenth century; soon there were more Slavs than Greeks on the Holy Mountain: 5,500 out of a total population of 9,800 in 1910.[38]

Language and the Macedonian Question

From at least the late 1890s until the First World War, the language controversy was dominated by the Macedonian question: the struggle between Greece and Bulgaria for the hearts and minds of the inhabitants of Macedonia, which was part of the contest to decide who would take over the region once it was released from Ottoman control. The most intense phase of what Greeks call the Macedonian Struggle lasted from 1904 until the Young Turk revolution of 1908. Apart from guerrilla activity, the struggle was carried out on both sides through the Church and through education. As we have seen, since a separate national Bulgarian church (exarchate) had split from the Ecumenical Patriarchate in 1870, the latter had become closely allied to the cause of Greek nationalism, while the inhabitants of Macedonia had become divided into those who continued to adhere to the patriarchate and those who had shifted their allegiance to the exarchate. Both the Greek and the Bulgarian authorities expected the inhabitants of Macedonia to possess what was for most of them a novelty: a national consciousness. But the Greeks and the Bulgarians had different criteria for defining the nationality to which people belonged: while the Bulgarians tended to classify as 'Bulgarian' all those inhabitants of Macedonia who spoke a Slav language as their mother tongue, the Greek authorities tended to count as 'Greeks' all those who adhered to the patriarchate and all those who sent their children to Greek schools.

---

[37] Dialla 2005.   [38] Speake 2000: 199–200.

Both sides believed, however, that if the inhabitants of Macedonia were taught to read and write Greek (or Bulgarian), they would automatically gain access to Greek (or Bulgarian) national culture and history, would share the same feelings and thoughts as the rest of the Greeks (or Bulgarians), would consequently adopt a Greek (or Bulgarian) consciousness, and would feel an adherence to the Greek (or Bulgarian) national cause. The question for the Greek authorities was which kind of Greek to teach them. Only Ancient Greek and *katharévousa* were being taught in Greek schools in Macedonia at the time, as they were in Greece itself. Demoticists observed that in Greek schools Slav-speaking and Vlach-speaking children were attempting to learn to read Ancient Greek and *katharévousa* without being able to communicate in spoken Modern Greek; they also observed that many children preferred to attend Bulgarian schools because they found written Bulgarian easier to learn, since the vocabulary and grammar of the written language corresponded closely to the spoken, and it employed a more or less phonetic orthography.

At this time, efforts were made by some Greeks to demonstrate that the language of the Slav speakers in Macedonia was a dialect of Greek. The chief publication in support of this theory is *Contributions to the Bilingualism of the Macedonians from a Comparison of the Slav-seeming Macedonian Language with Greek* (1907) by Konstantinos Tsioulkas, headmaster of the Greek high school in Monastir [Bitola]. By a perversion of historical linguistics, the author, who claimed not to know any Slavonic language, set out to prove that basic items in the Macedonian vocabulary are not Slavonic but are derived from Greek. Tsioulkas concentrates purely on vocabulary (where it is easy to find Slavonic words that are cognate with Greek) rather than phonology, morphology, and syntax. To take one out of many examples, anyone with a knowledge of Indo-European philology recognizes immediately that Macedonian (and common Slavonic) *vino* 'wine' (like English *wine*) is derived from Latin *vinum*, and its similarity to Ancient Greek *oinos* is not due to the fact that the Macedonian word is derived from Ancient Greek but that both the Ancient Greek and Latin words are descended from a common Indo-European ancestor.[39]

---

[39] Tsioulkas 1907: 116. Tsioulkas' book was republished in Greece in 1991, without negative comment, during the new 'Macedonian crisis'; indeed, it was accompanied by a laudatory preface by former government minister Nikolaos Martis. A similarly unscholarly study (Georgiadis 1948) aimed at demonstrating that the 'mixed language' spoken by the inhabitants of Macedonia (including the author himself, another local schoolteacher) cannot be related to any Slavonic language was published during the Greek Civil War.

Educational demoticism: first phase

In November 1904 the first society aimed at promoting demotic in education and in public life generally was founded.[40] It was given the significant name *I Etaireia i Ethnikí Glossa* [The National Language Society], thereby appropriating the epithet 'national' from the supporters of *katharévousa*. The society's founding members included the writer and diplomat Ion Dragoumis (1878–1920), the poets Kostis Palamas and Miltiadis Malakasis, the fiction writers Andreas Karkavitsas and Grigorios Xenopoulos, the civil servant and author Zacharias Papantoniou, and the teacher Elisaios Gianidis. The society's proclamation, issued in 1905, blamed the lamentable state of the nation on Greek primary education, which insisted on teaching the knowledge of words (*lexignosía*) rather than the knowledge of things (*pragmatognosía*), arguing, in an echo of St Paul, that schools should teach the Ancient Greek 'spirit' rather than merely the 'letter' of the Ancient Greek language – which would entail the use of demotic rather than *katharévousa* as the medium of interpretation.[41] The proclamation claimed that, by teaching *katharévousa* rather than demotic at primary schools in Macedonia, the Greek nation was in danger of losing what they called 'the Slavophone and Vlachophone Greeks' to the Bulgarians.

In a speech he gave at the inaugural meeting of the society in January 1905, Palamas made a striking comparison between the demotic and *katharévousa* versions of the phrase 'My father died': while the demotic version (Πέθανε ὁ πατέρας μου) takes root in one's heart, in one's very being, he argued, the *katharévousa* version (Ἀπέθανεν ὁ ἐμὸς πατήρ) is like a piece of clothing that can be discarded. The demotic version 'has grown organically as the green branch of our national linguistic tree', while the *katharévousa* version is 'the dead branch..., which has been nailed to the linguistic trunk by willpower alone'. Extolling the Greek folk songs, he added, echoing Psycharis: 'The Greek Dante is the Greek people!'[42]

Very soon, the society ceased to function after Psycharis' supporters resigned because of a disagreement over which variety of demotic to

[40] Stavridi-Patrikiou 1989: 11 calls the Society 'the first institutionalized group effort by demoticists'.

[41] *Etairia* 1905. Compare 2 Cor. 3.5: 'the letter killeth but the spirit giveth life'.

[42] Palamas n.d.: VI 255–6. Krumbacher 1902: 101 had already used almost the same example as the one chosen by Palamas ('Our father died'). However, Palamas' choice is especially poignant in view of the fact that he lost both his parents when he was six years old; he was probably expected to inform his teacher of this fact in *katharévousa*.

use.[43] But an important new dimension had already been introduced into the language question: this was the movement, known as 'educational demoticism', that aimed to base education (at least at primary level) on the demotic language, Greek popular culture, and practical training. This was a bourgeois democratic reaction to the elitist ideals of the purists; the democratization of education was seen as an agent of social and economic progress. The first to argue specifically for educational reform based on demotic was Fotis Fotiadis in his book *The Language Question and our Educational Renaissance*, which was published in Athens in 1902. Most of its contents had been published as a series of articles in the Constantinople newspaper *Tachydromos* in 1899–1901, before the Gospel riots had taken place; these articles were a reaction to the fact that the teacher and writer Alexandra Papadopoulou had been excluded from teaching in schools by the educational committee of the patriarchate for publishing a story in demotic in the same paper.[44]

At this time the Greek population of Constantinople was larger than the total population of any town in Greece, while the Greeks of Smyrna were about as numerous as the entire population of Athens. Fotiadis (1849–1936) was born and bred in Constantinople and trained as a doctor in Germany and Austria, where he qualified as an ear, nose, and throat specialist. He practised as a doctor in the Ottoman capital, where he served as one of the personal physicians of Sultan Abdül Hamid and his two sons, who became sultans in their turn. Thus, like other leading demoticists, Fotiadis was a privileged member of an elite class. As a wealthy doctor rather than a poor schoolteacher, Fotiadis could afford to support demoticism and oppose the patriarchate.[45]

In his book, the basis of Fotiadis' argument is that, because Greek children do not study their own language, they do not actually study anything at all. Claiming that it is easier for a Greek child to learn a foreign language than to master *katharévousa*, he calls for demotic to be established as the official language of the Greek state, education, and law.

---

[43] Frangoudaki 1977b: 44.

[44] Papakostas 1989: 41. The editor of *Tachydromos* himself attacked the language of Papadopoulou's story, claiming that 'when it is complete and regular, [a language] announces a nation that is morally able-bodied and sensible, but when it is mutilated and barbarized, it bears witness to a people that is morally and intellectually inferior' (quoted ibid., 48 from Fotiadis 1902: 128).

[45] A sign of Fotiadis' social confidence – and perhaps his eccentricity – is the fact that he appears to have been the first Greek to have the invitations to his daughter's wedding printed in demotic.

As a doctor and a father, Fotiadis was able to present a psychological view of the traumatic effect of Greek education on children, who were taught at school that everything they had known so far was mistaken. As a result, he claims, their minds become confused and disordered, and they are unable to do anything in a natural manner, instead becoming self-conscious and hesitant, not only in their linguistic expression but in everything else they do. Fotiadis argues, like other demoticist educationalists after him, that national education should be a process of national self-knowledge and self-development: instead, by imposing an alien, static, and 'inorganic' form of language, Greek education is distorting the 'national soul', which has developed naturally over the generations. He sees the solution as being the establishment of new schools, independent of the state and the patriarchate, in the mountains and by the sea, far from the miasma of the modern city. He makes a clear distinction between the vacuous and oppressive Greek *kratos* [state] and the living *ethnos* [nation], and presents the *laós* [people] as being 'the heart of the nation'.[46] He urges that 'national poetry' and 'popular music' (meaning rural folk poetry and folk music), which reveal the 'soul of the people', should become an essential part of the curriculum.[47] Both the Herderian emphasis on the 'people' as the true bearers of the 'national soul' and the rural orientation are typical manifestations of demoticism at this time.

One of the most important aspects of Fotiadis' book, however, was that it shifted the focus of language and education from the nation as a whole to the psychology of the individual child. Children, he wrote, are an inexhaustible treasure for the nation. He also claims that women, in their role as mothers, are 'the keyholders of the language. It is they that we must win over in every way, it is they who will nurture and strengthen [linguistic] orthodoxy'.[48] He was the first to argue that Ancient Greek literature should be taught in translation in both primary and secondary schools – a view that was promoted by later demoticists.

Shortly afterwards Fotiadis founded a demoticist society in Constantinople known as the *Aderfato* [Brotherhood], which began to function clandestinely in 1905 and was able to operate openly after the Young Turk revolution of 1908. The leading members of the Brotherhood, which was inspired by what Giannis Papakostas calls 'romantic bourgeois liberalism', consisted of doctors, lawyers, and merchants.[49] Its aims were to disseminate demoticist ideas through education and the press. However, although the Brotherhood helped to publish a newspaper in

---

[46] Fotiadis 1902: 42.   [47] Ibid., 43.   [48] Ibid., 89.   [49] Papakostas 1989: 76.

Constantinople for a few months in 1908–09 with financial help from Pallis and others, it was never able to fulfil its aim of setting up its own school, and nothing came of its plan in 1907 to produce school readers in demotic, which were intended partly to help 'Greek children who speak other languages' (meaning Orthodox Christians in the Ottoman empire who spoke Turkish, Slavonic, and Aromanian) to become an integral part of the nation.[50] The Brotherhood was finally wound up in 1909.

Demoticism and socialism: the *Noumas* debate

In April 1907 a law was passed by the Greek parliament providing for the state monopoly of the production of school teaching books and for the approval of a single book for each subject for each class in all primary and secondary schools throughout the kingdom.[51] In parliamentary debates concerning this bill, and in similar debates the following year – the first time the language question had been debated in parliament[52] – proposals were made to introduce legislation protecting school teaching books from 'vulgarism' and imposing *katharévousa* in all branches of the civil service. During these debates Konstantinos Papamichalopoulos argued that *katharévousa* was 'the foundation stone of our national unity'. An opposition member of parliament, Kyriakoulis Mavromichalis, even proposed that the Greek government make a *démarche* to the French government protesting about Psycharis' propagation of demoticist ideas at the Ecole des Langues Orientales in Paris. Although these proposals were not passed, the minister of education, Stefanopoulos, reprimanded Kostis Palamas for his demoticist position, and his successor issued a decree imposing disciplinary penalties on teachers who manifested a tendency contrary to the variety of the Greek language that was deemed appropriate for schools and teachers.[53]

Later in 1907 yet another dimension was introduced into the political profile of the demoticist movement when Georgios Skliros (*nom de plume* of Georgios Konstantinidis, 1878–1920) published the first Marxist manifesto in Greek, *Our Social Question*, which was written in simple *katharévousa*.[54] Born in Trebizond and having studied medicine

---

[50] For the planned school readers see Papakostas 1989: 79n.   [51] Drosinis 1907: 229–38.

[52] Stavridi-Patrikiou 1999: 36–7.

[53] Much of the information contained in this paragraph is based on Stavridi-Patrikiou 1976: pp. xiii–xix.

[54] It may be that the title of Skliros' book is a deliberate reference to the phrase 'our language question', suggesting that the demoticists are fixated on the language issue, which was only a part of a more general social question.

in Moscow and Germany, Skliros, like Psycharis, was able to look at Greece from the outside, to make a (perhaps simplistic) diagnosis of her ills and to propose a radical cure for them. Having expounded Marx's theory of the three classes and their historical succession (aristocracy, bourgeoisie, and working class), Skliros argued that, after the War of Independence, instead of becoming a progressive liberal bourgeois demo-cratic state, Greece had preferred to follow the 'great historical traditions' of an aristocratic past with the aim of reviving the Byzantine empire. In keeping with his Marxist beliefs, he stated that in Greece the dictatorship of the proletariat would be an inevitable outcome of the class struggle, and he called upon the progressive elements of the Greek nation to collaborate with the historical process.

Most importantly for the language question, Skliros singled out the demoticists as being living proof of 'the vitality of the Greek race': they were potentially the most effective instruments of social progress, if only they would realize that they could not solve the language problem without changing the whole structure of Greek society. They had to face the fact that the language problem was the direct consequence of the social system, and that therefore it was not an academic question but a social and political one. He called the demoticists 'the best and the most sensible, brave and enthusiastic sons of our bourgeoisie', claiming that amid 'such a pedantic, corrupt and satanically selfish atmosphere', they were 'practically the only healthy elements in our country, capable of positive social activity'. 'The demoticists,' he continued, 'have been called upon by history to play an important role in the rebirth of our soci-ety.'[55] Skliros argued that the ruling class was not willing to listen to the demoticists' message because it wanted to keep people in ignorance. In order to win their argument, he concluded, the demoticists must address themselves not to the upper class, which would never be convinced, but to the working class, whose allies they must become and whose plight they must attempt to improve. Thus, whereas most demoticists had hitherto envisaged reform from above, Skliros promoted revolution from below.

With its concentration on the need for radical social change within the Greek state, Skliros' book greatly intensified the politicization of the language question. Hitherto 'political' had meant 'national' (the expansion of Greece's frontiers), whereas soon, and especially after the First World War, the language question was to become a party-political issue in the struggles between Left and Right and between Venizelism

[55] Skliros 1976: 128.

and Monarchism. Skliros' challenge gave rise to a protracted debate in the columns of the demoticist magazine *Noumas* (1907–09) between bourgeois demoticists who believed that reforming the language of Greek education would automatically lead to a liberalization of Greek society, and socialists who argued that social reform or revolution was a necessary prerequisite for the solution of the language question.

The debate in *Noumas*, which began with a favourable review of Skliros' book by the teacher and educationalist Αlexandros Delmouzos (1880–1956), who was studying child psychology and education in Germany and was going through a socialist phase in his intellectual career, was carried on at a remarkably high level, in both intellectual and personal terms. The use of demotic was now taken for granted by almost all of the participants as the appropriate medium for such a debate, as well as the most effective medium of education. The participants used it in practice and promoted it in theory as an instrument of communication, irrespective of the actual differences in grammar, vocabulary, and spelling among them. In the *Noumas* debate, in contrast to debates among purists (and any debate involving Psycharis), there was hardly any discussion (let alone criticism) of linguistic details. In fact, Psycharis, Eftaliotis, and Pallis, who were, linguistically speaking, among the most extreme practitioners of demoticism, kept out of the *Noumas* debate, which suggests that they felt out of their depth when it came to such ideological discussions, especially since the armchair socialism sometimes espoused by Psycharis and Pallis had been trumped by Skliros' Marxism.

With regard to the variety of demotic that the participants in the debate wrote in, the racist nationalist Petros Vlastos used an 'orthodox' (Psycharist) version of demotic, while the socialist Skliros used a variety of demotic that made a number of concessions to *katharévousa*, and the socialist Konstantinos Hatzopoulos stood somewhere in between. For example, some participants followed Psycharis in using recently coined demotic terms such as ξετυλιξιά [evolution] (Vlastos), while others preferred to make the already existing purist term (ἐξέλιξις) conform to demotic morphology as ἐξέλιξη (Skliros and Hatzopoulos);[56] it is the latter form that has prevailed today.

Most of the participants were influenced by Nietzschean, Darwinian, and Marxian ideas concerning the 'struggle for existence'. The socialists

---

[56] Stavridi-Patrikiou 1976: 29, 125, and elsewhere.

argued that social progress depends on evolution, which is based on the struggle between social classes, while the nationalists, like the purists, claimed that national progress was best served by the struggle to unify the Greek nation and to combat its rivals. The nationalists saw language as the force uniting all Greeks and capable of leading to the liberation of the Orthodox Christians currently living in Turkey. While the nationalists saw demotic as a potential weapon of the people (*laós*), the nation, and the state in the national struggle against neighbouring nations, the socialists saw it as a potential weapon of the proletariat in the class struggle within Greece.[57]

In order to explain why so many members of the working class and the petty bourgeoisie had taken part in the anti-demotic demonstrations in 1901 and 1903, Hatzopoulos argued that the real supporters of *katharévousa* were the educated classes, who deliberately kept such people in ignorance.[58] For the nationalist Ion Dragoumis, the only bastion capable of repelling European cultural penetration, and the sole ideological foundation for national consciousness and the development of the national struggle, was modern Greek culture, based on popular oral tradition, which could only be perfected and articulated through the demotic language.[59] However, in contrast to the members of the literary Generation of 1880, the nationalist demoticists in the *Noumas* debate, in their attempts to combat the socialists' focus on the urban proletariat, laid surprisingly little emphasis on specific features of rural folk language and traditions – a sign, perhaps, that the Greek bourgeoisie was beginning to gain greater confidence in its own capabilities.

In the event, Skliros was mistaken in thinking he could harness the demoticist movement to the chariot of social revolution. As Emmanouil Moschonas pointed out, 'Demoticism... sought not to overthrow but to renew the system and render it more efficient.'[60] Demoticism never became a mass movement, and its progress was effected largely through pressure exerted on governments by members of the bourgeois elite; outside literature, the greatest successes of demoticism were achieved through educational reform rather than social revolution. By 1915 even Skliros himself had declared his support for Venizelos' reformist government.[61]

---

[57] Ibid., p. lxxxvi.   [58] Ibid., 233.   [59] Ibid., p. lxxxvii.
[60] Moschonas 1975: p. xiv.   [61] Ibid., p. xxxix.

Educational demoticism: second phase

In 1908 Delmouzos began putting demoticist educational theory into practice as principal of the newly founded Municipal Girls' High School in Volos. This school was an innovative initiative, given that it was the first time that the Greek state was providing girls with secondary education.[62] Although he taught both *katharévousa* and demotic, Delmouzos placed particular emphasis on training his pupils to express themselves freely in written demotic; previously they had only been trained to write in *katharévousa*. For the first time in a Greek school, he taught Ancient Greek literature in demotic translation – particularly Pallis' version of the *Iliad*.

It was not a propitious time to be adopting such measures. Demotic had already been associated with anti-national and anti-religious activity. The debates on language and education, mentioned above, had taken place in parliament shortly before Delmouzos took up his post. In the same year, the first translation of a Marxist text, the *Communist Manifesto* by Marx and Engels, appeared in Greek, in an incomplete demotic translation by Konstantinos Hatzopoulos, in the socialist newspaper *Ergatis* [Worker], published in Volos, the very town where Delmouzos was carrying out his educational experiments.

On 16 March 1911 patriarch Ioakeim and the Holy Synod of the Ecumenical Patriarchate issued an encyclical urging that the appropriate measures be taken 'for protection from any *malliarós* or vulgar influence'.[63] Dimitrios Stamatopoulos has argued that by this time Ioakeim, a relentless opponent of demoticism, had come to espouse the nationalist ideology of the 'continuity of Hellenism', and now saw demoticism less as a threat to Orthodox Christianity than as a threat to the Greek nation.[64] Encouraged by the patriarch's encyclical and by the language debate in parliament, and urged on by the local bishop, some of the citizens of Volos succeeded in having Delmouzos' school closed down, and in 1914 he and his associates were tried at Nafplion for spreading atheism both within and outside the school. In court the bishop identified *malliarismós*

---

[62] Dimitrios Saratsis in *Diki* 1915: 269, quoted in A. Dimaras 1974: 55.

[63] The text of the patriarch's encyclical of 16 March 1911 is published in Fotiadis 1911: 47ff. The term *malliarós* [hairy] had come to be applied jocularly to those who used an extreme variety of demotic in their writings, because some of the demoticists in the 1890s wore their hair long. According to Xenopoulos, the term was applied to demoticists in the Athens magazine *Estia* on 26 November 1898, after it was used by Ioannis Kondylakis in an Athens café (Xenopoulos, lecture to *Foititikí Syntrofiá* in 1921, reproduced in A. Dimaras n.d. (*c*.1980): 14). See also Petrounias 1997.

[64] Stamatopoulos 2007: 299–300.

with 'anarchism, socialism, atheism, and freemasonry', while the slander-
ous allegations made against Delmouzos included the sexual molestation
of some his pupils.[65] The defendants were acquitted of all charges.
Like the other demoticist educationalists, Delmouzos had realized that
the education of children was the most effective way to disseminate
demoticist ideas on Greek language and culture, but he understood that
educating future mothers was the most effective of all. It is clear that there
was a strong anti-feminist feeling behind the accusations against him – a
feeling that women should not be too highly educated.

In 1909 a demoticist student movement named the *Foititikí Syntrofiá*
[Student Company] was founded by students at Athens University. In its
proclamation, the Company argued that '[s]chools don't have a mission
to make the children of a nation into wise men or into the descendants
of the ancestors, but to form human beings rather than animals'.[66] The
proclamation goes on to assert that 'we have a right to live and to
grow strong as a nation not because we are descended from the ancient
Greeks but because we are alive'.[67] The majority of students published a
declaration anathematizing the Company and the demoticists in general.

During an unofficial visit made by the linguist and educationalist
Manolis Triantafyllidis (1883–1959) to schools in Thessaly in the same
year, one teacher justified the use of the 'corrected' Korais-type hybrid
form *opsárion* 'fish' (based on the vernacular word *psári*) in primary
schools by exclaiming: 'We can't write *psári*. Can we go out into the
street with dishevelled hair and dirty nails? Well, it's the same with
language.' Triantafyllidis argued that, using the alphabet book by Chari-
sios Papamarkou that had been used in Greek primary schools since at
least 1891, children emerged from school able to say 'nose', 'ears', 'pig',
'horse', and 'house' in Ancient Greek but without having broadened their
repertoire of concepts.[68] These glimpses into Greek primary education
enable us to understand why the pedagogical pressure group known as
the *Ekpaideftikós Omilos* [Educational Association] was set up.

The foundation of the Association was encouraged by the reformist
bourgeois putsch carried out after the Young Turk revolution of 1908
by a group of army officers at Goudi barracks in Athens in 1909. The

---

[65] A. Dimaras 1974: 106–7.   [66] *Prokiryxi* 1910: 9.   [67] Ibid., 28–9.
[68] Triantafyllidis 1912: 300 [= Triantafyllidis 1963: IV 83–4]. The Ancient Greek word for
'fish' is not *opsárion* but *ichthýs*. Glinos too wrote in 1914 that Greek life is dominated by
'verbalism'. Echoing Vizyinos twenty years previously (see Chapter 7), Glinos writes that, in
Greek society, '[t]he naming of things replaces the knowledge of them' (quoted in Bagionas
1985: 16).

putsch succeeded in marginalizing the political elite centred around the palace and led to Venizelos becoming prime minister for the first time in 1910. The Educational Association conformed to the spirit of Venizelos' concept of a national *anórthosis* [recovery; lit. 'raising up again'] after the military defeat by the Turks in 1897. Despite the fact that it centred around Venizelos himself, the Liberal Party (which he founded in 1910 in order to fight the general election of that year) was seen by many as the first 'party of principles' in Greece as opposed to parties that represented the vested interests of a small clique. In the view of most of the demoticists – Psycharists and non-Psycharists, socialists and non-socialists – Venizelos seemed to be achieving the successful combination of liberal reform at home and national expansion abroad that had eluded every political leader before him. This is why most of them were keen to associate themselves with his policies and his authority.

The work of the Educational Association, which was founded in May 1910, continued that of the Constantinople Brotherhood, and its foundation indicated that the intellectual centre of demoticism had moved from Constantinople to Athens.[69] Like the Brotherhood, the Association originally placed less emphasis on demotic and more on education than the National Language Society had done. The stated aim of the Association was the founding of a model primary school in Athens as a testing ground for demoticist ideas such as the teaching of the demotic language and popular traditions and values, and providing a more practical education. At this time, only a tiny percentage of Greeks went on to secondary education; thus the Association viewed primary education not so much as a preparation for secondary education but rather as a preparation for life. For this reason, as Anna Frangoudaki has pointed out, their concentration on primary education was not a sign of modest aims but a matter of shrewd targeting.[70] Founder members of the Association included Fotiadis, Delmouzos, a number of literary figures (including Andreas Karkavitsas, Lorentzos Mavilis, and the youthful Nikos Kazantzakis), doctors, lawyers, military officers, and politicians (among them four future prime ministers). It was as though the bourgeoisie were trying to snatch the initiative for education from the hands of the state, just as they had from the hands of the Church in Korais' time. The Association's proclamation declared that the linguistic purpose of their proposed school would be to render children conscious of the grammatical rules that came unconsciously to their lips; no changes should be made to children's

[69] Papakostas 1989: 104; Kriaras 2004: 47.   [70] Frangoudaki 1987: 128.

language as long as it did not deviate from the 'Panhellenic Common Oral Language'.[71] The Association's official bulletin soon became an important forum for demoticist ideas on language and education.

Demoticism had by then become a sufficiently broad movement for the Association to include moderate socialists such as Delmouzos and the anti-Venizelist right-wing ideologue Dragoumis, though most of the members were upper-middle-class liberals. No fewer than twenty members of parliament were members of the Association in 1911. Soon Delmouzos and two other men who joined the Association shortly after its foundation, Triantafyllidis and Dimitris Glinos (1882–1943), became its leading members.[72] This new demoticist triumvirate, established in Greece, opposed and eventually superseded the diaspora triumvirate consisting of Psycharis, Pallis, and Eftaliotis.[73] With the notable exception of Psycharis, most of the members of the first generation of demoticists were not professional linguists or educationalists, and Psycharis had little contact with school teaching. By contrast, the three leaders of the following generation had carried out postgraduate studies in linguistics and education in Germany and went on to gain practical classroom experience in Greece.

Opposition to the Educational Association came from conservatives such as Hatzidakis and Mistriotis, who saw its aims as undermining the social and cultural establishment. Mistriotis and others founded a rival pressure group named the 'Committee for the Legal Protection of the National Language'. Official reaction to the growing threat posed by demoticism to the linguistic *status quo* was soon to come. Palamas was suspended from his post at the university for one month in April 1911 for having published an article two months previously in which he declared that he was 'absolutely, roundly and soundly, a *malliarós*'.[74] His declaration led to a demonstration against him by university students, and Mistriotis, who had urged them on, was subsequently disciplined in his turn for doing so.

The conciliatory report of the 'Investigative committee of Parliament into the language question', which met while the constitution was being debated and to which Mistriotis denounced the demoticists as being in the

[71] Eidikous 1911: 12–13. The adjective 'Panhellenic', like the term 'national language', had been appropriated by the demoticists from the purists.

[72] All three were out of Athens when it was founded, Delmouzos in Volos and the other two in Germany.

[73] Stavridi-Patrikiou 1999: 126.

[74] Triantafyllidis 1982: pp. xxxvix–xl. For *malliarós* see n. 63 to this chapter.

pay of the enemies of Hellenism, found no evidence for his allegations. In fact, the committee implied that Mistriotis and his supporters were using the language controversy to cover up their desire for political change (presumably referring to their desire to overthrow the Venizelos government). The committee's report distinguished between two varieties of *katharévousa* and two varieties of non-*katharévousa*, one good and one bad: Mistriotis, it found, was defending hyper-*katharévousa*, and his attacks were really intended to undermine *katharévousa*; he openly attacked the *malliaroí*, whereas in fact it was the latter, according to the report, who threatened to undermine demotic. The report declared that demotic was the genuine language of the people and the direct descendant of Classical Greek, whereas *malliarí* was 'a peculiar linguistic construct, repulsive and incomprehensible'. Finally, the committee looked forward to a future merger between the two less extreme varieties.[75] In sum, the committee concluded that the extremists in both camps were undermining their own side.

However, despite Venizelos' sympathy for the demotic movement, pressure from public opinion, whipped up by Mistriotis and the conservative press, led to an article being inserted for the first time in the new Greek constitution of 1911 (approved in February of that year, just nine months after the foundation of the Educational Association) specifying the official language of the state. Article 107 stated that '[t]he official language of the State is that in which the constitution and the texts of Greek legislation are drawn up; any intervention aimed at corrupting it is forbidden'. This clause, though omitted from the Republican constitution of 1927, was reintroduced into the monarchist constitution of 1935 and was included again in the constitutions of 1952 (in the early years of the Cold War) and 1968 (during the Colonels' dictatorship); it was omitted from the present constitution (1975). As a consequence of the Gospel riots ten years earlier, and particularly in view of the fact that a second edition of Pallis' translation of the Gospels had been published in Liverpool in 1910,[76] the 1911 constitution also included, for the first time, a clause prohibiting the publication of translations of the Bible without the permission of the patriarchate of Constantinople and the Holy Synod of the Church of Greece; this clause has remained in subsequent constitutions, including (in a slightly modified form) the current one.

---

[75] The text of the committee's report is published as Ekthesis 1912.

[76] The full text of Pallis' translation was first published in book form in Liverpool in 1902, and copies of it were smuggled into Greece.

The minister of education in 1911, Apostolos Alexandris, was a founder member of the Educational Association; he absented himself from the parliamentary debate on the language clause, supposedly due to illness.[77] A phrase uttered by the aristocratic and patriotic Heptanesian poet Lorentzos Mavilis (1860–1912) during the debate has gone down in history: 'There is no vulgar language, but there are vulgar people, and there are many vulgar people speaking *katharévousa*.'[78] This phrase, which could have been uttered by the Poet in Solomos' 'Dialogue', was specially biting when it was addressed by Mavilis to his fellow members of parliament.

While Psycharis and certain other demoticists attacked Venizelos for his 'compromise' in agreeing to the inclusion of the language article, the Educational Association remained silent, accepting the compromise as an unfortunate necessity.[79] In a 1915 interview Venizelos claimed that the insertion of the language clause was intended to ensure 'national unanimity' in the run-up to the Balkan wars, and that the indirect definition of the official language, in which *katharévousa* was not specified by name, was 'sophistic' and might allow the form of the official language to be changed in future.[80]

The insertion of the language clause in the constitution and the closure of the Volos school put paid to the plans of the Educational Association to set up a model primary school. Nevertheless, despite the constitutional provision, in 1913 – as Greece was completing its victories in the Balkan wars against Turkey and Bulgaria – texts in a conservative version of the vernacular known as *kathomiloumeni* ['generally spoken'] were introduced into primary school readers for the first time. Thereby official education policy acknowledged the importance of teaching children to read and write the vernacular before going on to introduce them to *katharévousa* and Ancient Greek.[81] In an article published at the time Triantafyllidis presented the crucial victories in the Balkan wars, which greatly increased the territory and population of the Greek state, as the Greek equivalent of the unification and *apokatástasi* [restoration, rehabilitation] of Germany in 1870, which gave the Germans the opportunity and

---

[77] Frangoudaki 1977b: 33.   [78] Mavilis 1990: 214.

[79] Frangoudaki 1977b: 52. Among those Psycharists who objected was Eftaliotis, in Delta 1956: 184.

[80] Stavridi-Patrikiou 1999: 108; Moschonas 1975: p. xxix.

[81] Galateia Kazantzaki (and possibly her husband Nikos Kazantzakis) produced two of these readers.

the incentive to standardize their language and thereby consolidate their political unification.[82] After 'the great national movement of the last few months,' he wrote, 'the Greek soul has begun to come to a fuller and more sincere self-awareness', and now that 'the *new state* has to ponder the problem of how quickly and best *it will linguistically assimilate the new Greek populations* that it has enclosed within it', the great national question of education was taking on an even greater significance than before.[83] Whereas Psycharis affected to despise all 'schoolmasters', Triantafyllidis wrote that 'the primary school teacher [is] the first creator of the national soul'.[84]

In August 1916 a provisional government was set up in Salonica following a military revolt in protest against King Constantine's refusal to bring Greece into the First World War on the British and French side. For a time, Greece had two governments (Venizelos soon became prime minister of the Salonica government), two armed forces, and two civil services. This situation has become known as the *Ethnikós Dichasmós* [National Schism]. One of the leading members of the Educational Association, Glinos, joined Venizelos in Salonica and persuaded him to initiate legislation aimed at introducing demotic into primary schools.

In June 1917 King Constantine left Greece without abdicating, and Venizelos assumed power in Athens without elections. His justification for not holding elections was that the legally elected parliament of June 1915 had been dissolved by the king in October of the same year after Venizelos had resigned in protest at what he claimed to be unconstitutional actions taken by the king aimed at establishing absolute monarchy. In Athens Venizelos found himself wielding sufficient authority to put some demoticist reforms into practice. He appointed the three leading members of the Educational Association (Triantafyllidis, Delmouzos, and Glinos) to newly-created senior positions in the Ministry of Education, which placed them in charge of primary education.[85] The teaching of Ancient Greek was removed from primary schools. Demotic alone was taught in the first four forms, and in parallel with *katharévousa* in the last two.[86] New school readers 'in the common spoken (demotic) language'

---

[82] See Triantafyllidis 1965a: 58 [1913].   [83] Ibid., 5; his emphasis.   [84] Ibid., 54.

[85] Triantafyllidis and Delmouzos were appointed Supreme Superintendents of Education, while Glinos was appointed General Secretary of the Ministry of Education (Moschonas 1975: p. xlv).

[86] Frangoudaki 1977a: 36.

were introduced for the first four forms, using a slightly reformed orthography that Triantafyllidis had proposed in 1913.[87]

Triantafyllidis later wrote, with some exaggeration, that the introduction of demotic into schools in 1917 was the first ever official recognition of the mother tongue.[88] Now that Greece had successfully gained Macedonia and other hitherto contentious regions, Venizelos no longer considered it dangerous to introduce demotic into schools; indeed, one of the chief reasons why the triumvirate was appointed was the problem of integrating the non-Greek-speaking populations of Greek Macedonia.[89] Venizelos had already argued in parliament in 1914 that only by teaching the spoken language could the populations of the New Lands (the areas incorporated into Greece as a result of the Balkan wars) learn Greek.[90] Triantafyllidis observed in 1915 that, because of *katharévousa*, not even the Albanian-speaking populations of Attica – on Athens' doorstep – had been linguistically Hellenized.[91]

Ironically, it was the institution of the state-published single book for each subject in each class, introduced by the government in 1907 with the illiberal intention of asserting greater state control over education, that enabled the Venizelos government to impose teaching books in demotic in 1917. However, the educational reforms were short-lived. Because of the war-weariness of the electorate – Greece had been on a war footing since 1912, with conscripts serving in the Balkan wars, the First World War and now, since 1919, in Asia Minor – Venizelos was decisively defeated in the 1920 elections, and the three education reformers resigned from the Ministry of Education; Triantafyllidis and Delmouzos even left for Germany.[92] In 1921 a Ministry of Education committee recommended that the 1917 demotic schoolbooks be burned (in the event they were not, but their use in schools was banned), and that the 1913 books in *kathomiloumeni* be reintroduced. Describing the three men who masterminded the educational reforms as 'the new linguistic emperors', the committee's report alleged that the language used in the 1917 school books was 'a completely artificial language, their own peculiar creation, not spoken by anyone and incomprehensible to pupils'. One of the

---

[87] Triantafyllidis 1913. Triantafyllidis called his orthographic principles 'evolutionary', in contrast to the 'anachronistic' nature of the traditional orthographic system (Triantafyllidis 1965a: 161 [1917–19]).

[88] Triantafyllidis 1965a: 204 [1932].   [89] See Triantafyllidis 1982: pp. xliv–xlv.

[90] Frangoudaki 1977b: 70.   [91] Triantafyllidis 1915.

[92] Triantafyllidis stayed in Germany until he was reinstated in his post at the Ministry of Education in 1923 (Triantafyllidis 1982: 1).

features of the brief school grammar guidelines provided to teachers in 1917 that the Committee objected to was the use of 'vulgar' words in declension paradigms, such as *kafés* [coffee], on which the committee commented: 'All the mire of the streets, everything foreign, barbaric and vulgar that has ever been introduced into the mouths of the lowest social strata, has been fondly picked up and imposed as the form and model of the language of primary school'.[93] Meanwhile, in Constantinople, the patriarchate continued to take measures against demoticists and to attack publications that promoted the demoticist cause.[94]

There were, however, members of the Educational Association who believed that the 1917 school language policy was misconceived. In the view of such people the Association had been set up specifically to found a model primary school where demoticist ideas could be tested, not to try to impose their ideas by law on all primary schools in the country without sufficient planning and preparation.[95]

The 1917 reform demonstrated that in order to see their arguments put into practice, progressive linguists and educationalists had to harness their ideas to the power of government. Through their co-membership of the Educational Association with members of parliament, and through their access to Venizelos himself, they assured that their policies would be implemented – even though this meant that these policies might be overturned once their favoured political leader was voted out of office. These lessons were learned especially by Triantafyllidis, as was shown in the 1930s, when he successfully lobbied two opposing governments to commission him to write his monumental grammar of demotic. Psycharis, on the other hand, living in Paris and without involvement in Greek power politics, soon proved incapable of ensuring that his version of demotic was accepted by the political and cultural establishment.

Scholarly arguments against demoticism: G. N. Hatzidakis

In 1908, during the Macedonian Struggle, Professor Georgios Mistriotis gave a speech in which he argued that 'our national language' (by which he meant *katharévousa*) was a rampart against the assaults of the enemies of the Greeks, because 'it rejects foreign words and linguistic forms', while 'the language of the vulgarists' is like clay and mud in its

---

[93] Sakellaropoulos 1921, quoted in Triantafyllidis 1938: 517–18.   [94] Kriaras 1987: 72.
[95] These criticisms were expressed by one of the Association's founder members, the naval officer, civil servant, and poet Markos Tsirimokos (1927).

readiness to accept alien features.[96] In the same year Mistriotis published a series of newspaper articles attacking his colleague Hatzidakis' plans for a historical dictionary of Modern Greek, which, he claimed, would be a 'Babel-like dictionary of barbarisms and vulgarisms' and would provide weapons to the 'traitors of the Greek race', by which he meant Psycharis and Pallis.[97] In 1910 Mistriotis opposed plans to found a chair of medieval and modern Greek literature at Athens University on the grounds that this subject was not worthy of being taught and studied.[98] The following year, during the debate in parliament on the drafting of the constitution, he argued that '[t]he language of the vulgarists is unusable in both poetry and prose. Since poetry seeks out beauty, the mutilations, the vulgarities and mire of barbaric words are incapable of producing a linguistic work of art, just as one cannot build a Parthenon out of filthy materials'.[99] The metaphors used by Mistriotis to refer to *katharévousa* have connotations of immobility and staticness, while the metaphors he uses in relation to demotic allude to the changeable nature of oral language. Mistriotis depicted the Greek nation as being timid, turned in on itself, beleaguered, conservative, and bound by tradition. By contrast, demoticists of the same period connected the demotic language with life, feeling, spontaneity, originality, and creativity.

The steadfast refusal of Mistriotis and others to acknowledge the existence of modern Greek culture as an autonomous entity is summed up in the following statement of his, dating from 1908:

Modern Greek grammar does not exist, because our language has been assimilated to the ancient.... When we create a new grammar we create a new nation.

A similar statement was made in the same year by Pavlos Karolidis:

A grammar of the Modern Greek language cannot exist. [The difference between the ancient and the modern] is so small that there is no need for two grammars.[100]

Mistriotis may have been on the lunatic fringe with regard to the language question, but he commanded considerable influence over his students, and he was at least consistent in his fanaticism. However, the most effective opponent of both Psycharis and the educational demoticists was Hatzidakis, professor of linguistics at Athens University and one of

[96] This was the adjudication speech given by Mistriotis as chairman of a committee awarding a prize for the 'improvement of the Greek language' (Mistriotis 1908). The text of the speech was co-signed by Hatzidakis.

[97] Glinos 1983: 549–50. For more details of the historical dictionary see below.

[98] Kriaras 2004: 353.   [99] Mistriotis 1911: 8.

[100] Both passages are quoted in Triantafyllidis 1926: 46–7 [= 1963c: 209].

most authoritative linguists of modern Greece, whose style was far less rhetorical, emotive, and rabble-rousing than that of Mistriotis. Like other purists, Hatzidakis rejected the claim that there was a common spoken language, arguing that spoken Greek was fragmented into dialects and therefore unsuitable for written communication.[101]

Before looking at Hatzidakis' campaign against demoticism, it is worth mentioning his initiative, mentioned briefly above, for compiling a dictionary that would cover the whole chronological span of the Greek language. Hatzidakis announced this initiative in a magazine article entitled 'An urgent national duty' in 1907. In this article he reminds the reader that spoken Modern Greek derives from the *koine*, in which the New Testament was written. The language of the New Testament, he continued, is not a 'special, divinely inspired language, separate from the rest of Greek, but part of it'. Thus, he argued, in order to understand the language of the New Testament one needs to study the older, contemporary, and later phases of the Greek language.[102] A royal decree was issued the following year, specifying that the dictionary would be published in 1921, the centenary of the outbreak of the War of Independence. As early as 1910, however, it was decided to confine the project to Modern Greek alone. According to the Byzantinist Faidon Koukoules, the reason why it was decided to begin with the modern period was that Ancient and Medieval Greek survived in texts, whereas the modern spoken language was in danger of being altered and lost under the pressure of social change.[103] In an address to the king, the committee appointed to compile the dictionary (with Kontos as chairman and Hatzidakis as vice-chairman) wrote that the aim of the dictionary was to demonstrate that Greek had been spoken constantly through the ages, that there had always been a Greek nation that spoke it, and that the changes that had taken place in the language did not constitute corruption and barbarization but 'a natural and necessary development' that conformed to laws that are essential to every living spoken language. It also aimed to show that the Greeks are a single nation from Agamemnon to George I and from the Caucasus to Italy, and that they worship one God and possess one fatherland and one language.[104] This is one of the clearest statements

---

[101] Hatzidakis 1905a: 792; Hatzidakis 1920: 32. For more details on Hatzidakis' career and linguistic views see Mackridge 2004.

[102] Hatzidakis 1907a.

[103] Koukoules 1933: 2. The title of each published volume begins: *Dictionary of the Greek Language. I. Historical Dictionary of Modern Greek*, implying that Part I will be followed by a part or parts covering earlier phases of the language, but plans for these have now been abandoned.

of the maximalist ambitions of Greek nationalism based on language. According to this view, even Greek-speaking Catholics living in southern Italy (and possibly even Greek-speaking Muslims in Greece and Turkey) would form part of the Greek nation, though Turkish-speaking Christians in Anatolia would not.

Hatzidakis had published a series of articles in 1890–95 attacking Psycharis' linguistic ideas, but the frequency and vehemence of his interventions in the language controversy increased after the Gospel riots of 1901. Although both he and Psycharis were influenced by the *Junggrammatiker*, their views were based on two contradictory approaches within the same movement. The linguists who particularly influenced Psycharis believed that language was a natural phenomenon and could therefore be studied scientifically in the same way as other natural phenomena. Karl Brugmann, for instance, argued that sound changes occur according to mechanical laws that allow of no exception.[105] By contrast, Hatzidakis was influenced by linguists such as W. D. Whitney, who argued that language is an institution, a historical product of man's action, and by Hermann Paul, who saw linguistics as a 'cultural science', that is, a social science, and consequently not subject to the exact laws of the natural sciences.[106] Hatzidakis, then, saw language as a cultural phenomenon, influenced, or even controlled, by social factors, including (in the case of Greek) a desire to adhere to older linguistic models.

His chief argument against demoticism, however, was a purely conservative one, similar to Kodrikas' argument against Korais' proposals a century previously: that written Modern Greek was a reality that must be accepted. He claimed that by his time, *katharévousa* had become the natural medium of written communication throughout the Greek-speaking world, whereas each demoticist wrote in a different language, each of which was characterized by anomalies. After all the efforts of learned Greeks to develop the written language over the centuries, he argued, it would be absurd, if not impossible, to abandon it and start all over again.

Hatzidakis tended to repeat the same arguments in a plethora of polemical books and articles. He presented his views most succinctly in writings intended for a foreign scholarly audience. He wrote one of these in 1902, shortly after the Gospel riots.[107] Here he asserted that the Greeks had

---

[104] Chronika 1908.   [105] Davies 1998: 231–2.   [106] Ibid., 191, 207, 249.

[107] This article (entitled 'On the language question in Greece') was originally written for publication in the *Revue des études grecques*, but it proved too long for that journal; it was first published in full in Hatzidakis 1905a: 774–843.

awoken from the torpor of slavery (i.e. in 1821) by fixing their gaze on their past, which orientated them as if it were the Pole Star.[108] He went on to argue that, because the Greeks were divided by their loyalty to two different ecclesiastical authorities (the patriarchate of Constantinople in the Ottoman empire and the Church of Greece in the Greek kingdom), it was only in their language that they could find their national unity. Therefore, they had to adhere as closely as possible to Ancient Greek in their written language, since ancient language and literature were their only source of enlightenment: unlike the works of Dante and Renaissance authors in Italy, there was no more recent body of Greek literature that could be used as a model. Besides, he argued, the Greek language was conservative by nature. Nevertheless, he continued, it was not true to say that modern written Greek employed the whole of Ancient Greek grammar: in fact it took many features from what he called 'la langue des salons'[109] – what in English might have been called 'the language of polite society'.

In the same year Karl Krumbacher, professor of Byzantine literature at the University of Munich, gave a lecture (published in book form immediately afterwards) in which he defended Psycharis' linguistic theory and practice. The German scholar supported the 'natural language', attacked the use of *katharévousa*, which he described as a *Mumiensprache* [language of mummies], and called for 'the unfortunate situation of *Doppelsprachigkeit* to be brought to an end.[110] He argued that ancient forms are no more 'pure' than modern forms and claimed that 'Italian, French, and Spanish are nothing other than the accumulation of a vast and constantly increasing mass of errors in Latin grammar and vocabulary, which would have made an ancient Roman grammarian tear his hair'.[111] Even more provocatively, Krumbacher grouped the Greeks together with other 'Oriental' peoples, such as the Arabs and the Turks, because of their adherence to an older form of their language rather than espousing the living language as the forward-looking peoples of Europe do.[112] From this last reference and other details in Krumbacher's lecture it is clear that he was drawing some of his arguments from Psycharis' writings.

In 1905 no fewer than three books by Hatzidakis appeared in the Maraslis Library series as part of a campaign to attack the written use of demotic and justify the continuing use of *katharévousa*. One of these

[108] Ibid., 819, repeated from Hatzidakis 1890 [= Hatzidakis 1901: 260].

[109] In Greek he used the terms 'γλώσσα των συναναστροφών' [the language of social gatherings] (Hatzidakis 1905a: 808; also Hatzidakis 1895 [=Hatzidakis 1901: 510–11]) and 'γλώσσα των αιθουσών' (Hatzidakis 1893 [=Hatzidakis 1901: 346]; Hatzidakis 1907d).

[110] Krumbacher 1902: 46; 47.　　　[111] Ibid., 63–4, 67.　　　[112] Krumbacher 1902: 95–7.

was the first volume of his monumental work *Medieval and Modern Greek*, consisting of reprints of various articles in which he presented his findings on the historical development of the spoken Greek dialects.[113] Another was a work that he wrote in German expressing his views on the language question for a foreign audience, *Die Sprachfrage in Griechenland*; this was subsequently published in French and Greek translations in 1907.[114] A third large volume appeared consisting of a Greek translation of Krumbacher's lecture followed by a lengthy series of ripostes by Hatzidakis.

In *Die Sprachfrage in Griechenland*, in particular, Hatzidakis claimed that the linguistic situation in Greece was utterly different from that in western Europe, since Greece had experienced no Dark Ages and therefore had no need for a Renaissance; Greek cultural continuity had never been broken, and the spoken and written languages had always existed side by side, each influencing the other.

In general, linguistic conservatives such as Hatzidakis viewed language as if it were an object to be admired and preserved: their attitude was based on a visual, spatial, attitude to a fixed, written language. It is indicative that Hatzidakis' arguments, like those of his admired Korais, tended to concentrate on individual words rather than on grammatical structures. Hatzidakis argued that if a writer used Ancient Greek words, the reader could ascertain their meanings by looking them up in a dictionary, whereas spoken words were semantically fluid.[115] For Hatzidakis, both the form and the meaning of a word were defined and dictated by its history: one could not understand a word fully unless one knew its etymology. Whereas the demoticists recognized the inevitable fluidity of language and believed that the forms and meanings of words were a matter of constant negotiation among speakers within the community, the purists saw linguistic forms and meanings as being fixed by some external authority, namely the authority of texts from the past.

Hatzidakis bewailed the fact that the 1911 Constitution did not specify that *katharévousa* should be compulsory in schools and that demotic should be excluded. He defended what had by now come to be known as *diglossía*, arguing that it had existed in all highly literate societies, from ancient Greece to modern Germany. Writing was an artificial activity, and it required an artificial language that must be constantly adjusted

---

[113] Hatzidakis 1905c, 1907c.

[114] German original Hatzidakis 1905b; French and Greek translation Hatzidakis 1907b, 1907d.

[115] Ibid., 87.

according to Ancient Greek rules, though it should also be written in a form that is readily comprehensible to the people. *Katharévousa*, he argued, was no more difficult to learn than any foreign language – an odd way to describe one's own national written language. In all this he seems to have been advocating simple *katharévousa*, while he himself continued to write in a more archaic variety till the 1920s.

Hatzidakis condemned the new school readers in demotic introduced into primary schools as a result of the 1917 reforms. He alleged that, instead of the 'common spoken language', whose existence he had earlier denied,[116] the reformers had used 'their own *idiótefkton* [concocted] demotic'.[117] He focused his attack on the third-year reader *The High Mountains* by the poet and prose writer Zacharias Papantoniou (1918), a charming and environmentally sound story of a group of schoolboys who spend their summer holiday in a camp in the mountains, where they organize their own lives and learn, through their experiences, to live as an organic community that functions in harmony with the natural environment; this is yet another example of the anti-urban orientation of demoticism. Hatzidakis branded this community a 'soviet'[118] – the Bolshevik revolution had taken place the previous year – and criticized the book for failing to mention the 'great ideals of fatherland and religion' and for not depicting the children even once writing to their families; this was the first of many allegations that demoticism was allied to Communism.[119] His arguments were highly influential in bringing about the withdrawal of the 1917 schoolbooks in 1921.

Although demotic retained a foothold in the lower years of primary school from 1923 onwards, the 1917 reforms were vitiated by the fact that they had been introduced by a government whose constitutional legitimacy was questioned by its opponents; demoticism could thus be easily identified with Venizelism, and even with Bolshevism. Opponents of demoticism could reasonably argue that the three educationalists of the Educational Association had been appointed to their powerful posts in the ministry by *coup d'état*; in the view of such conservatives, a small clique had used undemocratic means to impose their ideas by force. The involvement of the language question in the schism between Venizelists

---

[116] Hatzidakis 1905a: 792.   [117] Hatzidakis 1920; see A. Dimaras 1974: 127–8.

[118] Hatzidakis 1920: 51.

[119] In fact, Papantoniou's book contains references to the children attending church every Sunday, as well as an extensive description of their visit to a monastery, where they stay overnight and take part in the services.

and anti-Venizelists paved the way for its even more intense politicization from the late 1920s to 1974.

Demoticism: orthodoxy or compromise?

Following the linguistic polarization of the early 1890s, by the end of that decade most literary writers showed their preference for what Dimitris Gounelas calls 'a free mixture', which he defines as the combination of vernacular morphology with a 'learned way of thinking' and with vocabulary taken from both the learned and popular traditions, as well as newly coined compound words.[120] Poets, in particular, showed how this enriched variety of demotic could be used for complex and subtle expression.

Both before and after the Gospel riots, there was considerable controversy within the demoticist movement between those, led by Psycharis, who were determined to impose demotic orthodoxy on the Greek nation and those who recognized that it was impossible to eradicate the learned vocabulary and grammatical features that had already become entrenched in the spoken language. While Psycharis claimed to respect the style and content of the work of creative writers, he demanded, as an expert linguist, that they respect his system of orthography, phonology, and morphology, which, he claimed, had been devised on the basis of general linguistic rules.[121]

Despite the fact that he had earlier written that 'The *Taxidi* opened our eyes',[122] Giannis Kampysis, in an article entitled 'Psycharism and life' (1900), was one of many writers to protest at the stifling effect of Psycharis' linguistic orthodoxy on literary creativity.[123] Kampysis' criticism of Psycharis also reflected a rivalry between German-orientated and French-orientated Greek intellectuals. Kampysis had recently spent some months in Germany, where he had been deeply influenced by Nietzsche. At a time of the stereotypical antithesis between the 'robust Germans' and the 'effete French' before the First World War, Psycharis was a robust and decidedly anti-German Frenchman.

In the summer of 1901 there appeared a new literary magazine, *Dionysos*. The editors, Konstantinos Hatzopoulos' brother Mitsos (using the *nom de plume* Bohème) and Kampysis (until his death in November of that year), left contributors free to write in whatever version of Greek

---

[120] Gounelas 1984: 63–5.
[121] Psycharis to Pallis, 21 May 1900, in Karatzas 1985: 503 ff.
[122] Kampysis 1899: 160.   [123] Kampysis 1900.

they chose. In the first issue Bohème wrote, in *katharévousa*, that, as far as 'the poetic [i.e. creative] work of the demotic language' is concerned, Psycharis was not a revolutionary but one who falsifies and misleads, and he characterized Psycharis' ideas and attitudes as *daskalismós* [school-masterliness].[124] The following year Konstantinos Hatzopoulos, who was living in Germany at the time, claimed that 'Psycharism... is the highest expression of *daskalismós*, whose principle is to stifle every genuine and noble feeling and every free and brave impulse of the soul'.[125] These attacks must have been particularly wounding to Psycharis, who, though a teacher himself, tended to use the word *dáskalos* as a term of abuse, associating it with linguistic archaism.

Following Kampysis' lead, Xenopoulos wrote in a review of a book by Psycharis in 1903 that creative writers cannot subject themselves to Psycharis' 'chemically pure demotic grammar', a phrase that he attributed to Palamas; literary creativity, argued Xenopoulos, requires not only 'linguistic wisdom' but 'linguistic feeling'.[126] In response, Palamas, who during the first years of the twentieth century was a staunch supporter of Psycharis' linguistic theory, attacked the 'anarchic eclecticism' of Xenopoulos' attitude to the language, claiming that, though he himself had previously practised such eclecticism, he had now become enthusiastically convinced that his duty as a writer was to subject his creativity 'to the exclusively and chemically pure demotic grammar which the author of *My Journey* means to impose'. He adds, using a theological-sounding phrase, that such submission brings freedom.[127] He praised Psycharis' novels, characterizing one of them in 1899 as 'the novel of the Hellenic soul'[128] and describing the author in 1903 as 'the greatest writer of fiction that we have acquired so far'.[129] During this phase in his career, Palamas himself used a number of linguistic features typical of Psycharis' language, including even certain features of Constantinople dialect.

In an interview published in the newspaper *Estia* a few days after the foundation of the National Language Society in 1905, Karkavitsas explicitly distanced the Society from 'the curious Anglo-French idiom of Messrs Psycharis and Pallis'. The newspaper's editor presents Karkavitsas as a 'reasonable demoticist', unlike Psycharis and Pallis, whose

---

[124] Bohème 1901: 75.   [125] Vasilikos 1902: 249.   [126] Xenopoulos 1903: 243.
[127] Palamas 1975: 71, 273.
[128] This is the title of Palamas' review of Psycharis 1897; now in Palamas n.d.: VI 125.
[129] Palamas n.d.: XVI 220. This was in a review of Psycharis 1903 published shortly after Xenopoulos' review of the same book. Palamas repeated almost the same statement in 1909 (Palamas n.d.: VI 523). Thanks to Pantelis Voutouris for these references.

extreme ideas have 'rendered their struggle so unpopular, so unpleasant and so futile, and for a number of years have ... harmed – buried, I would dare to say – the very idea for which they are struggling'.[130] As was to be expected, Psycharis condemned the proclamation of the National Language Society.[131]

In the same year the naval doctor and moderate demoticist author Pavlos Nirvanas gave a lecture entitled 'Linguistic autobiography', in which he expressed the view that Art, rather than Science, would solve the language question: 'Art will create the perfect [linguistic] instrument, will raise it and ennoble it, because Art springs directly from life.'[132] Now, he claims, the Greeks have been liberated from the twin idols of *katharévousa* and demotic. He continues:

I have seen pages written under the terror of the linguistic law, frightened, frozen by religious awe, sterilized in a disinfecting oven. Their every word has been brought out of a microbiological laboratory, with the analysis label stuck to it.[133]

He forbears to specify which kind of linguistic orthodoxy he has in mind, since his words apply equally to the effects of both of the extreme linguistic dogmas. As for the purists' argument that, by using an archaized variant of Modern Greek, they are approaching the ancient language, Nirvanas comments that, just as our grandfathers live within us more truly than they do in their portraits, so Ancient Greek lives within us rather than in modern books.

The nationalist Ion Dragoumis, a member of a leading political family from Macedonia, felt uncomfortable with Psycharis' linguistic orthodoxy and preferred to write 'naturally'. He wrote to his friend Petros Vlastos that demotic 'will *xesklavosei* [liberate, literally 'de-enslave'] the brain of the *Romiós*',[134] whereas the revolution of 1821 had presumably only liberated their bodies. As a diplomat and politician, and unlike Psycharis and Eftaliotis, Dragoumis believed that to bring about the desired result, demoticism needed to resort to Machiavellian means, including under-hand tactics, compromises, and alliances with people who did not think or write exactly as they did.[135]

Vlastos (Calcutta 1879–Liverpool 1941) lived mainly in India and England. He married Pallis' daughter Aziza (thus both his mother and his wife's mother were Rallis) and succeeded his father-in-law as a

---

[130] Kyrou 1905. Thanks to Josep Maria Bernal for providing me with a copy of this text.
[131] Papakostas 1989: 17.   [132] Nirvanas 1988: 37.   [133] Nirvanas 1988: 39.
[134] Dragoumis to Vlastos, 14(27) Sept. 1909, in Karatzas 1985: 118–19.
[135] Dragoumis to Pallis, 22 March 1911, ibid., 126.

director of Ralli Brothers in Liverpool. In language he remained a faithful follower of Psycharis. In a revealing letter, written in 1908 after spending a fortnight in Athens, he tells Fotiadis that he has met various actual or would-be demoticists, but almost all of them have 'a strange antipathy towards us, the orthodox, the Psycharists, the *malliaroí*'. While demotic is gaining ground in people's minds, he continues, this seems to be happening without 'us'. He concludes that their mistake is to present demotic as an end rather than as a means: their tactic should not be linguistic but national.[136]

This view was shared by Pinelopi Delta (Alexandria 1874–Athens 1941), daughter of Emmanouil Benakis, a banker and close associate of Venizelos. Delta occupies an especially important place in the history of Greek identity formation because of her extremely popular children's books, which were influenced by those produced in Britain. Delta insisted that children needed not only school readers but entertaining books.[137] Four of her most popular novels are wholly or partly about Macedonia: *For the Fatherland* (1909), *In the Time of the Bulgar-Slayer* (1911), *Mangas* (1935), and *In the Secret Places of the Marsh* (1937). The first two of these are set in Byzantine times. All of these books contributed both to familiarizing generations of children with written demotic and to making them aware of the national importance of Byzantine history and of the Greek national claims on Macedonia. In this respect Delta's children's novels were far more effective than any overt propaganda campaign.

Like her friends Dragoumis and Triantafyllidis, Delta did not subscribe to Psycharis' linguistic orthodoxy. When criticized by Pallis, Eftaliotis, and Fotiadis for not toeing the line, she claimed that in her books she used the language actually spoken by children, which was not the standardized version devised by Psycharis.[138] This important point was lost on Psycharis and his supporters: because his language did not faithfully represent the language of children, it was unsuitable for school readers and children's literature. Delta attracted many more readers than Psycharis, and her literary success allowed her to more or less ignore the language question from 1911 onwards.

As was to be expected, Psycharis expressed his opposition to the Educational Association right from the start, objecting to the Association's use of the form σχολείο /sxolío/ [school] instead of what

---

[136] Vlastos to Fotiadis, 7(20) March 1908, in Papakostas 1989: 199.
[137] Delta to Fotiadis, 30 Nov. 1907, ibid., 184.   [138] Ibid., 279.

Psycharis insisted was the only 'correct' form, σκολειό /skoljó/.[139] (The Association's version, which uses the *katharévousa* form of the word minus the final /n/, is the standard form used today.) Psycharis' response shows that 'orthodox' demoticists could be as dogmatic and pedantic as the supporters of *katharévousa*. Pallis and Eftaliotis either attacked the Association or at least distanced themselves from it; like Psycharis, they were fearful of losing their control over the language and their cultural authority in general. Palamas at first expressed mild disapproval of the compromise language in which the Association had written its founding proclamation,[140] but he came to admire and support the work of its members during the period 1917–20,[141] when he defended the Association from the attacks of the 'schoolmasters', among whom he now included Psycharis.[142]

With his characteristic immodesty, Psycharis wrote in 1919 that 'Psycharis is to demoticism what Marx is to socialism', thus implicitly condemning the school language reform currently under way as bourgeois.[143] Lest there be any doubt in anyone's minds, Delmouzos wrote in the same year that in certain areas, particularly phonology, the conception according to which the linguistic reform in education was being undertaken was *metapsycharikí* [post-Psycharic],[144] thus effectively consigning Psycharis to history.

Thought and feeling

During this period there are signs that many moderate supporters of the linguistic *status quo* were trying to lay down clearer lines of demarcation between the functions of *katharévousa* and demotic. A characteristic instance of this is the report of the parliamentary committee investigating the language question in 1911, which refers to 'the development of modern *katharévousa* as the means for the expression of thought, but simultaneously the evolution and predominance of the *dimodis* [vernacular] in the expression of emotion'.[145] A similar, and highly suggestive, distinction was made by Hatzidakis between the learned written tradition as *patroparádotos* [handed down by the father] and the popular tradition

---

[139] Psycharis 1909.
[140] See Palamas n.d.: VIII 42–3, an open letter written in decidedly Psycharist language.
[141] Kriaras 1997: 45–6.
[142] Palamas in *Noumas*, 25 July 1910, reprinted in Palamas 1975: 188 (see also ibid., 315 n. 7).
[143] Stavridi-Patrikiou 1999: 130.   [144] Delmouzos 1917–19: 228.
[145] Ekthesis 1912: 78.

as *mitrodídaktos* [taught by the mother].[146] Here thought is being associated with the male, and feeling with the female.

Outside literature, the purists failed to develop a lively and interesting style, replete with vivid images and metaphors. This condemned non-literary *katharévousa* to remain little more than a utilitarian instrument for the expression of facts and ideas, with no creative dimension and no emotional colouring. That is why it was suitable for use as a bureaucratic language. Hatzidakis, for instance, writes in a style that appears to carry the weight of objective academic authority, whereas the discourse of demoticists such as Psycharis is full of both humour and metaphor, and it delights in expressing the authors' emotions. It is characteristic that the title chosen by Gianidis for the book in which he summed up his arguments in favour of demotic was *Language and Life* (1908). In the following emotional passage written by Delmouzos in 1911, we can almost hear the voice of Herder, the herald of romantic nationalism, who had died a hundred years earlier: 'the folk songs, legends, proverbs etc. reflect the pain, desire, hope, wit, grace – all the merits and faults, in other words the character, of the modern Greek soul.'[147]

In 1912 Gianidis wrote that '*katharévousa* isn't derived from Ancient Greek; it is artificially transformed demotic'. Gianidis goes on to argue that '*[k]atharévousa* was born through the method of replacement. Word by word. The original plan of the feeling is demotic, but the model is ancient grammar. The replacement goes forward just as long as the feeling doesn't revolt violently, that is, when the forms don't differ much'.[148] This had been precisely Korais' aim, as Solomos had pointed out. As we have seen, the views expressed here had already been voiced by literary writers when describing their experience of writing their early works in *katharévousa* before deciding to write in demotic.

The arguments of the educational demoticists take on a moral dimension when in 1914 Delmouzos describes his experience of teaching in demotic to his female high school pupils who had hitherto been educated entirely in *katharévousa*. *Katharévousa*, he writes, is a 'mask for the soul', while demotic is a mirror that leaves the child free to 'externalize its inner logos'.[149] Delmouzos contrasts the hypocrisy and deceit encouraged by *katharévousa* with the authenticity and sincerity encouraged by demotic. He relates how his pupils proceeded from a state of *ragiadismós* [enslavement: a term implying the mentality of subjection

---

[146] Hatzidakis 1920: 4, 10.   [147] Delmouzos 1911b: 275–6.
[148] Gianidis 1912: 25, 27.   [149] Delmouzos 1914: 266.

to the Turks during the Ottoman period] to 'spiritual/intellectual and moral *xesklávoma* [freedom from slavery]'.[150] Here Delmouzos recalls Solomos' prediction that liberation from the Turks would automatically bring about liberation from the pedants. For Delmouzos, the very moral fibre of the Greeks was at stake in the language controversy: demoticism aspired to mould a dynamic, lively nation made up of a new type of Greek, who acts freely, feels freely, thinks freely, and expresses himself freely as the worthy citizen of a free state. It is precisely such characteristics that seemed, to the demoticists, to connect the modern Greeks, in a natural and unbroken line of cultural descent, with the ancient Athenians. Given this outlook, it is not surprising that the educational demoticists tended to follow their senses and their feelings when steering a course between the linguistic science of both Hatzidakis and Psycharis.

Folklore and national geography

In 1907 Nikolaos Politis gave a public lecture 'On the national epic of the modern Greeks'. By this Politis meant the Byzantine heroic romance of *Digenis Akritis* and the so-called 'akritic cycle' of oral folk songs, still sung in modern times, that appeared to be thematically related to it. His claim that the Greek folk had composed and preserved a medieval epic lent powerful support to the demoticist cause by enhancing the prestige of the language and culture of the traditional rural population. Before the manuscripts of *Digenis Akritis* had been discovered from 1875 onwards, the only national Greek epics were the poems of Homer. Like Hatzidakis and unlike Mistriotis, Politis showed a sense that there was a specifically medieval and modern Hellenism. Like the *Kalevala* in Finland, the romance of *Digenis Akritis* was read by Politis and others as a historical document of a specific place and time, and the songs of the 'akritic cycle' seemed to demonstrate a living awareness of medieval Greek history and culture among the present-day Greek folk.

In the same lecture Politis used the Greek folk songs to provide support and inspiration for Greek irredentism:

From the farthest reaches of Cappadocia to the Ionian Islands, and from Macedonia and the lands of the western shores of the Black Sea, from which through barbarous violence the Bulgarians are attempting to uproot and annihilate Hellenism, to Crete and Cyprus, songs are still sung today relating the feats and adventures of Digenis and his struggles against the *apelatai* [bandits] and Saracens.

---

[150] Delmouzos 1913: 229. Compare the words of Dragoumis quoted above, p. 280.

At the time, all of the places mentioned by Politis except the Ionian Islands lay beyond the frontiers of the Greek state. This heavily ideological statement renders the Greek folk songs directly relevant to contemporary issues: 'the western shores of the Black Sea' refers to Eastern Rumelia, while the medieval *apelatai* are the equivalent of the *komitadjis* (Bulgarian guerrilla fighters in Macedonia) and the Saracens are the equivalent of the Turks.[151] Macedonia and Crete were incorporated into Greece as a result of the Balkan wars in 1912–13, but British rule in Cyprus since 1878 and the defeat of Greece by Turkey in 1922 ensured that the other 'unredeemed' regions that Politis referred to remained outside the Greek state borders.

In the preface to his monumental *Selections from the Songs of the Greek People* (1914), Politis explained that, like a Classical textual scholar, he had tried to establish for each song, out of the multifarious variants that had been recorded in writing, the archetype, in other words the putative original text of which the songs that were being performed in his time were variations. Just as Korais had used the terms and techniques of the textual scholar to 'correct' and 'establish' the Modern Greek language, so Politis used them to emend the folk songs.[152] This gave him ample leeway for standardizing their language, on the grounds that each song belonged to the whole of the Greek people, not only to those of the regions where it happened to have been recorded. However, there were some songs, only found in Greek dialects distant from the common core such as Cypriot, Pontic, Cappadocian, and southern Italian, whose language was not susceptible to standardization; these he relegated to an appendix entitled 'Songs in Greek dialects', implying that the rest of the songs were in a Panhellenic poetic language. Despite, or because of, these scholarly failings, Politis' book was to have a tremendous ideological impact, supplying the folk song texts that were incorporated into school readers and reminding Greeks that their brothers and sisters within and

---

[151] N. G. Politis 1906 [1907]: 11. Eastern Rumelia, a large proportion of whose urban population was Greek or Hellenized, was set up as an autonomous province within the Ottoman empire by the Congress of Berlin in 1878. In 1885, the province was annexed by the Principality of Bulgaria, which was still tributary to the Ottoman empire. In 1908 it was absorbed into the newly independent state of Bulgaria. In 1946, during the Greek Civil War, G. A. Megas published a booklet with the revealing title *Do the Bulgarians Possess a National Epic?* He used his conclusion – that they do not – to demonstrate the cultural inferiority of the Bulgarians (G. A. Megas 1946). It should be pointed out, however, that parts of Greek Macedonia and Thrace had recently been liberated from a particularly brutal Bulgarian occupation, which attempted to efface all traces of Greek culture in those regions.

[152] In his prologue he talks of carrying out '*emendatio (diórthosis)*' and '*recensio (apokatástasis)*': N. G. Politis 1914: p. vii.

beyond the borders of the state shared the same language and culture as themselves.

The defeat of national historical and geographical aspirations

As we have seen, with the National Schism of August 1916 to June 1917 the language question became inextricably linked to party politics: demotic came to be identified with Venizelist liberalism, *katharévousa* with monarchism and the Right. During the National Schism, in early December 1916, the Athens regime took repressive and violent measures against Venizelists. In retaliation, the return of Venizelos to power in 1917 was accompanied by extensive dismissals of judges, civil servants, military officers, and members of the security forces from their posts, and their replacement with people who were thought to be supporters of Venizelos. This kind of tit-for-tat bullying continued to take place during the 1920s and 1930s each time an anti-Venizelist government succeeded a Venizelist one, and vice versa.

On 12 August 1920 Venizelos was shot and wounded in Paris by two royalist officers who had been dismissed from the army, and in retaliation Ion Dragoumis was murdered in Athens the following day by members of the security forces. After the defeat of Venizelos in the November 1920 elections, King Constantine returned to Greece, and the monarchist government (newly renamed *Laïkón Komma* [Populist Party]) set about undoing as many of Venizelos' policies as possible, except – most significantly – the pursuit of the military campaign against Turkish nationalist forces in Asia Minor. It was inevitable that this fanatical rivalry would not only perpetuate the bad blood between the supporters of the two opposing Greek political factions but would also have an impact on the language question, each successive government altering educational language policy in order to be different from the previous one.

After the defeat of the Greek army by Turkish forces in Asia Minor in September 1922, the government resigned and was replaced by a Venizelist one. The king abdicated, and six of those held responsible for the military defeat (three former prime ministers, two other former ministers, and the commander-in-chief of the Greek forces) were executed. Greece was declared a republic on 25 March 1924. The Treaty of Lausanne between Greece and Turkey the previous year incorporated an agreement for the compulsory exchange of religious minorities between Greece and Turkey. This meant that, with some clearly circumscribed exceptions, all Orthodox Christians resident in Turkey were compulsorily removed to Greece, and all Muslims resident in Greece were removed to Turkey. In fact, a large proportion of those Orthodox Christian inhabitants of Asia Minor who had survived the hostilities between Greece and Turkey (which lasted, on and off, from 1912 to 1922) had already left Turkey, while the rest were removed during the period 1922–24. It is estimated that by the end of this protracted process 1.2 million Orthodox Christians had moved from Turkey to Greece, and 380,000 Muslims had moved from Greece to Turkey.[153] These devastating events radically altered the demographic situation of both countries. The Asia Minor Disaster and the exchange of populations changed Greece's national outlook for ever. With few significant pockets of ethnic Greeks living in neighbouring countries, Greece no longer had any serious irredentist aims or prospects: she had to be content with the national borders set by the Lausanne treaty. At the same time, the Lausanne exchange, together with a voluntary exchange of minorities between Greece and Bulgaria and the sporadic unofficial ethnic cleansing that took place between 1912 and 1924, ensured that Greece came to have one of the most ethnically homogeneous populations in the world. For instance, Greeks made up 44 per cent of the population of Greek Macedonia in 1913 according to the official Greek census, whereas in 1926 the Refugee Settlement Commission calculated that the population of the same region was 88.8 per cent Greek.[154]

The Greek landing in Smyrna in May 1919 and the Turkish military victory in September 1922 spelled the end of the Orthodox Christian communities in Asia Minor. Between them, Greek and Turkish nationalism had destroyed the multicultural co-existence of the various groups who had lived there for centuries. The logic of nationalism, perhaps even unbeknown to the actors themselves, made this inevitable, since nationalism is in the business of separating nations, and of emphasizing and exaggerating the differences between them.

---

[153] The figure of 1.2 Christians is from Hirschon 2003: 14–15, who gives a figure of about 350,000 Muslims. The figure of 380,000 Muslims is from Clogg (1992b: 101), who gives a figure of 1.1 million Christians. For more on the exchange of minorities between Greece and Turkey see Clark 2006.

[154] Pentzopoulos 1962: 28, 134.

9

The political polarization of the language question, 1922–1976

Historical background

A crucial factor that entered Greek public life during these years was the emergence of the Communist movement. The Socialist Workers' Party of Greece (SEKE), founded in 1918, changed its name to the Communist Party of Greece (KKE) in 1924. In the same year, under instructions from the Comintern in Moscow, the Party announced that its policy was to promote the creation of two new independent secessionist states in Macedonia and Thrace. For this reason, in addition to the already existing royalist/republican split, there came to be a fundamental division in Greece between communists and anti-communists. After 1922, in the absence of foreign enemies and 'unredeemed Greeks' in neighbouring countries, right-wing nationalist governments turned their attention to 'the enemy within'. The Communist Party returned ten members of parliament in the 1926 elections, eight of them elected from Macedonia and Thrace, where a large proportion of the refugees from Turkey had been settled. In 1936, a year after the monarchy had been restored, fifteen KKE members of parliament held the balance of power between the Venizelist and Monarchist blocs. This was the chief reason why King George II and Ioannis Metaxas decided to suspend parliamentary democracy and set up a dictatorship in August of that year – a suspension that eventually lasted for the next ten years.

All these developments helped to ensure that the already highly politicized language question remained a deeply contentious national issue. Demoticism had already been demonized by nationalists who connected it with the Slav threat and accused it of collaborating with Greece's enemies to divide and destroy the nation. Once the existence of a 'communist threat' had been established, the transition from Bulgarian nationalism to Russian-dominated communism as the greatest threat to the Greek nation was easily made. Claiming to be the sole guardians of national values, the supporters of *katharévousa* began to use it more overtly as an instrument of power and oppression.

The impact of politics on the language controversy, 1922–30

Venizelos' educational reforms, which had been overturned in 1921, were re-applied by the Venizelist government that took power immediately after the Asia Minor Disaster in 1922: demotic was reinstated in primary education, while the educationalists of 1917 returned to favour. In 1923 Triantafyllidis returned to his post at the Ministry of Education, while Delmouzos was appointed director of the newly founded *Marásleion Didaskaleion*, a primary teachers' training college in Athens; the fact that the college had a model primary school attached to it meant that the original aim of the Educational Association seemed to have been fulfilled. At the same time Glinos was appointed director of the *Paidagogikí Akadimía*, which opened in 1924 with the purpose of providing in-service further education for selected secondary teachers and of training staff for the *Marásleion* and educational administrators such as head teachers. In 1922 Glinos published, in book form, his most ethnocentric work, entitled *Nation and Language*. Here he argued that it is demotic, not *katharévousa*, that preserves and strengthens the cohesion and unity of the Greeks and keeps alive, by means of translation, the ancient Greek and ecclesiastical traditions.[1]

Now, with the king deposed and elected ministers executed, conservative anti-Venizelists could claim that demotic was once again being imposed in education by *coup d'état*. For such people, the fact that Ioannis Limperopoulos, the minister of education in Alexandros Papanastasiou's liberal republican government in 1924, was a member of the Educational Association[2] seemed to confirm suspicions that there was an unholy alliance between Venizelism and demoticism. In 1925 a 'National Conference for combating the enemies and corruptors of Religion, Language, Family, Property, Morals, and the National Consciousness of the Homeland', organized by a large coalition of professional and scholarly associations, called for the withdrawal and destruction of the school books in 'vulgar language' that had recently been reinstated and for the teaching of simple *katharévousa* to be reintroduced into the first two years of primary school.[3]

---

[1] Frangoudaki 1977b: 68. The text was written in 1915–16 and first published as Foteinos 1915–22.

[2] See A. Dimaras 1994: 215.   [3] See A. Dimaras 1974: 143–4.

During the dictatorship of General Theodoros Pangalos from June 1925 to August 1926, the authorities made a concerted effort to link demotic and the demoticist movement with communism, and there was much debate in the press in 1926 between supporters of demotic and supporters of *katharévousa*. The dictator himself pronounced that a large proportion of the *malliaroí* [extreme demoticists] were communists.[4] Demotic was removed from primary schools, and the demoticist student society, *Foititikí Syntrofiá*, was abolished by the university authorities. All members of the Educational Association were dismissed from the civil service. The *Paidagogikí Akadimía* was closed down indefinitely. An attempt was made to expose the *Marásleion Didaskaleíon* as part of a communist plot. Delmouzos was not only dismissed from the directorship of the *Marásleion* but he was subsequently investigated for having promoted 'anti-national teaching', 'the abolition of or disregard for religious instruction', and 'the cultivation of moral dissolution'.[5] The judicial investigation, however, whose findings were published after the fall of Pangalos, concluded that these allegations were unfounded.

The allegations that all demoticists were communists led non-communist demoticists such as Delmouzos and Triantafyllidis to attempt to depoliticize demoticism in their writings, chiefly the book *Demoticism and Education* by Delmouzos, and the pamphlet *Demoticism – a Letter to our Teachers* by Triantafyllidis, both of which were published in 1926. By this time Delmouzos had espoused a liberal form of nationalism, fostering a national education aimed at promoting a Greek national consciousness based on 'genuine' modern Greek culture, which excluded not only purism but also 'foreign imports' such as communism. At the same time, Triantafyllidis was producing a huge output of scholarly work on the linguistics of demotic.

Few new arguments were put forward during this period. Instead, the proponents of the different varieties of written Greek continued to consolidate their positions. Most of them, whether purists or demoticists, asserted equally that national unity ensured strength in the face of potentially hostile neighbours and ideologies, and that this unity should include cultural homogeneity. Demoticists claimed that the written use of demotic was a more efficient way of achieving this. In 1926 Delmouzos diagnosed what he called a *psychikós dichasmós* [psychological split] within people taught *katharévousa* (and in *katharévousa*) at school. This schism on the individual level, he argued, militated against national unity;

---

[4] Moschonas 1975: p. lix.   [5] A. Dimaras 1994: 146–7.

the term *dichasmós* was the one used to denote the National Schism of 1916–17.[6] Pangalos' allegation of communism implied that demoticism was threatening to divide the nation, whereas the demoticists countered that it was *katharévousa* that was socially – and therefore nationally – divisive.

Anastasios Megas' *History of the Language Question* (published in two volumes in 1925–27) was itself part of the debate at the time, arguing in favour of the continued use of *katharévousa* and justifying his argument by claiming that the purist language continued the noble national educational and cultural tradition initiated by Korais. On the communist side, Gianis Kordatos' *Demoticism and Pedantry: Sociological Study of the Language Question* (1927), perhaps written in response to Megas' book, was a history of the language question that also attempted to separate demoticism from communism, arguing that, although all communists should be demoticists, most demoticists were not communists. Regarding the actual use of language by communist writers, however, it is telling that in 1921 a Greek translation of Lenin's *The Role of Communist Youth* was published in Constantinople in simple *katharévousa*, together with a preface in demotic by the anonymous translator claiming that he wrote the translation in *katharévousa* so that all workers would be able to read it without being put off by unusual linguistic forms.[7] Kordatos, who from 1920 to 1924 served as general secretary of the Socialist Workers' Party of Greece (SEKE) and was a founding member of its successor, the Communist Party of Greece (KKE), until his expulsion in 1927, had also written a book in *katharévousa*, *The Social Significance of the Greek Revolution of 1821* (1924). In an epilogue (written in demotic) he excused the language of his book by claiming that, since he lacked the financial means to publish it himself, he had had to succumb to pressure from his publisher, who preferred *katharévousa*. But, he added, he too preferred to use *katharevousa*, since '[t]he student and scholarly world hasn't yet rid itself of its hollow linguistic tooth – *katharévousa* – and, because of linguistic prejudice, it often doesn't read a useful book written in the language of the people'. 'The *Idols* of Roïdis,' he concludes, 'achieved far greater linguistic propaganda than many articles by Psycharis.'[8]

The last official texts of the KKE to be written in *katharévousa* were published in 1927 in *Rizospastis* [*The Radical*], which had become the

[6] Delmouzos 1926: 47.   [7] Lenin 1921, quoted in Moschonas 1975: pp. lxxv–lxxvi.
[8] Kordatos 1924: 170. He is alluding to the fact that Roïdis wrote his book in *katharévousa*.

official newspaper of the SEKE in 1920 and then the official organ of the KKE.[9] The official texts of these parties during the first ten years of their existence (1918–28) had made little reference to the language controversy,[10] and at this time the broad masses of the people seem to have remained largely indifferent to the debate, which was mostly carried out within the 'bourgeois world'. Outside the official Party texts, the change from demotic and *katharévousa* in the columns of *Rizospastis* was gradual: some articles appeared in demotic right from the early issues, but most of the material at that time was in *katharévousa*. Editorials gradually changed from *katharévousa* to mixed language and then to demotic, but it was not until 1932 that the whole newspaper was definitively written in demotic. The variety of demotic used by the paper in those years was closer to that of the educational demoticists than that of Psycharis. Be that as it may, the change of language in the Party newspaper and its other official documents was taken by the enemies of demotic as confirmation that demoticism was a communist plot. Meanwhile other newspapers continued to be written in simple *katharévousa*.

By 1926 Glinos had espoused Marxism, chiefly perhaps out of disillusionment with the republic's reforms. The following year he split the Educational Association – now numbering about three hundred members – by insisting that it espouse the Marxist principle of class struggle as opposed to the preservation and homogeneity of the nation. Delmouzos and about fifty of its other members (mostly nationalists) resigned, since to abandon the principle of the 'homogeneity of the state' would have meant acceding to the KKE's demand for the secession of Macedonia and Thrace. The Association eventually collapsed in disarray in 1929 when its communist members refused to work with the socialists.

In 1926, Glinos had founded a magazine, *Anagennisi* [*Renaissance*], which hosted a lively debate on spelling reform, focusing on the possibility of replacing the old polytonic system, which used multiple diacritics, with the simpler monotonic (single-accent) system.[11] At the same time, in the Soviet Union from 1926 to 1937, books and newspapers were being printed for the ethnic Greek populations of the southern USSR. The language variety of these publications varied (demotic, Pontic, and Mariupol dialect), but they were all printed in a specially devised phonetic system using the monotonic system and twenty of the twenty-four letters of the Greek alphabet. This development, which was aimed partly at

---

[9] Moschonas 1975: p. lxxviii.   [10] Ibid., p. lxxiv.

[11] For more on the inter-war debates on spelling reform, including proposals to replace the Greek alphabet with the Latin script, see Bernal 2007b.

culturally separating the Greek populations of the USSR from the Greeks of Greece, ensured that in Greece any proposal for orthographic reform tended to be met with the suspicion of communist connections.

The practical progress of the demoticist movement in the inter-war period

Meanwhile considerable practical progress was being made within a very short time by leading proponents of demoticism. The University of Salonica – Greece's second university after Athens[12] – was founded in 1925, and demotic became the usual language of instruction in the Arts Faculty. Triantafyllidis was appointed professor of linguistics there in 1926 (though he resigned in 1934 to devote himself to research and writing), while Delmouzos served as professor of education from 1928 until his resignation during the Metaxas dictatorship in 1937. In 1926 Kostis Palamas, who in his prime had been the leading exponent and proponent of demotic in literature, was elected a member of the newly established Academy of Athens, and even became its president in 1930. In 1928 he wrote (in demotic) that his verse was 'poetry itself mathematically measured according to the demoticist ideal' but that, with regard to prose, he had always 'nurtured an illicit secret care and sympathy for *katharévousa*':

Little by little, as my mind matured and life around me pressed on me, together with the tyranny of *katharévousa* that I sensed day by day to be falling away in the domain of its subjects, who were now free to use colloquial features within *katharévousa* without being stigmatized as illiterate or anathematized as irreligious, I saw the tyranny of Psycharism similarly breaking down within my consciousness. The thought grew stronger within me that demoticism was not an exclusive logical construct absolutely subjected to the rule of linguistic science.... There is an urban [or bourgeois] demoticism, which isn't always compatible, within the complex gait of sensible and convincing prose, with the voice of the agriculturalist and the highlander, much as this may be distilled and sanctioned by ecstatic and charming verses.

[12] The second university to be established on territory administered by the Greek state was in fact set up in Smyrna during the Greek occupation in 1919–22, but the expulsion of the Greek authorities and the Greek population from the city in September 1922 took place a few days before it was due to be inaugurated. The University of Salonica, founded in the city where the largest concentration of refugees from Turkey was settled, was conceived partly as a substitute for the ill-fated Ionian University of Smyrna. For more details see Solomonidis 1997.

'There are *katharévousa* usages alive within our blood and demoticist usages that are repellent and insufferable', he concludes.[13] As a sophisticated and sensitive creative writer, Palamas felt the need for a range of stylistic registers in demotic that Psycharis' rigid linguistic outlook tended to preclude. However, his use of the word 'illicit' in the above passage indicates how Psycharis' orthodoxy could make even such a well-established literary figure as Palamas feel guilty when he was being unfaithful to the master's precepts.

In 1927 Grigorios Xenopoulos founded what went on to become Greece's longest-running literary magazine, *Nea Estia*, which has continued to be published, without interruption, to this day. Although successive editors were tolerant towards the linguistic varieties used by the magazine's authors, the vast majority of contributions were in demotic from the outset. The magazine's social respectability among the middle class helped to enhance the prestige of written demotic. However, when Xenopoulos was elected a member of the Academy of Athens in 1932, he delivered his inaugural address in *katharévousa*.

Venizelos' long premiership (1928–32) was a rare period of comparative calm amid the turbulent inter-war years. Beginning from Konstantinos Gontikas' and Georgios Papandreou's terms of office as minister of education from 1929 onwards, demotic was used in all six years of primary school, and was even taught and used alongside *katharévousa* in the first two years of the *gymnásion* [high school], while Ancient Greek texts were taught in demotic translation.[14] In 1931 Papandreou commissioned Triantafyllidis to write a grammar of demotic for the use of teachers, writers and publishers,[15] though the plan fell through with the change of government in the following year. Nevertheless, even the government of the monarchist Populist Party, which came to power in 1933 under the leadership of Panagis Tsaldaris, retained demotic in primary schools, though from 1935 onwards it was confined to the first three years, while the variety of demotic used in schoolbooks was slightly altered – or adulterated, according to the demoticists – through the replacement of certain spoken morphological forms by the equivalent *katharévousa* forms. Also, in a purge after a Venizelist coup attempt in 1935, a number of university professors, including (temporarily) Delmouzos, were dismissed from their posts on the grounds that they were demoticists.

---

[13] Palamas 1928 [= Palamas n.d.: X 11–13].

[14] Stavridi-Patrikiou 1999: 133.

[15] Thanks to Stesi Athini for providing me with a photocopy of Papandreou's letter to Triantafyllidis, dated 6 June 1931.

Psycharis' death in 1929 removed the leader of the extremist demotic camp from the scene and helped a conciliatory and tolerant version of demotic to become more widely accepted. This was the variety used by leading members of the literary Generation of 1930, including the poet Giorgos Seferis (1900–71) and the novelist and essayist Giorgos Theotokas (1905–66). In 1929 Theotokas published a book entitled *Free Spirit*, which has been described as the manifesto of the Generation of 1930.[16] In this book Theotokas promoted a new kind of Greek literature as a force for renewal and as the most effective way of developing and expressing a Greekness that would be less ethnocentric and more European than the variety of national identity promoted in Psycharis' *My Journey*.[17] The work of several other authors of the Generation of 1930 explored and expressed a new Greek national identity after the end of the *Megali Idea*. The poets Seferis and Odysseas Elytis (1911–96), in particular, focused on the Greek landscape, including its ancient ruins and its reminiscences of Odyssean quests, as the other great cohesive factor contributing to Greek cultural continuity along with language. The same poets rediscovered the Aegean and the Greek islands, which had been marginalized since they were first exploited in the poetry of Kalvos more than a century previously, as sites and symbols for poetic expression.

As far as language is concerned, the new fiction of the 1930s presented two varieties, one exploiting the expressive capabilities of the rural demotic to the full, as in the work of Stratis Myrivilis (1892–1969), the other attempting to employ a standardized urban language, as in the work of Theotokas and Angelos Terzakis (1907–79). In poetry, however, the fertile linguistic pluralism of the time can be illustrated by four collections published in 1935. At one linguistic extreme stand Seferis' poem sequence *Mythistorima* and the first set of published poems by Elytis, which employ many images referring to traditional rural and seafaring life and a standardized demotic grammar, but whose sensibility is suffused with intertextual references to a wide range of readings in Ancient Greek and modern European literature. At the other extreme is the collection of prose poems by the surrealist Andreas Empeirikos (1901–75), who claimed to have written them according to the method of

---

[16] Psycharis died in Paris on 29 September 1929. The manuscript of *Free Spirit*, which Theotokas wrote in Paris, is dated July 1929 (Dimaras in Theotokas 1979: x), and it was published in Athens in November (Moschonas 2004: 3). While it is impossible to say whether the genesis of Theotokas' book was related to Psycharis' death, it could well have been read as a manifesto for Greece's post-Psycharist future.

[17] Tziovas 1986: 12.

'automatic writing'; their morphology displays a significant proportion of *katharévousa* forms, while the vocabulary includes a large number of technical terms, with the result that some of these texts read like parodies of journalistic or scientific reports. Effie Rentzou interprets the Greek surrealists' use of *katharévousa* as 'une réaction à l'ordre établi par le démoticisme uniformisant'.[18] In between these two extremes stands the first complete edition of the hundred and fifty-four poems of C. P. Cavafy (Alexandria 1863–1933), which employ a variety of urban spoken vernacular as a basis on which to weave a complex tapestry that includes an admixture of vocabulary and forms from various historical stages of Greek.[19]

The influence of the young literary writers of the 1930s on the stabilization and dissemination of the demotic written standard, through their elaboration of a markedly non-Psycharist variety of demotic in poetry and fiction of the highest quality, was enormous. In 1937 a number of young writers decided to draw up a scheme for the morphological standardization of literary demotic, and they invited Triantafyllidis to advise them. However, this effort was halted when the Ministry of Education set up its own committee, headed by Triantafyllidis, to draft a grammar of Modern Greek in 1938.[20]

During this period a number of impressive scholarly works on the Modern Greek language were published, significantly raising the level of public awareness concerning the Greek language in general and increasing the acceptability of demotic. In 1928 Achillefs Tzartzanos (1873–1946) published the first ever syntax book of 'demotic and commonly spoken' Greek, albeit written in *katharévousa*. This was based on spoken varieties of the language, on the folk songs, and on literary texts. In 1930 Tzartzanos published a *Grammar of the Modern Greek Language (Simple Katharévousa)*. In his prologue to this volume, which he wrote on his own initiative and published without official backing, he was careful to point out that he was not arguing in support of the continuing use of *katharévousa*, but that, since it was the official language, all Greeks should be able to understand it and write it properly without having to learn Ancient Greek. Tzartanos insists that *katharévousa* is a variety

---

[18] Rentzou 2002: 114.

[19] Seferis 1935; Elytis 1935; Empeirikos 1935; Cavafy 1935. Jacques Bouchard has written that Empeirikos' *katharévousa* acts like an incantation and – using a phrase that gives the lie to the allegedly artificial character of *katharévousa* – that it draws on 'the aquifers of the Greek subconscious' (Bouchard 1995: 179).

[20] For the texts of the magazine articles in which this scheme was mooted see Seferis 1987: 135–58.

of Modern Greek and criticizes those who confuse it with the ancient language.[21]

Tzartzanos was a member of a middle-class circle in Athens (including intellectuals and politicians) who claimed that the language question had moved on not only since Psycharis but also since the 1917 education reforms, and that a 'neo-demotic' language had developed among the urban educated classes, which had incorporated more grammatical features of *katharévousa* than were catered for by leading members of the Educational Association such as Triantafyllidis.[22] In 1931 members of this circle published a book entitled *Grammar: Forms and Rules of Common Spoken Modern Greek, Written by Athenians* and with a prologue by Maria Argyropoulou, wife of a minister in the Venizelos government.[23] Those who produced this book were clearly uncomfortable that demotic had tended thus far to be identified with traditional rural culture; instead of this, they felt, it should become the standard-bearer of modern bourgeois liberal attitudes. For his part, Triantafyllidis criticized such 'Athenians' for being foreign-educated and out of touch with 'national life', by which he meant traditional rural language and culture.[24]

In 1931 Petros Vlastos, a leading member of the cosmopolitan diaspora Greek bourgeoisie who remained a demoticist of the Psycharist tendency, published a comprehensive dictionary of vocabulary related to arts and crafts (*Synonyms and Cognates*). This was the first dictionary of concepts – with entries laid out according to their semantic connections rather than in alphabetical order – that had ever been produced for Modern Greek. In his prologue, Vlastos takes a conservationist attitude – almost unique in Greece at this time – when he likens Greeks' contempt for and destruction of their mother tongue to their destruction of forests and birds, ancient columns and statues. His Psycharist convictions are apparent in his statement that languages are saved by a combination of art (literature) and science (linguistics).[25] In all of these activities we observe a split, within the progressive Greek bourgeoisie, between those who felt that, because the majority of the Greek population was rural, the most effective

---

[21] Tzartzanos 1930: 5–9.

[22] For details of Tzartzanos' credo and the membership of his linguistic circle see Tzartzanos 1935. The terms 'neo-demotic' and 'neo-*katharévousa*' had already been used in 1901 by Bohème [Mitsos Hatzopoulos] to refer to the new phases of the two variants of Modern Greek which, he claimed, would merge in the future (Voutouris 2006a: 256). 'Neo-demotic' was also used by Tsirimokos in a lecture given in December 1910 to refer to what he called 'the unaffected spoken language of today's capital of Hellenism' (Ramas 1911: 77), the 'capital of Hellenism' being Athens rather than Psycharis' Constantinople.

[23] *Grammatiki* 1931.   [24] Triantafyllidis 1965a: 292.   [25] Vlastos 1931: 3.

mode of action was to appropriate rural tradition, and those (including Palamas, as we saw above) who saw urban bourgeois culture as having rendered rural culture obsolete.

In the year of Psycharis' death (1929) there appeared the first volume of his *Great Romaic Scientific Grammar*; the other two volumes were published in 1935 and 1937. The first two volumes were intended for teachers, while the third was for pupils. The muddled structure of Psycharis' grammar bears witness to the fact that it was written during his declining years, and it was left incomplete at his death. The three volumes extend no further than phonology, and the highly detailed and pedantic analysis of the history of the Modern Greek sound system, coupled with the highly personal rants that punctuate the scholarly exposition, render the grammar virtually unusable. It is regrettable that this important linguist, in his old age and in the face of major health problems, had completely lost sight of his readership.

Now that Psycharis was gone, demoticists became keener to dissociate themselves publicly from his extreme variety of demotic. In 1932 the young linguist Nikolaos P. Andriotis (1906–76) published an article entitled 'The demotic language in science/scholarship' in *Nea Estia*. Contrary to Psycharis' teaching, Andriotis wrote:

Unfortunately the idea that it would be possible for the demotic language, as it has been handed down to us through oral tradition, to enrich itself from its own resources and to develop into a modernized language of a civilized people, at the same time preserving all its virginal demotic chastity, has proved to be romantic and impracticable.

Even if the Greeks had started writing demotic in the time of Korais, he continued, they would have borrowed from Ancient Greek and French just as *katharévousa* did. As it is, what he called the 'deplorable parenthesis' of *katharévousa* would perhaps find some historical vindication in 'the language-forming task that demoticism is now going to carry out with very little effort': by adapting ancient words to modern grammar, the Greeks will do the equivalent of what the French, Italians, and Romanians have done in adapting Latin words to the morphology of their own languages.[26] Andriotis gives the impression here that, after the end of Psycharism, he is conscious of being part of a new beginning in the Greek language-building process.

The year 1933 saw the publication of the first volume of two hugely ambitious dictionaries, the aims of one of them being purely scholarly

---

[26] Andriotis 1976: 316–17.

and those of the other at least partly commercial. As I have already mentioned, the *Historical Dictionary of the Modern Greek Language* was the brainchild of Hatzidakis. In 1926–27 the dictionary project had been placed under the aegis of the Academy of Athens. Its then editor, the Reverend Anthimos Papadopoulos, wrote in his prologue to the first volume that, like all civilized nations, the Greek nation must acquire 'the dictionary of its spoken language; . . . a nation's dictionary, in which the words spoken by it are treasured up, is a rich archive of its descent and history and a splendid mirror in which its civilization is brightly depicted'. The dictionary's aim was to demonstrate the immortality of the Greek race and the unbroken unity of the Greek nation as a monument to the immortality of the richest language in the world. The Greeks, continued Papadopoulos, have a duty to the civilized world to help it to understand the written monuments of 'our old [i.e. ancient and medieval] language'. Only those who know vernacular Greek can understand the medieval and ancient writers, he concluded.[27] In this way, Papadopoulos claimed that, because their spoken language was directly and naturally descended from Ancient Greek, the modern Greeks had privileged access to aspects of the ancient language that remained a closed book to foreigners.

At the time of writing (one hundred years after Hatzidakis first made his proposal), the publication of the *Historical Dictionary* is only about one-quarter complete.[28] The *Historical Dictionary* – unlike the dictionary of the Académie Française, for instance – is based on uncompromisingly descriptive (as opposed to prescriptive) principles. However, while its full title specifies that it is a dictionary of 'the common language and the dialects', it has proved to be almost exclusively a dictionary of the dialects, whose vocabulary (including all its recorded variant forms and meanings) is covered in such minute detail that it is only consulted by specialists.

The perceived failings of the *Historical Dictionary* were intended to be remedied by a largely commercial venture undertaken by the publisher Ioannis Dimitrakos. This was the *Great Dictionary of the Greek Language*, published in nine volumes from 1933 to 1951. This dictionary, compiled by a group of linguists and literary figures on the basis of

---

[27] Papadopoulos 1933: pp. vii–xiv.

[28] The first volume was published at the expense of Emmanouil Benakis. Vol. 3 appeared in 1941 and vol. 4 in 1953, but the first fascicle of vol. 5 was published as late as 1984. The most recent volume to be published is vol. 5, fasc. 2 (1989), which goes up to *dachtylotós*. All material in each volume, apart from the vocabulary items being discussed, is in *katharévousa*.

existing dictionaries, aimed to include the whole of the recorded Greek vocabulary from Homer to the present day. In his prologue, G. P. Anagnostopoulos, Hatzidakis' successor as professor of linguistics at Athens University, quoted the older linguist as claiming that, while the grammar of Greek had changed since Homer's time, the vocabulary of the whole language was a single unity.[29] Laying out the vocabulary in strictly alphabetical order, this dictionary attempted to render the diachronic synchronic by analysing, in a single corpus, the meanings and uses of vocabulary from widely different periods of Greek linguistic history. From a strictly linguistic point of view, the Dimitrakos dictionary was quite unscholarly, and indeed totally misguided, attempting, as Kriaras has written, to create 'a totality out of clearly incompatible elements'.[30] Nevertheless, the dictionary indicated in many of the entries, perhaps for the first time in a dictionary of Greek, whether the word belonged to ancient, later, modern (i.e. *katharévousa*), or demotic Greek. It also appealed to a wide Greek educated readership, not only flattering their national pride by suggesting that Ancient and Modern Greek constituted a single language but also making them realize the radical changes of meaning that had taken place over the centuries in familiar words that were superficially conceived of as being identical in the ancient and the modern languages.

In the same year a *Dictionary of the Greek Language* was published by the Athens daily newspaper *Proia*; this could be said to be the first ever monolingual dictionary of Modern Greek. It was compiled by an impressive group of linguists and literary scholars, and the fact that the title of this dictionary did not include the indication 'Modern' was a sign that some Greeks, at least, were sufficiently confident in their national identity to accept that the word 'Greek' alone could legitimately be applied to their own modern language. In his prologue to the dictionary, the same G. P. Anagnostopoulos implied that there were currently three varieties of Modern Greek, namely 'spoken', 'written vernacular', and *katharévousa*, and that, while the Academy's dictionary was concerned with the first, the *Proia* dictionary covered the second and third, that is, the two varieties of the written language.[31] The dictionary included vocabulary belonging to both demotic and *katharévousa*, although the fact that 'vernacular and regional' words were marked by an asterisk

---

[29] Anagnostopoulos in *Mega* 1933–51: I v. For some reason this prologue was omitted from a second and slightly revised edition of the first volume of this dictionary, published in 1936 without any indication that it was a second edition.

[30] Kriaras 2004: 110.   [31] Anagnostopoulos in Zevgolis 1933: 5–7.

while *katharévousa* words were not marked at all showed that the editors thought of *katharévousa* as being the basic variety.

In October 1936 the minister of education in the dictatorial regime of Ioannis Metaxas, Konstantinos Georgakopoulos, sent a circular to all schools describing the demoticists as 'anti-nationals who serve foreign interests' and condemning the education reform as 'an unholy effort' and 'a means for preparing the imposition of communism'.[32] Delmouzos, who had been reinstated to his university post in January of the same year, resigned under political pressure in September.[33]

The attitude of the dictator himself towards the language question was unexpected, yet it showed an acuteness of judgement and vision that other Greek dictators have lacked. Only a month after he had become dictator, Metaxas claimed in an interview to a newspaper that demoticism was a purely national movement and had no connection with communism. Later, following the resignation of Georgakopoulos, Metaxas appointed himself minister of education (1938–41), and, although he used *katharévousa* publicly himself and never considered making demotic into the official language of the Greek state, he almost immediately set up a committee, chaired by Triantafyllidis, to draw up a *Modern Greek Grammar (of Demotic)*, which was published in June 1941. Metaxas even drafted a prologue (eventually omitted because of his death in January 1941), in which he claimed that grammatical rules would bring about the 'linguistic discipline' of the Greeks and curb their 'over-developed individualism'.[34]

Often known as the 'state grammar' or 'official grammar' because it was commissioned by the government, the Triantafyllidis grammar has not yet been superseded as the most authoritative account of Modern Greek morphology. (In common with previous Greek grammars, it does not cover syntax.) This standard grammar of demotic does not claim to describe a spoken variety of Greek but a standardized literary variety: Triantafyllidis makes it clear in his introduction that the language described (and in practice prescribed) in his grammar is that of the folk songs and of literature. This implies that the first steps in moulding a standardized Greek literary language had been taken in the folk songs, and that the task of continuing to develop this standard language has since been undertaken by literary writers. Triantafyllidis' statement and its implications have led critics to denounce his grammar as insufficiently

---

[32] Kriaras 2004: 122.   [33] Papanoutsos 1978: 112–17.
[34] Quoted in Triantafyllidis 1963d: 61–2.

tolerant of the learned features that have entered the language spoken by educated Greeks. As Horrocks writes, it 'preserved an already rustic-seeming "purity" that was fast becoming a thing of the past in the speech of ordinary urban Greeks'.[35]

Triantafyllidis' achievement in having his grammar officially commissioned by Metaxas as minister of education continued the educational demoticists' successful strategy of courting government leaders in order to further their cause. Their first great success had been with Venizelos in 1917, while their second began when Venizelos' minister of education Papandreou commissioned the grammar from Triantafyllidis in 1931 and was completed under Metaxas in 1938–41. Triantafyllidis' grammar was published by the state-run Organization for the Publication of Teaching Books (OEDV) and was produced in a large print-run of cheap copies. However, the fact that it appeared two months after the beginning of the German occupation meant that its full impact was not widely felt at the time.

Triantafyllidis had previously published his other major work, *Modern Greek Grammar: Historical Introduction* (1938), which covers the history of Greek, including the Greek language question, since ancient times and contains many passages quoted from earlier texts, some of them as samples of different varieties of the language and others as samples of the arguments used by participants in the language controversy. This compilation of texts is still useful today. The *Historical Introduction* can be seen as Triantafyllidis' response to Hatzidakis' *Concise History of the Greek Language* (1915): Hatzidakis' book was a history of the Modern Greek dialects, whereas Triantafyllidis was attempting to write the history of the common spoken language.[36]

Greeks and others revisited: minority languages

As a result of the territorial expansion of the Greek state brought about by the Balkan wars of 1912–13, Greek citizens included a sizeable number of people who spoke languages other than Greek as their mother tongue. The chief of these languages were Slavonic, Albanian, Aromanian, Turkish, and Judaeo-Spanish (Ladino) – the last being spoken by the Jews of Salonica.

Systematic efforts were made by the Greek authorities to assimilate the Christian populations. As Dimitris Livanios has written, '[a]fter 1913

---

[35] Horrocks 1997: 360.   [36] Cf. Kriaras 1987: 187.

the Greek nation had to speak only the "national" language, and in the interwar years neither Greece nor any other Balkan state tolerated "minority" languages that were considered a threat to the nation'.[37] Eyal Ginio argues that in the immediate wake of the Balkan wars the Greek authorities displayed tolerance to minorities in the newly-acquired territories in order to impress the western powers and thus further their ambitions in Asia Minor, but that after 1922 the Greek state embarked on a policy of cultural homogeneity.[38] As I have already said in Chapter 2, it is not my intention to cover linguistic minorities in detail. Here I shall say a few words about the two Christian linguistic groups that were ideologically the most contentious because they spoke languages that were associated with the enemies of Greece, namely Slavonic and Turkish. The members of one of these groups, the Slavophones of Macedonia, were speaking their language when the Greek state incorporated them in 1912–13. The other, the *Karamanlides*, brought their Turkish language with them when they were expelled from Asia Minor to Greece after 1922.

Until the 1930s it seems to have been acceptable for Greeks to talk about the Slav language spoken in Macedonia as 'Macedonian' and about its speakers as 'Macedonians'. I will cite three literary testimonies here. In his book about the struggle for Macedonia, *Martyrs' and Heroes' Blood* the nationalist writer Ion Dragoumis argues that 'Macedonian' is the correct term for this language, which the Bulgarians, he says, misleadingly call 'Bulgarian'.[39] In the first edition of *Life in the Tomb* (1924), a novel based on his experiences of trench warfare against the Bulgarians in the First World War, Stratis Myrivilis includes a scene in which the narrator is recuperating at the house of a Slav-speaking family who live north of the Greek border. After saying something about their language, he tells the reader that 'they don't want to be either *Bulgar*, or *Srrp*, or *Grrts*. Only *Makedon ortodox*'. In later editions, Myrivilis excised the last sentence because he no longer felt it to be politically advisable to include it.[40] In her patriotic children's novel about the Macedonian struggle, *In the Secret Places of the Marsh*, which was first published under the Metaxas regime in 1937, Pinelopi Delta refers to the local Slavonic language as 'Macedonian dialect', though in another passage she refers to it inaccurately as 'Macedonian, a mixture... of Slavonic

---

[37] Livanios 2006: 67.   [38] Ginio 2002: 239.   [39] Dragoumis 1914: 98.
[40] Myrivilis 1924: 147 [= 1991: 104–5]. The subsequently excised sentence is still present in Myrivilis 1930 [= 1993: 305; Chapter 34], and Myrivilis 1931: 196. The novel was banned from 1936 until the end of the Second World War; subsequent editions do not include this sentence.

and Greek'.[41] Since then, however, it has become politically incorrect in Greece to talk about the Slav speakers as 'Macedonians' (except in so far as they are inhabitants of the Greek province of Macedonia) and their language as 'Macedonian'.

From the 1920s onwards the Greek authorities operated a policy of linguistic assimilation on the Slav speakers, on the grounds that an individual's language was inextricably bound up with their national consciousness. Among other measures, night schools were provided for adults. Greek officials were, however, divided on the question whether it was more efficacious to teach them *katharévousa* or demotic. There was a significant amount of resistance from members of the Slav-speaking population who saw their language as a central feature of their group identity.[42]

The Metaxas regime was more repressive than previous governments in this respect: it issued directives prohibiting the public use of languages other than Greek and specifying relevant penalties. In practice, this applied chiefly to the use of Slavonic languages in Greek Macedonia. One directive stated that 'all municipal and township councils would forbid...the speaking of other idioms of obsolete languages within the area of their jurisdiction for the reconstruction of a universal language and our national glory'. In some places, imprisonment and corporal punishment were employed to achieve what Anastasia Karakasidou has called 'the construction of Greek linguistic hegemony'. Whereas descendants of immigrants from western Europe have been permitted to preserve their foreign names, Slav speakers living in the Greek state were obliged to Hellenize both their baptismal names and their surnames and have not been allowed to use their Slav names in public. During the Second World War, however, strong efforts were made by the Bulgarian occupation forces in eastern Greek Macedonia and Thrace to Bulgarize the local Slav-speaking population, with the use of propaganda and torture. A sense of their difference from the Bulgarians led many of them to gain a firmer sense of their Greekness. In this way the nation became ethnically (though not socio-politically) more homogenized.[43]

Turkish was spoken not only by most members of the Muslim minority that remained in Western Thrace after 1922 but by the *Karamanlides*

[41] Delta 1993: 70, 286, 44.

[42] For state language policy towards the Slav speakers of Greek Macedonia in the inter-war period see Apostolakou and Carabott 1999.

[43] For more details of the efforts to Hellenize the Slav speakers of Greek Macedonia see Karakasidou 1997.

who arrived from Asia Minor. At the time of the Greek offensive against Turkey in 1921, priests and members of the congregation of some *Karamanlí* communities sent telegrams to the Turkish Great National Assembly (the provisional government of Mustafa Kemal) claiming that they were patriotic Turks, distancing themselves from the patriarchate's involvement in the Greek national cause, and stating that they wished to replace Greek with Turkish as the language of their liturgy.[44] During discussions over the drafting of the 1923 exchange agreement with Greece concerning the compulsory exchange of populations, the Turkish authorities considered exempting the Turkish-speaking Christians from the exchange. It was finally decided that the exclusive criterion for deciding which people would stay in their homelands and which were to be expelled should be religion rather than language, and the *Karamanlides* living elsewhere than Istanbul were removed to Greece. However, a significant proportion of the Orthodox Christians who have remained in Istanbul till the present day come from a *Karamanlí* background.

In their new homeland the *Karamanlides* faced prejudice and discrimination from many native Greeks because they spoke the language of the age-old enemy of Hellenism; indeed, they were sometimes taunted with the allegation that they were of Turkish racial stock. During the Metaxas dictatorship some of them were punished as a result of the law forbidding the speaking of any language but Greek in public. Nikos Marantzidis writes that the myth of the Turkish-speaking Christians from western Pontus now living in Greece is that the Turks had forced them to choose between abandoning their language and renouncing their religion, whereupon they decided to preserve their religion. They thus saw their speaking of Turkish as an acquired characteristic forced upon them by the conquerors, at the expense of their Greek language. This myth resolved the antithesis between the two poles of nationality: language and religion.[45]

Mention should also be made of the Jewish minority, which was almost completely obliterated as a result of deportations to the death camps during the German Occupation. Katherine Fleming writes that the additions to Greek territory in 1912–13 'increased Greece's Jewish population tenfold: at the end of the nineteenth century, it stood at around

---

[44] Johannes Kolmodin to Swedish Foreign Minister, 9 May 1921, in Özdalga 2006: 152–3. The letter mentions telegrams from Havza (south-west of Samsun), Kayseri [Caesaria], Gömüş-Haci-Köy (west of Amasya), İsparta and Tosya (in the *vilayet* of Kastamonu). Thanks to Jon Van Leuven for bringing this material to my attention.
[45] Marantzidis 2001: 46–7.

12,000; at the end of the 1912–1913 Balkan War, Greece was home to at least 100,000 Jews.... In Salonica there were 56,000 Jews in 1943. In 1945, the next year for which population figures are available, there were 1,950.'[46] The vast majority of the Jewish community of Salonica spoke a variety of Spanish based on the language their ancestors had brought with them after being expelled from Spain around 1492. Most of the other Jews settled in Greece, the so-called Romaniots, spoke Greek as their mother tongue. In the 1920s and 1930s, a concerted effort was made by Greek governments to persuade the Salonica Jews to use the Greek language and adopt a Greek consciousness so as to enable them to participate fully in Greek public life. The younger generation were taught Greek language, history, and geography as obligatory subjects in community schools, while Greek books were translated into Judaeo-Spanish for the benefit of adults. On the whole, the leaders of the Jewish community appear to have encouraged assimilation as a safeguard for its future survival.[47]

Occupation: the 'Trial of the accents'

No member of the Arts Faculty at the University of Athens had been invited by Metaxas to serve on the committee to produce the Triantafyl-lidis grammar. After the death of Metaxas and the German invasion of 1941 the conservative majority in the faculty took its revenge in the so-called 'Trial of the accents'.[48] In November 1941, at a time when thousands of Greeks were dying of starvation, the dean of the faculty, the eminent Byzantinist Faidon Koukoules, wrote to the vice-chancellor accusing a young professor of ancient Greek literature, Ioannis Kakridis (1901–92), of 'criminal activity against the nation, which threatens to bring about a rift in national opinion and a dangerous commotion'.[49] Calls were made for his dismissal from his post.

---

[46] Fleming 2001, referring to Cohen 1998: 12, 194.

[47] This is a very simplified account based on Ginio 2002.

[48] *The Trial of the Accents* was the title of the book containing a transcript of the proceedings and published without the permission of the Arts Faculty (*Diki* n.d. [1942/3]). The book was probably edited by Kakridis himself, and it was probably he who provided the title, which is likely to have been based on Lucian's comic text 'Trial of the vowels', in which the vowels gang together to try the letter T for being a troublemaker. In 1944 some of Kakridis' accusers published a riposte to claims made by his supporters during the proceedings (*Antidikia* 1944).

[49] A. Dimaras 1974: 194. Kakridis was later to gain an international reputation as a distinguished Classicist.

What Kakridis had done to provoke these allegations was to publish two small books on ancient Greek culture, written in demotic and printed in the monotonic (single-accent) system, and – in accordance with normal Greek university practice – to make one of them compulsory reading for his students. One of these books was an excellent stylistic analysis of Pericles' funeral speech entitled *Interpretive Commentary on the Funeral Oration in Thucydides.* Although it was not mentioned during the disciplinary proceedings, it is significant that Kakridis had chosen to comment on an ancient text (Pericles' speech at the funeral of the Athenian dead at the end of the first year of the Peloponnesian War) whose democratic ideology had caused it to be banned by the Metaxas dictatorship, which promoted Spartan rather than Athenian ideals as the most appropriate ancient models for the modern Greeks. The book that Kakridis made compulsory reading for his students was the second edition of a pair of lectures that he had given in 1936 on Greek classical education.[50] Koukoules alleged that Kakridis' orthographic system severs 'a bond uniting the ancient and the modern Greek worlds and opens a chasm between the Ancient Greek language and the modern'. Reading his books, students 'will notice how deep is the difference between the orthography of the Ancient Greek language and the modern. The ancient texts are thus calumniated, since it is indirectly suggested that they should be despised as being full of orthographic difficulties.'[51] Koukoules disregarded the fact that the Greek accent system was invented after the end of the Classical period, at a time when Greek was undergoing such radical phonological changes that it was thought necessary to indicate intonation by means of accent marks in order to help students to pronounce Ancient Greek in the traditional manner.

For more than a century, Greek intellectuals had adopted German ideas regarding the modern legacy of Classical Hellas. The University of Athens had been set up on a German model, and some of the members of the Arts Faculty, including Kakridis himself, had studied in pre-Nazi Germany. Several participants in the 'Trial of the accents' refer to German scholars such as Ulrich von Wilamowitz in order to support their views. But whereas the nationalist tradition of Johann Gottlieb Fichte (1762–1814) and others had argued that it was the Germans that were (or should be) the true heirs of the ancient Greeks, the modern Greeks attempted to show that they themselves were the only modern people to

---

[50] Kakridis 1941b; Kakridis 1941a. The latter had originally been published in a journal in the traditional accent system in 1936.

[51] A. Dimaras 1974: 195.

possess this privilege. It is not insignificant that, a hundred years earlier, as we have seen, it was an Austrian settled in Bavaria (Fallmerayer) who, by alleging that there was no racial continuity between the ancient and modern inhabitants of Greece, had provoked a huge and enduring complex of activities among Greek intellectuals, aimed at demonstrating the cultural continuity of the Greeks from antiquity to the present. The *katharévousa* tradition was founded on the outward imitation of the Ancient Greek language, while demoticism was grounded in a German-influenced assertion that the Greek *Volk* was the genuine bearer of the continuity of Hellenic civilization.

It is difficult to imagine what the members of the Arts Faculty must have felt when the nation from whom they had learned the humanistic values of ancient Greek civilization became the brutal invaders and occupiers of their country. For the conservative members, Kakridis' action was especially treasonable, since his texts, which, according to the allegations, implied that Ancient and Modern Greek were two distinct languages, were published during the German occupation. His accusers may have hoped that the occupation authorities would treat the Greeks well as long as they believed them to be the descendants of the ancients. In their view, Kakridis was undermining this belief. During the proceedings, Koukoules read out the transcript of a programme recently broadcast by Berlin radio about the way that professors, writers, journalists, and other intellectuals in Germany were working to adjust German cultural life according to ancient Greek models;[52] he was clearly implying that this was what should have been happening in Greece too.

Although the disciplinary tribunal set up to examine the charges found Kakridis not guilty of attempting to challenge the value and usefulness of ancient culture, it pronounced him guilty of abusing his position as a professor by disseminating his ideas on orthography and imposing demotic on his students,[53] and he was punished by two months' temporary suspension. One of Kakridis' accusers was Nikolaos Exarchopoulos, professor of education and president of the Academy of Athens, who twenty years previously had been a member of the committee that had recommended the withdrawal and burning of the 1917 schoolbooks. Now he asserted that the demoticists 'have always attempted to impose their ideas by *coup d'état* and during periods when either dictatorial regimes were functioning in our country or irregularities prevailed'.[54] Exarchopoulos and his colleagues seem to have been using the foreign occupation as

[52] *Diki* n.d.: 41.   [53] *Antidikia* 1944: 8–10.   [54] Moschonas 1975: p. xcix.

an opportunity to reassert their cultural authority over the Greek nation, which had been undermined during the previous twenty-five years. On the other hand, it is true that the (anti-German) 1917 government was set up under Anglo-French pressure and without elections; the demotic teaching books were withdrawn in 1921 by a democratically elected government; the 1922 reversal of this anti-demotic stance was a result of a coup, and only the 1929 pro-demotic reforms were carried out by an elected government; yet even then Venizelos had altered the electoral laws in advance in order to ensure a large majority in the 1928 election. It was certainly unwise of Kakridis to choose a period of brutal enemy occupation in order to introduce his monotonic system into his work.

In his prologue to the volume containing a transcript of the proceedings in the 'Trial of the Accents', Petros Charis, the editor of the pro-demotic and pro-Venizelist magazine *Nea Estia*, wrote that the language controversy was a mask for the rivalry between two worlds: 'the Greeks who want to appear Greek and the Greeks who want to be Greek'[55] – a neat, though biased, summary of the relationship between the language question and national identity. The transcript shows that several professors made the totally unfounded assertion that the use of the monotonic system would inevitably lead to the adoption of the Latin alphabet. But the discussion covered much more than simply diacritics. In his books, Kakridis had dared to adopt a creatively critical stance towards Classical Greek antiquity in place of the uncritical admiration that his accusers demanded of a professor of Classics. The historian Apostolos Daskalakis (1900–82) said as much when he likened Kakridis to an Orthodox archbishop who does not believe in Christian dogma;[56] it is clear from this that Kakridis' accusers thought of the Classics as a revealed religion rather than as an object of critical study.

After the disciplinary case was over, Spyridon Marinatos (1901–74), who was later to win an international reputation as an archaeologist, gave a long speech in which he trotted out the old arguments of the purists that spoken Greek is divided into dialects and each demoticist writes in his own language, whereas only *katharévousa* is a nationally unified and unifying variety: *katharévousa*, he said, has 'formed... a rich and unified language out of a barbarous hotchpotch within a single century'.[57] In fact, the language of Marinatos' own speech consists of a jumble of morphological forms from various historical stages and stylistic levels. Marinatos also claims that the misspellings, misuses of words, and

[55] *Diki* n.d.: p. xi.   [56] Ibid., 31.   [57] *Antidikia* 1944: 45.

factual errors found in scripts submitted to the Greek university entrance examinations are such that, if the scripts were subjected to the idiocy test used in Germany, most Greek pupils would be classified as imbeciles and sent for sterilization.[58] He blames these failings on the fact that demotic was taught at primary school, whereas it is more likely that the candidates' linguistic difficulties stemmed from the fact that they were obliged to write in *katharévousa*.

Other professors, however, supported Kakridis' case. In particular, Ioannis Theodorakopoulos (1900–81), a professor of philosophy, Kakridis' brother-in-law and a known demoticist, expressed the hope and the prediction that demotic would eventually come to embody and express the totality of Greek culture from Homer to the present.[59] This implies that the modern Greeks themselves embody the totality of Greek culture throughout its duration.

Meanwhile, in the Greek mountains, both of the important resistance organizations expressed their support for demotic: the anti-communist EDES [National Democratic/Republican Greek League] proclaimed in 1943 that demotic was to be the sole language of education, while in 1944 the communist-dominated EAM [National Liberation Front] was able to announce that demotic was already the sole language used in schools in the areas under its control. EAM also expressed its support for the monotonic system. Demotic was supposed to be used for all purposes – education, legislation, judicial decisions, military orders, and other official documents – by the provisional 'government of the mountains' that was set up with EAM backing in March 1944 under the name PEEA [Political Committee of National Liberation]. Although there were many exceptions in practice,[60] these developments combined to give the impression that the language controversy was part of the intense struggle between nationalism and Communism.

Cold War developments

As early as 1945, when Triantafyllidis applied for the chair of linguistics at Athens University, he was excluded on the grounds that, 'once the demoticists had organized demoticism into a GAM [Linguistic Liberation Front], with activities and a system completely parallel with those

---

[58] Ibid., 91.   [59] *Diki* n.d.: 23.

[60] Moschonas 1975: pp. c–ci. Glinos was probably the chief inspiration behind the language policy of EAM. He was the author of the EAM's manifesto (Glinos 1944), which was published immediately after the end of the Occupation.

of EAM, demoticism became a conspirator and revolutionary and was placed outside the law in the consciousness of the Greeks'.[61] In fact, Triantafyllidis seems to have had no contact with EAM.

With the Civil War (1946–49), the reaction against demotic became even more entrenched, and the 1952 Constitution included the same article specifying the official language as that of 1911. The extreme nationalism underlying this constitution is manifested in the fact that for the first time a clause was introduced laying down the aims of primary and secondary education: '[T]eaching is aimed at the moral and intellectual training and development of the national consciousness of the young, on the basis of the ideological directions of Helleno-Christian civilization.'[62] In 1948, while parliament was debating whether to include the language article in the constitution, the demoticist novelist and lawyer Giorgos Theotokas, who had been born and bred in Constantinople, wrote that the article should be abolished, 'for the same reason that Kemal's Turkey abolished the fez. The fez, too, had no legal or practical significance; it was a symbol. *Katharévousa* is our fez.'[63] Theotokas' humorous analogy had a certain justification, since the fez, like *katharévousa*, was an institution which had been adopted in the nineteenth century as a symbol of modernity, but which by the twentieth century had come to be considered by many to be a sign of backwardness.

During the period 1945–64 demotic was the language of instruction in the first four years of primary school, and *katharévousa* was introduced from the fifth onwards; this was more or less the situation that had been imposed in 1917. Nevertheless, the struggle for demotic continued. In 1946 the Organization for the Publication of Teaching Books published, in an easily affordable edition, the first volume of a radically revised, expanded, and updated second edition of Tzartzanos' *Modern Greek Syntax*, which was now written in demotic and included references to the work of poets as young as Seferis and Elytis (the latter born in 1911).[64] In 1947–49 the left-wing intellectual Giorgos Valetas published his monumental three-volume *Anthology of Demotic Prose*, presenting literary and non-literary prose works written in the vernacular between the years 1340 and 1847. Valetas' book made available many texts that

---

[61] Triantafyllidis 1963d: 333–4 [1945].

[62] 1952 Constitution, art. 16, para. 2, quoted in Stavridi-Patrikiou 1999: 40.

[63] Theotokas 1948: 1012. Theotokas' text was a response to a memorandum from the Arts Faculty of Athens University urging that the language article be included.

[64] Tzartzanos died a few months after the publication of the first volume; the second volume did not appear until 1963. On Tzartzanos' syntax book see Kakridis 1946.

were either entirely unknown or known to only a few, and implied that there was an unbroken tradition of writing in demotic going back half a millennium before the mid-nineteenth century. In 1949, in a series of books intended to assist the teaching of demotic in schools, Triantafyllidis published his *Small Modern Greek Grammar*, a condensed and simplified version of his 1941 grammar suitable for use in schools, although in the event it was not used officially in teaching until 1964–67.

In 1955 the novelist Nikos Kazantzakis and the classical scholar Ioannis Kakridis published a translation of Homer's *Iliad* which they had drafted during the German occupation; their translation, which they dedicated to Pallis' memory, has found more favour with the public than Pallis' older version. While Pallis used the traditional fifteen-syllable verse of the Greek folk songs, Kazantazakis and Kakridis decided to use a seventeen-syllable line, as Kazantzakis had used in his own *Odyssey*, a sequel to Homer's poem published in 1938; they felt that this metre corresponded more closely to the Homeric hexameter, which contains a number of syllables varying between thirteen and seventeen. A similar translation of Homer's *Odyssey* in the same metre, first drafted by Kazantzakis in 1942 and completed by Kakridis after his collaborator's death, appeared in 1965.

In the 1960s literary demotic was finding favour with an increasing public, especially through regular essays in daily newspapers written by members of the Generation of 1930 such as the literary and cultural historian K. Th. Dimaras (1904–92),[65] Theotokas and Terzakis. Dimaras' magisterial *History of Modern Greek Literature*, whose first edition was published in two volumes (1948–49), had already presented, from a broadly demoticist perspective, an authoritative history of Greek literary culture since late Byzantine times but with special emphasis on the period since 1774. Having gone through numerous revisions, it still remains the classic history of modern Greek literature. In 1962 the poet Giorgos Seferis published the first Athens edition of his *Dokimes [Essays]*.[66] The essays and articles by such writers created a widely accepted and fairly homogeneous language that took on an objective and substantive identity as well as conforming to educated readers' perceptions of what demotic was and should be.

Demotic became more universally acceptable in Greece as a written language outside literature as it became de-ruralized. In 1963 the

---

[65] Dimaras published regular essays in the Athens newspaper *Eleftheron Vima* (later renamed *To Vima*) from the 1930s until the 1980s.

[66] The first edition of his *Dokimes* was published in Cairo in 1944.

demoticist lawyer Christoforos Christidis published a demotic translation of the Greek Civil Code to demonstrate that demotic was capable of being used in the most complex legal documents. As Christidis wrote in his introduction, legal texts should not smell either of 'mountain and thyme, or of the coffee-house and grocer's shop'.[67] In a negative sense, de-ruralization meant that demotic ceased to represent the rural origins of the majority of Greeks, while in the positive sense it meant that it ceased to be associated with illiterate peasants. Yet, as Christidis wrote, instead of bringing about a revolution to replace *katharévousa* with demotic, demoticism had by then achieved only the 'peaceful coexistence' of the two varieties.[68]

In poetry and fiction written from the 1950s onwards by authors born since 1920, the literary language became more standardized, losing both its lyricism and the rhetorical gestures that deliberately drew attention to the fact that it was demotic. From now on, the emphasis could be on the message rather than the linguistic medium. The language question had long been solved in literature, which waited for other discourses to catch up. While using demotic morphology, poets no longer felt that there were vocabulary items (e.g. learned or technical words) that were inappropriate for poetry.[69]

The award of the Nobel Prize for Literature to Seferis in 1963 was often justifiably interpreted as a tribute not only to this particular poet but also to all the poets before and during his time who had succeeded in moulding demotic Greek into a supreme instrument of poetic expression. But another development led to an even greater bourgeois acceptance of demotic in the 1960s, namely the extraordinary flowering of popular song in the works of composers such as Manos Hadjidakis and Mikis Theodorakis, who succeeded in wedding traditional Greek urban popular rhythms to high-quality lyrics, many of them poems that were not originally intended to be set to music. Suddenly everyone in Greece, whether rural folk or middle-class or working-class urbanites, was listening to – and singing – the poetry of Greece's greatest modern poets.

An illuminating insight into demoticists' views of the national importance of demotic during the Cold War period is provided by a public lecture, entitled 'Language and nation', given by Nikolaos Andriotis as vice-chancellor of the University of Salonica in 1963.[70] Andriotis, a

---

[67] C. Christidis 1984: 18.   [68] C. Christidis 1984: 43.

[69] The surrealists of the 1930s shared the same view about vocabulary, but they often used *katharévousa* morphology.

[70] Andriotis 1976: 331–45 [1963].

lifelong demoticist, was born on the island of Imbros in Turkey and grew up after 1922 on the island of Samothrace, which was claimed and occupied by Bulgaria in the two world wars. Salonica was only 70 and 135 kilometres by road from the borders of communist Yugoslavia and communist Bulgaria respectively. In this lecture Andriotis expresses his anxiety about Greece's position in the far corner of a Slav-speaking and politically pan-Slavic continent extending from the Adriatic to Vladivostok. He talks about a thousand-year-old struggle between the Greek and Slav languages, which he likens to the struggle between the hero Digenis and Death in the Greek folk songs. Andriotis' linguistic chauvinism borders on racism when he talks about the 'pungent breath' of the Slavonic languages and claims that the 'Slav element' of the population has imbued and melted Hellenism in the Balkans as water melts sugar. Slavonic, he claims, is 'a foreign language of monolithic simplicity, grammatically and orthographically easy, and for this reason it is transmitted like the microbe of an epidemic'. Here Andriotis adheres to the Greek nationalist narrative that the majority of the Slav speakers of the southern Balkans are descended from Greeks who were obliged to change their language when the Slavs invaded, since the Slavs were incapable of mastering the intricacies of the Greek language.[71] Greek is a bourgeois language par excellence, he argues, while Slav languages are suitable for simple peasants. Quoting the German Classical scholar Wilhelm Schulze, Andriotis describes Ancient Greek as 'the highest manifestation of the human language-forming spirit'. 'The vocabulary of Greek,' he adds, 'its inflections and its syntactic structure are bearers of superior spirituality'. Yet it is this very virtue of Greek, namely its complexity, that makes it vulnerable.[72]

In the same lecture Andriotis claims that language, in the form of the Modern Greek dialects, is the greatest monument to 'the racial survival of ancient Hellenism' – greater than any work of literature or visual art. In an earlier text, refuting Fallmerayer, he had argued that studies of the Modern Greek dialects 'convince even the most incredulous that Greek life in our lands has never experienced an interruption'.[73] Here he reveals the ideological motivation behind much of the dialectological

---

[71] For the theory, dating from the 1870s, that the Slav speakers of Macedonia were the descendants of Greeks who had lost their language see Chapter 6, note 97.

[72] Two propagandistic works by Andriotis dating from the Cold War period are the pamphlets Andriotis 1952 and Andriotis 1957; the latter argues that the southernmost of the federative republics of Yugoslavia has no right to use 'Macedonia' for its name and 'Macedonian' for the name of its official language.

[73] Andriotis 1976: 326 [1939].

research carried out by Greeks until the 1970s or 1980s: the attempt to prove the unbroken continuity of Greek-speaking populations in the lands claimed as Greek by Greek nationalism.[74] In his 1963 address he presents demoticism as a democratic movement that would both oppose the totalitarian regimes of neighbouring countries and allow all social classes in Greece to gain equal access to the national language and national culture, thus making Greece a more homogeneous and therefore a stronger entity, more capable of putting up ideological, political, cultural, and military resistance against attacks from beyond its borders. Finally, Andriotis' argument for teaching demotic in schools to the speakers of Greek dialects in northern Greece is similar to the one used by Triantafyllidis in favour of teaching demotic to children who spoke other languages: *katharévousa* prevents dialect speakers from learning the Panhellenic language that would enable them fully to realize their nationality.

The absolute majority gained by Georgios Papandreou's Centre Union Party in the 1964 elections (after a tight win in 1963) allowed it to proceed with educational reforms, with the prime minister himself as minister of education, as he had been in 1930. By a law of 1964 demotic was introduced into all levels of education, though on equal terms (*isotimía*) with *katharévousa*. This meant that all teachers and students were permitted, without discrimination, to speak and write in whichever variety they wished to use. The concise version of Triantafyllidis' grammar was introduced into primary schools.[75] Constitutionally, however, *katharévousa* remained the sole official language, and the officially recognized *isotimía* perpetuated the use of *katharévousa* in education. In 1965 demotic, which was not the official language of the state, became the official language of the Greek state broadcasting service.

Another aspect of educational reform of relevance to the language question was that Classical texts were to some extent taught in demotic translation – much to the enjoyment and relief of many pupils and their parents. During the 1960s, alongside new demotic translations of ancient texts, there was a spate of translations of Modern Greek literary works from *katharévousa* into demotic aimed at a young audience. These were mostly selections of short stories by Papadiamantis, but they also included stories by Vizyinos.

---

[74] Andriotis was one of the leading Greek dialectologists of his time. His dialectological work culminated in his monumental dictionary of archaisms in Modern Greek dialects (Andriotis 1974), published in German for a non-Greek readership. Among his many other works is the classic etymological dictionary of Standard Modern Greek (Andriotis 1951).

[75] Triantafyllidis 1965b.

The educational reforms introduced by the Papandreou government were even more short-lived than those of 1917. The 1964 readers were abandoned after Papandreou's resignation in 1965 over a constitutional dispute with the king concerning the demarcation of power between monarch and prime minister – a similar dispute to the one that had brought about the National Schism of 1916–17. The collapse of democracy with the military coup of 1967 completely reversed what remained of the 1964 reforms. Under the Colonels' dictatorship, the teaching of what was called the 'mother tongue' was once again confined to the first three years of primary school, while the 'mother tongue' used in the textbooks was adulterated with the aim of making it easier for children to learn *katharévousa* later. In this way, the educational language policy returned to the pre-1917 situation.[76] The Junta's constitution of 1968 specified *katharévousa* as the official language not only of the state but also (for the very first time) of education. Many academics were dismissed from their posts, including professors at Salonica University who were open supporters of demotic. The armed forces now saw themselves as the guardians of *katharévousa*: in 1972 and 1973 the General Staff published an anonymous booklet entitled *National Language*, which circulated widely free of charge and alleged that demoticists were aiding the communist cause by decrying *katharévousa*, which was the true national language. It also claimed that the spoken vernacular was a jargon or slang that did not possess grammar. In particular, it criticized the version of Triantafyllidis' demotic grammar that had been introduced into schools by the previous regime, alleging that it was so inconsistent that it could not be taught.[77] The allegations against demotic in this book take us back to Mistriotis – and even further back to Samuel Johnson's description of colloquial language as 'fugitive cant'.

There was plenty of linguistic opposition to the Colonels' benighted policies. Liberal and left-wing intellectuals took the opportunity to

[76] A. Dimaras 1974: 297.

[77] There were at least three versions of this booklet, one published in 1972 (*Ethniki* 1972) and two in 1973 (*Ethniki* 1973); the first two were published by the General Staff of the Armed Forces, while the third was published by the 'Society of the Friends of the People'. This society, founded in 1865 with the aim of furthering 'Helleno-Christian civilization' by providing lectures, books and libraries for working people but with little to show for its activities during the first hundred years of its existence, was revived as an organ of nationalist propaganda with financial assistance from the Colonels' government. One of the society's advisers was Georgios Kourmoulis (1907–77), professor of linguistics at Athens University from 1949 to 1977 and a former minister of education, who, if not the author of this text, was no doubt one of its inspirers. Moschonas' conjecture (1975: p. cxi), that the author may have been the Chief of the Armed Forces, Odyssefs Angelis, does not seem plausible to me.

publish or republish older texts that were relevant to the language question. In 1970 K. Th. Dimaras produced the first edition of the writings of Dimitrios Katartzis, who could be claimed to have been the first demoticist. Republications included Gianidis' *Language and Life* (1969), Psycharis' *My Journey* in its original 1888 form, Glinos' *Nation and Language*, Delmouzos' *Demoticism and Education* (all three in 1971), and Kordatos' *History of our Language Question* (1973, first published in 1943). K. Th. Dimaras' son Alexis published his two-volume work *The Reform that Never Took Place* (1973–74), a valuable collection of documents pertaining to the history of official Greek education policy between 1821 and 1967 and the various (mostly unsuccessful) attempts at educational reform.

In 1969 the newspaper *Estia*, long a bastion of reactionary views, challenged the demoticists to translate the *Politikí Dikonomía* [manual of civil legal procedure] into demotic. This was a conscious repetition of the same challenge, issued to Psycharis by Agisilaos Giannopoulos in 1888, in the firm belief that it was not feasible to translate a precise and complex technical text into such a poverty-stricken language. What the editors of *Estia* did not know was that Christoforos Christidis had already begun translating the *Politiki Dikonomia* into demotic in 1963; he completed the translation in 1971 and published it in 1974.[78]

In 1968 the first volume of Emmanouil Kriaras' *Dictionary of Medieval Greek Vernacular Literature* was published.[79] The story behind this dictionary is revealing. At the Second International Byzantine Conference, held in Belgrade in 1927, the Austrian linguist Paul Kretschmer proposed that a dictionary of Medieval Greek be compiled, but the matter was not pursued until the Academy of Athens announced at the international Byzantine conference held in Athens in 1930 that it would undertake to establish a service for this purpose.[80] Kriaras served as director of this Medieval Archive from 1939 to 1950.[81] In 1948, in contrast to the Academy's ambitious plan to produce a dictionary of the whole of medieval Greek writing, Kriaras proposed that the dictionary produced by the Medieval Archive should be limited to vernacular Greek from 1100 to 1669, but his proposal was not accepted.[82] In 1955, five years after he had been appointed professor of medieval Greek literature at

[78] Kriaras 1993: 138.
[79] At the time of writing, fifteen volumes have been published.
[80] Kriaras 1998: 158.   [81] Kriaras 2004: 101.   [82] Ibid., 102.

the University of Salonica, Kriaras decided to undertake the task of producing the dictionary of medieval vernacular Greek.[83]

The difference between a dictionary of Byzantine Greek and Kriaras' medieval dictionary is that the former would have concentrated on the overwhelming majority of texts that were written throughout the Byzantine period in more or less archaic Greek (and would have been of interest to an international audience of Byzantinists), while his medieval dictionary not only covers the last part of the Byzantine period but extends its chronological reach to cover the period up to the Ottoman capture of Crete. The reasons for Kriaras' choice were not only practical (the number of texts to be studied, while large, was far more manageable) but ideological: he was intending to produce a dictionary not of Byzantine Greek but of the medieval and pre-modern vernacular as recorded in texts. His view of Medieval Greek can be summed up in his statement that 'the medieval vernacular language had taken on a modern form that in time developed into Modern Greek'.[84] Thus his dictionary, even though it is consulted only by specialists, has made an invaluable contribution to the understanding and acceptance of the continuity of the Greek vernacular language since the Middle Ages, with the implication that the demotic written by Psycharis from 1888 onwards and by the more moderate demoticists since 1910 is not some new-fangled construct but the natural development of the long history of written vernacular Greek.

The post-1974 democratic regime

As Maro Kakridi-Ferrari has written, 'the prestige of *katharévousa* was totally discredited by the use – both ideological and actual (linguistic) – that the Colonels' regime made of it'.[85] When the dictatorial regime fell in July 1974, *katharévousa*, in terms of its use as a distinct variety of Greek, began to collapse remarkably quickly.

In December 1974, after an election campaign during which most of the candidates used demotic in their speeches, the conservative New Democracy government led by Konstantinos Karamanlis began using demotic for most of its official announcements, and the prime minister

---

[83] Kriaras 1998: 164

[84] Ibid., 158–9. The fact that Kriaras' medieval dictionary anachronistically adopted the modern monotonic system from vol. 5 (1977) onwards shows that he considers the medieval vernacular language to belong to the Greeks of his own day. By contrast, dictionaries of learned Byzantine Greek are printed in the traditional polytonic system that was used in its time.

[85] Kakridi-Ferrari 2008.

himself addressed parliament in vernacular Greek on 11 December. A referendum had already been carried out in which an overwhelming majority of the Greek electorate voted against the re-establishment of the monarchy, which had been abolished by the Colonels' dictatorship. The day after Karamanlis' first parliamentary speech in demotic, the leader of the opposition, Georgios Mavros, addressed parliament in *katharévousa*, saying that of the two great problems that had beset the Greek people, the constitutional question (monarchy or republic) and the language question, the first had just been solved, while the second must be solved urgently, and he proposed that the new constitution be written in demotic. But this initiative soon petered out, and, in the parliamentary debate on the constitution, not a single deputy spoke in favour of his proposal. Nevertheless, only one deputy argued for the retention of *katharévousa* as the official language of the state.[86]

In the event, although the 1975 constitution was written in *katharévousa*, it contained no reference to the official language of the state or of education. Article 2 of Law 309, written in *katharévousa* and enacted on 30 April 1976, stipulated that, starting from the school year 1977–78, 'Modern Greek' should be the sole language of education at all levels. The text continued:

'Modern Greek' is defined as the Demotic that has been developed into a Panhellenic instrument of expression by the Greek People and the acknowledged writers of the Nation, properly constructed, without regional and extreme forms.

This wording represents the final triumph of the efforts made by the Educational Association in the 1910s to persuade Greek public opinion that there was a common Panhellenic vernacular.[87] Concealed behind the phrase 'developed . . . by the Greek People' lies the demoticist assumption that the origins of this Panhellenic language lie in the folk songs. In the same year an abridged and slightly revised version of Triantafyllidis' grammar was officially introduced into schools, where it is still in use today.[88] In an extraordinarily radical move, the teaching of Ancient

[86] C. Christidis 1984: 242–4, 258.

[87] Cf. the definition of the 'pure Panhellenic demotic language, free of all . . . dialectal . . . features' in Delmouzos 1911a: 23.

[88] Two confusingly similar 'small grammars' were published almost at the same time: the second edition of Triantafyllidis 1949, produced by the Triantafyllidis Institute in Salonica (Triantafyllidis 1975), and an adapted version produced by the Organization for the Publication of Teaching Books in Athens (Neoelliniki 1976); it is significant that most of the authors of the latter were attached to Salonica University (Kriaras 1987: 217). The state-approved 1976 version was stricter than the unofficial 1975 version, i.e. it allowed for fewer alternative forms, even when they are used in everyday speech (Manesis 1999: 56).

Greek, hitherto a compulsory subject in the *gymnásio* (first three years of secondary education) was to be taught only in the *lýkeio* (last three years of secondary education) and only as an optional subject.

It is not surprising that the official abolition of *katharévousa* coincided with the establishment of the first entirely stable democratic republic in the history of Greece. The Communist Party of Greece, which had been outlawed since 1947, was legalized immediately after the fall of the Colonels' regime. A few years later, in the 1980s, the Greek state officially recognized for the first time that the communist-led resistance organization during the Axis Occupation formed part of the so-called 'national resistance'. These measures succeeded in healing the breaches in Greek society caused by the civil war. The linguistic civil war came to an end at the same time. With the abolition of *katharévousa* as a discrete variety in 1976, Greeks officially became free, in their writing, to mix colloquial and learned words, forms, and constructions, words of ancient and modern origin, and native and foreign words. The transition from writing *katharévousa* to writing demotic paralleled the passage from dictatorship to democracy. It was not simply a matter of dropping the one and adopting the other as the natural default position. On the contrary, it needed care, discipline and hard work – as Delmouzos' pupils at the girls' school in Volos had found in 1908.

10

Epilogue

Developments since 1976

The fact that it was a conservative government that introduced the 1976 educational reforms meant that it became practically impossible to reverse those aspects that concerned the Modern Greek language, particularly since the virtual abolition of *katharévousa* was aimed partly at facilitating Greece's entry into the European Economic Community (now the European Union). When this took place in 1981, Greek became one of the Community's official languages. Today all the political parties employ demotic, as do all newspapers – even *Estia*, which was the last to hold out for *katharévousa*. Since 1976, according to the late Tasos Christidis, 'the "language question" has ceased to be one of the strategic fronts on which wider political and social conflicts are played out'.[1] Nevertheless, the language question in its broadest sense has continued to exercise the minds and pens of intellectuals, politicians, and many other Greeks.

In 1977 demotic was officially recognized as the language of administration, and the first Greek law (on agricultural cooperatives) was enacted in demotic. In the same year a government ministry issued instructions to all departments of the civil service on drawing up official documents in demotic;[2] it also organized seminars in which civil servants were trained to draft documents in demotic. These activities were followed by the publication of a privately produced style guide to writing in demotic for administrative and scientific purposes.[3]

Nevertheless, most legal texts continued to be drafted in *katharévousa* until a 'Committee for demotic' was established at the Ministry of Justice by law 1406/1983. The committee consisted of lawyers and *filólogoi* [literature experts] and was chaired by the veteran demoticist *filólogos* and lexicographer Emmanouil Kriaras. The committee translated the

---

[1] A.-F. Christidis 1999: 80.   [2] These instructions were contained in Ypourgeio 1977.
[3] Dormparakis 1979.

basic legal codes into demotic. The same law established demotic as the language to be used by both attorneys and notaries and made the use of demotic obligatory in legal documents and actions. The fact that the 1976 school grammar had become the official state grammar by means of legislation meant in practice that those who drafted legal texts were supposed to follow its dictates. It was the first time that the Greek state had ever laid down the specific morphological forms that should be used for official purposes. These stipulations caused considerable practical problems and provoked some frustration and opposition on the part of those who were bound by them.[4] In 1986 the Greek Parliament ratified for the first time a demotic translation of the constitution (of 1975), but it ruled that the original text in *katharévousa* retained legal precedence for the purposes of interpretation.[5]

In the early years after the restoration of democracy, the variety of Greek one used, including certain quirks of vocabulary or grammar, continued to define one's political and ideological allegiances. During the period 1981–89 the government of PASOK (Panhellenic Socialist Movement), starting from the charismatic prime minister, Andreas Papandreou, was responsible for creating and disseminating some usages that resulted from the automatic translation of *katharévousa* forms and phrases into pseudo-demotic by simply altering the inflections of words. A prime example of this was the expression of dates, e.g. στις έξι Μάη 'on the sixth of May', a hybrid between the traditional 'high-register' στις έξι Μαΐου (without the definite article and with the learned genitive form of the noun) and the 'low-register' στις έξι του Μάη (with the definite article and the colloquial form of the noun).

As an indication of how far the language question had moved on since the beginning of the twentieth century, it is worth mentioning that in 1901, when faced by the problem of translating the feminine version of όνος [donkey] in the biblical episode in which Christ enters Jerusalem in triumph (Matthew 21.2), Alexandros Pallis coined the word όνισσα in order to avoid the vernacular word for a female donkey, γαϊδούρα, which he considered too vulgar to be acceptable. By contrast, the United Bible Societies' demotic translation of the New Testament, published in 1985, used the word γαϊδούρα, and this choice did not meet with any adverse reaction.[6]

---

[4] Manesis 1999.

[5] *Greece: Background – News – Information* (Greek Press and Information Office, London), no. 8 (10 April 1986).

[6] *Kaini* 1985: 46.

Maro Kakridi-Ferrari, referring to Article 2 of Law 309/1976, has talked about 'the progress towards the standardization of demotic as (common) Modern Greek'.[7] According to this law, in other words, demotic officially became Modern Greek and vice versa. Many intellectuals and others were far from satisfied with this identification, which, in their view, narrowed the definition of Modern Greek and consequently narrowed the limits of the language itself. Such people have preferred to describe the contemporary written language as Common Modern Greek rather than demotic. I prefer to call it Standard Modern Greek.

As we have seen, the official language reform continued after the electoral victory of PASOK in 1981. The following year the monotonic (single-accent) system was imposed in education by presidential decree. Despite the linguistic reforms that had taken place in the educational and administrative fields, literary writers, journalists, and others have continued to feel free to use *katharévousa* features in their work, and many writers and publishers still continue to use the polytonic system today, although *Estia* is the only newspaper in Greece that currently uses it. They do so because they are used to the traditional writing system and because, in their view, words written according to the monotonic system look somehow incomplete. A few new publications even appeared in *katharévousa*, including Andreas Empeirikos' massive erotic novel in *katharévousa, The Great Eastern*, published posthumously in 1991–92, which met with considerable critical and popular success. In this novel, set on a transatlantic liner during the Victorian era, a significant amount of humour is generated by the incongruity between the traditionally strait-laced and euphemistic nature of *katharévousa* and the explicit nature of the sexual descriptions.

The decree imposing the monotonic system in education was yet another example of official state intervention in the use of the Greek language, and it proved to be the last straw for a number of Greek intellectuals who were growing increasingly frustrated by what they saw as the state's imposition of one kind of Greek to replace the variety that had been imposed hitherto, instead of letting the language develop naturally. On 15 February 1982, immediately after the official introduction of the monotonic system, twenty-eight authors signed a declaration protesting at what they called the 'complete dislocation of the Greek language' and asserting that the introduction of the monotonic system was wrenching the modern language away from a 2,000-year-old tradition of writing in

---

[7] Kakridi-Ferrari 2008: 368.

Greek. It should be made clear that all the signatories of this declaration were supporters of demotic.

Later in the same year an *Ellinikós Glossikós Omilos* [Greek Language Association] was founded, and its first proclamation, formulated in a distinctly rhetorical style and signed by the Nobel-prize-winning poet Odysseas Elytis, the professor of linguistics at Athens University Georgios Babiniotis, and other leading intellectuals, implied that the government was attempting to reduce the rich variety of the Greek language. The proclamation announced that the Association's aim was the defence of Greek in its *diachronikótita* [diachronicity]. However, the Association faded away after three years of debate and after having produced two volumes containing articles published in newspapers and magazines in the wake of its proclamation.[8] Ironically, when the new school grammar of 1976 had tacitly abolished the grave accent by replacing it with the acute, no one seems to have noticed; at least, no one pointed it out in print until the authors of the grammar revealed, some time later, what they had done.

From the late 1970s to the early 1990s, Babiniotis made a number of polemical statements in newspapers and other publications about the language problem. He frequently talked of language (meaning particularly the Greek language) as an *axía* [value] and about an alleged decline in linguistic 'quality' in Greece;[9] he also talked about 'linguistic terrorism exercised in the name of political ideology by semi-ignorant amateurs'.[10] Another member of the Greek Language Association claimed that 'the fanatical insistence on linguistic uniformity, the levelling of all shades of meaning, the lack of articulation, the violation of cadence of rhythm, could lead to totalitarianism'.[11]

By the 1980s many educated Greeks were complaining about the allegedly sloppy use of Greek (in terms of grammar, vocabulary, and semantics) in the mouths of the young and in the media (especially on television).[12] Parents claimed that they could no longer understand their children, though this was probably the result of a deliberate tactic on the children's part, a symptom of a generation gap that had been experienced

---

[8] Babiniotis et al. 1984–6.

[9] See, for instance, the title of Babiniotis 1999 (*Language as Value*).

[10] Quoted in an article by Neocosmos Tzallas syndicated by Reuters, 20 Apr. 1986.

[11] Stelios Ramfos, quoted by Neocosmos Tzallas, ibid.

[12] The media felt it necessary to make good the damage they had been accused of causing, by inserting short programmes about good usage on television and radio, and from 1986 onwards there was a spate of books on 'correct usage' aimed at a wide public.

in America and Western Europe for at least the previous thirty years. Another cause for concern was the substantial number (often described as an 'invasion') of indeclinable words from American English that had been entering the language in recent years. This shocked speakers of a language in which the majority of words are of proven 'native' origin, and which depends – unlike English – on a complex inflectional system. In 1978 Babiniotis wrote that

the unjustified, irresponsible and unrestrained introduction of foreign words, which alters the character of our language, adulterates its structure and impoverishes its expressive power, constitutes yet another source for the erosion of our Greekness,[13]

while Giannis Kalioris published a book in 1984 warning against what he called 'linguistic de-Hellenization'.[14]

In 1986 there was a public outcry when the examiners in the national university entrance examinations announced that in their opinion the standard of Greek in the candidates' scripts gave cause for serious concern. One aspect that caused widespread dismay was the large proportion of candidates who appeared not to know the meaning of two nouns, namely αρωγή [succour] and ευδοκίμηση [prosperity]. Greek newspapers carried extensive reports of this announcement on their front pages, and the ensuing journalistic investigation and public debate went on for several months. It became customary for Greeks to complain that the vocabulary of young people had been reduced to a few hundred words (this spawned a new and widely used term, *lexipenía* [vocabulary deficiency]), and that the younger generation did not employ syntax; the consequence of this situation – Korais' argument that a corrupt language harms the mind – was that young people's minds were in danger of becoming atrophied as a result of using an atrophied language.

Many Greeks, including members of the government, attributed what they saw as the decline of the Greek language to the abolition of Ancient Greek lessons at the *gymnásio*. For this reason the chief demand voiced by such people was that the ancient language should be reintroduced as a compulsory subject into the *gymnásio*, since it was only by studying Ancient Greek that one could understand the 'roots' of Modern Greek and realize, through etymology, the 'correct' and 'true' meanings of Modern Greek words.

The question whether or not Ancient Greek should be taught as a compulsory subject split Greek linguists and educationalists into two

[13] Quoted in A.-F. Christidis 1999: 47.   [14] Kalioris 1984.

opposing camps, one claiming that, without the compulsory teaching of Ancient Greek, Modern Greek would be cut off from its past, the other arguing that Modern Greek should be allowed to develop as a self-contained language without interference from earlier stages of the language. Those who supported the compulsory teaching of Ancient Greek had an additional argument in their favour: that the vast majority of Greeks are, actually or nominally, Orthodox Christians, that Orthodox church services use the original Ancient Greek texts of the Bible and the liturgy, and that therefore Greeks should be taught to be able to understand this language.

In 1987 the minister of education, Antonis Tritsis, announced that compulsory lessons in Ancient Greek would be reintroduced into the *gymnásio*, arguing that Greeks cannot use their language properly unless they possess a good knowledge of Ancient Greek. In 1993 a new series of textbooks was introduced into the *gymnásio*, entitled *Greek Language through Ancient, Byzantine and Learned Texts*.[15] These books did not teach Ancient Greek systematically; instead, they introduced pupils to texts in earlier stages of their language, including nineteenth-century *katharévousa*. These widely differing varieties of Greek were lumped together under the label 'our older Greek'.[16] The books provided pupils with a smattering of Ancient Greek vocabulary and grammar that was intended to be sufficient to enable them to read the relevant passages with a significant degree of comprehension. According to one of the co-ordinators of this policy, its ulterior purpose was to enable pupils 'to attain a more essential knowledge and, as a consequence, a more efficient use of Modern Greek'.[17]

Since 1993, the content and focus of the books for teaching 'older Greek' in the *gymnásio* has gradually shifted, to the extent that nowadays the equivalent books are entitled *Ancient Greek Language*. Nevertheless, the chief aim of Ancient Greek teaching in the Greek *gymnásio* continues to be to increase the pupils' knowledge of the Greek language as a whole in the hope that this will improve their use of Modern Greek.

In the arguments in favour of the compulsory teaching of Ancient Greek we can see the views of Korais and Hatzidakis being recycled. Various metaphors – some of them rather misleading – have been used

---

[15] *Elliniki* 1993.

[16] The phrase '*ta palaiótera elliniká mas*' was borrowed by Babiniotis (1991 [=1992]: 71) from Seferis (*Apokalypsi* 1966: 15). Thanks to Nikos Petropoulos for tracking down the Seferis reference for me.

[17] Rankousis 1999: 364–5.

over the centuries to convey the relationship between Modern Greek and Ancient Greek, including Ancient Greek as the mother or the *trofós* [nursemaid] of Modern Greek. But most persistent in recent times has been the one involving 'roots': Modern Greek is likened to a tree whose roots are Ancient Greek and which will wither and die if it is cut off from them. This view results from a widespread view in Greece that the Greek language exists not merely by virtue of its living contemporary usage, but by virtue of its historical past as well.

The linguistic consequences of the learned/popular distinction

The underdevelopment of vernacular Greek for non-literary uses in the past is similar to the way some economists and political scientists, such as Andre Gunder Frank, have viewed underdeveloped countries. According to Frank, the development of First World countries is dependent (in both the colonialist and globalist economies) on the deliberate under-development of Third World countries.[18] Similarly, the Greek vernacular was kept in a state of underdevelopment by those who devoted their linguistic energies exclusively to the development of *katharévousa*. Just as proponents of colonialism could claim that colonized peoples were inherently incapable of economic and cultural advancement, so some Greek language purists could claim that the Greek vernacular was inher-ently incapable of being developed to serve all the expressive needs of the Greek nation.

The most harmful consequence of the learned/popular distinction has been a number of dichotomies within the Greek language: a dichotomy between town and country (*katharévousa* was *par excellence* an urban language variety, while older demotic tended to have a rural flavour); a dichotomy between everyday discourse and technical and official dis-course; a dichotomy between literal and figurative discourse and between concrete and abstract discourse; and a dichotomy between the expres-sion of thought and the expression of feeling. These dichotomies have only begun to be transcended during the past thirty years. In vocabu-lary the legacy of the learned/popular distinction has left a significant amount of synonymy in today's language. For instance, there are two words for 'moon', namely the vernacular term φεγγάρι /fengári/ and the ancient/*katharévousa* term σελήνη /selíni/, and two words for 'liver',

---

[18] See, for instance, Frank 1967.

the vernacular συκώτι /sikóti/ and the learned ήπαρ /ípar/. As regularly happens in such cases of Greek lexical dualism, the vernacular term is the everyday word for the object, whereas the learned term is used especially in scientific discourse. There are also pairs of verbs, such as vernacular πάω /páo/ and learned μεταβαίνω /metavéno/ 'go', the first being used in oral communication, while the latter is often used in more formal contexts.

With regard to the literal/metaphorical distinction, *katharévousa* used Ancient Greek words in both literal and figurative meanings, while today's Standard Modern Greek often uses vernacular words for literal meanings while retaining *katharévousa* words for figurative meanings. Demotic words have been needlessly protected or prevented from metaphorical extension through the use of *katharévousa* words in figurative senses. To take one example among many, the nouns φτερούγα /fterúγa/ and φτερό /fteró/ are used in the vernacular to mean the wing of a bird. When educated Greeks needed to talk about the wing of a building, however, they resorted to the Ancient Greek word for a bird's wing, namely πτέρυξ /ptériks/. With the advent of post-Psycharist demotic, the morphological suffix of this word was demoticized, with the result that the word used today for the wing of a building is πτέρυγα /ptériγa/. Thus, while the literal meaning of the English word 'wing', like its French equivalent *aile*, has been extended to cover the metaphorical wing of a building, neither of the vernacular Greek words has been permitted such an extension; instead, separate but etymologically related words are used for the two different meanings.

To take an example from syntax, the word τάξη /táksi/ means both 'order' and 'class, classroom'. Spatial expressions such as σε τάξη /se táksi/ 'in order' (as in putting one's room in order) and στην τάξη /stin táksi/ 'in the classroom' use the demotic preposition σ[ε] /s[e]/ + accusative. In Ancient Greek and archaic varieties of *katharévousa* the preposition εν /en/ + dative meant 'in' in both literal (spatial) and metaphorical (abstract) senses. In Modern Greek today, εν + dative is not used in a spatial sense, but it is often used instead of σ[ε] + accusative in metaphorical (abstract) senses, for instance in the expression (now written as one word) εντάξει /endáksi/ 'OK', which originated in the early nineteenth century as a literal translation of the German phrase *in Ordnung* into pseudo-Ancient Greek. The example of εντάξει also illustrates another consequence of the historical influence of *katharévousa*, namely that foreign influences in Standard Modern Greek often manifest themselves in the form of pseudo-archaisms. It is difficult to know what is gained by making formal linguistic distinctions between concrete and metaphorical discourse. Only in poetry has the metaphorical potential of demotic been exploited to the full; indeed, this may be one of the reasons why, until recently, poetry has been so central to Greek culture.

In some pretentious writing today, such as one finds every day in Greek newspapers, superfluous archaisms seem to be included as a kind of 'value added'. Fanis Kakridis has described the use of archaisms in contemporary Greek as post-modern cherry-picking.[19] It is certainly true that in the post-modern age, the boundaries between the different varieties of Greek have become fluid. Roderick Beaton sees this in a more positive light when he writes that '[f]rom the *Babel* [the comedy of that title] of the 1830s, (written) Greek has evolved towards the polyphony of the 1980s and 1990s'.[20]

There is indeed cause for optimism. The outcome of all these developments, disputes, and compromises is that today the *katharévousa* and vernacular linguistic traditions, together with their different ways of viewing the relationship with the ancients, have been combined into Standard Modern Greek, and the antithesis turns out to have produced a synthesis. As a result of negotiation and compromise, the struggle between the supporters of the rival varieties has both enriched and enlivened the language. The Greeks now possess a rich and supple written language whose vocabulary consists overwhelmingly of words inherited from Ancient Greek and of constructs based on Ancient Greek morphemes, and in which the rules governing derivational morphology make it comparatively easy to create new words. Most of the existing word stock from the learned tradition has been adjusted according to demotic morphological rules, while those ancient words that cannot be so adjusted are largely inflected according to ancient morphological patterns. Conversely, some of the word stock from the popular tradition has been phonologically adjusted according to the learned tradition. The syntax of Standard Modern Greek has developed, through the interplay between *katharévousa* and demotic and under the influence of various western European languages, into an instrument capable of expressing the most complex relations.

The supporters of extreme *katharévousa* and extreme demotic were equally aiming at a uniform national language that was homogeneous in terms of phonology, morphology, and vocabulary. Yet the majority of Greek speakers and writers have preferred to use a language that

[19] F. I. Kakridis 1997.   [20] Beaton 1999: 346.

mixes phonological, morphological, and lexical features from both the learned and the popular traditions. Both *katharévousa* and demotic were defined as much by the features they excluded as by those they included. One result of the abolition of the official division of the modern Greek language into *katharévousa* and demotic is that Greeks at last possess a rich stylistic repertoire that, until recently, had been restricted by the necessity to choose between either *katharévousa* or demotic. This unified language expresses and embodies modern Greek culture by inscribing not only the perceived continuity of the cultural tradition from ancient Greece, through the Roman occupation, Christianity, Byzantium, and Frankish and Ottoman rule to the post-independence period, but also the intense desire of Greek intellectuals since the eighteenth century to establish a direct connection with both ancient Greek culture and the culture of modern western Europe. In short, the Greeks of today have the best of both worlds, since their contemporary language offers them potentially the most expressive and productive features of both demotic and *katharévousa*.

Language and national identity in Greece today

The late Emmanouil Moschonas concluded his history of the demoticist movement in 1975 as follows:

The only safe finding is that the demands of demoticism were born in the bourgeois world and – despite the dangers of extreme generalization – did not aspire to aims that were different from those of the bourgeois conservatism by which *katharévousa* was supported.

The tactics of both sides, in other words, served the same end of promoting a Greek national identity that included the connections with the ancients.[21]

Today, the 'language controversy' has been replaced by a widespread perception among Greeks that the Greek language is in crisis. Many Greeks see their language as being an endangered species, threatened with extinction by the global domination of English. In Greece and Cyprus today the Greek language is being used side by side with English, which is omnipresent in the media and on the internet. Time will tell whether the use of Greek is going to be reduced as a result. In the meantime, those who feel anxious about the survival of the Greek language tend to be especially those who insist on the compulsory teaching of

[21] Moschonas 1975: cxvii.

Ancient Greek and on efforts to remove or reduce the indeclinable words of foreign origin that are commonly used within an otherwise Greek linguistic context. The perception of a language crisis is more universal in the developed world than most Greeks are aware, resulting from the demand for instant communication and information and the influence of the mass media, and of visual stimuli such as television, video, email, and text messaging, all of which seem to militate against the careful and precise use of language.

A number of writers, including some distinguished linguists, have raised their voices against what Tasos Christidis called the *katastrofología* [doom-mongering] of so much contemporary discourse about the state of the Greek language.[22] Some have publicly opposed the widespread ideology of the 'diachronicity of the Greek language'. One of these is the novelist and cultural commentator Takis Theodoropoulos, who, on the occasion of the republication of Dimitrakos' dictionary of the Ancient, Medieval, and Modern Greek language in 2001, wrote that the dictionary

is something like the ark in which the most enduring and interesting modern Greek fantasy is preserved – that which lays down that, even if the blood of Pericles and Lykourgos doesn't flow in our veins, our grey matter is tilled by words that were once uttered with the prosody of the [ancient] bards and were heard from the mouth of Palaiologos [the last emperor of Byzantium] shortly before the Fall of Constantinople.

The same writer went on to assert:

There is no doubt that in order to speak and write Modern Greek one doesn't need to know the ancient language. Even to create literature in Greek you don't need to be able to read a text in Attic dialect, although I believe that the great [Greek] poetry of the modern age would have been different if our great poets had not had a sense of the diachronicity of their language.[23]

For many educated Greeks, the assertion that one does not need to have studied Ancient Greek in order to handle Modern Greek fully and correctly is highly contentious.

The linguist Maro Kakridi, commenting on a recent turn against the monotonic system and towards older, 'etymological' spellings, writes as follows:

These developments seem to be an immediate function of the more conservative turn in Greek society in the last few years, especially after the post-dictatorship dynamic had subsided and after the realignments on the international

[22] A.-F. Christidis 1999: 48.   [23] Theodoropoulos 2001.

and European scene more generally. Here too, as in other linguistic . . . conflicts, what is at stake remains the same: (a), with respect to the content of national identity, the specific form that will be taken by the relationship with the historical past, and (b), with respect to the content of social and cultural identities, the attitude towards the *distinction* guaranteed to those who possess the knowledge of the specific complexities of the written language.[24]

Here Kakridi deftly connects attitudes towards national identity (distinction from non-Greeks) with social and cultural identities (distinction among Greeks).

There is a common Greek saying, when jocularly addressing foreign friends: 'When we were writing philosophy, you were swinging from the trees.'[25] Although it is intended to be comic, this saying encapsulates a widespread assumption in Greece that the modern Greeks are somehow superior to other people because of their direct connection with the language and culture of Classical Greece, which are thought to be unsurpassable. Nationalism encourages people to say 'we' and 'you' to refer not only to synchronic imagined communities of their own time, but to diachronic imagined communities that include people who lived thousands of years ago.

A much-quoted passage in Odysseas Elytis' poem *The Axion Esti* (1959) goes as follows:

> I was given Greek as my language;
> a meagre house on Homer's sandy shores.[26]

The implication is that, even though, in comparison with Ancient Greek, the modern language may be poor in synchronic terms, it is diachronically rich because it stretches back to Homer. For modern Greeks, Hellenic is no longer the language of their ancestors (as it was until about 1800), but their own. Greek nationalists, unlike Katartzis in the late eighteenth century, taught their compatriots that they did not have to *claim* to be Hellenes; they *were* Hellenes. But it was chiefly the demotic movement, with its emphasis on the continuity of popular language and culture since antiquity, that taught the Greeks that vernacular Modern Greek was not a corrupt form of Hellenic; it *was* Hellenic.

Because Ancient Greek did not split into several distinct modern languages, the modern Greeks can see themselves as the sole possessors and

---

[24] Kakridi-Ferrari 2008: 377.

[25] There are other versions of the first part of this saying, e.g. 'When we were building Parthenons . . .'.

[26] Elytis 1959: 28.

guardians of the diachronic Greek language from Homer to the present day. This gives them a sense of great privilege and grave responsibility. For this reason a sense that their language is declining in international prestige and becoming internally impoverished seems more tragic for them than in the cases of other languages; indeed, they see it as a tragedy of world proportions. Some Greeks feel they have a mission not only to keep the Greek language alive but also to exploit to the full its lexical richness and its expressive subtlety.

Pierre Bourdieu has talked about the knowledge of Classical languages as 'linguistic capital'.[27] To some extent, those in Greece today who cherish their archaisms and bewail the dominance of 'restricted demotic' do so because they see their (linguistic) cultural capital being devalued. Tasos Christidis, following Bourdieu, wrote about

the traditional overrating of more ancient...forms of the Greek language as proof...of the Europeanness of the modern Greeks by way of their rightful participation, through descent, in the powerful 'symbolic capital' of Classical antiquity, which was being controlled by the powerful West....In the new environment, according to a characteristically a-historical interpretation, this traditional overrating is being converted into an assertion of the superiority of the Greek language and Greek culture.[28]

Such attitudes provide the background to Greek responses to the declaration of independence by the former Yugoslav Republic of Macedonia in 1991. This was met with forceful reactions from the Greek government and with displays of popular indignation from Greeks around the world. Greek officials, along with many academics, continue to refuse to use the word 'Macedonian' to denote the official language of FYROM and the language spoken by the majority of its inhabitants. Since the official Greek line is that ancient Macedonia was entirely Greek in language and culture, the words 'Macedonia' and 'Macedonian' can only be used to refer to Greek geography, culture, and history. A large province of northern Greece is called Macedonia. Therefore, according to this line, the use of these words by FYROM and its citizens is tantamount to claiming part of the territory of the Greek state – a part that was fiercely and heroically fought for against rival neighbours in the early twentieth century. Instead, many Greeks describe the official and majority language of FYROM as '*to skopianó idíoma* [the Skopian idiom]', after Skopje, the republic's capital; as we have already seen, the term *idíoma* is used

---

[27] Bourdieu 1991: 57.   [28] A.-F. Christidis 1999: 11.

in Greece to denote a language variety that is considered to be something less than a full language.

Greek language debates no longer take the form of battles between the supporters of two varieties of Greek that are perceived to be in contrast but among people who promote different nuances within a unified language. Today the two tendencies in the debates about the Greek language are represented by those who respect (even if they do not follow faithfully) the standardized demotic devised by Triantafyllidis and his collaborators and used by literary authors of the Generation of 1930, and those who espouse freedom from standardization, a 'diachronic Greek' that leaves speakers and writers at liberty to employ features from every historical stage of the Greek language. Many Greeks, both in the past and in the present, have challenged dualities such as those between Ancient and Modern Greek, and between the synchronic and the diachronic, as being artificial and unnecessarily constricting. The standardization of the written language by demoticist grammarians and authors – especially the linguistic 'discipline' espoused and propagated by leading intellectual and political figures of the extreme right such as Petros Vlastos and Ioannis Metaxas – is often interpreted as an infringement of individual linguistic freedom and a restriction on creativity. In addition, the reaction against 'state demotic' since 1976 – apart from being an inevitable reaction against something that has been officially imposed – is also a reaction against the traditionally rural-orientated populism of demoticism. For a long time, most Greeks have not wanted to live in rural areas, but have aspired to live in cities. Besides, by using *katharévousa* features – and by supporting their use – Greeks feel they are defending traditional values and enacting the continuity of Hellenism from Classical through Byzantine times.

For a few years now, Juan Coderch, a non-Greek Classicist teaching in Britain, has been producing an online newspaper called 'Akropolis World News', which features articles on the latest world news written in Ancient Greek.[29] What is particularly interesting is that Coderch resorts to the normal Modern Greek terms for hundreds of modern concepts such as buses, terrorists, and computers. In this sense, it could be said that the Modern Greek learned tradition has kept Ancient Greek alive by providing it with words denoting phenomena and concepts of modern life. Greek purists and archaists of the nineteenth century would have

[29] See http://www.akwn.net

been pleased to know that their method of creating neologisms would come to be viewed in this way.

The vast majority of the neologisms of Modern Greek have been based on Ancient Greek morphemes and Ancient Greek derivational rules. By contrast, the neologisms (compound and complex words) that were coined by demoticist poets and other writers on the basis of demotic stems in the late nineteenth and early twentieth centuries have been largely forgotten.[30] With hindsight, we can see that the role of *katharévousa* was to enrich the written (and to some extent the spoken) language of modern Greece. Yet it had clearly served its linguistic purpose and had begun to outlive its usefulness decades before it ceased to be the official language.

For most of the second half of the twentieth century Greeks were able to continue to develop and refine their national identity on the basis of earlier developments, because their country existed in splendid isolation from its northern neighbours, from whom it was artificially separated by the 'Iron Curtain'. At the present moment, however, Greek national identity, as it has been formed, elaborated, and disseminated over the past two centuries, is facing its greatest challenge from the large number of immigrants who have settled in Greece since the fall of communism. It is estimated that more than 10 per cent of the population of Greece now consists of immigrants. Large numbers of people who have settled in Greece now have children who were born there, and these children are often torn between the national identity of their parents and that of their country of birth. As a result of this massive immigration into Greece, the use of the Greek language is ceasing to be the almost exclusive preserve of people who originate from geographically or ethnically Greek family backgrounds. I can make no predictions about precisely what impact this situation is going to have on Greek national identity in the coming decades, except to say that it is bound to be immense. The national identity of a country whose intellectual and political leaders have often proudly pronounced it to be one of the ethnically, culturally, and linguistically most homogeneous nation-states in the world is now being seriously challenged and tested. For this reason, I believe that a historical account of the role of language in the development of that national identity has been timely.

---

[30] In Greek, unlike in Turkish, no new roots were invented during the language reforms.

Glossary

Abstand **language**: language that is not closely related to the languages spoken around it; cf. *Ausbau* **language**.

accent: in the **polytonic system**, one of the three diacritics (acute [ά], grave [ὰ], and circumflex [ᾶ]) written over one of the vowels in almost every word; in words of more than one syllable the accent indicates the stressed syllable; see also **monotonic system**.

Aromanian: [speaker of a] romance language closely related to Romanian; non-Aromanians use the term 'Vlach' to denote this language and its speakers (Aromanians prefix the sound /a/ to initial /r/, hence the name).

Arvanite: speaker of an Albanian dialect settled for centuries in Greece.

Athonite Academy: school founded on Mount Athos in 1749 by patriarch Kyrillos V.

Ausbau **language**: language that is deliberately made to be as different as possible from the related languages that are spoken around it; cf. *Abstand* **language**.

breathing: one of two marks (rough [ἁ] and smooth [ἀ]) written over an initial vowel, indicating whether the vowel was preceded by an /h/ sound in Ancient Greek or not (the /h/ is not pronounced in Modern Greek).

demotic (Greek *dimotikí*): (generally) spoken Modern Greek; (more particularly) standardized version of the spoken language used in writing (in both cases contrasted with *katharévousa*); **demoticism**: cultural movement in the late nineteenth and twentieth centuries aimed at using demotic for all written purposes; **demoticist**: adherent of demoticism.

Educational Association: see *Ekpaideftikós Omilos*.

Ekpaideftikós Omilos (Educational Association): **demoticist** pressure group in Athens (1910–29).

Ethnikós Dichasmós (National Schism): the split of Greek territory between the jurisdictions of two governments in 1916–17, based in Athens and Salonica respectively.

ethnos: nation; cf. *genos*.

Fanariot: (in particular) member of a group of Orthodox Christian families living in the Fanari district of Constantinople who held high posts in the Ottoman administration; (in general) person closely associated with members of the Fanariot families.

Filikí Etaireia (Friendly Society): secret Greek national revolutionary society founded in Odessa in 1814.

filólogos (pl. *filólogoi*): teacher of or expert in literature.

Foititikí Syntrofiá (Student Company): **demoticist** student association in Athens (1909–26).

genos: nation, especially in the sense of the Orthodox Christian community in the Ottoman empire; cf. *ethnos*.

gymnásio[n]: high school (according to period, either covering the whole of secondary education or the first three years of it); pupils graduate from primary school to the *gymnásio* at about the age of twelve.

Hellenic: Greek, especially Ancient Greek.

Heptanese (Greek *Eptánisos* [Seven Islands]): see **Ionian Islands**.

Ionian Islands: group of islands under Venetian rule till 1797, under French and Russo-Turkish rule 1797–1814, and under British protection from 1814 to 1864, when they became united with Greece; the seven chief islands are Kerkyra (Corfu), Paxoi, Lefkada (Santa Maura), Cephalonia, Ithaki, Zakynthos (Zante), and Kythera (Cerigo).

iota subscript: diacritic in the form of a miniature iota written under certain vowels (e.g. ᾳ) in the **polytonic system**.

Karamanlí (pl. *Karamanlides*): Turkish-speaking Orthodox Christian from Asia Minor; *karamanlídika*: Turkish written in the Greek alphabet.

katharévousa: written form of Greek consisting of a mixture of ancient and modern words and forms; the official language of the Greek state, 1911–76.

kathomiloumeni ('generally spoken'): slightly archaized version of the vernacular.

koine ('common'): the geographically non-specific variety of Ancient Greek used in writing throughout the Greek world in Hellenistic and Roman times (fourth century BC to fourth century AD); (in modern times) spoken variety that is claimed to be common to all areas of the Greek-speaking world, or else local variant of spoken Greek that is in wider geographical use than a particular dialect.

laós: [common] people, folk (sometimes in the German romantic sense of *Volk*).

lógios (pl. *lógioi*): learned person.

lýkeio: school covering the last three years of secondary education, after *gymnásio*.

malliarós (literally, 'hairy'; pl. *malliaroí*): orthodox **demoticist** (follower of Psycharis); *malliarí*: extreme variety of demotic; *malliarismós*: ideology that supports the use of *malliarí* (see Chapter 8, note 63).

Megali Idea: Greek nationalist ideology, first formulated in 1844 and aimed at incorporating into the Greek state as many areas inhabited by Greeks as possible.

monotonic (single-accent) system: system of diacritics in which an acute **accent** is written over the stressed vowel in words of more than one syllable.

National Schism: see *Ethnikós Dichasmós*.

polytonic system: traditional system of diacritics in which all three **accents** and both **breathings** are employed.

prólipsi[s]: preconceived idea (French *préjugé*); this word is frequently used as a pejorative term by authors of the Greek Enlightenment.

purism: movement aiming to purge a language of features considered foreign or vulgar; **purist**: adherent of linguistic purism.

revolution, Greek: the military struggle for independence from the Ottoman empire (1821–29).

Romaic: old term for **vernacular** Modern Greek.

Romiosyni: term referring to the Greeks as a totality, especially in the Byzantine, Ottoman, and modern phases of their history (now largely replaced by *Ellinismós*, which includes the ancient phase).

Standard Modern Greek: the official language of Greece today, based mostly on the grammar of **demotic**.

vernacular: spoken language, or a variety of written language that is moderately close to it.

Vlach: see **Aromanian**.

War of Independence: see **revolution, Greek**.

yfos: style; often used in the eighteenth and nineteenth centuries to refer to each of the different varieties of Greek available for written use.

Bibliography

AGAPIOS and NIKODIMOS (1800). *Pidalion tis noitis nios . . .* Leipzig.

AGER, DENNIS (2001). *Motivation in Language Planning and Language Policy.* Clevedon.

AKOLOUTHIA (1816). 'Akolouthia tis kriseos tou syngrammatos tou Anglou Leake', *Ermis o Logios*, 1 May: 395–402.

ALEXIOU, MARGARET (1982). 'Diglossia in Greece', in W. Haas (ed.), *Standard Languages, Spoken and Written.* Manchester: 156–92; reprinted in Alexandra Georgakopoulou and Maria Spanaki (ed.), *A Reader in Greek Sociolinguistics* (Oxford, Bern, and Berlin 2001), 89–118.

AMILITOU, AMALIA (2002). Introduction to Grigorios Xenopoulos, *Nikolas Sigalos.* Athens: 11–93.

ANDERSON, BENEDICT (1991). *Imagined Communities: Reflections on the Origin and Spread of Nationalism*, revd edn. London [1st edn. 1983].

ANDRIANOU, ELSA (2005). 'I "lexis" tou Georgiou Sotiriadou stin *Oresteia*: poso varia itan i "petra tou skandalou" ', in Evangelika: 129–40.

ANDRIOTIS, N. P. (1951). *Etymologiko lexiko tis koinis neoellinikis.* Athens.

——(1952). *I glossa kai i ellinikotita ton archaion Makedonon.* Salonica.

——(1957). *The Confederate State of Skopje and its Language.* Athens.

——(1974). *Lexikon der Archaismen in neugriechischen Dialekten.* Vienna.

——(1976). *Anticharisma ston kathigiti Nikolao P. Andrioti: anatyposi 88 ergasion.* Salonica.

ANEMOUDI-ARZOGLOU, KRISTA (ed.) (1986). *Anekdota grammata tou Alexandrou Palli.* Athens.

ANGELOU, ALKIS (1954). 'I neoelliniki skepsi kai o John Locke', *Angloelliniki epitheorisi* 7: 128–49.

——(1963). 'To chroniko tis Athoniadas', *Nea Estia*, Christmas: 84–105.

——(1971). *Oi logioi kai o Agonas.* Athens.

——(1994). Introduction to Korais 1994: 13*–53*.

——(1998). 'Mia diafotistiki diamachi', in Kodrikas 1998: 17*–168*.

ANTHIMOS (1798). *Didaskalia patriki.* Constantinople.

Antidikia (1944). *I antidikia ton tonon. Ek ton synedrion tis Filosofikis Scholis tou Panepistimiou Athinon.* Athens.

Apokalypsi (1966). *I Apokalypsi tou Ioanni. Metagrafi Giorgos Seferis.* Athens.

APOSTOLAKOU, LITO, and CARABOTT, FILIPPOS (1999). ' "Omileite ellinika": Slavomakedones kai kratos stin Ellada tou Mesopolemou', in Argyriou, Dimadis, and Lazaridou (ed.): I 121–32.

APOSTOLOPOULOS, DIMITRIS (ed.) (1995). *Neoelliniki paideia kai koinonia: praktika Diethnous Synedriou afieromenou sti mnimi tou K. Th. Dimara.* Athens.

APOSTOLOPOULOS, DIMITRIS (2005). ' "Neoi Ellines": o neologismos kai ta syndiloumena tou sta 1675', *O Eranistis* 25: 87–96.

ARGINTEANU, IOAN (1904). *Istoria românilor macedoneni*. Bucharest.

ARGYRIOU, ASTERIOS, DIMADIS, KONSTANTINOS A., and LAZARIDOU, ANAS-TASIA DANAI (eds.) (1999). *O ellinikos kosmos anamesa stin Anatoli kai ti Dysi 1453–1981: praktika tou A' Evropaïkou Synedriou Neoellinikon Spoudon, Verolino, 2–4 Oktovriou 1998*, 2 vols. Athens.

ASOPIOS, KONSTANTINOS (1853). *Ta Soutseia, itoi o Kyrios Panagiotis Soutsos en grammatikois, en filologois, en scholarchais, en metrikois kai en poiitais exetazomenos*. Athens.

AUGUSTINOS, GERASIMOS (1992). *The Greeks of Asia Minor: Confession, Community, and Ethnicity in the Nineteenth Century*. Kent, OH.

BABINIOTIS, G. (1991 [= 1992]). 'Diachroniki prosengisi tis ellinikis glossas', *Platon* 43: 69–80.

——(1999). *I glossa os axia: to paradeigma tis ellinikis. Meletimata, dialexeis kai arthra 1978–1993*. Athens.

——et al. (eds.) (1984–86). *Elliniki glossa: anazitiseis kai syzitiseis*, 2 vols. Athens.

BAGIONAS, AVGOUSTOS (1985). 'I filosofiki skepsi tou Dimitri Glinou kai i symvoli tou stin anaptyxi tou Marxismou stin Ellada', in *Dimitris Glinos: ekato chronia apo ti gennisi tou. Epistimoniko diimero, 1 kai 2 Dekemvri 1982*. Athens: 13–32.

BALTA, EVANGELIA (1987a). *Karamanlidika: XXe siècle. Bibliographie analytique*. Athens.

——(1987b). 'Oi prologoi ton karamanlidikon vivlion pigi gia ti meleti tis "ethnikis syneidisis" ton tourkofonon orthodoxon plithysmon', *Mnimon* 11: 225–33.

BARTLETT, ROSAMUND (2004). *Chekhov: Scenes from a Life*. London.

BATALDEN, STEPHEN (1982). *Catherine II's Greek Prelate: Eugenios Voulgaris in Russia, 1771–1806*. Boulder, CO.

BEATON, RODERICK (1982–83). 'Realism and folklore in nineteenth-century Greek fiction', *Byzantine and Modern Greek Studies* 8: 103–22.

——(1999). *An Introduction to Modern Greek Literature*, revd edn. Oxford [1st edn. 1994].

——(2007). 'Antique nation? "Hellenes" on the eve of Greek independence and in twelfth-century Byzantium', *Byzantine and Modern Greek Studies* 31: 76–95.

——and RICKS, DAVID (eds.) (2009). *The Making of Modern Greece: Nationalism, Romanticism, and the Uses of the Past (1797–1896)*. Aldershot.

BECK, HANS GEORG (1978). *Das byzantinische Jahrtausend*. Munich.

BERNAL, JOSEP MARIA (2007a). 'O Korais, o Triantafyllidis, kai i diamorfosi tis Neas Ellinikis: simeia synklisis', in Dimadis (ed.): 583–93.

——(2007b). 'Spelling and script debates in interwar Greece', *Byzantine and Modern Greek Studies* 31: 170–90.

BESHEVLIEV, V., TODOROV, N., and KIRKOVA, T. E. (eds.) (1968), *D-r Nikola S. Pikolo: izsledvaniia i novi materiali, izdadeni po sluchai sro godini ot smurtta mu (1865–1965)*. Sofia.

BIEN, PETER (1972). *Kazantzakis and the Linguistic Revolution in Greek Literature*. Princeton.

—— (2005). 'Inventing Greece', *Journal of Modern Greek Studies* 23.2: 217–34.

BILLIG, MICHAEL (1995). *Banal Nationalism*. London.

BIRTEK, FARUK (2005). 'Greek bull in the china shop of Ottoman "Grand Illusion": Greece and the making of modern Turkey', in Faruk Birtek and Thalia Dragonas (eds.), *Citizenship and the Nation-State in Greece and Turkey*. London: 37–48.

BLINKHORN, MARTIN, and VEREMIS, THANOS (eds.) (1990). *Modern Greece: Nationalism and Nationality*. Athens.

BLOMMAERT, JAN (1999). 'The debate is open', in Jan Blommaert (ed.), *Language Ideological Debates*. Berlin and New York: 1–28.

—— and VERSCHUREN, JEF (1998). 'The role of language in European nationalist ideologies', in Schieffelin, Woolard, and Kroskrity (eds.): 189–210.

BOHÈME [= MITSOS HATZOPOULOS] (1901). 'I "Istoria tis Romiosynis", para tou k. Argyri Eftalioti', *O Dionysos* 1: 75–6.

BOIATZIS, MICHAIL G. (1813). *Grammatiki romaniki itoi makedonovlachiki... Romanische, oder Macedonowlachische Sprachlere...* Vienna.

BOMPOU-STAMATI, VASILIKI (1982). *O Vikentios Damodos: viografia–ergografia, 1700–1752*. Athens.

BOSWELL, JAMES (1980). *Life of Johnson*. Oxford [1st edn London 1791].

BOUCHARD, JACQUES (1970). *Georgios Tertsetis: viografiki kai filologiki meleti (1800–1843). Didaktoriki diatrivi*. Athens.

—— (1995). 'I enedrevousa sagini tis poiisis tou Andrea Empeirikou', *Diavazo* 358 (Dec.): 178–83.

BOURDIEU, PIERRE (1991). *Language and Symbolic Power*. Cambridge.

BREUILLY, JOHN (1993). *Nationalism and the State*. Manchester.

BROWNING, ROBERT (1982). 'Greek diglossia yesterday and today', *International Journal of the Sociology of Language* 35: 49–68; reprinted in Browning, *History, Language and Literacy in the Byzantine World* (London 1989).

BUCKEN-KNAPP, GREGG (2003). *Elites, Language, and the Politics of Identity: the Norwegian Case in Comparative Perspective*. Albany.

CAMARIANO-CIORAN, ARIADNA (1974). *Les Académies princières de Bucharest et de Jassy et leurs professeurs*. Salonica.

CARABOTT, PHILIP (1993). 'Politics, Orthodoxy and the language question in Greece: the Gospel Riots of November 1901', *Journal of Mediterranean Studies* 20.1: 117–38.

CHARALAMPAKIS, CHRISTOFOROS (2006). 'I neologiki deinotita tou Kosti Palama', in *Kostis Palamas. Exinta chronia apo ton thanato tou (1943–2003). B' Diethnes Synedrio... Praktika*, vol. 1. Athens: 221–37.

CHARILAOU, NEOFYTOS (1999). 'O Neofytos Doukas kai i paradosi tou politikou rizospastismou sta Vaklania', in Argyriou, Dimadis, and Lazaridou (eds.): II 439–57.

——(2002). *O Neofytos Doukas kai i symvoli tou sto neoelliniko Diafotismo*. Athens.

——(2004). 'The critical stance of Neophytos Doukas towards the social structure of the Danubian Principalities', in Kitromilides and Tabaki (eds.): 179–87.

——(2007). 'Ekdoseis archaion keimenon tin periodo tou neoellinikou Diafotismou: oi ekdoseis tou Neofytou Douka', in Dimadis (ed.): II 289–97.

CHASAPOPOULOS, N. (1988). 'Enas Ellinas stin "avli" tou Kahfetzi', *To Vima*, 11 Sept.: 11.

CHILANDARINOS, PAÏSIOS (2003). *Slavovoulgariki istoria*, tr. with notes by Vaïtsa Chani-Moysidou. Salonica [Greek translation of Ivanov 1914].

CHOULIARAKIS, MICHAIL (1973). *Geografiki, dioikitiki kai plithysmiaki exelixis tis Ellados, 1821–1971*, vol. 1, pt. 1. Athens.

CHOURMOUZIOS, AIMILIOS (1929). 'Dimotikismos kai pezos logos', *Nea Estia*, 1 Nov.: 1440–52.

CHRISTIDIS, A.-F. (1999). *Glossa, politiki, politismos*. Athens.

CHRISTIDIS, CHR. (1984). *Dimotiki kai nomika*. Salonica.

CHRISTOPOULOS, ATHANASIOS (1805). *Grammatiki tis Aiolodorikis i omiloumenis torinis ton Ellinon glossis*. Vienna.

——(1853). *Ellinika archaiologimata*. Athens.

Chronika (1908). 'Chronika: Ellas', *I Meleti*, December: 570–2.

CHRYSOVERGIS, G. (1839a). *Grammatiki tis kath' imas ellin. [sic] glossis kata parathesin pros tin archaian...* Athens.

——(1839b). *Tis grammatikis tis kath' imas glossis to praktikon meros, itoi i grammatiki tis neoellinikis glossis*. Athens.

CLARK, BRUCE (2006). *Twice a Stranger: How Mass Expulsion Forged Modern Greece and Turkey*. London.

CLOGG, RICHARD (1969). 'The *Dhidhaskalia Patriki* (1798): an Orthodox reaction to French revolutionary propaganda', *Middle Eastern Studies* 5: 87–115; reprinted in Clogg 1996.

——(1976a). 'Anti-clericalism in pre-independence Greece c.1750–1821', in Derek Baker (ed.), *The Orthodox Churches and the West*. Oxford: 257–76; reprinted in Clogg 1996.

——(1976b). *The Movement for Greek Independence, 1770–1821: a Collection of Documents*. London.

——(1979). 'Elite and popular culture in Greece under Turkish rule', *Indiana Social Studies Quarterly* 32: 69–88; reprinted in Clogg 1996.

CLOGG, RICHARD (1982). 'The Greek *millet* in the Ottoman Empire', in Benjamin Braude and Bernard Lewis (eds.), *Christians and Jews in the Ottoman Empire: the Functioning of a Plural Society. I: the Central Lands.* New York: 185–207; reprinted in Clogg 1996.

—— (1985). 'Sense of the past in pre-independence Greece', in Roland Sussex and J. C. Eade (eds.), *Culture and Nationalism in Nineteenth-Century Eastern Europe.* Columbus, OH: 7–30; reprinted in Clogg 1996.

—— (1992). *A Concise History of Greece.* Cambridge.

—— (1996). *Anatolica: Studies in the Greek East in the 18th and 19th Centuries.* Aldershot.

—— (ed.) (1999a). *The Greek Diaspora in the Twentieth Century.* Basingstoke.

—— (1999b). 'A millet within a millet: the Karamanlides', in Dimitri Gondicas and Charles Issawi (eds.), *Ottoman Greeks in the Age of Nationalism: Politics, Economy and Society in the Nineteenth Century.* Princeton: 115–42.

—— (ed.) (2002). *Minorities in Greece: Aspects of a Plural Society.* London.

CODRIKA, P. (1804). *Observations sur l'opinion de quelques hellénistes touchant le grec moderne.* Paris.

COHEN, RIVKA (1998). *Pinkhas hakehillot: Yavan.* Jerusalem.

COOPER, ROBERT L. (1989). *Language Planning and Social Change.* Cambridge.

CORAY (1803). *Mémoire sur l'état actuel de la civilisation dans la Grèce.* Paris; English translation in Elie Kedourie (ed.), *Nationalism in Asia and Africa* (London 1971): 157–82.

Costituzione (1803). *Costituzione della Repubblica Settinsulare.* Corfu.

CRYSTAL, DAVID (2006). *The Fight for English.* Oxford.

DAKIN, DOUGLAS (1972). *The Unification of Greece 1770–1923.* London.

DALTAS, PERIKLIS (1994). 'The concept of diglossia from Ferguson to Fishman to Fasold', in Irene Philippaki-Warburton et al. (eds.), *Themes in Greek Linguistics.* Amsterdam and Philadelphia: 341–8.

DAMODOS, VIKENTIOS (1751). *Epitomos logiki.* Venice.

DANIIL (1802). *Eisagogiki didaskalia... para... Daniil tou ek Moschopoleos.* N.p. [Constantinople or Venice?].

DANTE (1890). *Dante's Inferno, Purgatorio and Paradiso, Translated into Greek Verse by Musurus Pasha, D.C.L.* London.

DARVARIS, DIMITRIOS (1806). *Grammatiki aploelliniki.* Vienna.

DASKALAKIS, AP. V. (1966). *Korais kai Kodrikas: i megali filologiki diamachi ton Ellinon 1815–1821.* Athens.

DAVIES, ANNA MORPURGO (1998). *Nineteenth-Century Linguistics* [*History of Linguistics*, ed. Giulio Lepschy, vol. 4]. London and New York.

DE BOEL, GUNNAR (1999), 'I neogrammatiki scholi tis glossologias os theoritiko themelio tou dimotikismou tou Psychari', in Argyriou, Dimadis, and Lazaridou (eds.): I 712–20.

—— (2003). 'L'Identité "romaine" dans le roman de Digénis Akritis', in Hero Hokwerda (ed.), *Constructions of the Greek Past: Identity and Historical Consciousness from Antiquity to the Present.* Gronigen: 157–83.

DE FRANCIS, JOHN (1950). *Nationalism and Language Reform in China*. Princeton.

DELL'AGATA, GIUSEPPE (1984). 'The Bulgarian language question from the sixteenth to the nineteenth century', in Riccardo Picchio and Harvey Goldblatt (eds.), *Aspects of the Slavic Language Question, vol. 1: Church Slavonic – South Slavic – West Slavic*. New Haven: 157–88.

DELMOUZOS, ALEXANDROS (1911a). 'To protypon dimotikon scholeion kai oi epikritai tou', *Deltio tou Ekpaideftikou Omilou* 1: 14–52.

——(1911b). 'Apo to kryfo scholeio', *Deltio tou Ekpaideftikou Omilou* 1: 271–92.

——(1913). 'Tria chronia daskalos' [pt. 1], *Deltio tou Ekpaideftikou Omilou* 3: 1–27.

——(1914). 'Tria chronia daskalos' [pt. 2], *Deltio tou Ekpaideftikou Omilou* 4: 197–283.

——(1917–19). 'I antidrasi', *Deltio tou Ekpaideftikou Omilou* 7: 225–36.

——(1926). *Dimotikismos kai paideia*. Athens; reprinted Athens 1971.

DELTA, P. S. (1909). *Gia tin patrida; I kardia tis vasilopoulas*. London.

——(1911). *Ton kairo tou Voulgaroktonou*. London.

——(1935). *Mangas*. Athens.

——(1956). *Allilografia*. Athens.

——(1993). *Sta mystika tou Valtou*, 39th edn. Athens [1st edn 1937].

DELVEROUDI, REA (1996). 'La question de la langue et les dialectes du grec moderne (1880–1910)', *Revue des Etudes Néo-Helléniques* 5.2: 221–39.

——(2008a). 'Apo ti *mixovarvaron* stin *katharevousa*: i diamorfosi enos orou', in Theodoropoulou (ed.): 353–63.

——(2008b). 'Les Avatars du purisme en Grèce et en France', *Le Français moderne* 76.1 [special issue: *Nouveaux regards sur le purisme*, ed. Laurence Rosier]: 24–37.

DIALLA, ANTA (2005). 'Evangelika kai panslavismos: o paradoxos syschetismos', in Evangelika: 43–61.

DIECKHOFF, ALAIN (2005). 'Beyond conventional wisdom: cultural and political nationalism revisited', in Dieckhoff and Jaffrelot (eds.): 62–77.

——and JAFFRELOT, CHRISTOPHE (eds.) (2005). *Revisiting Nationalism: Theories and Processes*. London.

Diki (1915). *I diki tou Nafpliou. Stenografimena praktika*. Athens.

Diki (n.d. [1942/3]). *I diki ton tonon (i peitharchiki dioxis tou kathig. I. Th. Kakridi)*. Athens; facsimile reprint Athens 1998.

DIMADIS, KONSTANTINOS A. (ed.) (2007). *O ellinikos kosmos anamesa stin epochi tou Diafotismou kai ston eikosto aiona: praktika tou G' Evropaïkou Synedriou Neoellinikon Spoudon (EENS), Voukouresti, 2–4 Iouniou 2006*, 3 vols. Athens.

DIMAKIS, IOANNIS (1991). *I politeiaki metavoli tou 1843 kai to zitima ton autochthonon kai eterochthonon*. Athens.

DIMARAS, ALEXIS (1973–4). *I metarrythmisi pou den egine*, 2 vols. Athens.

—— (ed.) (n.d. [*c*.1980]). *Dimotikismos: i poreia enos agona*. Athens.

DIMARAS, C. (1975). 'Les Transformations du langage en Grèce à partir du XVIIIe siècle', *Folia Neohellenica* 1: 27–37.

DIMARAS, K. TH. (1948–49). *Istoria tis neoellinikis logotechnias: apo tis protes rizes os tin epochi mas*, 2 vols. Athens.

—— (1953). *O Korais kai i epochi tou* [Vasiki vivliothiki, 9]. Athens.

—— (1970). 'Konstantinos Paparrigopoulos: i akmi kai to telos tou', in Konstantinos Paparrigopoulos, *Prolegomena*. Athens: 9–33.

—— (1982). *Ellinikos Romantismos*. Athens.

—— (1984). 'O Korais kai i glossa: i theoria', in Kentro: 9–28.

—— (1985). *Neoellinikos Diafotismos*, 4th edn. Athens [1st edn 1977].

—— (1986). *Konstantinos Paparrigopoulos: i epochi tou, i zoi tou, to ergo tou*. Athens.

—— (1996). *Istorika frontismata, B'. Adamantios Korais*. Athens.

—— (2000). *Istoria tis neoellinikis logotechnias: apo tis protes rizes os tin epochi mas*, 9th edn. Athens.

DIMITRAKOPOULOS, FOTIS (1996). *Vyzantio kai neoelliniki dianoisi sta mesa tou dekatou enatou aionos*. Athens.

DITSA, MARIANNA (1988). *Neologismos kai kritiki ston 19o aiona: neoplastoi logotechnikoi oroi apo ti "Synagogi" tou S. A. Koumanoudi*. Athens.

DORMPARAKIS, P. CH. (1979). *I neoelliniki stin epistimi kai to dimosio vio: grammatiki, lexilogio, syntaxi kai yfos tis Dimotikis*. Athens.

DOUKAS, NEOFYTOS (1804). *Grammatiki Terpsithea*. Vienna.

—— (1805). *Encheiridion peri diatheseos scholeiou ellinikou*. Vienna.

—— (1808). *Grammatiki Terpsithea*, 2nd edn. Vienna.

—— (1810). *Maximou Tyriou Logoi tessarakonta kai eis*. Vienna.

—— (1812a). *Grammatiki Terpsithea*, 3rd edn. Vienna.

—— (1812b). *Logoi ton Attikon ritoron: Dimosthenis*, vol 1. Vienna.

—— (1813a). 'Argo i Epistasiai tines kritikai eis tina neosti ekdothenton vivlion', prologue to *Irodianou tis meta Markon vasileias istorion vivlia okto*. Vienna.

—— (1813b). *Logoi ton Attikon Ritoron*, vol. 7 (Aeschines). Vienna.

—— (1813c). 'Filoi sympatriotai Ano Soudenitai, chairete!', in *Logoi ton Attikon Ritoron*, vol. 10 (Isaeus etc.). Vienna: 1–10 (separately paginated).

—— (1814). *Aischinou tou Sokratikou dialogoi treis*. Vienna.

—— (1815). *Epistoli pros ton Panagiotaton Patriarchin Kyrion Kyrillon peri ekklisiastikis eftaxias*. Vienna.

—— (1820). 'Tois ellogimois ton Neon Ellinon Neofytos Doukas ev prattein', *Kalliopi*: 87–91 (in Ancient Greek), and *Melissa* 2: 230–9 (in Modern Greek translation).

—— (1834). *Tetraktys, itoi Ritoriki, logiki, metafysiki, kai ithiki*. Aegina.

—— (n.d. [1811]). *Parainesis B' pros tous en Vienni Ellinas eis systasin scholeiou ellinikou*. N.p. [Vienna].

DRAGOUMIS, ION (1914). *Martyron kai iroon aima*, 2nd edn. Athens [1st edn 1907].

DRETTAS, GEORGES (1981). 'La *diglossie*: un pèlerinage aux sources', *Bulletin de la Société Linguistique de Paris* 76: 61–98.

DROSINIS, GEORGIOS (1880). *Istoi arachnis*. Athens.

——(1882). *Agrotikai epistolai*. Athens.

——(1884). *Eidyllia*. Athens.

——(1907). 'O nomos enos vivliou', *I Meleti*, April: 229–38.

EDWARDS, JOHN (1985). *Language, Society and Identity*. Oxford.

EFTALIOTIS, ARGYRIS [= KLEANTHIS MICHAILIDIS] (1894). *Nisiotikes istories*. Athens.

——(1901). *Istoria tis Romiosynis*, vol. 1 [and only]. Athens.

——(1911). *Nisiotikes istories*, 2nd edn. Athens.

Eidikous (1911). 'Se eidikous kai mi', *Deltio tou Ekpaideftikou Omilou* 1: 9–13.

Ekthesis (1912). 'Ekthesis tis epi tou glossikou zitimatos exetastikis ton pragmaton epitropis tis Voulis', *Deltio tou Ekpaideftikou Omilou* 2: 71–83.

Ellinika (1998). *Ta ellinika syntagmata, 1822–1975/1986*, ed. Evangelos Venizelos and Loukas Axelos. Athens.

Elliniki (1993). *I elliniki glossa mesa apo keimena archaia, vyzantina kai logia. A' Gymnasiou*, 2nd edn. Athens.

ELYTIS, ODYSSEAS (1935). 'Poiimata', *Ta nea grammata* 1 (Nov.): 585–8.

——(1959). *To Axion Esti*. Athens.

EMPEIRIKOS, ANDREAS (1935). *Ypsikaminos*. Athens.

——(1991–92). *O Megas Anatolikos*, 8 vols. Athens.

Ermou (1813). *Ermou tou Logiou apovlimata*. N.p. [Vienna].

Etairia (1905). *I Etairia 'I Ethniki Glossa' pros to elliniko ethnos*. Athens.

Ethniki (1972, 1973). *Ethniki glossa* (Athens).

Evangelika (2005). *Evangelika (1901) – Oresteiaka (1903): neoterikes pieseis kai koinonikes antistaseis*. Athens.

EVLAMPIOS, GEORGIOS (1843). *O amarantos, itoi, ta roda tis anagennitheisis Ellados: dimotika poiimata ton neoteron Ellinon...* St Petersburg.

FALLMERAYER, J. P. (1830). *Geschichte der Halbinsel Morea während des Mittelalters*, vol. 1. Stuttgart.

——(1845). *Fragmente aus dem Orient*, 2 vols. Stuttgart and Tübingen.

FARINOU-MALAMATARI, G. (1987). *Afigimatikes technikes ston Papadiamanti 1887–1910*. Athens.

FATSEAS, ANTONIOS (1952). 'Peri tis glossis kai paideias ton neoteron Ellinon', in *Choriatikes grafes*, ed. G. Valetas. Athens: 123–43 [1st edn. 1870].

FAUBION, JAMES D. (1993). *Modern Greek Lessons: a Primer in Historical Constructivism*. Princeton.

FAURIEL, CLAUDE (1824–25). *Chants populaires de la Grèce moderne*, 2 vols. Paris.

FERGUSON, CHARLES A. (1959). 'Diglossia', *Word* 15: 325–40.

——(1968). 'Language development', in Fishman et al. (eds.): 27–35.

FILINTAS, MENIOS (1902). *Grammatiki tis romaiikis glossas. Meros 1: fonologia kai grafi.* Athens.

——(1907–10). *Grammatiki tis romaiikis glossas,* 2 vols. Athens.

FILIPPIDIS, DANIIL (1801). *I logiki i ai protai anaptyxeis tis technis tou stochazesthai*... Vienna.

——(1816). *Geografikon tis Poumounias* [*sic*]..., vol. 1, pt. 2. Vienna.

——(1817). *Epitomi ton Filippikon tou Pompiiou Trogou*... Vienna.

——(1808). Epilogue to Florus, *Epitomi ton Romaikon.* Vienna.

——and KONSTANTAS, GRIGORIOS (1988). *Geografia neoteriki,* ed. Aikaterini Koumarianou. Athens [1st edn. Vienna 1791].

FILOLOGIA (1819). 'Filologia', *Ermis o Logios,* 1 and 15 June: 408–554.

FISHMAN, JOSHUA A. (1975). *Language and Nationalism: Two Integrative Essays.* Rowley, MA [1st edn. 1973].

——(2001a). 'Sociolinguistics', in Joshua A. Fishman (ed.), *Handbook of Language and Ethnic Identity.* New York.

——(2001b). 'Why is it so hard to save a threatened language?', in Joshua A. Fishman (ed.), *Can Threatened Languages be Saved?* Clevedon: 1–22.

——et al. (eds.) (1968). *Language Problems of Developing Nations.* New York.

FLEMING, K. E. (1999). *The Muslim Bonaparte: Diplomacy and Orientalism in Ali Pasha's Greece.* Princeton and Chichester.

——(2001). 'The paradoxes of nationalism: modern Greek historiography and the burden of the past', *Bulletin of the Royal Institute for Inter-Faith Studies,* 3.2 (Autumn/Winter): 221–37.

FLETCHER, ROBIN A. (1984). *Kostes Palamas: a Great Greek Poet.* Athens.

FOTEINOS, D. [=Dimitris Glinos] (1915 [= 1916]–1922). 'Ethnos kai glossa', *Deltio tou Ekpaideftikou Omilou* 5: 47–62, and 10: 47–93; reprinted as Glinos 1922.

FOTIADIS, FOTIS (1902). *To glossikon zitima k' i ekpaideftiki mas anagennisis.* Athens.

——(1911). *Sti foititiki syntrofia.* Athens.

FRANGOUDAKI, ANNA (1977a). *Ekpaideftiki metarrythmisi kai fileleftheroi dianooumenoi: agonoi agones kai ideologika adiexoda sto mesopolemo.* Athens.

——(1977b). *O ekpaideftikos dimotikismos kai o glossikos symvivasmos tou 1911.* Ioannina.

——(1987). *Glossa kai ideologia: koinoniologiki prosengisi tis ellinikis glossas.* Athens.

——(1992). 'Diglossia and the language situation in Greece: a sociological approach to the interpretation of diglossia and some hypotheses on today's reality', *Language in Society* 21: 365–81.

FRANGOUDAKI, ANNA (2001). *I glossa kai to ethnos 1880–1980: ekato chronia agones gia tin afthentiki elliniki glossa.* Athens.

—— (2002). 'Comment: Greek societal bilingualism of more than a century', *International Journal of the Sociology of Language* 157 [special issue: *Focus on Diglossia*, ed. Joshua A. Fishman]: 101–7.

FRANK, ANDRE GUNDER (1967). *Capitalism and Underdevelopment in Latin America: Historical Studies of Chile and Brazil.* London and New York.

FRANKISKOS, EMM. N. (1984). 'Proima schediasmata tou Korai gia mia "Grammatiki tis Graikikis"', in Kentro: 70–82.

——(1995). '"Mesi Odos" kai Dionysios Alikarnassefs: scholio se mia aftokritiki tou Korai gia ti glossiki tou theoria', in Apostolopoulos (ed.): 237–48.

GAVRIILIDIS, VLASIS (1901a) 'To Evangelion eis tin glossan tou laou', *Akropolis*, 9 Sept.

——(1901b). 'I vevilosis', *Akropolis*, 26 Oct.

——(1901c). 'Oi antevangelikoi', *Akropolis*, 27 Oct.

GELLNER, ERNEST (1983). *Nations and Nationalism.* Oxford.

Geniki (1801). *Geniki Konstitoutzione tis Eptanisou Politeias.* Constantinople.

GEORGAKOPOULOU, ALEXANDRA, and SILK, MICHAEL (eds.) (2009). *Standard Languages and Language Standards: Greek, Past and Present.* Aldershot.

GEORGIADIS, GEORGIOS DIM. (1948). *To mixoglosson en Makedonia idioma kai i ethnologiki katastasis ton omilounton touto Makedonon.* Edessa.

GEORGOUDIS, DINOS (1984). 'Ta lexikografika tou Korai: analysi perigrafiki tis "glossografias" tou', in Kentro 1984: 59–69.

GIANIDIS, ELISAIOS (1908). *Glossa kai zoi* (Athens 1908).

——(1912). 'I didaskalia tis katharevousis sto episimo scholeio', *Deltio tou Ekpaideftikou Omilou* 2: 13–30.

GINIO, EYAL (2002). '"Learning the beautiful language of Homer": Judeo-Spanish-speaking Jews and the Greek language and culture between the wars', *Jewish History* 16.3: 235–62.

GLINOS, DIMITRIS (1922). *Ethnos kai glossa.* Athens; republ. 1971 [originally published as Foteinos 1915–22].

——(1944). *Ti einai kai ti thelei to Ethniko Apeleftherotiko Metopo.* Athens.

——(1983). *Apanta,* ed. Filippos Iliou, vol. 1. Athens.

GOUNARIS, VASILIS K. (2007). *Ta Valkania ton Ellinon: apo to Diafotismo eos ton A' Pankosmio Polemo.* Salonica.

GOUNELAS, CHARALAMPOS-DIMITRIS (1984). *I sosialistiki syneidisi stin elliniki logotechnia 1897–1912.* Athens.

GRAMMATIKI (1931). *Grammatiki: typoi kai kanones tis koinis omiloumenis neas ellinikis. Grammeni apo Athinaious.* Athens.

GRIMM, JACOB (1851). *Über den Ursprung der Sprache.* Berlin.

GÜTHENKE, CONSTANZE (2008). *Placing Modern Greece: the Dynamics of Romantic Hellenism, 1770–1840.* Oxford.

HAMILAKIS, YANNIS (2007). *The Nation and its Ruins: Antiquity, Archaeology, and National Imagination in Greece.* Oxford.

HATZIDAKIS, G. N. (1881). 'Symvolai eis tin istorian tis neas ellinikis glossis', *Athinaion* 10: 3–28, 213–49; reprinted in Hatzidakis 1905c: 1–83.

——(1883). 'Diati den kalliergoun oi Ellines tin dimodi ellinikin glossan;', *Estia* 15: 390–4 (19 June), 423–6 (3 July).

——(1884). *Meleti epi tis neas ellinikis, i Vasanos tou Elenchou tou Psevdattikismou.* Athens.

——(1890–95). 'Peri tou glossikou zitimatos en Elladi', *Athina* 2–8 [4 instalments; 1 = 1890, 2 = 1893, 4 = 1895], republished in Hatzidakis 1901: 236–537.

——(1901). *Glossologikai meletai,* vol. 1. Athens.

——(1905a). *To provlima tis neoteras grafomenis ellinikis ypo K. Krumbacher kai apantisis eis afton ypo . . .* Athens.

——(1905b). *Die Sprachfrage in Griechenland.* Athens.

——(1905c). *Mesaionika kai nea ellinika,* vol. 1. Athens.

——(1907a). 'Epeigon ethnikon kathikon', *I Meleti,* June-July: 321–5.

——(1907b). *Kai palin peri tou glossikou zitimatos.* Athens [Greek tr. of Hatzidakis 1905b].

——(1907c). *Mesaionika kai nea ellinika,* vol. 2. Athens.

——(1907d). *La Question de la langue écrite néo-grecque.* Athens [French tr. of Hatzidakis 1905b].

——(1915). *Syntomos istoria tis ellinikis glossis.* Athens.

——(1920). *Gennithito fos: o malliarismos eis ta dimotika scholeia.* Athens.

HATZISTEFANIDIS, THEOFANIS (1986). *Istoria tis neoellinikis ekpaidefsis (1821–1996).* Athens.

HATZOPOULOS, KONSTANTINOS (1910). *Agapi sto chorio.* Athens.

HATZOPOULOS, KONSTANTINOS K. (1999). 'I "Ellas/Graikia" kata tous Ellines geografous tis epochis tis othomanikis kyriarchias', in Argyriou, Dimadis, and Lazaridou (eds.): II 357–70.

HAUGEN, EINAR (1965). 'Construction and reconstruction in language planning: Ivar Aasen's Grammar', *Word* 21: 188–207.

——(1966). *Language Conflict and Language Planning: the Case of Modern Norwegian.* Cambridge, MA.

——(1968). 'Language planning in modern Norway', in Joshua A. Fishman (ed.), *Readings in the Sociology of Language.* Berlin: 673–87.

HEILMAIER, JOHANN MICHAEL (1834). *Ueber die Entstehung der romaischen Sprache unter dem Einflusse fremder Zungen.* Aschaffenburg.

HENRICH, GÜNTHER S. (2007). 'I palaioteri elliniki parafrasi voltairikou ergou, o Memnon (1766) kai o Ellinas poiitis tis', in Dimadis (ed.): I 385–92.

HERZFELD, MICHAEL (1982). *Ours Once More: Folklore, Ideology, and the Making of Modern Greece*. Austin.

HIRSCHON, RENÉE (1998). *Heirs of the Greek Catastrophe: the Social Life of Asia Minor Refugees in Piraeus*, 2nd edn. New York and Oxford 1998 [1st edn. Oxford 1989].

——(1999). 'Identity and the Greek state: some conceptual issues and paradoxes', in Clogg (ed.) (1999a): 158–80.

——(2003). 'The consequences of the Lausanne Convention: an overview', in Renée Hirschon (ed.), *Crossing the Aegean: an Appraisal of the 1923 Compulsory Population Exchange between Greece and Turkey*. New York and Oxford: 13–20.

HOBSBAWM, E. J. (1992). *Nations and Nationalism since 1780*, 2nd edn. Cambridge [1st edn. 1990].

HOLLAND, ROBERT, and MARKIDES, DIANA (2006). *The British and the Hellenes: Struggles for Mastery in the Eastern Mediterranean, 1850–1960*. Oxford.

HOLTON, DAVID (1984–85). 'Ethnic identity and patriotic idealism in the writings of General Makriyannis', *Byzantine and Modern Greek Studies* 9: 133–60.

——(2002). 'Modern Greek: towards a standard language or a new diglossia?', in Mari C. Jones and Edith Esch (eds.), *Language Change: The Interplay of Internal, External and Extra-Linguistic Factors*. Berlin and New York: 169–79.

——MACKRIDGE, PETER, and PHILIPPAKI-WARBURTON, IRENE (1997). *Greek: a Comprehensive Grammar of the Modern Language*. London.

——————(2004). *Greek: an Essential Grammar of the Modern Language*. London.

HOMER (1875–81). *Odysseia*, tr. Iakovos Polylas, 4 vols. Athens.

——(1955). *Iliada*, tr. N. Kazantzakis and I. Th. Kakridis. Athens.

——(1965). *Odysseia*, tr. N. Kazantzakis and I. Th. Kakridis. Athens.

HORROCKS, GEOFFREY (1997). *Greek: a History of the Language and its Speakers*. London.

HUPCHICK, DENNIS (2001). *The Balkans: from Constantinople to Communism*. New York and Hounsdmills.

HUXLEY, GEORGE (1998). 'Aspects of modern Greek historiography of Byantium', in Ricks and Magdalino (eds.): 15–23.

IKEN, CARL (1825). *Leukothea*. Leipzig.

ILGEN, CARL (1796). *Hymni Homerici*. Halle.

ILIOU, FILIPPOS (1973). *Prosthikes stin elliniki vivliografia: ta vivliografika kataloipa tou E. Legrand kai tou H. Pernot*. Athens.

——(1984). 'Ideologikes chriseis tou koraïsmou ston eikosto aiona', in Kentro: 143–207.

——(1988). *Tyfloson Kyrie ton laon sou: oi proepanastatikes kriseis kai o Nikolaos Pikkolos*. Athens.

——(1997). *Elliniki vivliografia tou 19ou aiona*, vol. 1. Athens.

ILIOU, FILIPPOS (2005). *Istories tou ellinikou vivliou*. Irakleio.

Istorikon (1933). *Istorikon lexikon tis neas ellinikis glossis, tis te koinos omiloumenis kai ton idiomaton*, vol. 1. Athens.

IVANOV, IVAN (1914). *Istoria slavianobolgarskaia sobrana i narezhdena Paisiem Ieromonahom v liato 1762*. Sofia

JAFFRELOT, CHRISTOPHE (2005). 'For a theory of nationalism', in Dieckhoff and Jaffrelot (eds.): 10–61.

JOHNSON, SAMUEL (2000). 'Preface to *A Dictionary of the English Language* [1755]', in Samuel Johnson, *The Major Works*, ed. Donald Greene. Oxford.

JOSEPH, BRIAN (1985). 'European Hellenism and Greek nationalism: some effects of ethnocentrism on Greek linguistic scholarship', *Journal of Modern Greek Studies* 3.1: 87–96.

JOSEPH, JOHN E. (1987). *Eloquence and Power: the Rise of Language Standards and Standard Languages*. London and New York.

——(2004). *Language and Identity*. Basingstoke.

——(2006). *Language and Politics*. Edinburgh.

JUST, ROGER (1988). 'Anti-clericalism and national identity: attitudes towards the Orthodox Church in Greece', in Wendy James and Douglas H. Johnson (eds.), *Vernacular Christianity: Essays in the Social Anthropology of Religion Presented to Godfrey Lienhardt*. New York: 15–30.

K., KYRILLOS (1815). *Apologia istoriki kai kritiki yper tou ierou klirou tis Anatolikis ekklisias kata ton sykofantion tou Neofytou Douka*. N.p. [Pisa].

Kaini (1985). *I Kaini Diathiki se neoelliniki dimotiki metafrasi*. Athens.

KAISAREIA (1896). *Kaisareia mitropolitleri*. Constantinople.

KAKRIDI-FERRARI, MARIA (2008). 'Orthografikes metarrythmiseis: staseis kai antistaseis', in Theodoropoulou (ed.): 365–83.

KAKRIDIS, F. I. (1997). 'Ellinika kai ochi ellinikoures!', *To Vima*, 12 Jan.

KAKRIDIS, I. TH. (1941a). *Elliniki klassiki paideia*. 2nd edn. Athens [first publ. in *Archeion filosofias kai theoritikon epistimon* 8 (1936), 468–88].

——(1941b). *Ermineftika scholia ston Epitafio tou Thoukydidi*. Athens.

——(1946). 'O syngrafeas tou protou neoellinikou syntachtikou', *Nea Estia*, 1 Sept.: 922–8.

——(1963). *Fos elliniko: panepistimiakoi logoi*. Athens.

KALIORIS, GIANNIS M. (1984). *O glossikos afellinismos: peran tou misoxenismou kai tis ypoteleias*. Athens.

KAMPAS, N. G. (1880). *Stichoi*. Athens.

KAMPOUROGLOU, DIMITRIOS (1873). *I foni tis kardias mou*. Athens.

KAMPYSIS, GIANNIS (1899). 'Germanika grammata', *I techni* 6 (April): 159–60.

——(1900). 'O psycharismos ki i zoi', *To periodikon mas* 1: 33–7, 86–9, 159–63, 201–8; reprinted in his *Apanta* (Athens 1972), 415–36.

KAPSOMENOS, STYLIANOS G. (1985). *Apo tin istoria tis Ellinikis glossas: i elliniki glossa apo ta ellinistika os ta neotera chronia, i elliniki glossa stin Aigypto*. Salonica.

KARAKASIDOU, ANASTASIA N. (1997). *Fields of Wheat, Hills of Blood: Passages to Nationhood in Greek Macedonia 1870–1990*. Chicago and London.

KARATHANASSIS, ATH. (2004). 'Le Rôle culturel des Grecs dans les pays roumains', in Kitromilides and Tabaki (eds.): 251–7.

KARATZAS, STAM. K. (ed.) (1985). *562 grammata ton E. Gianidi, I. Dragoumi, A. Eftalioti, K. Palama, A. Palli, D. Tangopoulou, G. Psychari k.a.* Salonica.

——(ed.) (1988). *Gianni Psychari kai Argyri Eftalioti, Allilografia: 716 grammata, 1890–1923*. Yannina.

KARKAVITSAS, ANDREAS (1896). *I lygeri*. Athens.

——(1897). *O zitianos*. Athens.

——(1899). *Logia tis ploris*. Athens.

——(1904). *O archaiologos*. Athens.

——(1973). *Apanta*, ed. Stratos Chorafas, vol. 4. Athens.

[KAROLOU, IOULIA N.] (n.d. [1938?]). *Olga: i Vasilissa ton Ellinon, 22 Avgoustou 1851–19 Iouniou 1926*. Athens.

KAROULLA-VRIKKI, DIMITRA (2004). 'Language and ethnicity in Cyprus under the British: a linkage of heightened salience', *International Journal of the Sociology of Language* 168: 19–36.

——(2005). 'Language planning in Cyprus: a reflection of an identity conflict'. Unpublished PhD thesis, University of London.

——(2009). 'Greek in Cyprus: identity oscillations and language planning', in Georgakopoulou and Silk (ed.).

KARPOZILOS, APOSTOLOS (1984). 'The Cretan drama of *The Sacrifice of Abraham* in the dialect of the Mariupol Greeks', *Byzantine and Modern Greek Studies* 18: 155–85.

KASINIS, K. G. (1982–84). 'N. G. Politis – Kostis Palamas', *Laografia* 33: 332–45.

KATARTZIS, DIMITRIOS (1970). *Ta evriskomena*, ed. K. Th. Dimaras. Athens.

Katastasis (1804). *Katastasis tis Eptanisou Politeias*. Trieste.

KAVAFIS, K. P. (1935). *Poiimata*. Alexandria.

KAZAZIS, KOSTAS (1993). 'Dismantling Greek diglossia', in Eran Fraenkel and Christina Kramer (eds.), *Language Contact – Language Change*. New York: 7–26.

KECHAGIOGLOU, GIORGOS (1995–6). 'I spasmodiki synkritiki grammatologia tou Neou Ellinismou kai i "graikotourkiki" diaskevi tou *Polypathous* tou Gr. Palaiologou', *Deltio Kentrou Mikrasiatikon Spoudon* 11: 125–36.

KEFALLINAIOU, EVGENIA (1995), 'Michanismoi enischysis tis ethnikistikis ideologias sto teleftaio tetarto tou 19ou aiona', in Apostolopoulos (ed.): 451–72.

KELMAN, HERBERT C. (1975). Foreword to Fishman 1975.

KENTRO NEOELLINIKON EREVNON E. I. E. (1984). *Diimero Korai, 29 kai 30 Apriliou 1983. Prosengiseis sti glossiki theoria, ti skepsi kai to ergo tou Korai*. Athens.

KING, CHARLES (2004). *The Black Sea: a History*. Oxford.

KITROMILIDES, PASCHALIS M. (1983). 'The Enlightenment East and West: a comparative perspective on the ideological origins of the Balkan political traditions', *Canadian Review of Studies in Nationalism* 10.1: 51–70; reprinted in Kitromilides 1994.

—— (1984). 'Ideologika revmata kai politika aitimata: prooptikes apo ton elliniko 19o aiona', in D. G. Tsaousis (ed.), *Opseis tis ellinikis koinonias tou 19ou aiona*. Athens: 23–38.

—— (1985). *Iosipos Moisiodax: oi syntetagmenes tis valkanikis skepsis ton 18o aiona*. Athens.

—— (1989). ' "Imagined communities" and the origins of the national question in the Balkans', *European History Quarterly* 19: 149–92; reprinted in Kitromilides 1994.

—— (1994). *Enlightenment, Nationalism, Orthodoxy: Studies in the Culture and Political Thought of South-eastern Europe*. Aldershot.

—— (1996). *Neoellinikos diafotismos: oi politikes kai koinonikes idees*, tr. Stella Nikoloudi. Athens.

—— (1998). 'On the intellectual content of Greek nationalism: Paparrigopoulos, Byzantium and the Great Idea', in Ricks and Magdalino (ed.): 25–33; reprinted in Kitromilides 2007.

—— (2000). '*Philokalia*'s first journey?', in *Enthymisis Nikolaou M. Panagiotaki*. Irakleio: 341–60; reprinted in Kitromilides 2007.

—— (2007). *An Orthodox Commonwealth: Symbolic Legacies and Cultural Encounters in Southeastern Europe*. Aldershot.

—— and SKLAVENITIS, T. E. (eds.) (2004). *Istoriografia tis neoteris kai synchronis Elladas 1833–2002*, 2 vols. Athens.

—— and TABAKI, ANNA (eds.) (2004). *Relations gréco-roumaines*. Athens.

Kivotos (1819). *Kivotos tis ellinikis glossis . . .* vol. 1 [and only]. Constantinople.

KLOSS, HEINZ (1967). ' "Abstand languages" and "Ausbau languages" ', *Anthropological Linguistics* 9.7: 29–41.

Kodix (1816–17). *Kodix politikos tou Prinkipatou tis Moldavias*. Jassy.

KODRIKAS, PANAGIOTIS (1794). *Omiliai peri plithyos kosmon tou kyriou Fontenelle . . .* Vienna.

—— (1816). *Pros tous ellogimotatous neous ekdotas tou Logiou Ermou eis Viennan tis Aoustrias*. Paris; reprinted in Dasakalis 1966: 195–205.

—— (1817). *Pros tous oikeious*. Vienna and Paris; reprinted in K. Th. Dimaras 1953: 271–89.

—— (1818). *Meleti tis Koinis Ellinikis Dialektou*, vol. 1 [and only]. Paris.

—— (1988). *Meleti tis Koinis Ellinikis Dialektou*, ed. Alkis Angelou. Athens (facsimile of 1st edn.).

—— (1991). *Efimerides*, ed. Alkis Angelou. Athens.

KOHN, HANS (1946). *Prophets and Peoples: Studies in Nineteenth Century Nationalism*. New York.

KOLIOPOULOS, IOANNIS S. (2003). *I 'peran' Ellas kai oi 'alloi' Ellines: to synchrono elliniko ethnos kai oi eteroglossoi synoikoi Christianoi (1800–1912)*. Salonica.

KOMMITAS, STEFANOS (1800). *Paidagogos i praktiki grammatiki*. Vienna.

354   *Bibliography*

KOMMITAS, STEFANOS (1811) 'Peri tis idi ekdidomenis Enkyklopaideias', *Ermis o Logios*, 1 Apr.: 101–12.

——(1812–14). *Enkyklopaideia ellinikon mathimaton*, 12 vols. Vienna.

KONDYLAKIS, IOANNIS (1892). *O Patouchas*. Athens.

KONEMENOS, NIKOLAOS (1873). *To zitima tis glossas*. Corfu; reprinted in Konemenos 1993: 45–106.

——(1875). *Kai pale peri glossas*. Corfu; reprinted in Konemenos 1993: 107–50.

——(1895). 'To systima tou Psychari kai i mellousa attiki tou Kimonos', *Efimeris*, 20, 22, 23 May; reprinted in Konemenos 1993: 165–89.

——(1993). *To zitima tis glossas*, ed. Rinio Papatsaroucha-Missiou. Athens.

KONOMOS, DINOS (1964). 'Eptanisiakos typos 1798–1864 (imifylla, fylladia, efimerides kai periodika)', *Eptanisiaka Fylla* 5: 3–142.

—— (1984). *O Georgios Tertsetis kai ta evriskomena erga tou*. Athens.

KONORTAS, PARASKEVAS (1998). *Othomanikes theoriseis gia to Oikoumeniko Patriarcheio: veratia gia tous prokathimenous tis Megalis Ekklisias (17os-arches 20ou aiona)*. Athens.

KONSTANTAKOPOULOU, ANGELIKI (1988). *I elliniki glossa sta Valkania, 1750–1850: to tetraglosso lexiko tou Daniil Moschopoliti*. Yannina.

KONSTANTAS, GRIGORIOS (1804). Introduction to Francesco Soave, *Stoicheia tis logikis, metafysikis kai ithikis*, 4 vols. Venice.

KONTARIS, GEORGIOS (1675). *Istoriai palaiai kai pany ofelimoi tis perifimou poleos Athinis...* Venice.

KONTOS, KONSTANTINOS (1882). *Glossikai paratiriseis anaferomenai eis tin Nean Ellinikin*. Athens.

KORAIS, ADAMANTIOS (1798). *Adelfiki didaskalia pros tous evriskomenous kata pasan tin Othomanikin epikrateian Graikous: eis antirrisin kata tis pseudonymos en onomati tou Makariotatou Patriarchou Ierosolymon ekdotheisis en Konstantinopolei patrikis didaskalias*. 'Rome' [= Paris].

——(1805a). *Ti prepei na kamosin oi Graikoi eis tas parousas peristaseis: dialogos dyo Graikon...* 'Venice' [= Paris].

——(1805b). *Prodromos ellinikis vivliothikis*. Paris.

——(1829). *Atakta*, vol. 2. Paris.

——(1832). *Atakta*, vol. 4. Paris.

——(1888). 'Grammatiki tis koinis ellinikis glossis', in *A. Korai ton meta thanaton evrethenton syngrammation tomos ektos...* Athens.

——(1964). *Allilografia, I: 1774–1798*. Athens.

——(1966). *Allilografia, II: 1799–1809*. Athens.

——(1979). *Allilografia, III: 1810–1816*. Athens.

——(1982). *Allilografia, IV: 1817–1822*. Athens.

——(1984a). *Allilografia, VI: 1827–1833*. Athens.

——(1984b). *Prolegomena stous archaious Ellines syngrafeis*, vol. 1. Athens.

——(1994). *Yli gallo-graikikou lexikou*, ed. A. Angelou (Athens 1994) [1st edn. 1881].

KORDATOS, I. A. (1924). *I koinoniki simasia tis ellinikis epanastaseos tou 1821*. Athens.

KORDATOS, GIANIS (1927). *Dimotikismos kai logiotatismos: koinoniologiki meleti tou glossikou zitimatos*. Athens; 2nd edn Athens 1974.

KOUBOURLIS, IOANNIS (2005). *La Formation de l'histoire nationale grecque: l'apport de Spyridon Zambelios (1815–1881)*. Athens.

——(2009). 'European historiographical influences upon the young Konstantinos Paparrigopoulos', in Beaton and Ricks (ed.).

KOUKOUDIS, ASTERIOS I. (2003). *Studies on the Vlachs*. Salonica.

KOUKOULES, FAIDON (1933). 'The Athens Modern Greek lexicon'. London [offprint from *Journal of Hellenic Studies* 53].

KOUMANOUDIS, STEFANOS A. (1980). *Synagogi neon lexeon*, vol. 1 [and only], ed. K. Th. Dimaras. Athens [facsimile reprint of 1st edn, Athens 1900].

KOUMAS, KONSTANTINOS (1812). *Synopsis fysikis*. Vienna.

——(1832). *Istoriai ton anthropinon praxeon apo ton archaiotaton chronon mechri ton imeron mas*, vol. 12. Vienna.

KOUTRIANOU, ELENA (2003). Introduction to G. M. Vizyinos, *Ta poiimata*, vol. 1. Athens: 11–230.

KRIARAS, EMM. (1939–43 [1944]). 'I "Paidagogia" tou Moisiodakos kai i schesi tis me to paidagogiko syngramma tou Locke', *Byzantinisch-neugriechische Jahrbücher* 17: 135–53; reprinted in his *Glossofilologika: Ystero Vyzantio – Neos Ellinismos* (Salonica 2000), 8–27.

——(1968–). *Lexiko tis mesaionikis ellinikis dimodous grammateias, 1100–1669*. Salonica.

——(1973). 'Vilaras: glossika kai grammatologika', *Nea Estia*, Christmas: 2–50; reprinted in his *Filologika meletimata* (Athens 1979), 68–133.

——(1981). 'O Psycharis prin apo to "Taxidi": apo tin allilografia tis epochis', *Nea Estia*, 15 May: 635–41; 1 June: 735–41; 15 June: 791–9.

——(1987). *Logioi kai dimotikismos*. Athens.

——(1993). 'To glossiko kirygma tou Christidi (agones, diapistoseis kai kriseis)', in *Mnimi Chr. Christidi: deka chronia apo to thanato tou*. Salonica: 123–53.

——(1997). *Kostis Palamas: o agonistis tou dimotikismou kai i kampsi tou*. Athens.

——(1998). *Thiteia sti glossa*. Athens.

——(2004). *Anichnefseis: meletimata kai arthra; symvoli sto chronologio tou dimotikismou*. Salonica.

Krisis (1867). *Krisis tou voutsinaiou poiitikou agonos tou en etei AOXZ agonisthentos...* Athens.

KROSKRITY, PAUL V. (2000). 'Regimenting languages: language ideological perspectives', in Paul V. Kroskrity (ed.), *Regimes of Language: Ideologies, Polities, and Identities*. Santa Fe, NM, and Oxford: 1–34.

KRUMBACHER, KARL (1902). *Das Problem der neugriechischen Schriftsprachen*. Munich.

KURELEC, VESNA CJETKOVIĆ (1999). 'I rythmisi tis Neoellinikis kai oi Grammatikes tou Diafotismou', in Argyriou, Dimadis and Lazaridou (eds.): I 537–46.

KYRIAKIDIS, STILPON (1939). 'Laografia kai dimotikismos', *Nea Estia*, 1 Nov.: 1480–8.

—— (1953). 'I simasia tis laografias dia ton ethnikon agona', in his *Treis dialexeis* [Makedoniki vivliothiki, 13]. Salonica: 32–45.

KYRIAKIS, THOMAS (2007). 'I proslipsi "ethnikon axion" stin periptosi tou Ignatiou Oungrovlachias', in Dimadis (ed.): I 365–78.

KYROU, AD. (1905). 'To perifimon zitima tis glossis: logikai skepseis dimotikistou: mia synomilia me ton Karkavitsa', *Estia*, 5 Feb.; reprinted in Karkavitsas 1973: 313–15.

LADAS, GEORGIOS G., and HATZIDIMOU, ATHANASIOS D. (1970). *Elliniki vivliografia ton eton 1791–1795.* Athens.

—— —— (1973). *Elliniki vivliografia ton eton 1796–1799.* Athens.

LAMBROPOULOS, VASSILIS (1988). *Literature as National Institution: Studies in the Politics of Modern Greek Criticism.* Princeton.

LAMBRU, STELIU (2001). 'Narrating national Utopia: the case Moschopolis in the Aromanian national discourse', *Xenopoliana* 10, on website http://institutulxenopol.tripod.com/xenopoliana/arhiva/2001/pagini/7.htm

LASKARATOS, ANDREAS (1856). *Ta mystiria tis Kefalonias i Skepseis apanou stin oikogeneia, sti thriskeia kai stin politiki eis tin Kefalonia.* Cephallonia.

—— (1872). *Stichourgimata diafora.* Cephallonia.

—— (1886). *Idou o anthropos.* Cephallonia; new edn, ed. Giorgos G. Alisandratos, Athens 1970.

—— (1959). *Apanta*, 3 vols. Athens.

LAUXTERMANN, MARC (2007). 'Two surveys of modern Greek literature: Stephanos Kanelos (1822) and Iakovakis Rizos Neroulos (1826)', *Kampos: Cambridge Papers in Modern Greek* 15: 126–48.

LE PAGE, R. B., and TABOURET-KELLER, ANDRÉE (1985). *Acts of Identity: Creole-based Approaches to Language and Ethnicity.* Cambridge.

LENIN, N. [SIC] (1921). *O rolos tis kommounistikis neolaias.* Constantinople.

LIAKOS, ANTONIS (2008). 'Hellenism and the making of Modern Greece: time, language, space', in Zacharia (ed.): 201–36.

LIVANIOS, DIMITRIS (2000). 'Pride, prudence, and the fear of God: the loyalties of Alexander and Nicholas Mavrokordatos (1664–1730)', *Dialogos* 7: 1–22.

—— (2006). 'The quest for Hellenism: religion, nationalism and collective identities in Greece (1453–1913)', *The Historical Review/La Revue Historique* 3: 33–70.

—— (2008). 'The quest for Hellenism: religion, national, and collective identities in Greece, 1453–1913', in Zacharia (ed.): 237–69.

LUDASSY, MÁRIA (2004). 'Language and order: de Bonald's theory of language as a paradigm of traditionalist political philosophy', in Ronald Dworkin (ed.),

From Liberal Values to Democratic Transition: Essays in Honor of Janos Kis. Budapest and New York: 27–56.

MACKRIDGE, PETER (2004). ' "Sie sprechen wie ein Buch" ': G. N. Hatzidakis (1848–1941) and the defence of Greek diglossia', *Kampos: Cambridge Papers in Modern Greek* 12: 69–87.

—— (2010). "Modern Greek", in Egbert J. Bakker (ed.), *A Companion to the Ancient Greek Language* [Blackwell Companions to the Ancient World]. Malden, MA and Oxford: 564–87.

MAJUMDAR, MARGARET A. (2007). *Postcoloniality: the French Dimension.* New York and Oxford.

MAKRAIOS, SERGIOS (1797). *Tropaion ek tis Elladikis panoplias kata ton opadon tou Kopernikou.* Vienna.

MANESIS, ARISTOVOULOS I. (1999). 'I neoelliniki glossa sti nomiki epistimi', in Synedrio 1999: 47–80.

MANGO, CYRIL (1965). 'Byzantinism and romantic Hellenism', *Journal of the Warburg and Courtauld Institutes* 28: 29–43.

MANOLESSOU, IO (2008). 'On historical linguistics, linguistic variation and Medieval Greek', *Byzantine and Modern Greek Studies* 32: 63–79.

MANOUSOS, ANTONIOS (1850). *Tragoudia ethnika synagmena kai diasafinismena ypo . . .* Corfu; facsimile reprints Athens 1969 and Athens 1983.

MANTOUVALOU, MARIA (1983). 'Romaios-Romios kai Romiosyni', *Mantatoforos* 22 (November): 34–72.

MARANTZIDIS, NIKOS (2001). *Giasasin Millet. Zito to ethnos. Prosfygia, katochi kai emfylios: ethnotiki taftotita kai politiki symperifora stous tourkofonous ellinorthodoxous tou Dytikou Pontou.* Irakleio.

MARCELLESI, J.-B. (1981). 'Bilinguisme, diglossie, hégémonie: problèmes et tâches', *Langages* 61 (March) [special issue: *Bilinguisme et diglossie*]: 5–11.

MARCELLUS, M. DE (1851). *Episodes littéraires en Orient.* Paris.

MARGARITIS, GIORGOS (2005). *Anepithymitoi sympatriotes: stoichea gia tin katastrofi ton meionotiton tis Elladas.* Athens.

MARKORAS, GERASIMOS (1988). 'Apli kai katharevousa', in his *Poiimata* (Athens 1988), 205–14 [written 1872 and publ. in his *Poiitika erga* (Corfu 1890)].

MARTINET, ANDRÉ (1982). 'Bilinguisme et diglossie: appel à une vision dynamique des faits', *La Linguistique* 18.1 [special issue: *Bilinguisme et diglossie*]: 5–16.

M[ATESIS], A[NTONIOS] (1859). *O vasilikos.* Zakynthos; new edn, ed. Angelos Terzakis, Athens 1973.

MATESIS, ANTONIOS (1953). 'Pragmateia peri glossis', in G. T. Zoras (ed.), *Poiisis kai pezografia tis Eptanisou* [Vasiki vivliothiki, 14]. Athens: 323–6.

MAVILIS, LORENTZOS (1990). *Ta poiimata*, ed. G. G. Alisandratos. Athens.

MAVROFRYDIS, D. I. (1866). *Eklogi mnimeion tis neoteras ellinikis glossis*, vol. 1 [and only]. Athens.

MAVROFRYDIS, D. I. (1871). *Dokimion istorias tis ellinikis glossis.* Smyrna.

MAZOWER, MARK (2004). *Salonica, City of Ghosts: Christians, Muslims and Jews 1430–1950.* London.

Mega (1933–51). *Mega lexikon tis ellinikis glossis,* 9 vols. Athens.

MEGAS, ANASTASIOS E. (1925–27). *Istoria tou glossikou zitimatos,* 2 vols. Athens.

MEGAS, GEORGIOS A. (1946). *Echoun oi voulgaroi ethnikon epos?* Athens.

MENOUNOS, IOANNIS V. (n.d. [1979?]). *Kosma tou Aitolou Didaches.* Athens.

MICHALOPOULOS, FANIS (1940). *Kosmas o Aitolos* [Texte und Forschungen zur byzantinisch-neugriechischen Philologie, 43]. Athens; facsimile reprint Athens 1971.

MILLAR, ROBERT MCCOLL (2005). *Language, Nation and Power: an Introduction.* Basingstoke.

MIRAMBEL, ANDRÉ (1957). 'La doctrine linguistique de Jean Psichari', *La Nouvelle Clio* 3: 78–104.

——(1964). 'Les Aspects psychologiques du purisme dans la Grèce moderne', *Journal de psychologie normale et pathologique* 4 (October): 405–36.

MISAILIDIS, EVANGELINOS (1871–2). *Temaşa-i dünya ve cefakar-u cefakeş,* 4 vols. Constantinople; republished in a modern Turkish-script edition, ed. R. Anhegger and V. Günyol (Istanbul 1986).

MISTRIOTIS, GEORGIOS (1908) *Krisis tou Sevastopouleiou agonos tou idrythentos pros veltiosin tis simerinis glossis apangeltheisa ti 30 Martiou 1908 . . .* Athens.

——(1911). *Peri ennomou amynis tis ethnikis glossis.* Athens.

MOISIODAX, IOSIPOS (1761). *Ithiki filosofia.* Venice.

——(1781). *Theoria tis geografias.* Vienna.

MOLOKOTOS-LIEDERMAN, LINA (2003). 'Identity crisis: Greece, Orthodoxy, and the European Union', *Journal of Contemporary Religion,* 18:3: 291–315.

MOSCHONAS, E. I. (1975). 'Enas aionas dimotikismou: koinonikes kai politikes prosengiseis', introduction to A. Pallis, *Brousos.* Athens: xiii–cxxi.

——(1981). *Vilaras, Christopoulos k.a.: i dimotikistiki antithesi stin koraiki 'mesi odo'.* Athens.

——(2004). *Vivliografia Giorgou Theotoka,* 2nd edn, vol. 1. Salonica.

MOULLAS, PANAGIOTIS (1989). *Les Concours poétiques de l'Université d'Athènes, 1851–1877.* Athens.

——(1993). *Rixeis kai synecheies. Meletes gia ton 19o aiona.* Athens.

——(2006). 'I dekaetia tou 1850 mia tomi stin kardia tou aiona', in Voutouris and Georgis (eds.): 13–19.

MYRES, J. L. (1930). *Who were the Greeks?* Berkeley.

MYRIVILIS, STRATIS [= EFSTRATIOS STAMATOPOULOS] (1924). *I zoi en tafo.* Mytilini; reprinted as Myrivilis 1991.

——(1930). *I zoi en tafo,* 2nd edn. Athens; reprinted as Myrivilis 1993.

——(1931). *I zoi en tafo,* 3rd edn. Athens.

——(1991). *I zoi en tafo.* Athens [reprint of 1924 edn.].

—— (1993). *I zoi en tafo.* Athens [reprint of 1930 edn.].

Nea (1910). *I Nea Diathiki kata to vatikano cherografo metafrasmeni apo ton Alex. Palli.* Liverpool [1st edn. 1902].

Neoelliniki (1976). *Neoelliniki grammatiki: anaprosarmogi tis Mikris neoellinikis grammatikis tou Manoli Triantafyllidi.* Athens.

NEROULOS, IAKOVAKIS RIZOS (1816). *Kourkas arpagi: poiima iroikokomikon.* Vienna.

NEROULOS, IAKOVOS RIZOS (1813). *Korakistika, i Diorthosis tis romaikis glossas.* N.p. [Constantinople].

NÉROULOS, JACOVAKY RIZO (1827). *Cours de littérature grecque moderne.* Geneva.

NIRVANAS, PAVLOS [= PETROS APOSTOLIDIS] (1905). *Glossiki aftoviografia.* Athens; reprinted in his *Filologika apomnimonevmata*, 2nd edn. (Athens 1988), 13–35 [1st edn. 1929].

Nomothesia (1817, 1818). *Nomothesia tou Ypsilotatou kai efsevestatou, Afthentou kai Igemonos pasis Oungrovlachias, Kyriou, Kyriou Ioannou Karatza Voevoda.* Vienna (2 printings).

OIKONOMOS, KONSTANTINOS (1811). 'Logos peri tis ellinikis paideias', *Ermis o Logios*, 15 Dec.: 409–37.

ÖZDALGA, ELISABETH (2006), 'Excerpts from the diplomatic reports', in Özdalga, Elisabeth (ed.), *The Last Dragoman: the Swedish Orientalist Johannes Kolmodin as Scholar, Activist and Diplomat.* Istanbul: 145–60.

PALAMAS, KOSTIS (1886). *Tragoudia tis patridos mou.* Athens.

—— (1889). *Ymnos eis tin Athinan.* Athens.

—— (1892). *Ta matia tis psychis mou.* Athens.

—— (1901). *Thanatos pallikariou.* Athens.

—— (1904). *I asalefti zoi.* Athens.

—— (1907). *O dodekalogos tou Gyftou.* Athens.

—— (1910). *I flogera tou Vasilia.* Athens.

—— (1928). 'Prolegomena', in his *Pezoi dromoi.* Athens; reprinted in Palamas n.d.: X 9–15.

—— (1975). *Allilografia*, ed. K. G. Kasinis, vol. 1. Athens.

—— (n.d.). *Apanta*, 17 vols. Athens.

PALLIS, ALEXANDROS (1892–1900). *Iliada,* 2 vols. Athens.

—— (1904). *Iliada.* Paris.

PANTELIDIS, NIKOS (2001). 'Peloponnisiakos idiomatikos logos kai koini neoelliniki', *Meletes gia tin elliniki glossa... 21 (12–14 Maïou 2000).* Salonica: 550–61.

PAPADIAMANTIS, ALEXANDROS (1985). *Apanta*, vol. 4, ed. N. D. Triantafyllopoulos. Athens.

PAPADOPOULOS, A. A. (1933). 'Prolegomena', in Istorikon 1933: v–xix.

PAPAKOSTAS, GIANNIS (1989). *Ekpaideftikos dimotikismos: o Fotis Fotiadis kai to 'Aderfato tis ethnikis glossas'.* Athens.

PAPANOUTSOS, EVANGELOS (1978). *A. Delmouzos: i zoi tou, epilogi apo to ergo tou.* Athens.

PAPANTONIOU, ZACHARIAS (1918). *Ta psila vouna.* Athens.

PAPARRIGOPOULOS, KONSTANTINOS (1843). *Peri tis epoikiseos slavikon tinon fylon eis tin Peloponnison.* Athens.

——(1844). *To teleftaion etos tis ellinikis eleftherias.* Athens.

——(1860–74). *Istoria tou ellinikou ethnous apo ton archaiotaton chronon mechri ton neoteron,* 5 vols. Athens.

——(1886). *Istoria tou ellinikou ethnous apo ton archaiotaton chronon mechri ton kath' imas,* 5 vols. Athens.

——(1970). *Istoria tou ellinikou ethnous [i proti morfi: 1853],* ed. K. Th. Dimaras. Athens.

PAPAZOGLOU, CHRISTOS (1991). ' "Démotique": Dimotiki (glossa) et Dimotika (tragoudia)', *Molyvdokondylopelekitis* 3: 15–29.

PARLICHEV, GRIGOR S. (1929). *Avtobiografia.* Sofia.

PARLITSEF, GRIGOR (GRIGORIOS STAVRIDIS) (2000). *Aftoviografia,* tr. Antreas P. Andreou. Athens [Greek translation of Parlichev 1929].

PATERIDOU, GEORGIA (2004). 'Yannis Psycharis's Greek novels (1888–1929): didactic narratives, cultural views and self-referentiality'. Unpublished PhD thesis, University of Birmingham.

PATRINELIS, CH. G. (1997). 'O Georgios Kalaras kai i "Elliniki Nomarchia"', *O Eranistis* 21: 201–15.

——(2005). 'To "kryfo scholeio" kai pali', *O Eranistis* 25: 321–36.

PECKHAM, ROBERT SHANNAN (2001). *National Histories, Natural States: Nationalism and the Politics of Place in Greece.* London and New York.

PENTZOPOULOS, DIMITRI (1962). *The Balkan Exchange of Minorities and its Impact upon Greece.* Paris and The Hague.

PETMEZAS, SOCRATES (2009). 'From privileged outcasts to power players: the "Romantic" generation redefining the Hellenic nation and its attributes (circa 1840–1860)', in Beaton and Ricks (ed.).

PETROPOULOU, IOANNA (1988–9). 'O exellinismos-exarchaïsmos ton onomaton stin Kappadokia ton dekato enato aiona', *Deltio Kentrou Mikrasiatikon Spoudon* 7: 141–200.

PETROPULOS, JOHN ANTHONY (1968). *Politics and Statecraft in the Kingdom of Greece 1833–1843.* Princeton.

PETROUNIAS, EVANGELOS V. (1978). 'The Modern Greek language and Diglossia', in Speros Vryonis, jr. (ed.), *The 'Past' in Medieval and Modern Greek Culture.* Malibu: 193–220.

——(1997). 'Malliaroi kai Scapigliati: i genesi enos logotechnikou kai koinonikou orou', *Meletes gia tin elliniki glossa... 1996.* Salonica: 547–61.

PHILIPPAKI-WARBURTON, IRENE (1988). 'O Psycharis os glossologos', *Mantatoforos* 28 (December): 34–9.

POLITIS, ALEXIS (1974 [= 1980]). 'Korais kai Fauriel', *O Eranistis* 11: 264–95.

——(1984). *I anakalypsi ton ellinikon dimotikon tragoudion: proypotheseis, prospatheies kai i dimiourgia tis protis syllogis*. Athens.

POLITIS, ALEXIS (1993). *Romantika chronia: ideologies kai nootropies stin Ellada tou 1830–1880*. Athens.

——(2007). 'Glossa, Diafotismos kai ethniki syneidisi: antipales ideologies stis arches tou 19ou aiona', in Dimadis (ed.): I 463–74.

POLITIS, LINOS (1949). 'Argyris Eftaliotis', *Nea Estia* 15 Nov.: 1444–54.

——(1966). *Poitiiki anthologia*, vol. 4. Athens.

POLITIS, N. G. (1871–74). *Meleti epi tou viou ton Neoteron Ellinon*, vol. 1 (only): *Neoelliniki mythologia*, 2 parts. Athens.

——(1899–1902). *Meletai peri tou viou kai tis glossis tou ellinikou laou: Paroimiai*, 4 vols. Athens.

——(1904). *Meletai peri tou viou kai tis glossis tou ellinikou laou: Paradoseis*, 2 vols. Athens.

——(1906 [= 1907]). *Peri tou ethnikou epous ton neoteron Ellinon*. Athens.

——(1914). *Eklogai apo ta tragoudia tou ellinikou laou*. Athens.

——(1920). *Gnomodotiseis peri metonomasias synoikismon kai koinotiton*. Athens.

POLYCHRONAKIS, DIMITRIS (2002). *O kritikos idealismos tou Iakovou Polyla: ermineftiki parousiasi tou aisthitikou kai tou glossikou tou systimatos*. Irakleio.

——(2006). 'O "Ymnos eis tin Eleftherian" tou Dionysiou Solomou: tipote allo "parex eleftheria kai glossa" ', *Kondyloforos* 5: 39–65.

POLYLAS, IAKOVOS (1860). *Pothen i mystikofovia tou k. Sp. Zampeliou; Stochasmoi*. Corfu.

——(1892). *I filologiki mas glossa*. Athens; reprinted in Polylas 1959: 246–305.

——(1893). 'Kritiki "Eidolon" ', *Efimeris*, 10–11 May; reprinted in Polylas 1959: 308–21.

——(1894). 'Peri glossis', *Estia* 27: 257–62; reprinted in Polylas 1959: 322–36.

——(1959). *Apanta*, ed. G. Valetas. Athens.

POOL, JONATHAN (1980). 'Language planning and identity planning', *International Journal of the Sociology of Language* 20: 5–22.

Prokiryxi (1910). *Prokiryxi tis 'Foititikis Syntrofias'*. Athens.

PSALIDAS, ATHANASIOS (1791). *Alithis evdaimonia, i Vasis pasis thriskeias*. Vienna.

——(1794). Introduction to *Arithmitiki eis chrisin ton ellinkon scholeion*. Vienna.

——(1795). *Kalokinimata, itoi Encheiridion kata fthonou kai kata tis Logikis tou Evgeniou*. Vienna.; new edn., ed. Alkis Angelou, Tronken 1951.

PSICHARI, JEAN (1884). *Essai de phonétique néo-grecque: futur composé du grec moderne*. Paris.

——(1885). "Essais de grammaire historique néo-grecque", *Annuaire de l'Association pour l'Encouragement des Etudes Grecques en France* 19: 1–288.

——(1888). 'Questions d'histoire et de linguistique. Istorika kai glossologika', *Ellinikos Filologikos Syllogos Konstantinoupoleos*, appendix to vol. 18:

441–52, 463–96, and as offprint; reprinted with a new introduction in Psycharis 1902: 53–165.

PSIMMENOS, NIKOS K. (1995). ' "Eksyrikteon ta chydaïsti filosofein epangellomena vivliaridia": apopeira ermineias', *O Eranistis* 20: 36–46.

PSYCHARIS (1888). T*o taxidi mou*. Athens; reprinted as Psycharis 1971.

—— (1897). *T' oneiro tou Gianniri*. Athens.

—— (1902). *Roda kai mila*, vol. 1. Athens and Paris.

—— (1903). *Roda kai mila*, vol. 2. Athens.

—— (1905), *To taxidi mou*, 2nd edn. Athens.

—— (1906). *Roda kai mila*, vol. 3. Athens.

—— (1909). 'Pame skoleio', *O Noumas* 8: 257–62 (12 Dec.); 274–7 (26 Dec.).

—— (1929). *Megali romaiiki epistimoniki grammatiki, A meros. To vivlio tou daskalou*, vol. 1. Athens.

—— (1935). *Megali romaiiki epistimoniki grammatiki, A meros. To vivlio tou daskalou*, vol. 2. Athens.

—— (1937). *Megali romaiiki epistimoniki grammatiki, B meros. To vivlio tou mathiti*. Athens.

—— (1971), *To taxidi mou*, ed. Alkis Angelou. Athens [reprint of 1st edn.].

PUCHNER, WALTER (2001). *I glossiki satira stin elliniki komodia tou 19ou aiona: glossokentrikes stratigikes tou geliou apo ta 'Korakistika' os ton Karankiozi*. Athens.

RAMAS, STEFANOS [=MARKOS TSIRIMOKOS] (1911). 'Dialexis', *Deltio tou Ekpaideftikou Omilou* 1: 66–79.

RANGAVIS, ALEXANDROS RIZOS (1837). *Diafora poiimata*, 2 vols. Athens.

RANGAVIS, KLEON (1884). *Theodora*. Leipzig.

RANKOUSIS, NIKOLAOS (1999). 'I diachroniki didaskalia tis ellinikis glossas sto Gymnasio simera me nea methodo kai nea vivlia', in Synedrio: 361–72.

RENAN, ERNEST (1882). *Qu'est-ce qu'une nation?* Paris.

RENTZOU, EFFIE (2002). 'Surréalisme et littérature: une comparaison entre le surréalisme grec et français'. Unpublished PhD thesis, Paris IV-Sorbonne.

RICKS, DAVID, and MAGDALINO, PAUL (eds.) (1998). *Byzantium and the Modern Greek Identity*. Aldershot.

RITSOS, GIANNIS (1984). *Poiimata*, vol. 2, 17th edn. Athens.

ROÏDIS, EMMANOUIL (1866). *I Papissa Ioanna: mesaioniki meleti*. Athens.

—— (1885). *Parerga*. Athens.

—— (1893). *Ta eidola*. Athens.

—— (1913). *Meletai*. Athens.

ROSA, GEORG CONSTANTIN (1808). *Untersuchungen über die Romanier oder sogennanten Wlachen, welche jenseits der Donau wohnen... Exetaseis peri ton Romaion i ton onomazomenon Vlachon osoi katoikousin antiperan tou Dounaveos...* Pest.

ROTOLO, VINCENZO (1965). *A. Koraìs e la questione della lingua in Grecia*. Palermo.

ROUDOMETOF, VICTOR (1998). 'From Rum Millet to Greek nation: enlightenment, secularization and national identity in Ottoman Balkan society, 1453–1821', *Journal of Modern Greek Studies* 16.1: 11–48.

ROUDOMETOF, VICTOR (2002). *Collective Memory, National Identity, and Ethnic Conflict: Greece, Bulgaria, and the Macedonian Question*. Westport, CT and London.

SAKELLARIOS, GEORGIOS (1796). *Archaiologia synoptiki ton Ellinon*. Vienna.

SAKELLAROPOULOS, SOTIRIOS, et al. (1921). *Ekthesis tis Epitropeias tis dioristheisis pros exetasin tis glossikis didaskalias ton dimotikon scholeion*. Athens.

SALAVILLE, SÉVÉRIEN, and DALLEGGIO, EUGÈNE (1958). *Karamanlidika: bibliographie analytique d'ouvrages en langue turque imprimés en caractères grecs*, vol. 1. Athens.

SARTRE, JEAN-PAUL (1946). *L'Existentialisme est un humanisme*. Paris.

SATHAS, K. N. (1870). *Neoellinikis filologias parartima: istoria tou zitimatos tis neoellinikis glossis*. Athens.

SCHIEFFELIN, BAMBI B., WOOLARD, KATHRYN A., and KROSKRITY, PAUL V. (eds.) (1988). *Language Ideologies. Practice and Theory* [Oxford Studies in Anthropological Lingusitics, 16]. New York and Oxford.

SEFERIS, GIORGOS (1935). *Mythistorima*. Athens.

——(1944). *Dokimes*. Cairo.

——(1962). *Dokimes*. Athens.

——(1987). *To vyssini tetradio: anemologio, lexeis, votana kai orthografika*, ed. Fotis Dimitrakopoulos. Athens.

SFYROERAS, VASILEIOS VL. (1969–70). 'Ilarion Sinaïtis o Kris (1765?–1838) kai ai dyo epistolai tou peri tis metafraseos ton Agion Grafon', *Epistimoniki Epetiris Filosofikis Scholis Panepistimiou Athinon* 20: 225–301.

SIGALAS, NIKOS (2001). ' "Ellinismos" kai exellinismos: o schimatismos tis neoellinikis ennoias Ellinismos', *Ta istorika*, vol. 18, no. 34 (June): 3–70.

——(2004). 'Istoriografia kai istoria tis grafis: ena prooimio stin istoria tou schimatismou tis ennoias Ellinismos kai stin paragogi tis neoellinikis istoriografias', in Kitromilides and Sklavenitis (eds.): I 103–47.

SIMOPOULOS, KYRIAKOS (1971). *I glossa kai to Eikosiena: logiotatoi, Fanariotes, kotzampasides, titloi, axiomata kai prosagorefseis*. Athens.

SIOUZOULI, NATASA (2005). 'Apo ton Aischylo ston Sotiriadi: i peripeteia mias metafrastikis parathlasis', in Evangelika: 141–54.

SKENDI, STAVRO (1980). *Balkan Cultural Studies*. Boulder, CO.

SKLIROS, GEORGIOS (1976). 'To koinonikon mas zitima', in his *Erga*. Athens: 79–138 [1st edn Athens 1907].

SKOPETEA, ELLI (1988). *To 'protypo vasileio kai i Megali Idea: opseis tou ethnikou provlimatos stin Ellada (1830–1880)*. Athens.

SKOUVARAS, EVANGELOS (1965). 'Anekdota antikoraika keimena', in *Eranos eis Adamantion Korain*. Athens: 259–358.

SMITH, ANTHONY D. (1991). *National Identity*. London.

SOFIANOS, NIKOLAOS (1870). *Grammatiki tis koinis ton Ellinon glossis*, ed. Emile Legrand. Athens.

SOFOU, ALCESTE (2007). 'Les Fondements de la presse prérévolutionnaire et l'*Ephiméris* des frères Poulios', in Dimadis (ed.): I 81–8.

SOLOMONIDIS, VICTORIA (1997). 'The Ionian University of Smyrna, 1919–1922: "Light from the East" ', *Kampos: Cambridge Papers in Modern Greek* 5: 81–98.

SOLOMOS, DIONYSIOS (1859). *Apanta ta evriskomena*, ed. Iakovos Polylas. Zakynthos.

——(1955). 'Dialogos', in *Apanta, 2: Peza kai italika*, ed. L. Politis. Athens: 11–30.

——(1961). *Apanta, 1: Poiimata*, ed. L. Politis, 2nd edn. Athens [1st edn. 1948].

——(1964). *Aftografa erga*, ed. L. Politis, vol. 1. Salonica.

——(1991). *Apanta, 3: Allilografia*, ed. L. Politis. Athens.

——(2000). *The Free Besieged and other Poems*, ed. P. Mackridge. Nottingham.

SOPHOCLES, E. A. (1842). *A Romaic Grammar*. Hartford.

[SOTIRIS, LOUDOVIKOS] (1814). *Apologia istorikokritiki syntetheisa men Ellinisti ypotinos filogenous Ellinos epexergastheisa de eis tin koinin dialekton ton Ellinon... ypo Anastasiou iereos kai Oikonomou ton Ampelakion...* Trieste.

SOUTSOS, ALEXANDROS (1835). *O exoristos tou 1831: komikotragikon istorima*. Athens.

SOUTSOS, PANAGIOTIS (1831), 'O Odoiporos', in his *Poiiseis*. Nafplion.

——(1834). *O Leandros*. Nafplion.

——(1853). *Nea Scholi grafomenou logou i Anastasis tis archaias ellinikis glossis ennooumenis ypo panton*. Athens.

SPATHIS, DIMITRIS (2005). 'O skinothetis kai i parastasi tis *Oresteias* sto Vasiliko Theatro', in Evangelika: 229–6.

SPEAKE, GRAHAM (2000). 'Athos, Mount', in Graham Speake (ed.), *Encyclopedia of Greece and the Hellenic Tradition*, vol. 1. London and Chicago: 197–201.

STAMATOPOULOS, DIMITRIOS (2007). 'Ta oria tis "mesis odou": Oikoumeniko Patriarcheio kai glossiko zitima stis arches tou 20ou aiona', in Dimadis (ed.): II 287–300.

STAVRIDI-PATRIKIOU, RENA (1976). *Dimotikismos kai koinoniko provlima*. Athens.

——(1989). Introduction to Vlastos 1989.

——(1999). *Glossa, ekpaidefsi kai politiki*. Athens.

——(2001). 'Glossiko zitima', in A.-F. Christidis (ed.), *Enkyklopaidikos odigos gia ti glossa*. Salonica: 155–9.

——(2005). 'Palaies idees kai neoi fovoi', in *Evangelika*: 13–24.

STAVROU, THRASYVOULOS (ed.) (1966). *Eftaliotis kai Pallis: eklogi apo to ergo tous*. Salonica.

STEWART, CHARLES (2001). 'Immanent or eminent domain? The contest over Thessaloniki's Rotonda', in R. Layton et al. (eds.), *Destruction and Conservation of Cultural Property*. London: 182–98.

STOIANOVICH, TRAIAN (1960). 'The conquering Balkan Orthodox merchant', *Journal of Economic History* 20: 234–313.

STRAUSS, JOHANN (1995). 'The *millets* and the Ottoman language: the contribution of Ottoman Greeks to Ottoman letters (19th–20th centuries), *Die Welt des Islams* 35: 189–249.

SULEIMAN, YASIR (2003). *The Arabic Language and National Identity: a Study in Ideology*. Edinburgh.

Synedrio (1999). *Synedrio gia tin elliniki glossa, 1976–1996*. Athens.

TERTSETIS, GEORGIOS (1847). *Apli glossa*. Athens.

THEODOROPOULOS, TAKIS (2001). 'Lexeis vythismenes stin aperantosyni ton aionon', *Ta Nea*, 21 April.

THEODOROPOULOU, MARIA (ed.) (2008), *Thermi kai fos: afieromatikos tomos sti mnimi tou A.-F. Christidi/Lichte und Wärme: in Memory of A.-F. Christidis*. Salonica.

THEOTOKAS, GIORGOS (1948). 'To ypomnima diamartyrias tis Folosofikis Scholis', *Nea Estia*, 15 Aug.: 1010–12.

——(1979). *Elefthero pnevma*, ed. K. Th. Dimaras. Athens [1st edn. Athens 1929].

THEOTOKIS, NIKIFOROS (1796). *Kyriakodromion...* Moscow.

THIESSE, ANNE-MARIE (2005). 'National identities: a transnational paradigm', in Dieckhoff and Jaffrelot (eds.): 122–41.

THOMAS, GEORGE (1991). *Linguistic Purism*. London and New York.

ŢIPĂU, MIHAI (2004). 'Ethnic names and national identity in the Greek-Romanian historiography of the Phanariote era', in Kitromilides and Tabaki (eds.): 167–77.

——(2007). 'Ethni kai ethnika onomata stin *Istoria* kai to *Geografikon tis Roumounias* tou Daniil Filippidi', in Dimadis (ed.): III 117–30.

TODOROV, NIKOLAI (1964). 'La Participation des Bulgares à l'insurrection hétairise dans les principautés danubiennes', *Etudes balkaniques* 1: 69–96; reprinted in Todorov 1998.

——(1975). 'Le Développement social, économique et culturel de la ville bulgare du XVe au XIXe siècle', in *Structure sociale et développement culturel des villes sud-est européennes et adriatiques aux XVIIe-XVIIIe siècles*. Bucharest: 103–28; reprinted in Todorov, *La Ville balkanique sous les Ottomans (XVe-XIXe siècles)* (London 1977).

——(1983). *The Balkan City, 1400–1900*. Seattle and London.

——(1985). 'Social structures in the Balkans during the 18th and 19th centuries', *Etudes balkaniques* 4: 48–71; reprinted in Todorov 1998.

——(1998). *Society, the City and Industry in the Balkans, 15th–19th Centuries*. Aldershot.

TOLIAS, GIORGOS (1998). 'I "Charta" tou Riga kai ta oria tou "ellinismou" ', *Ta istorika*, 15, no. 28/29 (June–Dec.): 3–30.

TOMADAKIS, VASILEIOS FR. (1989). 'I emmetri parafrasi tou diigimatos "Memnon ou la sagesse humaine" tou Voltaire apo ton Evgenio Voulgari', *Neoellinikon Archeion* 3: 133–86.

TOUFEXIS, NOTIS (2008). 'Diglossia and register variation in Medieval Greek', *Byzantine and Modern Greek Studies* 32: 203–17.

TRIANTAFYLLIDIS, M. (1912). 'I paideia mas kai i glossa tis', *Deltio tou Ekpaideftikou Omilou* 2: 271–309; reprinted in Triantafyllidis 1963: IV 57–92.

——(1913). 'I orthografia mas', *Deltio tou Ekpaideftikou Omilou* 3, and separately, Athens; republ. in Triantafyllidis 1965: 3–155.

——(1915). 'I glossa mas sta scholeia tis Makedonias', *Deltio tou Ekpaideftikou Omilou* 5: 11–46; reprinted in Triantafyllidis 1963: IV 253–83.

——(1917–19). 'I neoelliniki orthografia kai oi antilogies tou Kou Skia', *Deltio tou Ekpaideftikou Omilou* 7: 74–85; reprinted in Triantafyllidis 1965: 156–66.

——(1926). *Dimotikismos: ena gramma stous daskalous mas*. Athens; reprinted in Triantafyllidis 1963c: 168–239.

——(1932). 'To provlima tis orthografias mas', in Triantafyllidis 1965: 167–238.

——(1938). *Neoelliniki grammatiki. Protos tomos: Istoriki eisagogi*. Athens.

——(1941). *Neoelliniki grammatiki (tis Dimotikis)*. Athens.

——(1949). *Mikri neoelliniki grammatiki*. Athens; 2nd edn Salonica 1975.

——(1963a). *Apanta*, vol. 1. Salonica.

——(1963b). *Apanta*, vol. 4. Salonica.

——(1963c). *Apanta*, vol. 5. Salonica.

——(1963d). *Apanta*, vol. 6. Salonica.

——(1965a). *Apanta*, vol. 7. Salonica.

——(1965b). *Mikri neoelliniki grammatiki dimotikou scholeiou*. Athens.

——(1982). *Epilogi apo to ergo tou*, ed. X. A. Kokolis. Salonica.

TRIKOUPIS, SPYRIDON (1821). *O Dimos: poiima kleftikon*. Paris.

——(1853). *Istoria tis ellinikis epanastaseos*, vol. 1. London.

TRYPANIS, K. A. (1984). *O attikismos kai to glossiko mas zitima*. Athens.

TSAOUSIS, D. G. (1983). 'Ellinismos kai ellinikotita: to provlima tis neoellinikis taftotitas', in D. G. Tsaousis (ed.), *Ellinismos – Ellinikotita: ideologikoi kai viomatikoi axones tis neoellinikis koinonias*. Athens: 15–25.

TSIOULKAS, K. I. (1907). *Symvolai eis tin diglossian ton Makedonon ek synkriseos tis slavofanous makedonikis glossis pros tin ellinikin*, 2 vols. Athens; reprinted, with a prologue by Nikolaos K. Martis, Athens 1991.

TSIRIMOKOS, MARKOS (1927). 'Istoria tou Ekpaideftikou Omilou', *Nea Estia*, 15 July: 401–10 and 468–78.

TSOPANAKIS, AGAPITOS G. (1983). 'I glossiki theoria tou Korai kai i glossa tou', *Nea Estia*, Christmas: 3–46.

TYPALDOS, IOULIOS (1953). 'I glossa', in *Apanta: poiimata, peza, grammata, metafrasmata, italika*, ed. Dinos Konomos. Athens: 324–9 [first published as epilogue to his *Poiimata diafora* (Zakynthos 1856)].

TZARTZANOS, ACHILLEFS (1928). *Neoelliniki syntaxis: itoi syntaktikon tis neas Ellinikis glossis (dimotikis kai koinis omiloumenis)*. Athens.

——(1930). *Grammatiki tis neas ellinikis glossis (tis aplis katharevousis)*. Athens.

——(1935). 'Dimotiki kai neodimotiki: i prospatheia enos syllogou', *Filologikos Neos Kosmos* 2 (Feb.), and offprint, Athens.

——(1946–63). *Neoelliniki syntaxis (tis Dimotikis)*, 2nd edn., 2 vols. Athens.

TZIOVAS, DIMITRIS (1986). *The Nationism of the Demoticists and its Impact on their Literary Theory (1888–1930): an Analysis based on their Literary Criticism and Essays*. Amsterdam.

URSINUS, MICHAEL (1993). 'Millet', in *Encyclopaedia of Islam*, new edn., vol. 8. Leiden and New York: 61–4.

VAGENAS, NASOS (1992). 'O poititis os kritikos: o Alexandros Soutsos, o Palamas kai i poiisi tou Kalvou', *To dentro* 67–8 (April–May): 50–74.

VALAORITIS, ARISTOTELIS (1857). *Mnimosyna*. Corfu.

——(1907). *Vios kai erga*. vol. 1. Athens.

VALETAS, GIORGOS (1947–49). *Anthologia tis dimotikis pezografias*, 3 vols. Athens.

——(1982). *Tis Romiosynis*. Athens [1st edn 1976].

VAMVAS, NEOFYTOS (1835). *Grammatiki tis archaias kai tis simerinis ellinikis glossis*. Ermoupoli.

VASILEIOU, ALEXANDROS (ed.) (1809). *Epistolai aftoschedioi grafeisai otan efani i deftera tis Terpsitheas ekdosis*. Vienna.

VASILIKOS, PETROS [= KONSTANTINOS HATZOPOULOS] (1902), 'Ex aformis tis metafraseos tou "Laokoontos" ', *O Dionysos* 2: 248–52.

VELESTINLIS, RIGAS (1797a). *Charta tis Ellados*. Vienna.

——[1797b]. *Nea politiki dioikisis ton katoikon tis Roumelis, tis Mikras Asias, ton Mesogeion nison kai tis Vlachompogdanias*. [Vienna]; reprinted in Velestinlis 2000: 31–77.

——(2000). *Apanta ta sozomena*, vol. 5, ed. Paschalis M. Kitromilides. Athens.

VENIERIS, DIMITRIOS (1799). *Epitomi grammatikis exigitheisa eis tin aplin romaikin dialekton...* Trieste.

VENTHYLOS, IOANNIS (1832). *Grammatiki tis neoteras ell. glossis*. Athens.

VEREMIS, THANOS (1997). 'Apo to ethniko kratos sto ethnos dichos kratos: to peirama tis Organosis Konstantinoupoleos', in Thanos Veremis et al., *Ethniki taftotita kai ethnikismos sti neoteri Ellada*. Athens: 27–52.

VERMEULEN, HANS (1984). 'Greek cultural dominance among the Orthodox population of Macedonia during the last period of Ottoman rule', in A. Blok and H. Driessen (eds.), *Cultural Dominance in the Mediterranean Area*. Nijmegen.

VERNARDAKIS, DIMITRIOS (1884). *Psevdattikismou elenchos, itoi K. S. Kontou Glossikon paratiriseon... anaskevi*. Trieste.

VERTSONI-KOKOLI, MARIA (1980). 'Grammata tou Psychari ston Konstantino Satha', *Nea Estia*, New Year: 83–105.

VIKELAS, DIMITRIOS (1997). *Apanta*, ed. Alkis Angelou, vol. 5. Athens.

VILARAS, GIANIS (1814). *I romeiki glosa*. Corfu.

VILARAS, IOANNIS (1827). *Poiimata kai peza tina*. Corfu.

——(1985). *Stoicheia ellino-alvanikis grammatikis kai ellino-alvanikoi dialogoi*, ed. Titos Giochalas. Salonica.

——(1995). *Poiimata*, ed. Giorgos Andreiomenos. Athens.

VITTI, MARIO (1959). 'Riflessi della questione della lingua italiana sul poeta greco Dionisio Solomòs', *Annali dell'Istituto Universitario Orientale di Napoli, Sezione Linguistica* 1.1: 79–94.

——(1991). *Ideologiki leitourgia tis ellinikis ithografias*, 3rd edn. Athens.

VIZYINOS, G. M. (1991). *Ta diigimata*, ed. Vangelis Athanasopoulos. Athens.

VLACHOS, GERASIMOS (1659). *Thisavros tetraglossos*. Venice.

VLASTOS, PETROS (1931). *Synonyma kai syngenika*. Athens.

——(1989). *Synonyma kai syngenika*, 2nd edn, ed. Rena Stavridi-Patrikiou, Athens.

VOGLI, ELPIDA K. (2007). *'Ellines to genos': i ithageneia kai i taftotita sto ethniko kratos ton Ellinon (1821–1844)*. Irakleio.

VOLTAIRE (1768). *Peri ton dichonoion en tais ekklisiais tis Polonias*, tr. Evgenios Voulgaris. Leipzig.

VOULGARIS, EVGENIOS (1766). *I Logiki*. Leipzig.

[VOULGARIS], EVGENIOS (1797). *Epistoli tou sofotatou kyriou Evgeniou...* Trieste.

——(n.d. [1770]). Introduction to *Eisigisis tis Aftokratorikis megaleiotitos Aikaterinas...* N.p. [Moscow].

VOUTOURIS, PANTELIS (2006a). *Agapimene mou Zaratoustra: Palamas – Nitse*. Athens.

——(2006b). 'I Megali Idea tou Kosti Palama', in Voutouris and Georgis (eds.): 76–97.

——and GEORGIS, GIORGOS (eds.) (2006). *O ellinismos ston 19o aiona: ideologikes kai aisthitikes anazitiseis*. Athens.

VRANOUSIS, LEONIDAS (1952). *Athanasios Psalidas*. Yannina.

——(1955). *Oi prodromoi* [Vasiki vivliothiki, 11] Athens.

——(1973). 'Keimena kai cheirografa tou Vilara kai tou Psalida', *Nea Estia*, Christmas: 51–70.

VYZANTIOS, D. K. (1972). *I Vavylonia, i i kata topous diafthora tis ellinkis glossis*, ed. Spyros A. Evangelatos. Athens [1st edn. Nafplion 1836].

VYZANTIOS, SKARLATOS D. (1835). *Lexikon tis kath' imas ellinikis dialektou metherminevmenis eis to archaion ellinikon kai to gallikon...* Athens.

——(1851–62). *I Konstantinoupolis, i perigrafi topografiki, archaiologiki kai istoriki tis perionymou taftis megalopoleos kai ton ekaterothen tou Kolpou kai tou Vosporou proasteion aftis*, vols. 1–2. Athens.

WEINREICH, URIEL (1974). *Languages in Contact*. The Hague.

WINCKELMANN, JOHANN JOACHIM (1755). *Gedanken über die Nachahmung der griechischen Werke in Malerei und Bildhauerkunst*. Dresden.

WOOLARD, KATHRYN A. (1998). 'Introduction: language ideology as a field of inquiry', in Schieffelin, Woolard, and Kroskrity (eds.): 3–47.

WRIGHT, SUE (2004). *Language Policy and Language Planning*. London.

XENOPOULOS, GRIGORIOS (1883). *Ta thavmata tou Diavolou*. Athens.

——(1888). *Nikolas Sigalos*. Athens.

——(1903). 'Filologiki zoi. Roda kai Mila apo Psychari. Tomos A'', *Panathinaia* 5: 242–4.

——(1906). *Margarita Stefa*. Athens.

——(1915). *O kokkinos vrachos*. Athens.

YAKOVAKI, NASIA (2004). 'O Daniil Filippidis kai i *Logiki* tou Condillac: mia "logiki" gia ti glossa', in Triantafyllos S. Sklavenitis and Konst. Sp. Staïkos (eds.), *To entypo elliniko vivlio, 15os–19os aionas. Praktika diethnous synedriou, Delfoi, 16–20 Maïou 2001*. Athens: 415–48.

——(2005). 'Kathomiloumeni kai typografia: oroi tis dievrynsis tou ellinikou anagnostikou koinou kata ton 18o aiona', in *Chriseis tis glossas*. Athens: 175–206.

YPOURGEIO PROEDRIAS KYVERNISEOS, GENIKI DIEFTHYSNSI DIMOSIAS DIOIKISEOS (1977). *I neoelliniki glossa sti dioikisi*. Athens.

ZACHARIA, KATERINA (ed.) (2008), *Hellenisms: Culture, Identity and Ethnicity from Antiquity to Modern Times*.

ZALLONY, MARC-PHILIPPE (1824). *Essai sur les Fanariotes...* Marseille.

ZAMPELIOS, IOANNIS (1860). 'Diatrivi peri tis Neo-ellinikis glossis', in his *Tragodiai*, vol. 2. Zakynthos.

ZAMPELIOS, SPYRIDON (1852). *Asmata dimotika tis Ellados ekdidomena meta meletis istorikis peri mesaionikou ellinismou*. Corfu.

——(1857). *Vyzantinai meletai: peri pigon neoellinikis ethnotitos, apo 8. achri 10. ekatontaetiridos m.Ch.* Athens.

ZEPOS, PANAGIOTIS I. (1936). *Syntagmation nomikon Alexandrou Ioannou Ypsilanti voevoda igemonos pasis Oungrovlachias 1780*. Athens.

——(1959). *Michail Foteinopoulou Nomikon procheiron (Voukourestion, 1765): to proton ekdidomenon ek cheirographou kodikos tou kratikou archeiou tou Iasiou*. Athens.

ZEVGOLIS, GEORGIOS (ed.) (1933). *Lexikon tis ellinikis glossis*. Athens.

ZIOGAS, PANAGIOTIS CH. (1974). 'Mia kinisi pnevmatikis anagennisis tou ypodoulou Ellinismou kata ton 16o aiona (1540–1550)', *Ellinika* 27: 50–78, 268–303.

Index

An asterisk next to an entry indicates a term that is defined in the Glossary on pp. 336–8. Main page references are printed in bold.